A CRUISING GUIDE TO

PUGET SOUND

A CRUISING GUIDE TO

P U G E T

OLYMPIA TO PORT ANGELES

Migael Scherer

S O U N D

INCLUDING THE SAN JUAN ISLANDS

International Marine
Camden, Maine

Published by International Marine®

10   9   8   7   6   5   4   3   2

Copyright © 1995 Migael Scherer.

Library of Congress Cataloging-in-Publication Data
Scherer, Migael.
   A cruising guide to Puget Sound : Olympia to Port Angeles, including the San Juans / Migael Scherer
             p.   cm.
   Includes index.
   ISBN 0-07-055285-1
   1. Boats and boating—Washington (State)—Puget Sound—Guide. 2. Puget Sound (Wash.)—Guidebooks.   I. Title.
   GV776.W22P846 1995
   797.1'0916432—dc20
                              94-27927
                              CIP

Questions regarding the content of this book should be addressed to:
   International Marine
   P.O. Box 220
   Camden, ME 04843

Questions regarding the ordering of this book should be addressed to:
   McGraw-Hill, Inc.
   Customer Service Department
   P.O. Box 547
   Blacklick, OH 43004
   Retail Customers: 1-800-822-8158
   Bookstores: 1-800-722-4726

A Cruising Guide to Puget Sound is printed on acid-free paper.

Printed by Quebecor/Fairfield, Fairfield, PA.
Design and Production by Molly Mulhern
Edited by Jonathan Eaton, John Vigor, Tom McCarthy

For my husband:
my captain,
my love,
my best friend.

CONTENTS

Writing this book has been a lengthy voyage—exhilarating, eye-opening, at times overwhelming. I am grateful to all who made it with me.

First and foremost, thanks to my husband, and to the captain and first mate on the good little ship *Jack.* Their skills as boaters and as readers, and especially their common sense, helped enormously. Somehow they never confused their loyalty to me with loyalty to my sentence structure.

Special thanks also to the cruising friends who reviewed and "road-tested" portions of the manuscript, and offered their experience and local knowledge: Jane Albee and Harold Anderson, Nancy and Don Decker, Janis and Jim Dyment, Eric Fagergren, Bob Howisey, Jim Jackson, Barbara Miles and Arne Anderson, Herm Moore, Lin Noah, Gloria and David Newman, Susan and Peter Risser, Mark Runions, and Liz Sipprell.

For sharing their "employee lounge," passing on packages, giving out lots of "attagirls," and in general making the work of writing less lonely, my thanks to the shipwrights in my marina: Ben Harry, Jim Martindale, Mike Pitman, Mike Powel, Darrel Olson, and Dave Tracy.

For their help in getting me close to those who work on the water, thanks to: Al Baird, Karin Johnson, Chris Murray, and Don Soriano.

Thanks to Neve Boyd, Bruce Dorn, and Sue Anne Sanders at Captain's Nautical Supplies, for letting me pore over their charts and page through their books, and for their encouragement all along the way.

In researching this book, I encountered many local, state, and federal agencies that were exceptionally helpful: Coast Guard Museum Northwest, Friday Harbor Laboratories, Lummi Tribal Office, National Oceanic and Atmospheric Administration, National Park Service, Nature Conservancy, Puget Sound Pilots Association, Seattle Engineering Department, Seattle Police Department Harbor Patrol Unit, Squaxin Tribal Enforcement, Suquamish Tribal Natural Resources, Tulalip Tribes of Washington, U.S. Army Corp of Engineers, U.S. Coast Guard and Puget Sound Vessel Traffic Service, U.S. Fish and Wildlife Service, U.S. Navy, Washington Sea Grant, Washington State Department of Fish and Wildlife, Washington State Department of Natural Resources, Washington State Parks and Recreation Commission, Washington State Ferries, Washington Toll Bridge Authority, and the parks departments of numerous counties and cities throughout Puget Sound. Thanks to all those who shared their knowledge, returned my calls, and referred me to others who were equally helpful. I am also indebted to the Chambers of Commerce and Visitors' Bureaus in just about every community in Puget Sound.

This book would never have happened were it not for my agent Elizabeth Wales and my editor Jon Eaton, who trusted me with this daunting project and encouraged my best work. Thanks also to managing editor Tom McCarthy, production director Molly Mulhern, and John Vigor. I have particularly appreciated their attention to detail, their level heads, and their good humor.

And finally, thanks to my parents, who first put the oars in my hands, and headed me out to sea.

ACKNOWLEDGMENTS

When this project was first suggested to me, I balked. How could I presume to describe every cove and harbor in Puget Sound? The book would have to be completed—researched and written—in a little over two years; where would my husband and I find the time around his "paying" job to do all the cruising necessary?

But I was also excited by the challenge; at that time no comprehensive cruising guide of the sound existed other than almanac-style publications peppered with advertising. Here was a chance to combine my boating experience and love of Puget Sound with fresh observations and notes on natural and human history.

I began in the early spring of 1992, 200 years after Vancouver's voyage to the sound. I felt like an explorer myself at first, but was soon humbled by the logistics of that early expedition: sail-powered mother ships, open boats powered by oars, lead-line soundings, pen-and-pencil drawings that still have the power to amaze. And, of course, absolutely no charts. I, on the other hand, had a comfortable sailing vessel with a dependable diesel engine, an inflatable dinghy with an equally dependable outboard, depth sounders for both, radios, a camera, and raingear that works. And charts more than 30 for the regions covered in this book. I used them all.

Incorporating the history of Puget Sound was simple until I looked back farther than two hundred years. Then all the complex, rich history of the Native Americans unfolded, two thousand years and more of permanent settlement. I could no more ignore this ancient culture than a writer cruising the Mediterranean could ignore the Roman Empire. So along with those of European explorers, I intertwined the names that Puget Sound tribes had given to the waters and landforms, and some of their accounts.

With very few exceptions, I have visited every cove and harbor described, and navigated every channel. Most, I also visited by land. I limited my exploration to navigable waterways, generally those suited to vessels drawing 4 feet or more, stopping short of going much upriver. Areas too shallow or risky for my own sailboat, I explored by inflatable. Early on, I decided that negative as well as positive observations were equally important to boaters, and recorded both.

In order to understand the ratings I have given for protection, it may help to know what and how I cruise. For 20 years my husband and I have been boating in a sailing ketch that draws almost 7 feet. Our anchor is a 75-pound cast Danforth, with all-chain rode. Because of the tidal extremes in Puget Sound, we rarely set an overnight hook in less than 3 fathoms. We don't trust the weather much. Thus, descriptions of "good" anchorages may seem too conservative for some boaters, especially those who can tuck into shallower areas where there is more protection. Another conservative element is the speed of our boat, around 7 knots. Those with fast boats who can quickly run for better cover might take the chance of more exposure.

The beauty and interest ratings have sparked many lively discussions in our cockpit and are entirely subjective. In general, I worked to balance the ratings within each region, and based them on such factors as physical beauty, shoreside access and amenities, historical interest, and things to do. In every case I rated them as a visitor who arrives by water, not by land.

It was impossible for me to experience fully every bay and harbor. I gleaned a great deal of information from local boaters, and welcome more. Your comments, corrections, and suggestions can help me improve subsequent editions of this book. Feel free to write me, c/o International Marine Publishing, P.O. Box 220, Camden, Maine 04843.

—Migael Scherer
September 1994

PREFACE

Information that applies to all of Puget Sound is provided in the Introduction. This includes information about cruising conditions (weather, tides, currents, vessel traffic, and so forth), public shorelines, state marine parks, protection of wildlife, and U.S. Customs. Specific cruising conditions are described in the introduction to each region.

Regions

This book divides Puget Sound into 11 regions, stretching from South Sound, north to Point Roberts on the Canadian border, and west to Port Angeles in the Strait of Juan de Fuca. These regions are shown on page xi.

Within each region, inlets and bays are generally described from the entrance to the head, and islands described clockwise beginning from the south. However, Puget Sound defies any attempt at structure, and there are many variations on this pattern.

To navigate quickly through this book, use the overview map on page xi (or use the table of contents) to locate the region. The small drawing at the top left corner of each left-hand page also shows you which region you're in. To help you navigate through the text of each region, use the headings in the top right corner of each right-hand page; these indicate the most important islands, bays, inlets, or anchorages that are described on the two facing pages.

The first page of each region gives a sketch map identifying the harbors rated most highly for beauty, interest, and protection.

HOW TO USE THIS BOOK

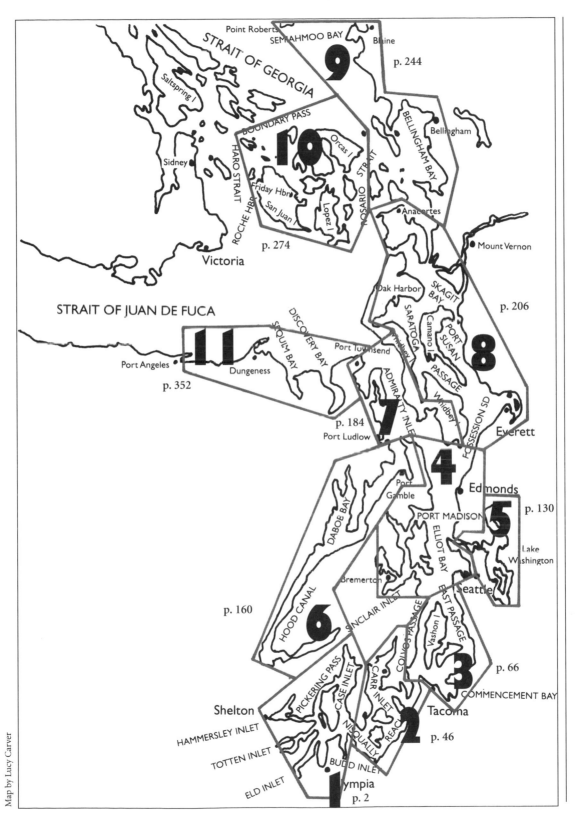

STRAIT OF GEORGIA

Point Roberts

SEMIAHMOO BAY

Blaine

p. 244

9

Saltspring I

BOUNDARY PASS

Bellingham

BELLINGHAM BAY

Sidney

HARO STRAIT

Orcas I

10

Friday Hbr

ROCHE HBR.

San Juan

Lopez I

ROSARIO STRAIT

Anacortes

Mount Vernon

p. 206

p. 274

Victoria

STRAIT OF JUAN DE FUCA

Oak Harbor

SKAGIT BAY

DISCOVERY BAY

SEQUIM BAY

Port Townsend

Whidbey I

SARATOGA

Camano I

PORT SUSAN

8

11

Port Angeles

Dungeness

PASSAGE

Whidbey I

POSSESSION SD

Everett

p. 352

p. 184

ADMIRALTY INLET

Port Ludlow

7

4

Edmonds

p. 130

Port Gamble

PORT MADISON

5

DABOB BAY

ELLIOT BAY

Lake Washington

HOOD CANAL

Bremerton

Seattle

EAST PASSAGE

p. 160

6

SINCLAIR INLET

COLVOS PASSAGE

Vashon I

3

p. 66

PICKERING PASS

CASE INLET

CARR INLET

COMMENCEMENT BAY

Shelton

NISQUALLY REACH

Tacoma

2

HAMMERSLEY INLET

1

p. 46

TOTTEN INLET

BUDD INLET

Olympia

ELD INLET

p. 2

Map by Lucy Carver

Coves and Harbors

For the most part, all the coves and harbors within each region are described individually. For inlets and bays, the order is generally clockwise, from the entrance to the head. For islands, the order is also clockwise, usually beginning from the south.

Charts are listed for all entries, with the preferred and most detailed chart or charts printed in bold. Small-craft folio charts are not listed unless they provide the best or only detail. The reader is assumed to be using official U.S. charts.

Coves and harbors suitable for overnight or short-term stays are rated for beauty/interest and protection. Symbols indicate facilities that are available for transient cruisers.

Beauty/Interest

The categories listed are:

★★★★★ Both beautiful and interesting; not to be missed

★★★★ Very attractive or interesting; definitely worth a visit

★★★ Attractive or interesting

★★ Nothing special, but OK

★ Not very attractive

Protection

The categories listed are:

5 Good refuge in a storm

4 Well protected under most conditions; good anchorage

3 Reasonably protected from prevailing wind; some exposure

2 Exposed in two or more directions; use in settled conditions or as a day stop only

1 No protection

Facilities

The facilities listed are:

Fuel (gas, diesel, or both; assume both unless specified)

Water (at a dock)

 Ice

 Repairs

Overnight moorings: buoys, slips, or both

 Shower

 Groceries within walking distance (1 mile)

 Laundromat within walking distance (1 mile)

 Restaurant and/or takeout

 Boat supplies or hardware

All Facilities—Indicates all the above facilities are available

Telephone Numbers

The telephone numbers in this book include the new area codes scheduled to go into effect on January 1, 1995. Marina phone numbers are given only for those that take advance reservations.

Sketch Maps

Sketch maps (chartlets) are provided to clarify tricky approaches, and to help identify anchorages, moorage, and shoreside facilities. Under no circumstances should these maps be used for navigation.

Disclaimer

In preparing this book, every effort has been made to provide information that is accurate and up-to-date, but it is impossible to guarantee accuracy, and there is no substitute for experience and prudent seamanship. This guide should be used as a supplement to official U.S. charts and other publications. The author and publisher disclaim any liability for loss or damage to persons or property which may occur as a result of the use or interpretation of any information in this book.

INTRODUCTION

"SO RICH A PICTURE"

The state's tall ship, the Lady Washington, *a replica of the original that explored the coast for the United States in 1792. The British Vancouver Expedition sailed similar ships into Puget Sound.*
(Paul Dudley photo)

P ut a chart of Puget Sound in front of any boater. Watch their eyes shine as they lean forward. Watch their fingers trace the labyrinth of channels, circle the bays and inlets. Try, if you can, not to do the same.

Almost two thousand miles of shoreline and more than three hundred islands lie between the state capital of Olympia and the Canadian border at Point Roberts. Protected coves and harbors are numerous. The scenery is breathtaking.

The first people to fall under the spell of Puget Sound called this inland sea the "Whulje." Over thousands of years they developed the richest, most populated culture north of Mexico, thriving on the abundant salmon, clams, berries, wild onions, and swordfern. Otter pelts attracted European explorers in the late 1700s; less than a hundred years later, the "inexhaustible" forest brought in homesteaders, the timber industry, and land speculators. A wealth of silvery salmon lured fishermen.

All these resources have been substantially diminished, but the sound is still a feast for the eyes, the palate, and the spirit. And the description written by Captain Vancouver more than two hundred years ago remains true: "The country before us exhibited everything that bounteous nature could be expected to draw into one point of view . . . I could not possibly believe that any uncultivated country had ever been discovered exhibiting so rich a picture."

Today, if you ask Puget Sound boaters to describe their fondest cruising memories, you probably won't hear about a resort or a restaurant. Instead, you'll hear about the way the sea smokes during sunrise in winter, about the otters along the shore in a secluded anchorage, a display of phosphorescence on a moonless night, or a harvest of Dungeness crab. Even days of heavy rain are forgiven at the sight of orca whales breaking the surface, porpoises playing in the bow wave, or a single, spectacular afternoon when all the mountains are in view.

In this book, Puget Sound is broadly defined to include the interconnected waters from Port Angeles, north to Point Roberts, and south to Olympia.

This introduction gives a brief overview of some of the common factors encountered throughout the sound. Regional specifics are provided in the introduction to each chapter.

Weather

Puget Sound weather is a complex interplay of ocean air, mountains, and channels. The *Coast Pilot* describes it as "mild and moderately moist," with "warm" winters and "cool" summers. For most of the year, boaters are likely to use stronger words: cloudy, rainy, and cold.

The prevailing flow of air in the sound is from the west, off the north Pacific Ocean. By the time this air reaches the Washington coast it is laden with moisture. Forced up by the Olympic Range, the saturated air cools and forms clouds. Precipitation results; lots of it—

more than 7 feet a year in Aberdeen, almost 12 feet in the Olympic Peninsula. No longer sodden but still moist, the air continues to flow inland over the Olympics, then across more water (where it picks up more moisture), up and against more mountains, down and around numerous channels and headlands.

These mountains, channels and headlands alter the direction and force of the wind, determining where clouds will gather and where rain is likely to fall. As a result, very different levels of precipitation occur within relatively short distances. Sequim Bay, in the rainshadow of the Olympics, averages only 17 inches per year, while some 40 miles away, in Everett, the average is 35 inches.

Temperatures, on the other hand, are remarkably even throughout Puget Sound—generally 60 to 80 degrees Fahrenheit in summer, 40 to 60 degrees in winter. Extremes of hot and cold do occur, but are short-lived. Winter daytime (about 45 degrees) and summer nighttime temperatures (about 55 degrees) average almost the same; likewise, water temperatures hold at a chilly 40 to 50 degrees year round.

Seasonal weather patterns for Puget Sound are based in large part on the location of pressure cells in the north Pacific. From October through March, the north Pacific is dominated by a low-pressure cell that circulates counter-clockwise to create moist, south-southwest winds. This pattern is altered in the summer, when (and if) a high pressure cell settles off the coast of British Columbia, to create north-northwest winds and drier, sunnier weather.

Generally speaking, most "bad" (wet) weather comes from the south, and most "good" (dry) weather comes from the north. However, some of the worst winter storms and some of the strongest winds come from the north, from the interior of Canada.

The daily thermal cycle tends to create calm mornings, with windier conditions in the afternoon, calm again toward dusk. Fog occurs throughout Puget Sound, forming mainly in the regions closest to the Strait of Juan de Fuca. It is most common in late summer and early fall, and again in January and February. Summer fog generally dissipates by mid-afternoon, and rarely lasts for more than a few days.

The Puget Sound Cruising Year

With a well-found boat, the proper gear, an eye to the weather and a flexible schedule, boating can be enjoyed year round in Puget Sound. For most, the cruising season is from May through mid-September, when high pressure is usually dominant and (usually) less than 20 percent of the annual precipitation falls. But there are no guarantees. Serious southerly gales can and do occur during this time.

The normal summer pattern is for a spell of warm, sunny weather, with north-northwest winds gradually shifting to west-southwest winds that bring in clouds and rain for a few days. The reverse is true in winter. At times, boaters enjoy splendid weather in March or October, while their summer counterparts cruise in a torrential downpour.

Doing Something About the Weather

While you can't do anything to change the weather, you can do a lot to prepare for it.

At any time of year, watch the weather and monitor local conditions. Don't ignore the obvious: increasing or shifting winds, thickening or lowering clouds, incoming fog. Listen to the 24-hour National Weather Service marine broadcast on VHF Channel 1 or 3. Pay attention to the synopsis (overview), the extended forecast, and the local observations that apply to the area you're in and the area you're heading into. Note whatever is happening off the Pacific coast—it's likely to be moving your way. Buy and use a barometer, and check it at regular times throughout the day. If you notice that the pressure is dropping, prepare for worsening weather; a sudden or severe drop is a dangerous sign. Alter your cruising plans accordingly. Be realistic about the abilities of your boat, your crew, and yourself.

Since rain is always a possibility, prepare for it. Good raingear, waterproof footwear, and warm clothes can make the difference between being miserable and enjoying yourself. They also help prevent hypothermia, which has detrimental effects on your mental and physical abilities—two critical elements when operating a boat.

Tides

Compared with most U.S. waters, Puget Sound tides are extreme. The difference between low and high varies from region to region. Port Townsend, at the entrance to Admiralty Inlet, has a daily tidal range of only 8 feet, while Seattle's is 11 feet. Olympia, at the far south end, experiences a sobering difference of 15 feet a day. These numbers increase when tides are extreme; in Olympia, for example, the difference between the highest high tide and the lowest low tide in a single day can be 20 feet or more.

There are two high tides and two low tides each day, with an occasional exception. Generally, one high and one low is more extreme (higher or lower) than the other.

Miscalculating tides can leave a boat high and dry.

Zero and Minus Tides

The height of the tide in the tide tables is given in feet ("ft") and centimeters ("cm"); some tide books use feet only. The stated height is measured above or below a datum (reference) known as "mean lower low water." This datum is commonly referred to as a "zero" tide. Tides that drop below this datum are called "minus" tides.

Calculating Actual Depths

Nautical charts for Puget Sound use the datum described above. That is, a depth shown on the chart as 2 fathoms means that water is 2 fathoms (12 feet) deep at zero tide. To figure the depth at high or low tide, add the height given in the tide table to the charted depth. In the case of minus tides, subtract the height from the charted depth.

Using this same example, a high of 9.1 feet (from the tide table) added to the 2 fathoms charted gives an actual depth at high tide of 21.1 feet. This may seem like enough for any boat, but a corresponding –2.7 low (from the tide table) gives an actual depth at low tide of only 9.3 feet.

In calculating depths, it is important to use the correct tide table. The major reference stations are Seattle and Port Townsend, generally referred to as "Seattle tides" and "Port Townsend tides." The times and heights of tides in other locations are calculated from these stations, using correction tables provided in most tide books. Some tide books do the corrections for you, providing separate tables for Olympia, Friday Harbor, Hood Canal, and other areas. Some also correct for Daylight Saving Time.

Tide tables are inexpensive insurance. Buy the ones you need and use them. Don't guess. Knowing the height of low and high tide is especially critical when navigating close to shore, when deciding where and how to anchor, and when passing under a bridge or power line. A foot or two of depth or clearance, an hour one way or the other, can save your boat, your propeller, your pride.

Seasonal Tidal Variations

Tidal extremes occur throughout the year in Puget Sound. Some of the lowest tides occur in summer. Fortunately for boaters, these lows are generally in mid-afternoon, when visibility (and presumably the skipper's ability to calculate) is good. In winter, the lowest tides occur toward the middle of the night.

Other Tidal Factors

Because other factors influence the tides, the heights predicted in the tide tables can be off by 2 feet or more. Unusually heavy rains (or dry spells) add or subtract to the predicted heights. Strong onshore winds add height, while offshore winds subtract height. When barometric pressure is low, waters are generally higher than predicted; the opposite is true when barometric pressure is high. A combination of these three factors can have significant results: An extended spell of hard rain accompanied by low pressure and onshore winds creates *higher* high and low tides. Dry weather, high pressure and offshore winds tend to create *lower* high and low tides.

Currents

Puget Sound has a complicated shoreline and an uneven underwater topography. It is surrounded by mountains and foothills that drain enormous quantities of fresh water. Twice a day the salt water flows in and out with the tide. These and other factors combine to create currents that range from "weak and variable" to "strong and dangerous." Even the most basic understanding of current can make the difference between a lumpy passage that never seems to end, and a smooth, relaxing run.

Using Current Tables

Though related, the ebb and flood of current does not correspond exactly with low tide and high tide. Separate current tables *must* be used to find the strength and direction of the current. These tables give predicted times and speeds (in knots) of ebb and flood, as well as the predicted times for slack water. In Puget Sound, these predictions are calculated for the Tacoma Narrows, Admiralty Inlet, Deception Pass, Rosario Strait, and San Juan Channel (Cattle Pass). Most books provide these; some also provide tables for the Strait of Juan de

Fuca and for Canadian waters. Correction tables help you calculate currents in other areas. Some books correct for Daylight Saving Time.

Working with the Current

Learning to use current wisely has two immediate advantages: increased speed and decreased fuel consumption. For example, a boater heading north from Seattle in the morning may benefit from a 4.2 knot ebb (measured off Bush Point); a late afternoon departure that same day can mean fighting a 3.3 knot flood. For boats that travel at 6 knots, these ebbs and floods make a big difference, but fast, planing hulls are also affected. Wave height is amplified when wind and current are opposed, making the smoothest ride during slack, or when both wind and current are moving in the same direction.

When navigating narrow passages, it is critical that you know the times of slack, maximum flood, and maximum ebb. Currents are strongest where channels are narrow and shallow, particularly when large bodies of water are close by. These strong currents are often accompanied by whirlpools and tide rips that make steering tricky if not hazardous.

Making the Best of an Opposing Current

With a little experience, most boaters learn to work with the current. However, there are times when you have no choice but to buck an unfavorable current. A few pointers—familiar to sailors and predicted log racers—can help you make the best of a difficult situation.

- As you move north from Olympia to Port Townsend, the current gets stronger.
- In straight channels, the current is strongest in the middle, weakest along the edges.
- In curved channels, the current is strongest on the outside of the curve.
- The current changes direction at the edges before it changes in the middle.
- Look for backeddies and countercurrents toward shore.

Current charts for the waters south of Port Townsend are provided in the Appendix.

Shipping

Commercial traffic is frequently encountered in Puget Sound. This traffic consists primarily of ferries, tugs and their tows, and ships weighing many thousands of tons. Regardless of the apparent freedom to go in any direction in your boat, for safety's sake you are restricted by the rules of the Vessel Traffic System, and you should always use common sense.

The Vessel Traffic System

The Vessel Traffic System (VTS) is the "highway control" providing safe passage for commercial shipping in and out of Puget Sound. It is monitored and enforced by the Coast Guard; Canada has a similar system in its waters. Generally, all commercial vessels must actively participate in the system. They must report their positions, arrivals, and departures via VHF radio to the Vessel Traffic Center, and they must navigate within the

Traffic Separation Scheme (TSS).

Pleasure boaters are not required to participate in the VTS system and can usually ignore it. However, a pleasure boat inside a Traffic Separation Scheme (TSS) is bound by VTS rules, regardless of whether it is motoring or sailing. The TSS is a network of one-way traffic lanes, with separation zones between the lanes and precautionary areas at the end points and where vessels normally enter, leave, or cross. These lanes are defined through the Strait of Juan de Fuca, Haro Strait, and Rosario Strait, and from Admiralty Inlet to Tacoma. They are marked with buoys and indicated on charts with purple dashes. The broad band charted between the lanes indicates the 500-yard separation zone.

There are many rules governing vessel movement in a TSS. Since 1993, these rules (sometimes referred to as "Rule 10") have applied to recreational as well as commercial boats. It should be noted that a boat under sail has no special privilege in a TSS. Rules that most directly affect pleasure boats are:

- Any vessel in a TSS, other than a crossing vessel, must move in the direction of traffic flow. One of the functions of the TSS is to provide predictability for ships and other vessels that have no choice but to navigate within them. Whether you are under power or sail, stay in the correct lane, or get out of the TSS altogether.
- A vessel of less than 66 feet, or a sailboat of any size, must get out of the way of a power-driven vessel following a traffic lane.

- A vessel of less than 66 feet, or a sailboat of any size, must not navigate in such a way as to risk the development of a collision with another vessel. Don't create a situation where a ship, or a tug engaged in towing, is forced to alter course in order to avoid you.
- Any vessel crossing a traffic lane must do so at right angles to the direction of traffic flow, as far as practicable. This not only gets you across the lanes quickly, it also makes your boat easier to spot, both by eye and by radar.
- All vessels are required to keep the precautionary areas to port. Precautionary areas are marked by yellow or yellow-and-black striped buoys, and charted with a circle of dashes. The buoys are often referred to as "turning buoys." Ships and tugs need room in these areas to make course changes.
- All vessels (other than crossing vessels) shall stay out of the separation zone. These zones provide areas where vessels can bail out in an emergency, and should be kept clear.
- A vessel engaged in fishing must get out of the way of any vessel following a traffic lane.

Some of the chart books on the market draw "suggested courses" that run against the flow of traffic in the TSS, or otherwise direct boaters to navigate in ways that violate VTS rules. If you use these courses, make the changes necessary to stay in compliance.

For an inside view of the Vessel Traffic Center, see page 109. The view from the bridge of a container ship is described on page 357.

Commonsense Guidelines

In addition to following VTS rules, boaters should use common sense around large ships and tugs with tow. A few simple guidelines are:

- Never cut between a tug and its tow. The cable connecting the tow—often partially submerged—can rip your boat in two. Towed barges can also unexpectedly move from side to side.

- Use caution around log tows. These flat, wide bundles are deceptively dangerous, and often difficult to see.
- Don't try to "outrace" a ship or tug with the intent of crossing ahead. The speed of a large ship is difficult to judge accurately.
- When traveling at night, keep a sharp lookout for large ships, which are easily masked by background lights on shore. Commercial

vessels display lights that indicate if they are towing or pushing; learn to recognize them.

• Make your intentions clear. If necessary, call the ship. Commercial vessels monitor VHF Channel 13, a bridge-to-bridge frequency reserved for navigational safety. Use low power, and keep your transmission short. Vessels participating in the VTS are not required to monitor Channel 16.

• Keep informed about commercial traffic in your area by listening to VTS communications on Channels 14 and 5A.

Logs and Deadheads

Puget Sound is an active timber-producing area, with sawmills, log booms (rafts of felled timber), and many tugs with log tows. Occasionally logs drift into the waterways. Sometimes they float vertically, and only the top of the log—if that—is visible; these are known as deadheads.

In the days when Pacific Northwest forests were more aggressively logged, often down to the water, logs and deadheads were a widespread navigational hazard. Today they are less numerous, but still present a serious problem. A deadhead can puncture your boat or tear out the bottom. Always keep a sharp lookout, and take special care when traveling at night or at high speeds.

Commercial Fishing

With local salmon and other stocks decreasing, most commercial fishing vessels work offshore or in Alaskan waters. However, some commercial fishing still takes place within Puget Sound.

To help recreational boaters stay out of the way of these working boats and to avoid their nets, a brief description of the most common commercial fishing methods is given here.

Gillnetters

Gillnetters catch salmon or herring with a net strung between a boat and a buoy or float. The net hangs below the surface from a corkline (a series of small floats), and is weighted on the bottom. After the net is strung out, the boat usually drifts, waiting for fish to become trapped by their gills in the mesh of the net. Nets are hauled aboard from either the bow or stern, depending on the boat.

Gillnetting periods occur from the end of July through November. During these seasonal openings, look for fishing boats that appear to be drifting, and look on the surface for the corkline; a buoy marks the end of the net, which is usually 1,800 feet from the boat. Often, many gillnetters work in the same area, and threading your way around their gear can be a challenge. The safest way is to head toward the fishing boat, parallel to the net; this also sends a clear signal that you see the net. When in doubt, slow down. Make sure you know where the net is before moving on.

At night, a gillnetter displays a red-over-white light on the mast. The buoy at the end of the net is also lighted, but the light may be dim and difficult to see.

Seiners

Seiners catch fish near the surface by surrounding them with a long, deep net suspended from small floats. When the circle is complete, the bottom of the net is closed ("pursed"), and the net is towed for a while. The catch is hauled aboard with a power drum or block.

The net is run around the fish by a skiff; this skiff also pulls the net away from the stern of the larger boat when the catch is hauled aboard, to prevent the net from fouling the propeller.

Seining periods occur from the end of July through November, generally during the daytime. If you see a skiff working around a fishing boat, assume it is purse seining. Head for the fishing boat, parallel to the net; this will also send a clear signal that you see the net. It is difficult to navigate through a purse seine fleet without fouling their nets; avoid the entire area if you can.

Trollers

Trollers catch fish on lines that hang from long trolling poles, one or two angled out on each side of the boat. The lines are weighted to keep them at a desired depth; each line usually has several lures. The boat itself moves at a relatively slow pace. Trollers are easy to recognize, and have no nets to worry about, but the lines may trail as much as 100 feet aft. In Puget Sound, trolling occurs in Hood Canal, Port Gamble, and the San Juan Islands.

Set Netting

Some of the Indian tribes in Puget Sound use a traditional fishing method called set netting. With this method, a gillnet is suspended on a float line between a buoy and the shore. The length of the net varies by tribe and by area. Nets are left in place and tended periodically.

During the season (usually July through November), be especially alert for these nets in narrow channels. The marker buoy at the end of each net is lighted, but the light may be dim and difficult to see.

Farming

In various parts of the sound, salmon, mussels, and oysters are raised in pens. Most pens are charted and marked. All should be avoided. Be aware that these floating pens are anchored with cables that may extend well out from the pens themselves. Salmon pens are often located where currents are strong.

Diving

A number of species are harvested commercially by diving. These include geoducks, sea urchins, and sea cucumber. When divers are working below the surface, two flags may be displayed. A red flag with a diagonal white stripe (the diving flag) may be attached to a float that follows the diver, but is often flown from the diving vessel instead. The international code "A" flag, a blue-and-white swallow-tail pennant or a solid cut-out replica, is shown aboard the diving tender. For the safety of submerged divers, stay 100 yards away.

Crabbing and Shrimping

Throughout Puget Sound, buoys marking crab or shrimp pots can be numerous, depending on the season. Take care that you don't run over the lines, or snag a pot with your hook when anchoring.

Public Shorelines

One of the pleasures of boating in Puget Sound is the relative scarcity of towns, cities, and housing developments. Much of the shoreline is deeply wooded, and the beaches seem deserted. Anchored cozily in an isolated harbor, with no one in sight, boaters often—and inaccurately—assume that the land is uninhabited and belongs to no one.

The increase of population and boaters in the past decade has led to an abundance of signs posted by property owners. Where boating pressure is highest—in the San Juan Islands, near state parks and public street ends—the signs are most numerous. Some are simply worded PRIVATE PROPERTY or NO TRESPASSING. Some cite ordinance numbers and threaten prosecution, or hint at surveillance. Others are more creative; one property owner, apparently deluged with unwelcome visitors, has posted a large sign that reads: ALL PROPERTY, BEACHES, AND TIDELANDS NORTHEAST AND WEST OF THIS SIGN ARE NOT FOR SALE NOW AND WILL NEVER BE FOR SALE.

As a boater, keep in mind that almost all the waterfront in Washington state is private property, not public. Private waterfront may include the tidelands, and always includes the beach to the mean high tide line. On a sandy beach, this

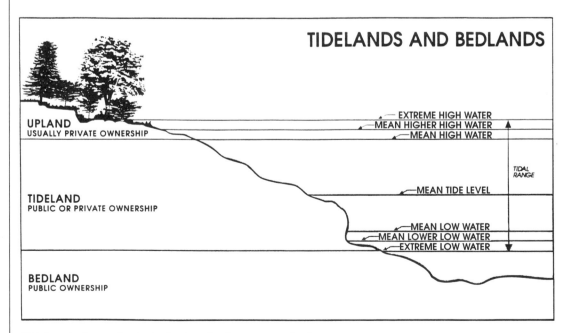

TIDELANDS AND BEDLANDS

EXTREME HIGH WATER
MEAN HIGHER HIGH WATER
MEAN HIGH WATER

UPLAND
USUALLY PRIVATE OWNERSHIP

TIDAL RANGE

MEAN TIDE LEVEL

TIDELAND
PUBLIC OR PRIVATE OWNERSHIP

MEAN LOW WATER
MEAN LOWER LOW WATER
EXTREME LOW WATER

BEDLAND
PUBLIC OWNERSHIP

Tidelands do not include the beach above mean high water.
(Department of Natural Resources)

line is roughly two or three yards seaward of the drift logs. On a rocky beach, the line is two or three yards shoreward of the uppermost barnacles. If you walk inland of this line, you are on private property. The owner may feel no more gracious about your presence than you would about strangers taking over the cockpit of your boat or having a barbecue in the backyard of your home.

Tidelands

Confusion arises regarding public tidelands. In Washington State, the term "tidelands" refers to the area between the mean high tide line as described above, and the extreme low tide line. Less than 50 percent of the tidelands in Washington are public. Where they exist, public tidelands are usually bordered on three sides by private property, and have no public access by land. Exceptions generally are at street ends, parks, or private facilities such as marinas and resorts catering to visiting boaters. Generally, these exceptions are posted as public. A good rule of thumb is to assume that a beach or dock is private unless posted otherwise.

In this book, public access to the shore is identified under the "Getting Ashore" heading provided for most coves and harbors. Occasionally, public tidelands are identified. A useful (and free) publication showing the location of public tidelands, *Puget Sound Shellfish Guide,* is available from the Department of Fisheries, the Department of Natural Resources, and the Department of Parks and Recreation.

Marine State Parks

The Washington State Parks and Recreation Commission provides facilities specially geared for Puget Sound boaters. Forty saltwater marine parks are located throughout the sound, including 12 in the San Juan Islands. With a few exceptions, all have mooring buoys or floats; some have both. Facilities such as showers, launching ramps, sewage pumpouts, and scuba areas (underwater parks) vary. Specifics about each park are given in the text. By region, these parks and their mooring facilities are:

Region 1, South Puget Sound—The Western Portion, including Olympia and Case Inlet:
- Hope Island—buoy only
- Jarrell Cove—buoys and floats
- McMicken Island—buoys only
- Stretch Point—buoys only

Region 2, South Puget Sound—The Eastern Portion, including Carr Inlet:
- Cutts Island—buoys only
- Eagle Island—buoys only
- Kopachuck—buoys only
- Penrose Point—buoys and float
- Tolmie—buoys only

Region 3—Point Defiance to Point Vashon:
- Saltwater—buoys only

Region 4—Blake Island to Kingston and Edmonds, including Port Orchard and Poulsbo:
- Blake Island—buoys and floats
- Fay Bainbridge—buoys
- Fort Ward—buoys
- Illahee—buoys and float

Region 5—Inside the Ballard Locks:
- No marine state parks

Region 6—Hood Canal:
- Kitsap Memorial—buoys only
- Pleasant Harbor—float only
- Potlatch—buoys only
- Twanoh—buoys and float

Blake Island State Park is a showcase for Native American art and dance.

Region 7—Admiralty Inlet, from Port Ludlow to Port Townsend:
- Fort Flagler—buoys and float
- Fort Worden—buoys and floats
- Mystery Bay—buoys and float
- Old Fort Townsend—buoys only

Region 8—Everett to Anacortes, including Deception Pass and La Conner:
- Bowman Bay/Sharpes Cove—buoys and float
- Cornet Bay—floats only
- Hope Island—buoys only
- Skagit Island—buoys only

Region 9—Guemes Island to Point Roberts, including Bellingham Bay:
- Saddlebag Island—no buoys or floats

Region 10—The San Juan Islands:
- Blind Island—buoys only
- Clark Island—buoys only
- Doe Island—float only
- James Island—buoys and float
- Jones Island—buoys and float
- Matia Island—buoys and float
- Patos Island—buoys only
- Posey Island—no buoys or floats
- Spencer Spit—buoys only
- Stuart Island—buoys and floats
- Sucia Island—buoys and floats
- Turn Island—buoys only

Region 11—The Strait of Juan de Fuca, from Discovery Bay to Port Angeles:
- Sequim Bay—buoys and float

Floats

Floats vary in length, and are not always in deep water. In some parks, floats are removed in winter to protect them from storms. Check the entry in the text for specific information. Rafting is permitted (within posted limits) but not required.

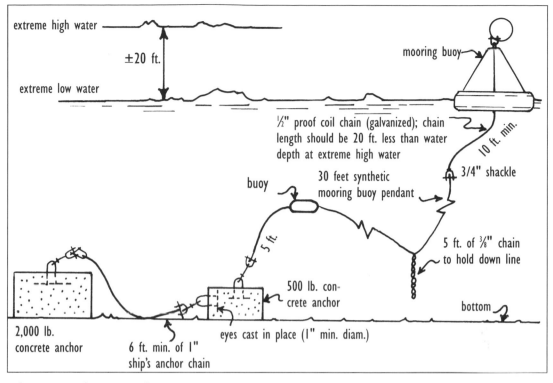

In the diagram:

extreme high water

±20 ft.

extreme low water

mooring buoy

½" proof coil chain (galvanized); chain length should be 20 ft. less than water depth at extreme high water

10 ft. min.

3/4" shackle

buoy

30 feet synthetic mooring buoy pendant

5 ft.

5 ft. of ⅜" chain to hold down line

500 lb. con-crete anchor

bottom

2,000 lb. concrete anchor

6 ft. min. of 1" ship's anchor chain

eyes cast in place (1" min. diam.)

The state park mooring buoy system. (Washington State Parks and Recreation Commission)

Buoys

State park buoys have pyramid tops above a white tire float. The buoy is secured with chain and line to a 500-pound concrete anchor block, which is chained in turn to a 1-ton concrete anchor block. The smaller block reduces the strain on the main block. The system, though stout, has its limits. The maximum number of boats allowed per buoy depends on the length of the boat: up to three 24-foot boats, two 25- to 36-foot boats, or one 37- to 45-foot boat.

Boats over 45 feet in length should not tie to these mooring buoys. Many of the buoys are set on narrow underwater shelves, and a boat that is too heavy may drag the anchor into deeper or shallower water. Your boat, or the next boat that ties to the buoy, may drift or go aground.

Don't assume a buoy is set in water deep enough for your boat. Check the tide tables and verify the depth yourself. Relative depths are approximated in the text.

Fees

From May 1 through September 30, many of the state parks charge fees for overnight use of mooring buoys and floats. A few charge all year round: Blake Island, Jarrell Cove, Fort Worden, Cornet Bay, and Mystery Bay. Self-service pay stations (fee boxes) are located on shore. Rafted boats each pay the full fee. A surcharge is added if park staff collect the fee. Instead of paying a nightly fee, you can buy an Annual Moorage Permit, valid from January 1 through

December 31 at all parks. To obtain a permit, call or write: Washington State Parks—Moorage Permit Program, 7150 Cleanwater Lane, Olympia, WA 98504-5711; telephone (360) 753-5771.

Boaters with permit stickers are asked to register their permit number at the pay stations, in order to help the parks keep accurate records of visitors.

Other Limitations

All mooring at buoys or floats is on a first-come, first-served basis. The state parks do not take reservations for buoys or floats. Leaving a dinghy or other property at a buoy or float does not reserve a moorage space. Stays are limited to 72 hours.

Closures

The dates when parks close are noted in the text, especially where they affect availability of showers or use of other facilities. Dates are subject to change, however; for a current list call the Washington State Parks 24-hour request line at (360) 753-2027.

Even if a park is officially closed, you may still use the mooring buoys and floats.

Other Parks

In addition to these marine parks, the state has others located on the water that may be accessible by boat. These are described throughout the text. Some counties and municipalities provide park facilities for boaters, others prohibit boat access; see the relevant chapters.

Respecting the Puget Sound Environment

Puget Sound is a biologically rich and productive area. Boaters are accustomed to sharing the waters with otters, seals, and porpoises, and to feasting on crabs, clams, salmon, and bottom fish. Birds are varied and many species are abundant. Eagles, once so rare, have grown to the largest population in the lower 48 states, and can be seen everywhere—including inside the Seattle city limits. This section suggests ways in which boaters can help preserve both the wildlife and the natural beauty of Puget Sound.

Wildlife Refuges and Biological Preserves

Refuges and preserves are for wildlife—not human—use. They provide areas where animals can rest, feed, and raise their young, and where plants and intertidal life can thrive. Many of these refuges, such as the San Juan National Wildlife Refuge (NWR) and the Nisqually Refuge, are on public lands. Others, such as those managed by the Nature Conservancy and the San Juan Preservation Trust, are on private lands.

Regardless of ownership, human access is usually prohibited. Those areas where boaters may go ashore are described in the text. If you visit these refuges, do not treat them as parks. Observe all restrictions. Occasionally, the Department of Natural Resources or other agency may close an area temporarily to protect seasonal habitat; pay attention to signs posted, and respect their stated restrictions.

Note the National Wildlife Refuges marked as "NWR" on charts, and stay 200 yards away—even if other boaters do not.

Guidelines to Watching Wildlife

Wildlife sightings are often the highlight of a cruise. In order to help these animals thrive in Puget Sound, it is important to observe them in ways that do not harm them.

Whales. Though gray, minke, and other whales are often seen in Puget Sound, the best-known and most acrobatic are orcas. Their tall dorsal fins are easy to recognize, and their black-and-white markings give them a distinguished, tuxedoed look.

Two main populations of orcas can be seen in Puget Sound: a transient pod that ranges from Alaska to California, and a resident pod that has become the most thoroughly studied in the world. Residents consist of three groups. Each member of the group—identified by its unique dorsal fin—has a name. You can even "adopt" one of them through a program sponsored by the Whale Museum in Friday Harbor.

Orcas range throughout Puget Sound, but are most regularly seen around the San Juan Islands, where they feed on Fraser River salmon runs. A thriving charter "whale watching" business has grown; private boaters, armed with cameras and video recorders, have understandably joined the "hunt."

Whales are protected by federal law. If you sight an orca or other whale from your boat, follow these rules:

- Do not approach closer than 100 yards.
- Approach slowly from the side, parallel to and no faster than the slowest whale.
- Never separate mothers from offspring.
- If a whale approaches, turn off your engine and drift (unless this puts your boat in jeopardy). Under sail, turn into the wind if you can to slow down, and don't do a lot of maneuvering.

Incidents of harassment should be reported, with the violator's vessel name and ID number, to the National Marine Fisheries Service, (206) 526-6133. Washington State has a Whale Hotline that takes reports of sightings and strandings—(800) 562-8832.

Seals. Harbor seals are the most common marine mammal in Puget Sound. Once hunted relentlessly for bounty, their major predator today is the orca. In the water, harbor seals are swift and curious, often surfacing and diving near boats, as though playing a game of hide-and-seek. However, when hauled out on rafts or rocks, seals are extremely wary of humans. They quickly enter the water when even the smallest, quietest boat is within 100 yards. Pups can be crushed in the rush. Pupping occurs during the height of cruising season, from mid-August to late September, but disturbing seals in their haulout areas at any time needlessly stresses them.

Where seals are hauled out, keep a minimum of 200 yards away. If you find a pup, do not assume it is abandoned. Leave it alone. Report strandings to the Whale Hotline—(800) 562-8832.

Northern and California sea lions, and the rarer northern fur seal, hunt and feed in Puget Sound waters, but do not breed here. Sea lions are large, move rapidly on land, and can be dangerously aggressive—do not approach them.

Birds. The wetlands, cliffs, rocks, and islands of Puget Sound are a rich feeding and nesting ground for birds. Some, like snow geese and black brant, are here only through winter. Others, including bald eagles, herons, cor-

17

If you find a seal pup that seems abandoned, leave the area. The mother is probably nearby, but will not approach when you are around.

morants, rhinoceros auklets, puffins, and many species of duck, are year-round residents.

Leave all feeding and resting birds alone. Whether in a boat or on foot, move slowly and quietly. Use binoculars or a telephoto lens if you want a closer look. Under no circumstances should you deliberately disturb birds in order to photograph flying scenes; such flights needlessly (not to mention cruelly) cause them to expend energy that should be reserved for migrating, nesting, or feeding young. For migrating species, continual disturbance during the critical feeding months (winter and spring) can lead to death from stress-induced disease, and eventual nesting failure on northern breeding grounds.

Sportfishing and Shellfish Gathering

One of the major activities of Puget Sound boaters—indeed, the only reason some take a boat out at all—is to fish or clam. The best places and methods for doing so are the subject of much debate, and beyond the scope of this book. Regulations are numerous. A few general guidelines are described below.

Licenses. All fishing (including bottom fish), and all shellfish and seaweed gathering, requires a license. Licenses are sold at most sporting-goods or hardware stores, at some marinas and boat charters, and at Department of Fish and Wildlife field offices.

Fishing Regulations. Different seasons apply to different species. For regulations regarding gear, open seasons, and catch limits, see the sportfishing guide published by the Department of Fish and Wildlife. This guide is obtainable where you pick up your license.

Shellfish and Seaweed. Per-person limits and seasonal openings vary by species; see the sportfishing guide published by the Department of Fish and Wildlife, obtainable where you pick up your license.

For clams, pay attention to periodic closures due to red tide—paralytic shellfish poisoning is real and serious. For up-to-date information call the Red Tide Hotline: (800) 562-5632. When digging clams, always back-fill your holes to protect exposed organisms from predators like seagulls and crows, and to promote continued clam population.

Shrimping is limited to specific places and times of year. There are also restrictions regarding the number of pots per person, and the type of pot that may be used.

Limits apply to all crabbing. For the popular Dungeness, only males 6¼ inches or more across the back may be taken; in Hood Canal, males 6 inches across may be taken. Limits vary from year to year. Throughout the year, restrictions apply regarding the type of pot that may be used.

Garbage and Sewage Disposal

The watery world so enjoyed by Puget Sound boaters may appear vast and forgiving, but is readily contaminated by oil, garbage, and by human sewage. The extreme tides do not "flush" the sound twice a day, as many suppose; Puget Sound waters are wholly replaced only twice a year, less often in South Sound and Hood Canal. Contamination affects the entire food chain, to say nothing of the appearance of beaches and the quality of harbors and coves.

Garbage. For Puget Sound boaters, local, federal, and international regulations concerning trash disposal are simple: *Nothing may be thrown overboard.* Not coffee grounds, not cigarette butts, not even apple cores. Certainly not waste oil, Styrofoam cups or plastics of any kind (which are harmful to boats as well, fouling props and clogging water intakes).

Make a place for garbage on your boat and dispose of it in trash containers on shore. Some marinas have waste-oil receptacles and recycling areas. At marina resorts, expect to be charged for each bag of garbage unless you are paying for moorage.

Sewage. The Coast Guard approves various marine toilets, but the regulations for the disposal of marine sewage are the same for all. *No untreated sewage may be dumped in Puget Sound waters, including the San Juan Islands and the American side of the Strait of Juan de Fuca.*

Sewage is considered "treated" only if it is properly processed by a Type I or Type II marine sanitation device (MSD); dumping even these is prohibited when the boat is moored in the city of Seattle. Boaters with other types of MSD must use a sewage pumpout station or service.

These pumpouts, once hard to find and unreliable, are becoming more plentiful. Currently there are more than 50 in Puget Sound, including the San Juans and the freshwater areas inside the Ballard Locks. For an updated list, see the *Washington State Boater's Guide*. This free publication is available at most state parks, wherever boat licenses are sold, and from local marine patrol units. You can also get a copy of this booklet by writing to: Boating Safety Program, Washington State Parks, 7150 Cleanwater Lane, Olympia, WA 98504-2654. The phone number is (360) 586-2166.

Getting Help on the Water

Depending on the nature of your problem, and the degree of danger you face, there are several avenues to pursue to get help on the water.

Distress Calls

A distress situation is defined as one where you or your boat are threatened by *grave* or *imminent* danger requiring immediate assistance. Under most circumstances, the Coast Guard does not consider running out of fuel or getting lost in the fog a distress situation.

In the event of a distress, call "Mayday, Mayday, Mayday" on Channel 16. The Coast Guard will take immediate steps to help you.

To do so, they will ask for the following information:

- Your location or position.
- Exact nature of the problem.
- Number of people on board.
- Description of your boat.
- Safety equipment on board (number of life jackets, etc.).
- Your boat name and registration.
- Any special problems.

Non-distress Calls

In situations where you need assistance but are not threatened by grave or imminent danger, simply call "Coast Guard" on Channel 16. Depending on the nature of the help you need, the Coast Guard may contact the Coast Guard Auxiliary or a vessel assistance company, and/ or make a marine broadcast that announces your location and invites other mariners to come to your aid.

You may also call another boat or a vessel assistance company yourself on Channel 16. Keep in mind that ships and other commercial vessels participating in the Vessel Traffic System (VTS) are not required to monitor Channel 16. When necessary, they may be contacted on Channel 13; use low power only.

Approaches to Puget Sound

There are several routes into Puget Sound from Canadian waters. Boaters entering via the Strait of Juan de Fuca will find the introduction to Region 11 helpful (page 354), as well as the description of the approach to Port Angeles (page 367). For those entering via Haro Strait or the Strait of Georgia, see Approaches to the San Juan Islands (Region 10), beginning on page 278. Additional information about the Strait of Georgia is given in the introduction to Region 9, on page 248.

U.S. Customs

When entering from a foreign port (including Canada), you must report to a designated U.S. Customs Port of Entry immediately after the boat has come to rest. You may report in person or from a dock phone at the Port of Entry. In either case, the boat must be available for inspection by a Customs agent.

Only one person (the vessel's master or designated representative) may go ashore to report arrival. No other person may leave the boat, and no baggage or merchandise may be removed from the boat, until release is granted by the Customs agent.

Have the following information ready

when you report your arrival:

1. Vessel number.
2. Vessel name and length.
3. User fee decal number, if you have one.
4. Canadian clearance number, for boats moored in U.S. waters.
5. Estimated date of departure, for boats moored in Canada.

You will receive a release number when you are cleared by the Customs agent. The U.S. Customs agency strongly recommends that you retain details of the release number, date, and port of entry for at least one year.

Ports of Entry

The designated Ports of Entry in Puget Sound are:

Anacortes—(360) 293-2331
Bellingham—(360) 734-5463
Blaine—(360) 332-6318
Everett—(206) 259 0246
Friday Harbor/Roche Harbor—(360) 378-2080
Olympia—(206) 593-6338 (serviced by Tacoma)

Point Roberts—(360) 945-2314
Port Angeles—(360) 457-4311
Port Townsend—(360) 385-3777
Seattle—(206) 553-4678
Tacoma—(206) 593-6338

On Sundays or holidays, and on weekdays before 8 A.M. and after 5 P.M., call the toll-free number: (800) 562-5943. If you can't reach the toll-free number, contact the local telephone operator for the appropriate access code.

Fees

Recreational vessels 30 feet or more in length are required to pay an annual processing fee, currently $25. If you report your arrival by telephone, a fee application will be mailed. Upon payment, a non-transferable decal is issued that is good for the calendar year.

SOUTH PUGET SOUND: THE WESTERN PORTION

A sloop ghosts along the entrance to Eld Inlet.

INCLUDING OLYMPIA AND CASE INLET

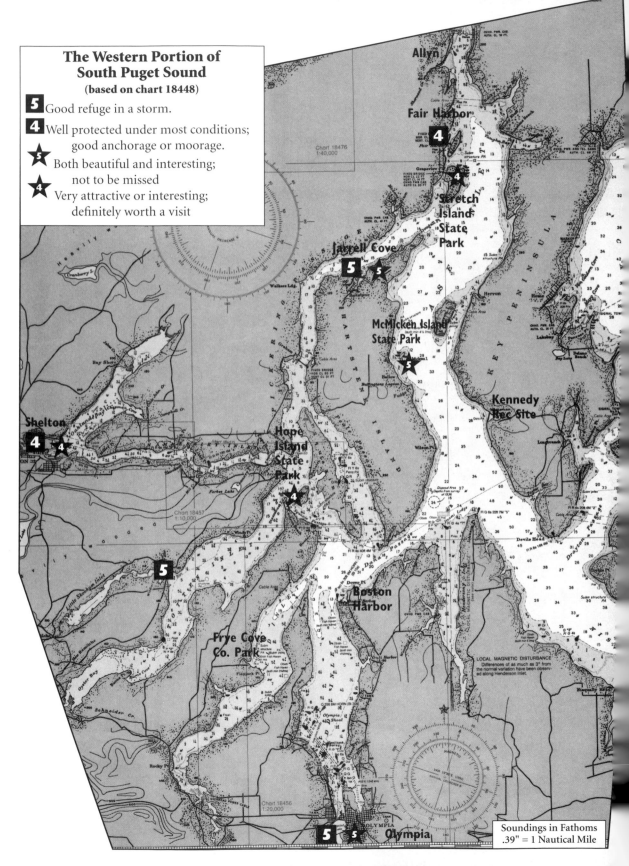

The Western Portion of South Puget Sound
(based on chart 18448)

5 Good refuge in a storm.

4 Well protected under most conditions; good anchorage or moorage.

★**5** Both beautiful and interesting; not to be missed

★**4** Very attractive or interesting; definitely worth a visit

Allyn

Fair Harbor **4**

4 Stretch Island State Park

Jarrell Cove **5** ★**5**

McMicken Island State Park

★**5**

KEY PENINSULA

Kennedy Rec Site

Shelton **4** **4**

Hope Island State Park **4**

5

Boston Harbor

Frye Cove Co. Park

Devils Head

LOCAL MAGNETIC DISTURBANCE
Differences of as much as 3° from the normal variation have been observed along Henderson Inlet.

5 **5** Olympia

Soundings in Fathoms
.39" = 1 Nautical Mile

24

West of the Key Peninsula, the channels of south Puget Sound multiply, winding this way and that in twisted fingers between narrow islands. The land is low and the inlets are shallow, terminating invariably in broad mudflats filled with oyster stakes or log booms, notched by tiny coves that dry at low tide or trap water in brackish lagoons.

At the extreme ends of this region are its only cities: the state capital of Olympia at the south end of Budd Inlet, and the timber center of Shelton at the west end of Hammersley Inlet. As elsewhere, the shores are more densely developed near these population centers, less so otherwise. But the waters are surprisingly empty.

There's a simple reason for this relative emptiness: rain. Olympia receives, on average, more than 52 inches of rain a year—18 inches more than Seattle. Shelton averages even more. Southwest winds and moist ocean air move almost unhindered from Grays Harbor, where Aberdeen, at 84.5 inches, is one of the rainiest areas in the state. Early explorers' accounts were filled with comments about the "weighty weather" here. Combine this with the fact that the large population centers of Seattle, Everett, and Tacoma are a fair distance away by water, and it's no surprise that most boaters cruise north. The result is a pleasing lack of boating pressure.

If you've never been to this region of Puget Sound, expect to be somewhat disoriented. Channels seem to branch off endlessly, like an immense river system. Familiar landforms, such as Mount Rainier and the Olympics, are in unfamiliar locations—east and northwest, rather than south and west. Tides here are even more extreme than in the eastern portion of South Sound, with highs as much as 3 feet 6 inches higher than in Seattle.

You may need to sharpen up your navigation skills: The only detailed charts are of Budd Inlet and Hammersley Inlet, which means careful reading of chart 18448 for everything else. Sometimes you'll find yourself in an anchorage so silent and untraveled you'll be reminded of the way boating was years ago. Often you'll feel like you're cruising upstream, against the current, away from the crowds.

Henderson Inlet ★★ No facilities

Charts: 18448

The narrow finger of Henderson Inlet points true south. This area is a suburb of Olympia, with many homes on shore and many private mooring buoys. Only the upper half of the inlet is navigable. The west shore, the site of a former log dump, is now a jam of pilings and booms, with an old rail spur and derrick still standing. Since the late 1980s the Department of Natural Resources has managed this as a wildlife conservation area. Seals lounge on the logs, but you won't be able to get close, or explore the inlet that branches to the northwest (locally known as Chapman Bay). A sign warns boaters to stay 200 yards away. The southwest inlet, Woodard Bay, is accessible to non-motorized craft only.

Approaches. Enter east or west of the Itsami Ledge mark, a green "7" on dolphin pilings. Watch for the two white buoys north of this dolphin that mark an obstruction at 5 fathoms.

Inside Henderson Inlet, stay in the middle. Watch for submerged pilings on the west side.

Anchorage. The bottom is mud and the depths are good in the upper half of Henderson Inlet, but there is no real protection from prevailing winter or summer winds. Shoreline access is in the southwest inlet, Woodard Bay, by non-

North Budd Inlet
(based on chart 18456)

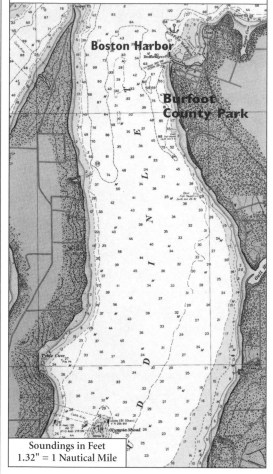

Boston Harbor

Burfoot County Park

Soundings in Feet
1.32" = 1 Nautical Mile

Budd Inlet South and Olympia Harbor
(based on chart 18456)

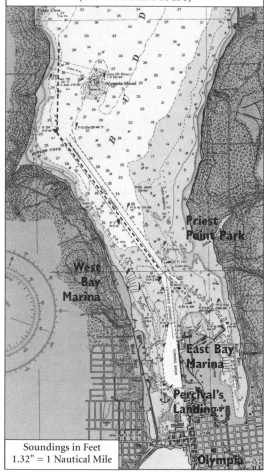

Priest Point Park

West Bay Marina

East Bay Marina

Percival's Landing

Olympia

Soundings in Feet
1.32" = 1 Nautical Mile

motorized craft only. Be prepared to walk in the mud; there is no launching ramp or other landing. The log booms and the northwest inlet of Chapman Bay are closed to provide refuge for wildlife.

Budd Inlet

Charts: 18448, **18456**

Budd Inlet points true south from the confluence of Dana, Peale, and Squaxin passages. The inlet is wooded and residential in its northern half; south of Butler Cove it is an industrial port (mainly forest products), accented by the state capitol dome.

Approaches. The capitol dome distinguishes Budd from the other inlets, and is visible from the south end of Squaxin Passage. If approaching from the east, a more prominent landmark is the white lighthouse at Dofflemyer Point. The entrance to Budd Inlet is clean on both sides as long as you keep about a quarter-mile away from shore, especially off Cooper Point, where shoals extend north and east.

Though deep at its entrance, Budd Inlet shallows out gradually from the east shore. Past Olympia Shoal—a dangerous marked reef—the east half bares altogether at the spoil bank.

If your destination is Olympia, keep to the west side. This will put you in a favorable position to enter either East Bay or West Bay via the dredged channel.

Inside Budd Inlet there are several choices for moorings and anchorage, both in and out of Olympia itself.

Boston Harbor ★★★

Charts: 18448, **18456**

Boston Harbor is a wide bight at the entrance to Budd Inlet, between Dover Point and Dofflemyer Point. Most of the harbor is taken up by a small private marina that welcomes visiting boats. The white lighthouse and the cottages along shore give it a picturesque, cozy feel. In summer, Boston Harbor is a busy resort; jet-skiers, board sailors, and skiffs swarm around the launching ramp west of the marina, and boaters from all over South Sound stop by for fuel and snacks.

Approaches. From the northeast, stay in deep water until past Dover and Jeal points, then head toward the west side of the floats. From the south, make a broad arc around Dofflemyer Point to avoid the shoals. On any approach, watch for private mooring buoys. The marina reports an approach depth to the fuel dock of 12 feet at a 5-foot tide.

Anchorage, Moorings. For overnight moorage, call ahead—(360) 357-5670. If your visit is brief, pull into an open space near the ramp south of the finger piers, or north of the finger piers on the west side of the outer floats. It's OK to anchor west and northwest of the marina itself, but be sure to keep clear of the launching ramp. Though locally regarded as a good harbor in the summer, there's no protection here from northerlies, and southerlies may gust around the point.

Getting Ashore. Use the marina guest floats.

For the Boat, Crew. Gas and diesel are at the north end of the marina floats, with some supplies at the store on shore. The nearest full-service facility is at West Bay Marina, four miles south in Budd Inlet. Groceries are suited to the drop-in boater.

Burfoot County Park ★★★ No Facilities

Charts: 18448, **18456**

Burfoot County Park lies behind a sandspit about a quarter-mile south of Dofflemyer Point. This popular day-use park has trails leading from the beach upland, where there is a large grassy area with picnic tables and shelters, play equipment, horseshoe pits, and other loop trails.

Approaches, Anchorage. The sandspit is low and may be difficult to find, but a black stone bulkhead at the park's north boundary is prominent, as is the notch in the trees that marks the lagoon and ravine. As you approach, look for the park sign on the north bluff. Anchoring may be difficult, as the underwater shelf is narrow and steep. Be sure your swing won't put you on the beach.

Priest Point Park ★★★ No Facilities

Charts: 18448, **18456**

This peaceful, thickly wooded city park two miles north of Olympia's capitol dome has a religious history. Used for centuries by Squaxin Indians for burial and spiritual gatherings, in the mid-1800s it was the site of a Catholic mission. Today its miles of trails—some quite steep—still promote contemplation. Upland is a viewpoint that overlooks Budd Inlet, and many picnic clearings. Over the bridge, on the east side of the divided road, are more picnic areas and a formal rose garden.

Approaches. Like Gull Harbor to the north, Ellis Creek is a silted estuary that is approachable only in beachable craft at high tide. The shoals from Ellis Creek extend halfway out to the dredged channel, making this park one that is best visited by land.

Olympia ★★★★★ (marina) (anchorage) All Facilities

Charts: 18448, **18456**

Olympia is one of the most pleasant cities on Puget Sound to visit by water. It has many attractions for the cruising boater: ample guest moorage, complete and convenient supplies, and a downtown within walking distance that's interlaced with historic capital grounds and parks.

Though Olympia was first developed for the timber trade, its primary business now is state government; the city has been the regional capital since Washington separated from Oregon territory in 1853. The capitol dome was the fourth tallest in the world when it was built, and is still the dominant feature. From the water, however, Olympia looks like a timber town, with towering stacks of logs on the piers between the East Bay and West Bay, and a lumber mill with extensive booming areas along the west shore.

Approaches. The southern half of Budd Inlet is shoal and in many areas foul with rocks or pilings. It's important to enter via the dredged channel. A black-and-white checked daymark on pilings marks Olympia Shoal; the main entrance to the channel begins west of nearby green buoy "1." Take care not to confuse "1" with "3," which is farther south. At "3," look southeast for the orange range markers set on pilings; these will set you on a clean course between the buoys toward the red-and-green junction mark, where the channel forks into East or West Bay. Beyond is a large radio tower that stands at the head of the peninsula.

Locals often approach east of Olympia Shoal, picking up the channel between green buoys "3" and "5." If you choose this route, use special caution in the vicinity of the unmarked but charted spoil bank.

Moorings. Olympia has two facilities for guest moorage: East Bay Marina in East Bay and Percival's Landing in West Bay.

East Bay Marina proudly affirms the Port of Olympia's commitment to high-quality marine facilities, with its stout concrete floats, crisp new restrooms with showers, a laundromat, ample parking, and groomed walkways. Plans are underway for a boat yard, a fuel dock, and a marine supply store. More than 500 pleasure and commercial craft can be accommodated here.

Enter East Bay via the marked dredged channel. All floats on "A" dock are designated for guest moorage; these floats are behind the breakwater, just south of the twin launching ramps. Moorage fees, which include power, are higher than those at Percival's Landing. Pay at the fee boxes or at the marina office at the head of "B" dock, where you can also get a key for

Percival's Landing in Olympia harbor. Guest moorage is beyond the information kiosk on the pier, slightly to the right of the capitol dome in this picture.

the restrooms and laundry. Maximum stay at East Bay Marina is 14 days. The major drawback to East Bay Marina is its location; it's a long walk from here to town.

Percival's Landing, at the southeast end of West Bay, is the more popular, though less secluded, guest moorage. You'll feel snuggled right up to the city, in sight of the capitol dome. Enter via the marked dredged channel. Once past the turning basin, head south and east of the boathouses (the boathouses and the floats south of them are part of the Olympia Yacht Club).

Guest slips begin along the east shore, south of the blue-roofed kiosk, and continue all the way to the bulkhead at the road. The floats at the far south end are about 10 feet shallower. Many of the guest slips are without power. Pay at the fee stations located at either of the two buildings, which house the restrooms and showers. Maximum stay at Percival's Landing is seven days. West Bay Marina, located about a mile north of Percival's Landing, has no overnight guest moorage.

Anchorage. The area in West Bay used as a small craft anchorage is south of the turning basin and just north of the Yacht Club boathouses. Holding ground is good in 2 to 3 fathoms. Keep the channel clear. For shore access, use Percival's Landing guest floats.

For the Boat. A hardware store is east of Percival's Landing, across Columbia Street. This store has an enormous inventory, and serves as a general information center, with bus schedules posted, mail service, and a photo display of locally caught "trophy" fish. Supplies are also available at the marine store facing the harbor across 4th Avenue. Currently, the nearest fuel is at West Bay Marina, a private facility about a mile to the north on the west shore. The fuel dock at West Bay Marina is between "F" and "G" floats. This dock dries at low tide. Deep-draft vessels should fuel at Boston

Harbor. At present the only marine repair yard in Olympia operates at West Bay Marina.

For the Crew. A wide variety of restaurants and shops are downtown, within a block of Percival's Landing. A supermarket is on 4th Avenue, west of the yacht club. From May through October, a festive open-air farmers' market operates Thursday through Sunday. This market is located across the street from Percival's Landing on Capitol Way, south of the hardware store. There's no laundromat close to Percival's Landing. A laundry is located at West Bay Marina.

Things to Do. Moored at Percival's Landing, you can immediately begin to entertain yourself. The floats and surrounding boardwalk park commemorate Olympia's first deep-water dock, then approachable only at high tide. Steamboats used the dock from the 1850s to the 1920s.

For a view of the harbor, walk north on the boardwalk and climb the tower; there's an outline drawing to help you identify the Olympic Mountains. Watch the log handling and ship loading on the commercial piers, and look south to the harbor spread below you, the capitol dome beyond. The capitol building itself is worth a visit; daily tours start from the main floor.

Capitol Lake, a tidal bog until it was dammed in the early 1950s, is surrounded by park. There's a swimming beach, dock, and fishing pier in the lower (north) lake, reachable via a promenade that begins at the boardwalk. The Washington State Capital Museum is south of the capitol building, on West 21st Street. On the west side of the lake are salmon pens and an interpretive center.

Those with time and energy for a long walk (about three-and-a-half miles from the harbor) can continue on into Tumwater, the first settlement of non-Indian Americans in the state. Tumwater is now a National Historic District.

Special events in Olympia include a Wooden Boat Fair on the second weekend in May and Harbor Days on Labor Day weekend—known for its tugboat races. Large portions of Percival's Landing are reserved for participating vessels during these events. In mid-July, Capital Lakefair draws crowds with limited hydroplane races, a carnival and food concessions at Capitol Lake, and an arts and crafts sale at Percival's Landing.

Butler and Tykle Coves ★★ No Facilities

Charts: 18448, **18456**

These two coves on the west side of Budd Inlet offer slight protection in 1 to 3 fathoms of mud. Approaches are clean. However, both are crowded with private mooring buoys and swim rafts, and ringed by homes. There is no public shore access.

Eld Inlet

Charts: 18448, **18456**

Eld Inlet snakes south and west from Dana and Squaxin passages. Its northeast shore is a display of large homes, with broad lawns and narrow beaches—a somewhat glamorous suburb of Olympia. The west shore is more wooded and the homes more modest. The inlet narrows about two miles south of Flapjack Point, quickly shallowing into mudflats that bristle with oyster stakes. Even a small boat will need to take care in this southern end to avoid grounding or disturbing the oyster beds.

Approaches. From the northwest, the green mark on Hunter Point is visible from Squaxin Passage. Before rounding the point, wait until you see the charted dolphin pilings about a half-mile south of the mark. Stay east of the pilings. As you approach Cooper Point, which divides Budd and Eld Inlet, slightly favor the west shore.

Arriving from the east via Dana or Peale passage, look south for the white lighthouse off Dofflemyer Point, then east for Cooper Point. Boats on this approach, and those traveling up from Budd Inlet, should take extra care to stay a quarter-mile off Cooper Point, as the beach extends north like a needle, farther than you'd expect.

The two anchorages worth noting are located north and south of Flapjack Point.

Cove North of Flapjack Point (Frye Cove) ★★★ 3   No Facilities

Charts: 18448, **18456**

Known locally as Frye Cove, the attraction here is a small, day-use county park. A groomed path leads from the rocky beach to a grassy meadow, where picnic tables and shelters are set among what appears to be the remains of an old orchard. Upland are restrooms and more trails that connect to a parking lot at the road. This is a lovely site, with tall evergreens and just enough room to stretch your legs, throw a Frisbee, and feel far away from nearby Olympia.

Approaches. The park is about a half-mile west of Flapjack Point, on the knuckle of land north of the unnamed inlet. From a mile or so away you can see the green lawn and tall, light-gray building that houses the restrooms. In contrast to the surrounding residential area, the park itself is heavily wooded.

Anchorage. Anchorage is off the park, east of the charted pilings. A sign on a nearby buoy reminds boaters that the park extends only halfway across the bay, so anchor accordingly. The mud bottom shallows gradually. There's no protection from the north, and little from prevailing southwest gusts.

Getting Ashore. All tidelands outside the park are private. The park beach is small and the bank steep.

Cove South of Flapjack Point (Young Cove) ★★ 2 🔧

Charts: 18448

Though the inlet southeast of Flapjack Point (also called Young Cove) seems to be an inviting anchorage, it is so shallow that locals place their own mooring buoys well outside in 2 fathoms of water or more, where there is no protection from the southwest. The private launching ramp on the north shore is available for a fee. A small boatyard that specializes in carefully crafted pleasure and passenger vessels operates upland from this ramp, and is available for repairs. There are no other facilities.

Approaches. Approaches to the anchorage outside Young Cove are clean. Enter the cove itself on a rising tide only, and watch for the charted rocks near both shores.

Evergreen State College Environmental Reserve

Charts: 18448

Just south of the notch on the east shore, across the inlet from Young Cove, is a wooded low-bank gravel beach, the site of the Evergreen State College Environmental Reserve. Despite its "public" appearance, this beach is reserved for faculty, staff, and students of the college. Signs posted on shore and on the nearby piling ask that the general public stay away.

Totten Inlet

Charts: 18448

When Captain George Vancouver's men explored Totten Inlet in 1792, they remarked on the "abundance of small oysters" found there. The same could be said of Totten Inlet today, though the oysters now are often the larger, Japanese variety rather than the smaller Olympia species. Along the shore, oyster shells are piled like haystacks beside small wooden shacks, and the beaches are bleached with their razor-like shards.

Totten Inlet is shaped somewhat like a crab's claw, the narrow, north pincer of Little Skookum Inlet curving toward the wider, south pincer that terminates in the mudflats of Oyster Bay. Primary anchorage is at the entrance to Little Skookum, though it's possible to anchor in a few other spots.

Approaches. From the east, give Steamboat Island a wide berth in order to avoid the shoals that extend northeast and northwest (the northwest shoal is marked). The bridge connecting Steamboat to Carlyon Beach is a low trestle; the marina east of this bridge is private. Inside Totten, stay alert for floating oyster pens and especially oyster stakes, which are often difficult to see.

Cove on the East Side of Totten Inlet ★★ No Facilities

Charts: 18448

About three miles south of Steamboat Island, north of a knob of land on the east shore, is a protective-looking cove with a clean entrance. The protective appearance is illusory, however, as southwesterlies funnel through the swale of land and on to Windy Point, north across the inlet. Oyster pens fill the best area for anchoring. All tidelands are private.

Burns Cove and Oyster Bay ★★ No Facilities

Charts: 18448

Shallow and obstructed with either oyster pens or stakes, most of the southern end of Totten Inlet, including Burns Cove and Oyster Bay, is unsuitable for anchoring. Even a skiff can eas-

Steamboat Island, an unmistakable landmark for navigating the western reaches of South Sound.

ily ground here. The charted mark on the west shore at the entrance to this area is a light on a tire float, maintained by the Coast Guard Auxiliary. Just beyond this mark there is deep water as charted, but you'll soon be in a fathom or less at low tide. A better anchorage is north of the mark against the west shore, where holding ground is good, there are few obstructions, and there is reasonable protection from the southwest. All tidelands are private.

Little Skookum Inlet ★★★ No Facilities

Charts: 18448

Narrow and twisted, too shallow for most boaters, Little Skookum Inlet feels timeless and removed from the rest of Puget Sound. There are a few new homes along the wooded shores, but most structures are farm-like, with weathered wooden oyster houses on pilings. Deer graze in the meadows, and herons stand elegant and motionless in the shadows. So much oystering goes on in Little Skookum that the bottom shoals white with discarded shells. It is difficult to imagine now that this inlet was once regularly served by steamboats transporting loggers and supplies to Kamilche.

Little Skookum is ideal for exploring by skiff while your boat is anchored at the entrance.

Approaches, Anchorage. Depths at the entrance to Little Skookum are 2 fathoms or less, as charted, and the approaches are clean. Protected anchorage is just inside, between Wildcat Cove and Deer Harbor. Enter mid-channel, slightly favoring the south shore. Wildcat Cove and Deer Harbor are themselves too shallow for most vessels. The tiny marina on the south shore is private, as are the mooring buoys.

Squaxin Island

Charts: 18448

This narrow island north of Budd Inlet takes its name from the Indian word meaning "alone." The name fits; not only does Squaxin stand apart as one of the few undeveloped areas in South Sound, but as reservation land since 1854, its beaches and harbors are for use by tribal members only. For many years the single glorious exception was a state park on the south tip. In 1993 the Squaxin Tribe and the

Getting Ashore. All tidelands in Little Skookum Inlet are private, including the grounds posted as "Southwest Division Headquarters" halfway up the inlet.

Parks and Recreation Commission were unable to settle a tidelands lease, leaving the state-owned upland parcel inaccessible to boaters. All buoys, floats, picnic shelters and other park buildings have been removed.

Respect reservation land and help protect its shellfish resources by not anchoring in any of the island's bays or coves.

Hope Island State Park ★★★★

Charts: 18448, **18457**

Between Steamboat and Squaxin islands lies small, almond-shaped Hope Island. Until recently Hope was privately owned; this, and the lack of a bridge to the mainland or a good harbor, saved it from the unrelieved development across Squaxin Passage. Now a day-use state park, plans are to keep Hope as unspoiled as possible. The island has no facilities for visitors other than a perimeter trail.

Approaches. When approaching from the southeast, stay west of nun buoy "2," which marks a reef and shoal. Approaches are clean from the north. Take extra care if passing between Hope and Squaxin islands, as the mudflats on the

Squaxin side are extensive and unmarked.

Anchorage, Moorings. A single mooring buoy is placed just outside the tiny notch at the island's southwest tip, within sight of the rustic "administration" building. The current here is strong, and the view of Carlyon Beach, with its many homes stacked up the hill, is unattractive. A more scenic and somewhat more protected anchorage is on the northwest side, in gradually sloping mud bottom. Expect currents to be strong here also.

Getting Ashore. The shoreline of Hope Island is public.

Hammersley Inlet

Charts: 18448, **18457**

Hammersley Inlet is narrow and beautiful, with a surprise around each bend. Some portions are wild and overgrown, so undisturbed

you'll feel like the first person ever there. Other portions are tamed, with tidy homes set back on trimmed lawns, their flower beds circled with stones. Now and then a large, carefully designed home with landscaped grounds announces its owner's wealth. Hammersley rolls on indifferently, a lovely green river.

The beauty of Hammersley Inlet disguises its many hazards. Navigating it the first few times is a challenge. The *Coast Pilot*'s warnings are grim: current velocities of 5 knots, numerous shoals and bars, "dangerous for strangers." Chart 18457 is essential. Study the tables and choose a rising tide with a moderate current. Some locals prefer the time just after low, when the dry spots are visible. Landforms are important—it's helpful to create your own navigational "ranges" from the many streams and points in order to clarify course and position—so don't attempt the inlet in darkness.

Be cautious, but don't be paranoid; a log tug regularly makes the run at high tide, and most Shelton boaters navigate with the course that's printed on their yacht club placemats. In 1920, a 50-foot humpback whale, seriously off its migration route, ended up in Oakland Bay by accident. If you're careful and alert, you should have no trouble.

Approaches. Alertness is needed right from the start. The buildings of Arcadia on the south shore of the entrance are easy to spot, but the mark charted there no longer exists. Nor does green "1," charted at 300 yards south of Hungerford Point. This, and the red "2" inside, west of Cape Horn, snagged so many log rafts the Coast Guard finally removed them altogether.

To enter, stay close to Hungerford Point, following the steep north shore to Cape Horn. Expect to feel like you're entering a dead-end bay. Once past Cape Horn, the channel becomes more obvious but no less deceptive, especially now that red "2" no longer exists. Avoid the shoal it once marked by favoring the south shore to Cannery Point, then go mid-channel for about three-quarters of a mile. Use the landforms and your depthsounder to determine when you should head for the south shore, which you should favor past Libby Point (marked) and Skookum Point (unmarked).

A shoal spreads westward of Skookum Point. Avoid this by favoring the north shore until you have passed Church Point. From here on a mid-channel course will keep you in deepest water. A privately maintained light is on the south shore between Church Point and Miller Point, on a shingled pyramid at the foot of a flagpole. This mark is more prominent and useful when you are eastbound, though in both directions it's a good reminder of the extensive shoal across from it on the north shore. You probably won't feel relaxed until past Munson and Eagle points.

Shelton ★★★★ 3 (anchorage) 4 (marina)

Charts: 18448, **18457**

Shelton's location in Oakland Bay, at the hairpin turn of Hammersley Inlet, isolates it from the rest of Puget Sound. You have to really want to get there, and be ready to navigate the long run in and out of Hammersley. Mention a cruise to Shelton, and other boaters will probably blink in disbelief.

Still primarily a timber town, Shelton is all business, its harbor jammed with log booms and pilings, its air pungent with the smell of fresh sawdust and pulp. Smoke and steam rise perpetually from the Simpson mill; at night it flashes white in the darkness. Though hardly oriented toward the rare boating visitor, Shelton is a walkable town that offers a pleasing array of services, supplies, and historic interest.

Moorings. The marina at Shelton is north of the mill, where a large fuel-storage tank hovers above the boathouses. The guest float sets east-west between the boathouses. Due to the mooring configuration, turning room may be tight. The float itself is only about 50 feet long, but there's often room. Tie either side. The first

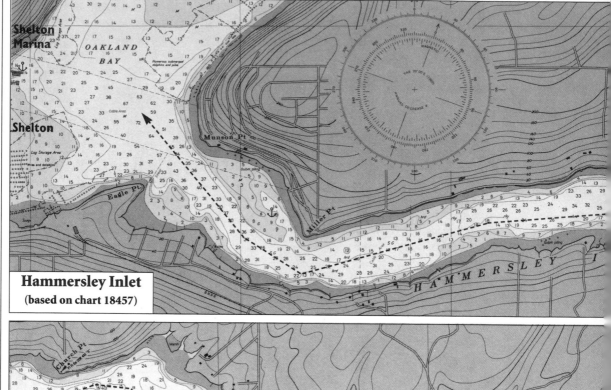

Hammersley Inlet
(based on chart 18457)

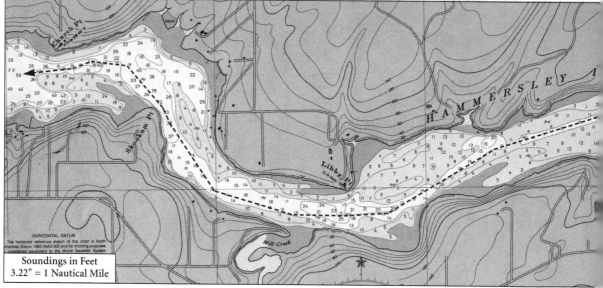

HORIZONTAL DATUM
The horizontal reference datum of this chart is North
American Datum 1983 (NAD 83) and for charting purposes
is considered equivalent to the World Geodetic System

Soundings in Feet
3.22" = 1 Nautical Mile

48 hours is free, with a small fee for electricity. Don't be surprised if you're personally welcomed. The yacht club at the head of the dock is especially friendly.

Anchorage. If the guest float is full, there's good anchorage just north of the marina. Another alternative is across Oakland Bay between Munson and Miller points, in a pocket of deep water that's reasonably protected. North of Shelton, Oakland Bay and Chapman Cove are too shallow for anchoring, and are obstructed with pilings and commercial oyster beds.

Getting Ashore. At the Shelton marina, tie your skiff to the guest float, as the others have locked gates. Public shore access is also available at a park across Oakland Bay, between Munson and Miller points. This park has a

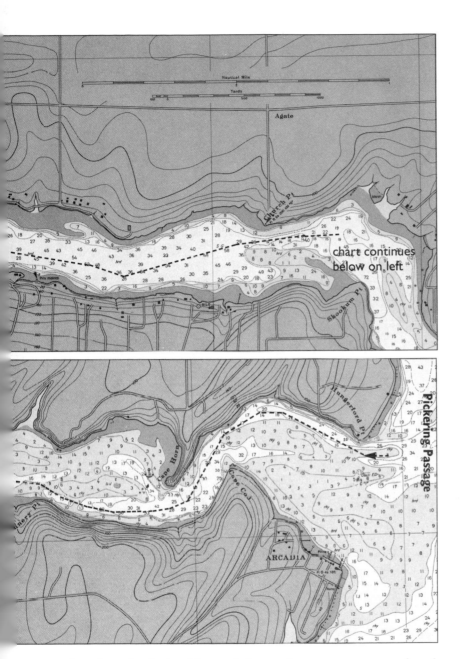

chart continues below on left

boat launch, picnic tables, and play equipment.

For the Boat. A marine repair shop is about a mile from the harbor, on Grove Street off 1st Street, south of Simpson's main gate. Marine supplies are not conveniently located in Shelton, but there are a number of well-stocked hardware, auto, and truck supply stores within walking distance that may have what you need. While there is no fuel dock, you can hand-carry gas or diesel from the pumps on the highway a few hundred yards west of the marina. The nearest fuel dock is in Boston Harbor at the entrance to Budd Inlet, or at Jarrell Cove at the north end of Hartstene Island.

For the Crew. A convenience store in a service station is close by, at the intersection of 1st Street and Highway 3. A supermarket is farther

The town of Shelton at the end of Hammersley Inlet, shown here between Eagle Point and Munson Point. The boathouses of the marina are to the right (north) of the mill.

into town, at Cedar and 6th—about a mile's walk each way. The laundromat is closer, on Franklin and 1st, and the post office another block south. Pick up a map at the yacht club to locate these. A free Chamber of Commerce map and tourist guide is also available at the visitor center on Railroad Avenue between 2nd and 3rd, with a complete list of local restaurants, banks, and entertainment.

Things to Do. The tourist map and guide includes a walking tour of Shelton's historical sites. Shelton was platted and developed for the mill in the mid-1880s, and in many ways the history of Shelton is the logging history of South Sound. The visitor center itself is an attraction, a caboose attached to the original Shay locomotive that once ran between the mill and the timber lands. In addition to designated historic buildings, Shelton has antique and junk shops that are as fascinating as museums.

Shelton considers itself the Christmas tree capital of the world; a Christmas village is displayed year round near the post office. Special events in Shelton include a heritage fair in mid-May, the Mason County Forest Festival on the first weekend after Memorial Day, and the West Coast Oyster Shucking Championship and Seafood Festival on the first weekend of October. The latter event takes place at the fairgrounds northwest of town, near the airport on Highway 101. Shelton's farmers' market operates year round on weekends, at Front and Railroad.

Pickering Passage

Charts: 18448

Pickering Passage runs between the mainland and the west side of Hartstene Island, and partly along the northwest side of Squaxin Island. It is deep and unobstructed, crossed by a fixed bridge with a vertical clearance of 31 feet. The *Coast Pilot* reports that the current in Pickering Passage sets south on the ebb and north on the flood. There are a few anchorages on the mainland shore, but the most popular and protected is on Hartstene Island, at Jarrell Cove.

Coves South of the Hartstene Bridge ★★ No Facilities

Charts: 18448

Two coves indent the west shore of Pickering Passage south of the Hartstene Bridge. Both are lined with private homes and crowded with private mooring buoys, floats, and swim rafts. Both are charted at 2 fathoms or less.

The southern cove offers some protection from the north behind its north hook, and from the south at the opposite end. A giant painted plywood eagle is a distinguishing landmark. Watch for the pilings charted off the south point. All tidelands are private.

The northern cove is a bit more hazardous in its approach, but also more interesting. The Olympia Yacht Club maintains a lovely outpost on the tiny island at the southern end of the cove, not quite one mile south of the bridge. The outpost has a clubhouse and docks. Watch for rocks off this island, and a shoal extending from the horns of land at the north end of the cove. This shoal is marked with a tall stick. A public launching ramp provides the only shore access.

Jarrell Cove ★★★★★

Charts: 18448

Jarrell Cove is one of the most beautiful and popular cruising destinations in South Sound. A state park is set under the tall evergreens on the east shore, with two docks and a dozen mooring buoys scattered throughout the cove. On the west shore is a private marina, with moorage, fuel, and other facilities for visitors. Tree-shadowed inlets perfect for exploring by skiff branch off the main cove. There are private homes here, but none seem to intrude on the natural beauty.

Jarrell Cove is heavily used, and some of its magic may be lost on busy, noisy weekends. Midweek or off-season, you'll find lots of excuses for lingering in its quiet waters. The campground facilities (including showers) are closed from Labor Day to the end of April.

Approaches. From Case Inlet, respect the shoals extending north and east from Dougall Point. As you round Dougall Point a private marina and residential development (Hartstene Pointe) will be visible. Southwest of this development, you may be able to make out the break in the shore that is the entrance to Jarrell Cove. More obvious are the two private pilings east of the entrance.

From the west, in Pickering Passage, look for a steep bluff topped with fir trees—the west point of the entrance to Jarrell Cove. The entrance itself is clean.

Anchorage, Moorings. The state park has two floats, the first long and T-shaped in deep water. The other, to the south, is slightly inside an inlet, L-shaped and more suitable for shallow-draft boats. About a dozen park buoys are placed throughout the cove; depths are steady, though the southernmost buoy is some 5 feet shallower than the others. Fees are collected year-round for the floats and buoys, at the box located at the head of each ramp. Maximum stay is three nights.

Jarrell Cove Marina has visitor moorage with electrical hook-ups on the west side of the main float. Check in at the office on the fuel dock. For summer weekends it's a good idea to call ahead to reserve a spot—(800) 362-8823.

There's good anchorage to about three-quarters of the way into Jarrell Cove, in a gradually sloping mud bottom.

Getting Ashore. The park floats and shore are public. The marina provides a dinghy dock. All other docks and tidelands in Jarrell Cove are private.

For the Boat. The fuel dock at the marina is on the outside, east float. The store up the ramp has a few marine supplies. There's a pump-out and portable toilet dump site at the state park.

For the Crew. A limited variety of groceries is available at the marine store. Showers and a laundromat are nearby. There are also showers in the upland restrooms at the state park.

Exploring the peaceful inlets of Jarrell Cove.

Things to Do. Trails lace throughout the state park; follow these north to vistas of Pickering Passage, and south to the finger-inlet. There are also picnic tables, shelters, and campsites. The shoreline is best explored by skiff, as the "beach" disappears at high tide and is deep, soft mud at low.

Visit the marine store even if you don't need to buy anything. You can learn a bit about the history of Hartstene from the memorabilia on the walls, and admire the collection of shells and starfish at the foot of the old-fashioned counter.

McClane Cove ★★ No Facilities

Charts: 18448

McClane Cove, located on the mainland a mile-and-a-half northeast of Jarrell Cove, is small and square, a reasonably secure alternative anchorage if Jarrell Cove is full. Private buoys and swim rafts occupy many of the best areas. The homes on shore are many but modest. All tidelands are private.

Approaches, Anchorage. Approaches are

Case Inlet

Charts: 18448

Case Inlet reaches north between Hartstene Island and the Key Peninsula, almost connecting with the tip of Hood Canal. The inlet is broad and deep, relatively unpopulated most of the year. In summer the water warms up, city dwellers move into the beach cabins, and the northern half of the inlet especially is busy with water-skiers and jet-skiers.

There are several good anchorages on the clean. Anchor mid-cove, slightly west, to avoid the charted shoal along the east side. Watch for the overhead power lines.

western side of Case Inlet, including two beautiful state parks.

Approaches. From the east, the approach to Case Inlet is clean. If arriving from the west, favor Hartstene Island. Watch for Itsami Ledge in Dana Passage, and the white buoys northwest of the ledge that mark a shallow, obstructed area.

McMicken Island State Park ★★★★★

Charts: 18448

McMicken Island lies off the middle of Hartstene Island, north of Fudge Point. All of the island is a state park, with the exception of the fenced land around the small house and outbuildings on the southern tip.

Approaches. From the southwest side of Case Inlet, McMicken emerges as you round the spit of Wilson Point. From the southeast, Fudge Point will be prominent. Within a mile or so, the silver-white roof of the house on the bluff is visible above the south beach. From the north, look for tiny McMicken south and west of low, broad Herron Island.

Watch for boulders all around McMicken Island. Do not pass between McMicken and Hartstene, as the sandspit that connects them dries at low tide.

Anchorage, Moorings. There are three state park buoys on the north side of McMicken and two on the south. All are close to shore, as the hard bottom rises steeply from the charted 18-fathom basin. If the buoys are full, set your anchor carefully to avoid swinging into the beach or dragging off the shelf into deep water.

The best protection is on the north side. At times the water here is so clear you can see your anchor 20 feet down, your boat tethered above, as though floating in jade-green air.

Getting Ashore. All of the beach on McMicken and on the sand bar is public. There is no immediate upland access to Hartstene Island; however, north of the anchorage, beyond the steep bluffs, is a public state Department of Natural Resources (DNR) beach with a steep trail to the road.

For the Crew. An outhouse is the only facility on McMicken Island. The buildings inside the fence are private.

Things to Do. Trails dense with fern braid the island. The trailhead is on the low, east end of McMicken, south of the outhouse. Follow

The north anchorage of McMicken Island State Park. Low tide exposes the spit to Hartstene. Note the boulders off the beach.

these out to viewpoints over the high sand bluffs. On a clear day you'll see the white, three-pronged crest of Mt. Rainier to the east. In any weather you can marvel at the sinewy madrona clinging by their roots to the steep bank.

At low tide the sand-and-gravel shore is one of the best for beachcombing anywhere in South Sound. Seals often sun themselves on the northwest side. Try your luck clamming, or gather the fragile currency of empty sand dollars.

The more ambitious may want to take a skiff to the DNR beach north on Hartstene. The public tidelands begin just beyond the steep bluff. Farther on is a break in the high wooded bank, where a footbridge to the beach marks the head of a trail that winds up the ravine to the road.

Cove South of Dougall Point ★★ 1 No Facilities

Charts: 18448

Halfway between McMicken Island and Dougall Point, a low knuckle of land extends into Case Inlet. The resulting cove is shallow at its south end, with a soft bottom as charted. Approaches are clean. There is little protection from the north or south. All tidelands are private.

Road maps name the rounded point that forms the south shore of this cove Fudge Point. This can be confusing, as the chart uses this same name to identify a point two miles south, beyond McMicken Island.

Stretch Island State Park ★★★★

Charts: 18448

A tiny state marine park is located on the southeast tip of Stretch Island. This is a beautiful site, with a sandy beach strewn with driftwood, silver-green beach grass, and a tidal lagoon. The park is heavily used in summer, and the bay noisy with water-skiers and jet-skiers. Off-season it is peaceful, with a remote feel despite the beach cabins and homes around and above; your eyes will be drawn north up Case Inlet, or southeast, where Mt. Rainier peeks over the Key Peninsula.

Stretch Island was once a wine-producing area; a few vineyards are still cultivated. Grapeview, on the mainland, was dubbed "The Detroit of the West" by settlers from the Great Lakes.

Approaches. From the southwest, a cluster of white buildings with red roofs on the west side of Stretch Island—the former winery, now a private maritime museum—is prominent. A low bridge connects the island to the mainland. This channel dries at low tide, and is not recommended as a short cut.

Approaching from the south, look for the flagpole near the northeast tip of the island. The flagpole and buildings around it are on private land; just beyond is the state park, with three mooring buoys visible offshore.

From the north, the park begins where the beach homes and their bulkheads end. Two park buoys are visible.

Anchorage, Moorings. Five mooring buoys are set around the spit, three on the east side and two on the north, all of them close to shore. The north buoys are in water about 5 feet deeper. The bottom rises steeply, so make sure your swing doesn't ground you at low tide. Anchorage between Stretch Island and Reach Island to the north is good. In the summer, expect heavy boat traffic in and out of Fair Harbor at Reach Island.

Getting Ashore. There is no upland access from Stretch Island State Park. The trail that leads over the lagoon stops at a gate about 100 yards up the bluff. The nearest road access is at Fair Harbor.

For the Boat, Crew. The park has no facilities. Some groceries and supplies, as well as gas, are available at Fair Harbor Marina.

Things to Do. The former winery on Stretch Island is now a private museum filled with local marine artifacts. The owner is pleased to open it by appointment and to help with shore access and transportation. Call ahead—(360) 858-7971.

Fair Harbor ★★★   (gas only)

Charts: 18448

A private marina that caters to visiting boats is located south of the bridge that connects Reach Island to the mainland. The marina is beautifully maintained, with a quaint new store at the fuel dock and bright flowers on shore. This is a busy place on summer weekends.

Approaches. Depths are good when approaching from the south. North of the marina it's shallow; beneath the bridge it's bare at low tide. Bridge clearance is charted at 16 feet.

Anchorage, Moorings. Call ahead for overnight moorage—(360) 426-4028—or check in at the gas dock. If the marina is full, the closest anchorage is south, between Reach and Stretch, or at Stretch Island State Park. There is anchorage north of Reach as well; approach this area from the north.

Getting Ashore. Marina floats are for customers only. The launching ramp just north of the marina is public, but there is no place to leave a skiff. All nearby tidelands are private.

For the Boat, Crew. The fuel dock sells gas only, and limited marine supplies. The nearest diesel fuel is at Jarrell Cove. The store sells mostly snacks and gift items, but does have a few groceries.

Allyn ★★ ▢2 🎁 ⚓ 🛒 🍽️

Charts: 18448

Although Allyn is the only community of any size on Case Inlet with water access, it caters more to highway motorists than to boaters. The public dock is in shallow water and useful only at high tide. Beyond Allyn the inlet shallows even more and soon turns to mudflats. Oyster stakes are everywhere.

This far end of Case Inlet comes within two miles of touching Hood Canal. The low isthmus was used by Indians as a canoe portage.

Approaches. Allyn is a suitable destination only for boats drawing less than 4 feet, and even then it's important to watch the tides. Approach along the east side of the inlet, where the water is deepest; aiming toward the middle of the overhead power cables may help you stay on course. When directly abeam of the public dock (line up the church steeple behind it), turn sharply toward it. Take care to stay out of the staked oyster beds.

Moorings. The public float is T-shaped and attached to stout pilings. A prominent sign reads: DANGER LOW WATER HAZARD. Moorage for the first 24 hours is free, with a fee box on the dock for longer stays.

Getting Ashore. The float and adjacent launching ramp are public, as is the waterfront park to the north.

For the Boat, Crew. A hardware store and gas station are about a quarter-mile south on the road. Nearby is a post office, supermarket, and restaurant. The waterfront park near the dock has picnic tables, a small rose garden, horseshoe pits, and portable toilets.

Rocky Bay ★ ▢1 No Facilities

Charts: 18448

This shallow bay at the northeast end of Case Inlet is well named. Rocks are strewn across the entrance, and you'll run out of water before you can tuck in anywhere for protection. There is a small pocket behind the sandspit that extends from Windy Bluff, but protection here is dubious and there is little swinging room. All tidelands are private.

Vaughn Bay ★★ ▢3 No Facilities

Charts: 18448

Vaughn Bay is almost completely closed off by a long sand spit, and ringed by homes set close together. Shallow, with a western exposure and a narrow entrance, the bay is like a warm lake in summer. Starfish are plentiful; in places the bottom is gold and purple, as though it has been tiled with their bright bodies.

Approaches. Enter on a rising tide, mid-channel. Watch for unexpected and unmarked shoals. Deep-draft vessels should not attempt to enter Vaughn Bay.

Anchorage. Holding is good in mud bottom.

Keep in mind that at high tide the spit won't give much protection from the southwest wind.

Getting Ashore. The sandspit is public, but all other beaches are private. There's a public launching ramp on the north shore, about the middle of the bay. A half-mile up the road is a post office and civic center, with a carved orca on display and a playground.

Herron ★ No Facilities

Charts: 18448

The small community of Herron clusters around the ferry dock. There is a public launching ramp, but no other facilities and no protected anchorage. Shoals extend from the north shore of Herron Island, all of which is private.

Robert F. Kennedy Recreation Site ★★★

Charts: 18448

Immediately north of Whiteman Cove, on the east side of Case Inlet, the state Department of Natural Resources has developed a 22 acre park. The setting here is striking, with a long, sloping beach beneath high bluffs. Upland are campsites, picnic tables, shelters, barbecues, and pit toilets.

Approaches. From the north, the park dock pilings are visible after rounding the point south of Herron Island. From the southwest the dock pilings and the galvanized railings of its ramp are prominent beneath the bluff. A launching ramp is immediately north of the park dock.

Anchorage, Moorings. Five mooring buoys are set southwest of the park floats, the outer two in deepest water. The inner three are 10 to 15 feet shallower. The park float is L-shaped, with fingers toward shore. Stays are limited to seven days. The floats are removed in winter.

Boats anchored or moored here are vulnerable to southwest weather. A sign warns that the dock and floats are closed when wave height exceeds 18 inches.

Getting Ashore. Tidelands outside the park are private. Note that Whiteman Cove itself is closed off by a private road that bridges the spit.

Taylor Bay ★ No Facilities

Charts: 18448

This open, shallow bay north of Devils Head is surrounded by private homes. The charted pilings offshore extend from the northwest, and private mooring buoys occupy the best anchorage. The inner bay dries at low tide.

Taylor Bay is completely exposed to the southwest. A public street-end on the north shore, once a ferry landing serving the Key Peninsula, provides the only shore access.

REGION 2

SOUTH PUGET SOUND:

THE EASTERN PORTION

The Tacoma Narrows Bridge is the gateway to South Sound. Vertical clearance at the center of this impressive structure is 180 feet. The pylons rise almost 500 feet above the water.

INCLUDING CARR INLET

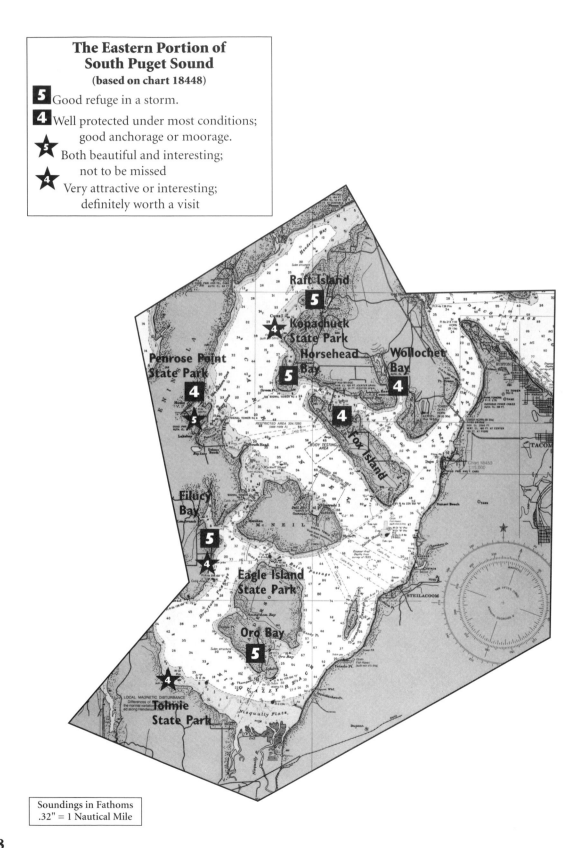

The Eastern Portion of
South Puget Sound
(based on chart 18448)

5 Good refuge in a storm.

4 Well protected under most conditions;
   good anchorage or moorage.

⭐**5** Both beautiful and interesting;
   not to be missed

⭐**4** Very attractive or interesting;
   definitely worth a visit

Soundings in Fathoms
.32" = 1 Nautical Mile

48

The waters between the Tacoma Narrows and the Key Peninsula are more actively boated than those west of Olympia. This eastern portion of South Sound is developed with residential and industrial areas from Tacoma south to Steilacoom and north to the head of Carr Inlet. Yet thanks to several state parks, the Nisqually Wildlife Refuge, and the McNeil Island penitentiary, some of the "uninterrupted wilderness" the Vancouver expedition described 200 years ago still remains. Salmon, seal, otter, eagle, heron, loons, and deer are abundant here. On the Key Peninsula, even black bear are not uncommon. It is uncanny that cruising south may put you closer to Puget Sound wildlife than cruising north.

In general, the channels and bays of South Sound are shallower and smaller than those to the north. The tidal range is also greater; in this eastern portion, highs are from 2 feet to 2 feet 6 inches higher than Seattle tides. Lows are about the same. Another difference is in the water itself. An underwater ridge—called a sill—at the Tacoma Narrows impedes the flow of water into and out of South Sound. It can take more than a month for these waters to flush completely. This contributes to their warmth as well as their productivity, but also means that dumping anything overboard is potentially more damaging to the ecology.

As with the western portion of South Sound, there are few detailed charts of this region, so you'll need to read chart 18448 carefully for most of your navigation. You can expect more rain here than falls in most of the Puget Sound area; southerlies bring moist ocean air over the lowlands of the Nisqually Delta, unhindered by the rain shadow of the Olympic Mountains. Along with this delta, Mount Rainier is a dominant feature here, huge and close, its volcanic cone clearly visible.

For most boaters, the gateway to South Sound is via the Tacoma Narrows, past the promontory of Point Defiance and beneath the towering suspension bridge. The channel itself is unobstructed, but currents can exceed 5 knots and must be respected. Time your passage near slack, or on an ebb or flood your boat can handle. According to the *Coast Pilot*, at the north end of the Narrows the current sets north on the east side and south on the west side—"most of the time."

The bold, high bluffs on both sides of the Narrows funnel and magnify winds here; the wind that caused the original Narrows bridge to writhe and collapse in 1940 was described as having a speed of "only" 42 miles an hour. When winds and current collide, expect a steep chop. Under all conditions, give tugs with tows room to navigate.

This eastern portion of South Sound attracts sport fishermen in large numbers, and many of the facilities here are geared for them. Four marine parks and several good anchorages make this area worthwhile for any boater.

Days Island ★★ 🖼 2 ⛽ (gas only) 🚰 🎁 🔧

Charts: 18448

Days Island, locally known as Day Island, is less than a mile-and-a-half south of the Narrows Bridge, on the mainland shore. Shaped like an inverted comma, the island is actually a peninsula that joins the mainland at its south end.

The area was once used by Indians for catching wild ducks; birds were driven from the inner bay into nets stretched on poles across the low isthmus. Today the area is a hub for sport fishing.

Approaches. From the south, Days Island is almost indistinguishable from the mainland, so tightly packed are the homes along its shore. The best clue from this direction is the sloping sand beach. From the north, the large turquoise building and hoist of the Narrows Marina are prominent.

For the Boat. There are two marinas here: Day Island Marina located inside the bay formed by the "island," and the Narrows Marina in the tiny cove to the east.

The Day Island Marina is quiet and private, with no overnight guest moorage. Entrance is from the north via a narrow, shallow channel, between a rock jetty and a timber breakwater. A tide gauge on the breakwater helps you determine if there's enough water for your boat. Inside the entrance—almost dead center—is an extensive reef; green daymarks guide you west of it. The marina has a surprising number of slips, many of them under cover. A repair yard with haulout service is on the peninsula.

The Narrows Marina is active with small craft. Entrance is to the east, past the braced pilings. There is no overnight guest moorage here, either. The gas dock is east of the hoist and large turquoise building (used for dry storage); live herring pens extend north of it. The gas dock provides access to the store, which has a few marine supplies. There's very little in the way of food at this store, but there's an impressive array of fishing lures. Even if you're lukewarm about the sport, the selection of rubber squid alone, arrayed in gum-drop colors from floor to ceiling, is inspiring.

A complete marine supply store is close by, westward toward the Days Island peninsula.

There's anchoring room outside these marinas, but little protection.

Hale Passage

Charts: 18448

Hale Passage branches northwest from the Narrows, between Fox Island and the mainland, to join with Carr Inlet. A fixed bridge with a vertical clearance of 30 feet spans the north end of the passage. Currents in Hale Passage are strong; the *Coast Pilot* reports velocities at times exceeding 3 knots. The entire area is developed, a Tacoma suburb, with almost no public shore access.

Hale Passage was named for a member of the 1838 Wilkes Expedition who compiled the first dictionary of the Chinook language.

Approaches. From the southeast, approaches are clean. From the northwest, watch for the blackened spine of a wreck east of Green Point, and a shoal extending from the north end of Fox Island. The wreck may blend in with the timber bulkhead behind it.

Cove South of Ketners Point ★★ ⬛ 3 No Facilities

Charts: 18448

The cove south of Ketners Point on Fox Island has good depth and a spectacular view of Mt. Rainier. Approaches are clean. You'll be somewhat exposed here to southeast weather, but otherwise reasonably protected. All shoreline is private.

Cove North of Ketners Point ★★ 　4　 No Facilities

Charts: 18448

The best anchorage on Fox Island is north of Ketners Point, a small U-shaped harbor that wraps around an islet known locally as Tanglewood Island. The unmistakable landmark is the lighthouse-shaped tower on the northwest tip of Tanglewood, part of a private resort and lodge. An obstruction in the west arm of the cove is marked with a privately maintained light. Entrance to the east arm is deepest toward Fox Island. Anchoring depth is good all around Tanglewood, as charted. All docks and mooring buoys are private.

Getting Ashore. All shoreline is private. The nearest public access is at the launching ramp on the southwest side of the Fox Island Bridge. Be prepared for strong current under the bridge.

Cove South of the Fox Island Bridge ★ 　3　 No Facilities

Charts: 18448

This cove is shallower than its neighbor to the southeast, and more exposed to current. The view and noise of the bridge also make this an unattractive anchorage. Approach east of green buoy "1" to avoid the rock shelf that lies southwest of this mark.

All docks and mooring buoys in this cove are private. Shore access is at the launching ramp on the southwest side of the Fox Island Bridge. Be prepared for strong current under the bridge.

Cove North of the Fox Island Bridge ★★ 　3　 No Facilities

Charts: 18448

Approaches, Anchorage. North of the fixed bridge, a low spit curves northeast from the tip of Fox Island. Anchoring is possible inside this hook, in 5 to 7 fathoms. The nearest public shore access is on the southwest side of the bridge.

Wollochet Bay ★★★ 　4　 No Facilities

Charts: 18448

Wollochet Bay is long and wide. Unlike other anchorages in Hale Passage, you'll feel some privacy here, and can row or motor your skiff without feeling obtrusive. Depths are good, with a gravel-and-mud bottom. Tucked inside, beyond the charted rock, you're well protected from most weather. Approaches to Wollochet Bay are clean.

Getting Ashore. All beaches here are private,

51

but there is shore access via two launching ramps. One is on the east shore, close to the entrance and south of the pilings (a former ferry landing and sawmill). The storefront building is a private residence. There are no public facilities up the narrow road.

Another public launching ramp is toward the head of the bay, on the west shore at the end of a steep downhill street. There are no facilities within walking distance.

Carr Inlet

Charts: 18448

Carr Inlet bends northwest to northeast from the Narrows, a deep, 12-mile waterway that terminates in the mudflats of Burley Lagoon. It has a somewhat split personality; its east shore, including Fox Island, is part of the Tacoma suburbs and densely populated, while its west shore has a quiet, country look. Carr Inlet offers a number of anchorages with good protection year round.

Approaches. Carr Inlet has three approaches. The cleanest is from the southeast, between Fox Island and McNeil Island. A second approach is through Hale Passage; boaters choosing this route should note the fixed bridge (30 feet vertical clearance) and the likelihood of strong current.

A third approach is from the west, via Pitt Passage. This narrow channel between McNeil Island and the Key Peninsula is tricky, with tiny Pitt Island in the middle surrounded by shoals and reefs. The island itself is state prison prop-

A rainbow highlights tiny Pitt Island in the narrow passage between McNeil Island and the higher shoreline of the Key Peninsula.

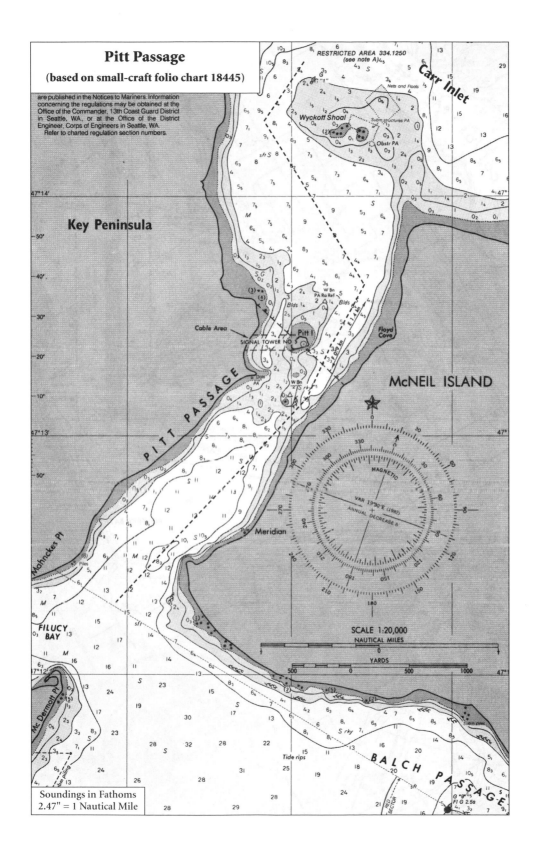

Pitt Passage

(based on small-craft folio chart 18445)

are published in the Notices to Mariners. Information concerning the regulations may be obtained at the Office of the Commander, 13th Coast Guard District in Seattle, WA, or at the Office of the District Engineer, Corps of Engineers in Seattle, WA.
 Refer to charted regulation section numbers.

RESTRICTED AREA 334.1250
(see note A)

Carr Inlet

Nets and Floats

Wyckoff Shoal

Subm structures PA

Obstr PA

Key Peninsula

Cable Area

SIGNAL TOWER NO

Pitt I

Floyd Cove

McNEIL ISLAND

PITT PASSAGE

MAGNETIC

VAR 19°30'E (1982)
ANNUAL DECREASE 6'

Meridian

Mahncke Pt

FILUCY
BAY

Mc Dermott Pt

SCALE 1:20,000

NAUTICAL MILES

0

YARDS

500   0   500   1000

Tide rips

B A L C H   P A S S A G E

RED
SECTOR

Fl G 2.5s

Soundings in Fathoms
2.47" = 1 Nautical Mile

erty. To appreciate—and avoid—the hazards of this passage, use the Pitt Passage detail in small-craft folio chart 18445. Choose a rising tide.

There are two routes through Pitt Passage. Regardless of the course you choose, note the *Coast Pilot*'s warning that the ebb, which runs north, can attain velocities of 2½ knots or more.

The *Coast Pilot* recommends the route east of Pitt Island. From a mid-channel course, head for red nun buoy "6" (this has been added since the 1993 chart). Stay east, past the white diamond-shaped mark on dolphin pilings 50 yards north of "6;" a rock and shoals extend from Pitt Island to this mark. Stay mid-channel between the mark and McNeil, and mid-channel between Pitt Island and McNeil.

Proceed on this same course until past the triangular red "4" mark set on a single piling about 250 yards north of Pitt Island. Continue well north of "4" before turning northwest. Change to a north heading past green can "3" (added since the 1993 chart). Buoys "3" and "1" mark the west edge of Wyckoff Shoal.

Some locals use the west passage. Once past the white diamond-shaped mark on dolphin pilings south of Pitt, dog-leg around the spit (known locally as Driftwood Point) in order to avoid shoals that extend south and east from the Key Peninsula. Stay mid-channel past Pitt Island, clear of the charted rocks off the Key Peninsula shore. Past the triangular red "4" mark north of Pitt Island, head west of the Wyckoff Shoal buoys.

From either the east or west passage, stay clear of South Head, where there are several charted rocks.

Penrose Point State Park ★★★★★   (gas only)

Charts: 18448

This 152-acre park one mile northwest of South Head is the chief attraction for boaters in Carr Inlet. Mooring buoys are set on both sides of Penrose Point, and a float for shallow vessels is located in the inner bay of Mayo Cove. Here also are a small marina and store. On shore are numerous trails that wander along the beaches and through second-growth forests of alder, fir, maple, and madrona.

Park facilities (including showers) are closed from Labor Day to early April.

Approaches. If your destination is Mayo Cove, be alert; an unmarked shoal peppered with rocks and boulders extends well north of Penrose Point. In addition, another, shorter spit parallels this shoal to the west. To avoid these dangers, give Penrose Point a wide berth.

If approaching from the south, stay in deep water (over 10 fathoms) until well north of the entrance. The white building of the Lakebay store should be fully visible before you make the turn into the cove. The mooring buoys are just west of the shorter spit, so be sure to stay west of them.

If approaching Mayo Cove from the north or east, the Lakebay store will be visible from the middle of Carr Inlet. Guard against drifting south toward Penrose Point, and stay in deep water until lined up north of the entrance and west of the mooring buoys.

From any direction, note that the signal tower shown on the chart no longer stands on Penrose Point.

The approach to Mayo Cove's inner harbor snakes between two sandspits and is advised only for shallow-draft boats.

The cove south of Penrose Point has a cleaner approach, provided you keep a safe distance from the north tip of Penrose Point. Note the charted rocks near South Head. The sandy bottom in this unnamed cove shallows gradually.

Looking east to Mount Rainier from Mayo Cove. The unmarked reef extending from Penrose Point is covered at high tide.

Anchorage, Moorings. In Mayo Cove, three state park mooring buoys parallel the sand spit. There is anchoring room and depth south and slightly west of the line of these buoys. The state park float in the inner harbor nearly dries at low tide. A fee box is at the head of the pier. Short-term moorage is also available at private Lakebay marina; call ahead (360) 884-3350. The marina operates daily in summer but from late fall through early spring it operates by appointment only.

On the south side of Penrose Point are five mooring buoys; the southernmost is set about 10 feet shallower than its counterpart to the north. Anchoring is good anywhere in this unnamed cove, but stay away from the pilings, which mark the edge of the shallows, and watch for the rock off Delano Beach.

Both these coves are exposed to northerlies.

Getting Ashore. Land at the park only, either side of Penrose Point. All other tidelands are private.

For the Boat. The marina at Lakebay sells gasoline and a few supplies. Call ahead—(360) 884-3350—from fall through spring, when it is open only by appointment.

For the Crew. Snacks and beverages are available at the Lakebay store. The state park restrooms have showers, and there is a public telephone near the ranger station.

Things to Do. In Mayo Cove the park beaches are steep and rocky; the mud and sand are pocked with clam holes, and the seaweed hides tiny creatures—ideal conditions for beachcombing. South of the point, the beach is sandy; below the tideline thousands of sand dollars, furred and reddish-brown, stand on end so closely they seem to be pushing each other over.

The Penrose Point State Park float. Extensive sandbars in this inner cove create a shallow and winding entrance.

Within the park itself are trails (including a "Touch of Nature" interpretive trail), picnic tables, shelters, and fire pits. Wildlife includes deer, raccoon, owls, woodpeckers, herons, and many migratory birds. Even black bear have been seen in the park.

Von Geldern Cove ★★★

Charts: 18448

Von Geldern Cove is best known for Home, the only real town on the Key Peninsula. Established by the Mutual Home Association in the late 1800s, Home described itself as a "community of free spirits, who came out in the woods to escape the polluted atmosphere of priest-ridden society." The practice of free love and nude swimming in the bay inevitably led to censure by outsiders, and legal battles forced the association to disband in 1919.

Home faces the highway, and with the exception of a launching ramp on the northwest shore of the cove, it has no provisions for boaters. From the water all that's visible of the town are simple, solid houses surrounded by lawn and garden. At the head of the cove, beyond the bridge, is a distinctive old barn on pilings.

Approaches. The navigable entrance to Von Geldern Cove is actually quite narrow. Charted rocks and a shoal that bares at low tide fan out from the north; favor the south shore.

Anchorage. This cove shallows fairly quickly. If you need protection from the southwest, you may run out of water before you can tuck in safely, especially during minus tides. Avoid anchoring south of the launching ramp, where depths are charted at 3 feet or less.

Getting Ashore. Take your dinghy to the launching ramp, located about halfway into the cove on the north shore. From here it's a pleasant half-mile walk to Home's main intersection.

For the Boat. There are no facilities for boats.

A gas station is at the intersection.

For the Crew. A post office and small grocery store are at the main intersection, as is a laundromat—the only one within walking distance of the water in this region of South Puget Sound.

Maple Hollow Recreation Site ★★★ No Facilities

Charts: 18448

A rustic day-use park is maintained by the Department of Natural Resources on the west shore of Carr Inlet, about a mile north of Von Geldern Cove. There are trails leading up the steep bank, as well as a few picnic tables and firepits overlooking the short gravel beach. Offshore, the bottom rises steeply from 10 fathoms, and there is no protection.

This park is most easily approached by land or from a beachable craft.

Approaches. The mooring buoy and lighted marker shown on the chart, which could help locate this park, no longer exist. Look for a break in the private homes, and for a set of stairs with railings of wood and galvanized pipe descending along a bulkhead. Watch for uncharted rocks and boulders on the beach.

Glencove

Charts: 18448

The complex inlet of Glencove is almost impassable at low tide and too shallow for anchoring. The entrance twists into an inner cove, over a sandy bottom virtually covered with sand dollars. Most of the cove is lined with private homes. YMCA Camp Seymour occupies the northeast shore. There are no public facilities.

Minter Creek

Charts: 18448

The cove at Minter Creek is entirely closed off to boats. The chart shows wrecks south of the entrance; these support extensive commercial oyster beds. Stakes are set closely across the entrance itself, and signs warn boaters to stay away.

A salmon hatchery located inside the cove at Minter Creek may be visited by land.

Henderson Bay ★

Charts: 18448

The northern reach of Carr Inlet, Henderson Bay, ends at the highway bridge between Wauna and Purdy. Beyond is shallow Burley Lagoon. The current over these shallows and

under the bridge can be swift, and the bottom rises steeply. Clearance beneath the power line is charted at 30 feet. Public access to the commercial development of Purdy is via the beach southwest of the bridge, where there is also a launching ramp. At the Purdy intersection is a grocery store and liquor store, a gas station, and several restaurants.

Raft Island and Lay Inlet ★★★ No Facilities

Charts: 18448

Like Horsehead Bay to the south, the cove behind Raft Island is an excellent anchorage, a good backup if you're blown out of the anchorage at Cutts Island or Kopachuck State Park. There is no privacy here, however. Homes of this Tacoma suburb are tightly packed along the shore, many with private docks. Boating through this area is like driving on a watery neighborhood street.

Approaches, Anchorage. Enter north of Raft Island, mid-channel. The best protection is slightly east of the island, in 5 to 8 fathoms.

At high tide, boats may enter south of Raft Island, under the low trestle. Aluminum rectangles on the bridge piles mark the preferred course. Vertical clearance is charted at 17 feet.

All docks and mooring buoys are private, and there is no public shore access.

Cutts Island and Kopachuck State Park ★★★★

Charts: 18448

Kopachuck State Park, which includes Cutts Island to the north, is the prime attraction on the east side of Carr Inlet. Though a short drive by car from Tacoma, the park itself feels remote and unspoiled. Views across the Key Peninsula and beyond to the Olympic Mountains are open and beautiful.

Kopachuck is a 109-acre park with campsites, picnic tables and shelters, and an underwater scuba-diving park. Cutts Island was once a sacred Indian site, where the dead were placed in the forks of trees to protect them from animals. Today poison oak discourages most explorers.

The campground facilities (including showers) are closed from Labor Day to the end of April.

Approaches. The most distinctive landform of the park is Cutts Island itself, with a west-facing, evergreen-topped bluff that makes it appear like a helmet or a hat. Approach the island from the south, and watch for rocks and boulders off the southern tip. From the north or west, avoid the long sandspit that almost connects it with Raft Island.

The mainland portion of Kopachuck State Park is a half-mile south of Cutts Island. The thick stand of tall, second-growth fir and rounded deciduous trees distinguishes Kopachuck from the surrounding developed land. As you approach, a concrete bulkhead with picnic tables will come into view. The stairs that lead down to the gravel beach may disappear altogether at high tide. Stay clear of the charted white buoy that marks the underwater park.

Anchorage, Moorings. Two mooring buoys are set in deep water off Kopachuck State Park. An additional nine are east of Cutts Island, with the deepest at the south end of the string. There's good holding ground east of these buoys.

Expect to be uncomfortable in blows from the north or south, as both anchorages are

Cutts Island from the east. Cutts is also known as Deadman's Island.

completely exposed. The nearest protection is north, behind Raft Island, or south in Horsehead Bay.

Getting Ashore. Land at Kopachuck beach or at Cutts Island. Adjoining properties are private.

For the Crew. At Kopachuck, an outside shower is at the restrooms halfway up the steep trail. The trail leads eventually to a campground, where there are hot showers. A public phone is up the road near the ranger station.

Cutts Island has no campsites or facilities other than a pit toilet.

Horsehead Bay ★★ ⬜5 No Facilities

Charts: 18448

Horsehead Bay is one of the most protected anchorages in Carr Inlet, a good place to run to if you're blown out of Cutts Island or Kopachuck State Park. The bay is deep, with a mud bottom. It is also densely populated, crowded with swim rafts, private docks, and mooring buoys. You may feel somewhat claustrophobic anchored here, especially at its narrow southern end.

Approaches. Enter mid-channel to avoid the many private mooring buoys and swim rafts. The mud bottom rises gradually.

Getting Ashore. Shore access is via the public launching ramp at the street end on the east shore. About a mile up the road is a small convenience grocery.

MCNEIL ISLAND

Whatever your cruising destination in South Sound, you're bound to encounter McNeil Island. From the north, the west, and the southwest, McNeil is thickly wooded and almost entirely uninhabited. In stark contrast, its southeast shore is developed as no other waterfront is in Puget Sound, with blank-faced buildings, massive walls, and glowering towers. This entire island is off-limits, and serves two strangely compatible functions: as a wildlife refuge and as a prison.

It was a prison before it was a refuge. In 1870, just 20 years after McNeil was homesteaded by white settlers, a 27-acre parcel was purchased for a territorial (and subsequently federal) penitentiary. By the 1930s, the prison had grown to include almost half the island. When the federal government decided to close the prison in 1981, the state of Washington purchased it, at first with the intention of turning it into a park and wildlife preserve.

Prison overcrowding—with resulting riots and litigation—persuaded the state to retain the prison. Environmental groups eventually joined forces with prison officials to form an unlikely but effective partnership. When the lands—which include Gertrude and Pitt islands—were officially transferred from the federal government to the state in 1986, they were transferred under a unique agreement of shared responsibility for wildlife.

Today, both the state Department of Wildlife and the state Department of Corrections manage McNeil as a true sanctuary. Wildlife feed and breed here undisturbed, inaccessible to the public. In the numerous creeks, wetlands, and 11 miles of shoreline reside 16 species of shellfish and 19 species of finned fish. Eighty bird species have been observed on McNeil. Waterfowl feed inland and offshore. Bald eagles perch on the cliffs overlooking Carr Inlet; Gertrude Island has an eagle's nest and a heron rookery.

McNeil is also home to 13 species of mammal, including a herd of about 500 blacktail deer, which regularly browse on the park-like slopes above Balch Passage. The harbor seals that slip gracefully through the water around Still Harbor total about 350, the largest remaining population in South Sound.

The island's human residents are more simply delineated: either prison staff, or inmates. Staff and their families live in the houses scattered around McNeil, some of which are visible from the water. Their children attend early elementary school on the island; in later grades they attend school in Steilacoom.

Inmates fall into two groups: medium- or minimum-security, for a total of just over 1,700 men. Medium-security inmates are confined to the area known as the Main Institution—the prominent structures on the southeast shore of the island, with their secure walls and guard towers. Minimum-security inmates live in the Annex to the north and work throughout the island.

Less than 100 acres of the almost 4,500 acres on McNeil is routinely used for prison purposes. The remaining land is managed as a sanctuary, its use restricted to protect wildlife. For example, mowing beneath powerlines or along the island's roads cannot be done during nesting season. Evergreens cannot be cut unless they are a hazard, and large deciduous trees must be girdled rather than cut down in order to provide bird habitat. Herbicides are not used on McNeil.

Further development of the island is also restricted; existing buildings and roads may be improved, but nothing new may be constructed outside the Main Institution parcel. Living in a wildlife refuge places extra restrictions on prison staff and their families as well: no beach or lake swimming, no free-roaming pets, no oystering and, in certain areas, no clamming.

Transportation to the mainland—primarily for prison staff and inmate visitors—is provided by scheduled passenger ferries that run all day between Steilacoom and the pier at the Main Institution. A cargo pier about a mile west of the Main Institution handles supplies and vehicles that come and go by tug and barge.

Still Harbor, on the northeast side of the island, is closed. Signs on floats warn boaters to stay 300 yards away. No anchoring is allowed. To avoid disturbing seals that beach themselves on the sandspit south of Gertrude Island, use of this harbor by the prison staff is restricted.

The cold, swift water around McNeil discourages escapes, but they have happened. The most popular legend surrounding these is of Driftwood Annie, an old woman on the Key Peninsula who welcomed escaped prisoners, giving them food and a change of clothes to help them on their way. Since the new fence was built in 1983, there have been no successful escapes from the Main Institution.

Access to McNeil by the general public is extremely limited. Signs posted on shore and on floats warn boaters to stay at least 100 yards away. If your boat is disabled and you find yourself drifting on to McNeil, call "McNeil 1" on VHF Channel 16 to advise the prison of your predicament; after working hours call "McNeil Island Passenger Boat" or "McNeil Island Tug Boat." If, despite your efforts, you land on the island, stay with your boat until prison staff arrive.

Steilacoom ★★ ▭² 🎁 🔧 🛒 ⚓ 🍽

Charts: 18448

Boaters cruising between the Narrows and Nisqually Reach aren't likely to be drawn to the mainland shore. Most of the area north of Steilacoom is industrial: an enormous gravel pit filled with symmetrical mountains of sand and graded rock, the tall stacks of a pulp mill, wharfs, and mooring buoys for barges. Railroad tracks that hug the narrow beach along this entire shore are noisy with the whistles, screeches, and clatter of freight trains. If you spot pleasure boaters here they are likely to be trolling for fish along the steep shelf; what few facilities exist are intended mainly for them.

Approaches, For the Boat, Crew. Visiting boaters have a choice in this area: to use the guest float at the ferry dock in Steilacoom, or to go south to Steilacoom Marina.

The guest float at Steilacoom is on the north side of the county ferry dock. The dock itself is prominent, as is the light gray building with a pergola roof that shares the pier (this building, and the attached floats to the south, are for McNeil Island Corrections Center use only). The guest float is for vessels 26 feet or less in length. Maximum stay is an hour.

Approaches are clean, but watch for boat activity around the trestle—there's a launching ramp just inside. An outboard and small boat repair shop is across the street from the launching ramp.

The restaurant at the head of the dock caters to ferry traffic. The nearest grocery stores are about two blocks uphill, past a small city park with play equipment. The town of Steilacoom is a National Historic District. The main street is a couple of blocks north, where there is a museum and several restaurants. A fine restaurant is located opposite the viewpoint on Commercial Street.

About a half-mile north of the ferry dock is a waterfront park, with picnic shelters and sand volleyball courts. It's possible to anchor off the park beach, but watch out for old pilings.

Steilacoom Marina is located south of town, at Gordon Point. Its square, over-the-water structure and hoist tower are distinctive from any approach. This marina specializes in boat rentals and dry storage; the marina store has fishing gear, snack foods, and a few supplies. Visitors may use the floats in front of the hoist, but there is no overnight guest moorage.

Immediately north of the store is a small, day-use state park that's perfect for stretching your legs. A stout stone picnic shelter stands guard over the sloping gravel beach. Carved signs along the paths bear playful messages from "Cujo Crab," "Sammy Sand Dollar," and "Sally Sea Star." The view is west up Carr Inlet and beyond to the Olympic Mountains.

The tiny marina about a mile north of Steilacoom, just inside the fixed bridge of the Chambers Creek "waterway," is private and has no facilities.

Ketron Island

Charts: 18448

Ketron Island lies southwest of Steilacoom. All of the island is private. A ferry dock is on the east side, off Cormorant Passage. The former fuel dock south of it and the launching ramp to the north are posted as private, as are all docks and tidelands on Ketron. VISITORS MAY BE QUESTIONED, reads one sign. PLEASE DO NOT BE OFFENDED.

Anderson Island

Charts: 18448

Anderson Island is private and rural. Its location between the state penitentiary of McNeil Island and the National Wildlife Refuge of the Nisqually River Delta isolates it from the suburban sprawl of Tacoma and Olympia. The island is served by ferry, but the absence of public land or shoreline access discourages outsiders from visiting.

Oro Bay ★★★ ⬜5 No Facilities

Charts: 18448

The best—some might say only—anchorage on Anderson Island is Oro Bay, located at the southeast end. The bay branches into two forks. The east fork shallows rapidly, ending in a labyrinth of saltwater marsh and duck blinds. Where there is anchoring depth it is exposed, suitable only in settled weather. The west fork, though tricky to enter, is sheltered, quiet, and deep enough for anchoring. A tiny marina and yacht club outpost are the only development. At Vega is a weathered building and dock, its SHELL sign barely visible in the faded paint.

Approaches. From the north, Cole Point is a steep sandy bluff. Stay in deep water, about a quarter-mile away, and pass completely around the point before turning in to the bay. From the south, the red "2" on pilings off Lyle Point is distinctive. Watch for rocks and shoals off the west shore as you turn in.

The two forks of Oro Bay aren't apparent when you first enter, and the submerged wreck that lies between them is not marked. Look for a green can and a red nun buoy—these mark the entrance to the inner west harbor. The green can may be difficult to spot against the foliage. Both buoys are privately maintained.

The channel to this inner harbor hugs the north shore in order to avoid a shoal that extends from the south point. Depths are steady through the entrance, slightly shallower once inside.

Anchorage. Anchorage is good in the southern branch of the harbor, north of the boat houses. The marina and mooring buoys are private.

You're reasonably protected outside the inner harbor, anchored slightly toward the west shore. You'll hear the train noise from the mainland, but on a clear day you will also have a splendid view of Mt. Rainier.

Getting Ashore. All tidelands are private.

Thompson Cove ★ ⬜2 No Facilities

Charts: 18448

This bight on the southwest tip of Anderson Island has little to recommend it. The cove may offer some protection from the north, but it is exposed to the south and to boat traffic along Nisqually Reach. Depths are OK to about a third of the way in. The inner cove shown on the chart dries at low tide. All tidelands are private.

Amsterdam Bay ★★ No Facilities

Charts: 18448

The finger of Amsterdam Bay indents the west side of Anderson Island. A bluff rises on the north shore. Homes are sited along the beach to the head of the inlet. The outer bay is exposed and shallow. The entrance to the inner bay is narrow, drying at low tide. All tidelands are private.

Nisqually Reach

Charts: 18448

Nisqually Reach curves around the south end of Anderson Island toward Case Inlet, skirting the mudflats of the Nisqually River. The river delta is the site of the Nisqually National Wildlife Refuge, more than 2,000 acres of estuaries, tidal flats, and freshwater marshes. This pristine wetland serves as a wintering area for waterfowl, as a spawning and passage area for fish, and as a year-round home to raptors, shorebirds, and songbirds. Visitors are welcome, but to protect the habitat they must arrive by land and explore on designated pathways. Visitors also pay a nominal fee.

Take care when boating near the delta. Mudflats extend north from the mainland almost a mile, and the edge, marked with two buoys, is steep. In places the bottom rises from 10 fathoms to nothing at all. It's a good idea to stay north, favoring Anderson Island west of green "1" and east of green "3." West and north of "3" are good depths and several attractions for boaters.

Tolmie State Park ★★★★ 🪝

Charts: 18448

West of green buoy "3," in a small cove marked on the chart with a mooring buoy and fish haven, is Tolmie State Park. This day-use park is close enough to the Nisqually Wildlife Refuge to share some of its biological richness, with a topography all its own. Within its 100 acres is a saltwater marsh spanned by a footbridge, a swamp, low wooded hills, more than two miles of trails, and a sandy beach ideal for wading. Offshore a sunken wreck provides an underwater park for divers.

Approaches. From the east, avoid the Nisqually Flats by favoring Anderson Island until west of green buoy "3." Scan the shore to find the flat sandy beach surrounded by woods; you may be able to make out the footbridge that arches over the salt marsh. A pair of white can buoys, striped orange, mark the underwater park; the mooring buoys are west of them.

Boaters approaching from the west have a cleaner approach south from Johnson Point, and can more readily spot the buoys.

Anchorage, Moorings. Five mooring buoys are set roughly parallel to shore in deep water. There's enough depth for most boats to anchor south of these buoys. The bottom slopes gradually. Stay clear of the fish haven.

Getting Ashore. The park beach is public; all adjacent tidelands are private.

For the Crew. Tolmie State Park is for day use only. There are picnic tables and shelters, but no camping facilities. An outdoor shower for swimmers and divers is near the restrooms, on the south side of the lagoon.

Coves South of Johnson Point ★

Charts: 18448

The two coves between Tolmie State Park and Johnson Point are unnamed on the chart but are important for local boaters. A launching ramp is east of the warehouse buildings in the south cove (locally referred to as Mill Bight or Puget Marina). The gas pump on shore operates during summer. Up the road is a repair shop for trailerable boats. The marine railway north of the pilings is no longer in service. Approaches are clean.

North of Mill Bight is Baird Cove, with a fuel dock, small-boat repair facilities, and a grocery. Locals refer to this cove as Zittel's. It can be identified by the charted dolphin pilings outside the entrance, and by the orange-and-white striped roof of the marina boathouse. The marina here is private and has no guest moorage. The entrance is shallow and narrow, with a log float to port and a log-and-tire raft to starboard. Deep-draft vessels should enter only on a rising tide. The fuel dock is just north of the boathouse. Stay clear of the floating bait pens.

Filucy Bay ★★★★

Charts: 18448

Filucy Bay, located at the southeast end of the Key Peninsula, is one of the most beautiful and protected anchorages in South Puget Sound. Much of the shoreline here is wooded. The town of Longbranch is little more than a country store and a cluster of homes. In early spring, the haunting music of loons can be heard over the still water; when the weather clears, Mt. Rainier fills the harbor entrance.

Filucy Bay is a popular destination on summer weekends.

Approaches. The entrance is wide and clean. The marina at Longbranch, just south of the charted wreck, is visible on entering.

Boaters approaching via Pitt Passage should use small-craft folio chart 18445, which contains a detail of the area. A northbound description of Pitt Passage is given in this chapter, under Approaches to Carr Inlet.

Anchorage, Moorings. The Longbranch Improvement Club, which owns and operates the marina, recently rebuilt and expanded the visitors' moorage. Tie up south of the boathouses, either outside or inside the large, horseshoe-like arrangement of floats. A fee box is located in front of the boathouses, near the dockmaster's shed. Electricity is available on all guest floats.

Anchorage is good in mud bottom throughout the bay. The northern inlet is often preferred for its peaceful surroundings.

Getting Ashore. Take your skiff to the marina. All other tidelands are private.

For the Boat. Other than moorage, Filucy Bay has no facilities for boats. An auto repair shop about a quarter-mile north on the main road may be able to help with a breakdown. The nearest fuel dock and boat repair facility is across Nisqually Reach, at Baird Cove.

The Longbranch Marina in Filucy Bay. On this cloudy day, only the base of Mount Rainier is visible across the entrance.

For the Crew. The Longbranch store has an extraordinary variety of goods, garden-fresh produce, and a meat counter famous throughout the Key Peninsula. Check here for events at the Improvement Club hall, which is a short walk north. Regrettably, the Chowder House Restaurant next to the store is closed, with no immediate plans to reopen.

Eagle Island State Park ★★★

Charts: 18448

This tiny island between McNeil and Anderson Islands is a rustic day-use state park, with trails and a few clearings. It is best suited for beachable craft, as currents in Balch Passage are swift. Views from the east side are of Mt. Rainier and the smokestacks near Steilacoom; from the west you can watch the seals haul themselves ashore on the tidal reef.

Approaches. Several hazards on the west side of Eagle Island are difficult to make out from the chart. Green buoy "9" marks the northern edge of a reef and shoal. Stay either north of this buoy or well south, favoring Anderson Island and watching for kelp. The black-and-white marker on the north end of Eagle Island is barely visible when approaching from the east. This side of the island is cleaner. From any direction, be prepared for strong current.

Anchorage, Moorings. One state park buoy lies east of the island; of the two on the west side, the south buoy is deeper. All buoys are set close to shore, with inadequate swinging room for large or deep-draft vessels at low tide. Anchorage is possible on the steep, rocky bottom, but current may cause you to drag.

Getting Ashore. All of Eagle Island is public. Watch for rocks and boulders on the beach. Anderson Island is private, and the state penitentiary of McNeil Island is strictly off-limits.

REGION 3

POINT DEFIANCE

TO POINT VASHON

Mount Rainier emerges from the low clouds beyond East Passage.
(Paul Dudley photo)

INCLUDING TACOMA AND GIG HARBOR

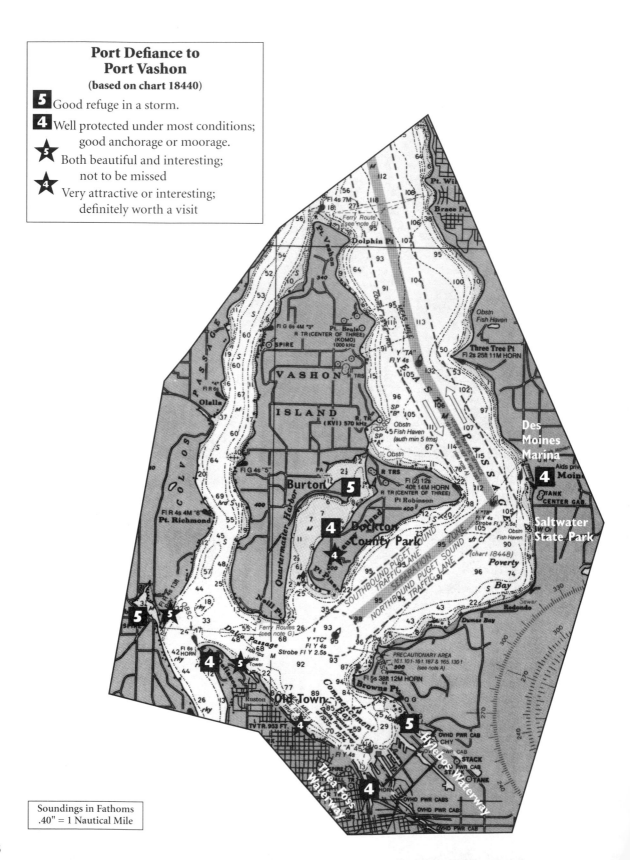

Port Defiance to Port Vashon

(based on chart 18440)

5 Good refuge in a storm.

4 Well protected under most conditions; good anchorage or moorage.

★**5** Both beautiful and interesting; not to be missed

★**4** Very attractive or interesting; definitely worth a visit

Soundings in Fathoms
.40" = 1 Nautical Mile

The waters north of the Tacoma Narrows and around Vashon Island are among the easiest to navigate in Puget Sound. Depths are good and the main channels are clean and deep. Currents are unusually consistent: Around the Narrows they ebb most of the time on the northeast side, and flood most of the time on the northwest. Colvos Passage almost always runs north, and currents in both East Passage and Commencement Bay are weak and variable. Weather patterns are similar to those around Seattle, including the occurrence of colliding winds when Pacific westerlies converge from around the Olympics.

This region has a pleasing, split personality. The mainland is heavily populated with Tacoma suburbs that spread north toward Seattle and west to surround Gig Harbor. By contrast, Vashon Island and Colvos Passage are undeveloped. In a circumnavigation of Vashon, you'll cruise between the green banks of river-like Colvos Passage, through the commercial traffic lanes in East Passage, and in view of industrial Tacoma. For such a short distance—only about 30 miles total—you'll feel like you've traveled much farther.

Ask boaters why they cruise here and they'll generally mention Gig Harbor or Quartermaster Harbor. These excellent anchorages, so different from one another, are a comfortable boating distance from Seattle's metropolitan area, and only seven miles from Tacoma—good weekend destinations in winter. With guest moorage also available in Des Moines, there's always a place to duck into if the weather turns bad.

This region is distinguished by its astonishing proximity to Mount Rainier. From Commencement Bay the mountain is less than 50 miles to the southwest. It seems to grow from the earth, as though its roots extend into the rich silt of the Puyallup River delta. Though most often hidden in a pile of cloud, when it reveals all of its 14,410 feet it is so unexpectedly huge that the mountains around it are reduced to a serrated horizon.

The mountain was named by Vancouver to honor his friend, Rear Admiral Rainier. The name stuck, but the spirit of its Indian name, Tahoma, has prevailed: thunderer, giver of spiritual wealth. One legend describes Tahoma as the estranged wife of Kulshan (Mount Baker), who stretched tall as she looked back toward her husband and the smaller mountains around him that are their children. Geologists explain its growth by fire through centuries of incremental eruptions, and its subsequent shaping by ice. In the drawings of the early explorers the mountain fills the sky, as the heart—not the eye—would see it. Here, you'll feel the same awe in its shadow, a combination of exhilaration and disbelief.

From the north watch for heavy tide rips around Allen Bank. East Passage is about one-and-a-half miles longer than Colvos, but as both ebb and flood tend to run north in Colvos, the longer route may be faster. Sailors generally make a clockwise voyage, tacking against the prevailing southerlies in wide East Passage, running with the wind and current in Colvos Passage.

Boaters approaching from the south should pay close attention to currents in the Narrows, which at times exceed 5 knots. A description of the Narrows is given on page 49, in the introduction to Region 2.

Gig Harbor ★★★★★

Charts: 18445, 18448, **18474**

This three-sided harbor west of Point Defiance was named by the Wilkes Expedition in the early 1800s for the ship's gig they used to explore this "pretty little bay concealed by the sound." The town was originally founded by Slovenians, Germans, and Scandinavians, and was for many years a thriving commercial fishing village, home port to a large purse-seine fleet. Today some of these vessels still nuzzle the wharves, but businesses cater mainly to those who make their living on land—Gig Harbor is essentially a Tacoma suburb—and to tourists, many of whom arrive by water.

Approaches. The narrow entrance to Gig

Harbor is easier to see from the Narrows than from Dalco Passage. Approaching from the northeast, look for a string of beach cabins below a housing subdivision on the high south bluff; a retaining wall topped with white railings is northwest of the beach cabins. The entrance will slowly become evident as you head for the far shore.

The entrance itself is constricted by a sandspit curling from the north shore and a shoal extending from the south. A privately maintained lighthouse stands on the spit. Slightly favor the south shore until abeam of the lighthouse, then curve around the spit, mid-channel. The shallowest area in the entrance is

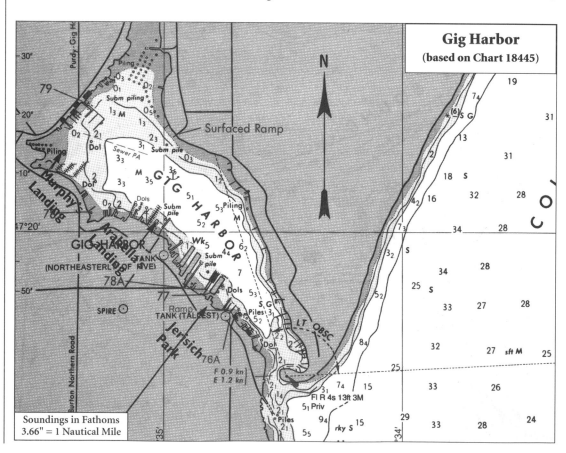

Gig Harbor
(based on Chart 18445)

Soundings in Fathoms
3.66" = 1 Nautical Mile

The entrance to Gig Harbor. This lighthouse was built by the community; the surrounding beach is public.

about halfway; the channel then steadies to depths of 2 fathoms. Inside, the harbor deepens toward the center, gradually turning to mudflats at its head.

Moorings. Gig Harbor is lined with marinas and floats. Guest moorage is available at three of these on the southwest shore.

A long guest float extends from the flagpole at Jerisich Park, immediately east of Pleasurecraft Marina's fuel dock. The pilings on the west side of this public float are spaced about every 40 feet; the other side is unobstructed, but its turning basin is narrow due to shallow water east of the float. No rafting is permitted. Depth at the float gradually rises to the ramp, 5 feet shallower on the west side, 10 feet shallower on the east side. A self-service pay box is on the pier, where there are also a few picnic tables and restrooms with showers. Maximum stay is 24 hours.

Guest slips are also available farther into the bay at Arabella's Landing. This marina is distinguished by its black pilings topped with dunce caps. Its two rows of finger floats are set north-south. Pull into an empty slip; the harbormaster will be down to register your boat. If you arrive after hours, use the fee box at the head of the ramp. Power is available at all the slips, and included in the moorage fee. On shore, signs direct you to the restrooms and showers, the laundromat, and the lounge area; you'll be given a code number to unlock these. The white house near the ramp is a private residence. Arabella's Landing takes reservations by phone (360) 851-1793.

At the southwest end of the harbor is Murphy's Landing Marina, with guest moorage May through October (during winter the float is rented out for long-term moorage). The guest float is on the far west side, past the permanent slips. The bay shallows rapidly here; signs remind you to stay east of the pilings as you approach. Tie up either side of the 80-foot float. The marina reports depths of 8 to 10 feet on a zero tide. Use the pay box at the head of the ramp. When the manager is on site, he or she will give you a key to the restrooms, showers, and laundry. Murphy's Landing Marina does not take reservations for guest moorage.

Anchorage. Anchorage is good in the middle of Gig Harbor, in 3 to 7 fathoms. Toward the northeast shore the bottom appears to rise more steeply.

Getting Ashore. Use the public float at Jerisich Park, located at the flagpole on the south shore. If you pay a dinghy-landing fee you can use the floats at Arabella's Landing, as well as their facilities. The Shoreline Restaurant at the head of the bay and the Tides Restaurant toward the entrance have floats for patrons (see For the Crew below). On the north shore of Gig Harbor, public access is at the street-end launching ramp.

All other floats and all mooring buoys in Gig Harbor are private.

For the Boat. The main fuel dock is west of Jerisich Park, at Pleasurecraft Marina. Inside the yellow building at the pumps is a fairly well-stocked marine store.

Fuel (gas and diesel) is also sold at Stutz's, located below the tank farm on the west side of the Tides Restaurant. The fuel here is gravity-fed, so there are no pumps on the dock. Tie up at either float (the outside is deepest) and walk through the warehouse to the office.

Marine repair facilities in Gig Harbor are fairly limited. Inquire at the Pleasurecraft Marina fuel dock.

For the Crew. The streets of Gig Harbor radiate from Jerisich Park like spokes from the hub of a wheel. The nearest supermarket is a short walk up Pioneer Way; a hardware store and post office are in this same mall. The closest laundromat is at the head of the bay, across the street from the Shoreline Restaurant.

Restaurants, delis, shops, and galleries fill the storefront buildings in town and line the road to the end of the harbor. The Peninsula Historical Museum is a block up Rosedale Street, in an old church. The Puget Sound Mariners' Museum, less than a block west of Jerisich Park, is open weekends in summer, and most any time by appointment—(360) 858-9395.

At least two restaurants have water access, the Shoreline Restaurant at the shallow head of the bay, and the Tides Restaurant toward the entrance. The outside floats at the Tides are in deep water; a red line about 20 feet from the ramp indicates where they go dry on a zero tide. Rafting is standard here, but there is no overnight moorage.

The facilities at Arabella's Landing (see above—Moorage) are available to anchored boaters for a fee.

Things to Do. In clear weather, walk west around the harbor to the viewing platform at the head of the bay. From here you'll see what makes this region so remarkable: Mount Rainier, massive and white above the blue water and brightly colored boats—silent, powerful, and close.

Special events in Gig Harbor include a parade in early June and a Christmas boat parade in early December. A farmers' market is held on summer weekends at the Methodist Church, uphill on Pioneer Way.

Colvos Passage

Charts: 18448, **18474**

Colvos Passage runs along the west side of Vashon Island, a virtual highway between the Narrows and north Puget Sound. The current in this pas- sage generally runs north on both ebb and flood, a condition used to advantage in southerly winds by sailboats and north-bound tugs with tows.

Both shores are minimally developed, with homes and a few beach-cabin resorts. The underwater shelf on both sides is fairly steep. Boats on private mooring buoys bob offshore in summer, minimally protected in the slight "coves."

Almost all tidelands are private. Two exceptions are at Olalla on the west shore, and Lisabuela on the east (Vashon) shore. Olalla is at the mouth of Olalla Bay, in a tiny V-shaped cove that dries at low tide. A rock is charted north of the bay's entrance. West of the road that bridges the bay is a public launching ramp; a convenience grocery and gas station are nearby. Unless your boat is beachable, stay at least 500 yards offshore. The steep bottom rises abruptly from 10 fathoms to less than 1 fathom. Olalla was the first landing site of Peter Puget, who explored for Vancouver in 1772. Its musical Indian name means "place of many berries."

Southeast across the passage from Olalla, on the Vashon side, is a small county park north of Point Sandford. The "cove" here also dries at low tide. A wreck is charted south of the beach. Anchoring may be more successful here than at Olalla, as the shelf, with depths between 5 and 20 fathoms, is somewhat broader. The park has no facilities other than a few picnic tables.

East Passage

Charts: 18448, 18449, **18474**

Wide and deep, East Passage is the main route for southbound commercial vessels. Along the mainland shore are the waterfront homes of Seattle and of the smaller cities that stretch in an almost unbroken chain south to Olympia. To the west is Vashon Island, spiked with radio towers but otherwise relatively undeveloped. Overhead is the low-flying traffic of the Seattle-Tacoma Airport. On a clear day Mount Rainier commands all attention.

East Passage is more thoroughfare than destination, with just a few notable stops for recreational boaters.

Approaches. All approaches are clean. Seas can be steep around Allen Bank at the north end of Vashon Island, especially when wind and current are opposed. Tide rips are charted west of Allen Bank.

Fauntleroy Cove ★★★

Charts: 18448, **18449**, 18474

This cove three miles south of Alki Point is best known for its ferry terminal, with routes west to Vashon and Southworth. North of the terminal are the thick evergreens and deciduous trees of Lincoln Park. From East Passage you can see the wind barrier that surrounds the park's Olympic-sized, saltwater swimming pool on Point Williams, and a few cook shelters along the seawall. Inland is an extensive trail system, picnic and play areas, tennis courts, horseshoe pits, and several ball fields. East, up the road from the ferry terminal, is a small commercial center with a bakery and grocery.

For all its attractions, Lincoln Park is best visited by land. Boats occasionally anchor in the cove, but Seattle city ordinances do not permit landing boats on park beaches. It's OK to use the street end that borders the north side of the ferry dock, and walk the short distance to the park from there. All other tidelands are private.

Fauntleroy Cove does not offer protection from north or south weather. Ferries come and go frequently, adding their wake to that of the shipping traffic in East Passage.

Ed Munro
Seahurst County Park ★★★ 1   No Facilities

Charts: 18448, **18474**

A mile north of Three Tree Point, at Seahurst, is a King County park distinguished from the water by its bulkhead and promenade, and by the doughnut-shaped metal sculpture above the beach. This day-use park has picnic shelters, play equipment, and several nature trails.

Approaching, watch for the fish haven charted toward the south end of the beach. The underwater shelf is steep, making secure anchorage in anything less than 10 to 20 fathoms somewhat difficult. The anchorage is open to the north and south.

Tramp Harbor ★★   2   🛒

Charts: 18448, **18474**

Tramp Harbor opens widely to the north from the narrow isthmus that connects Vashon and Maury islands. Much of this harbor is taken up by a cable area and the buoys and pens of an experimental seaweed farm. A fishing reef south of Point Heyer is marked by two white can buoys with rounded tops. A red-and-white radio tower stands on this point; others rise from Maury Island.

Approaches, Anchorage. Approaching from the north, stay clear of the fishing reef off Pt. Heyer. From the south, watch for the buoys of the seaweed farm south of the low slot of land at Portage, toward the middle of the bay.

A public fishing pier is on the northwest shore, but no tie-ups are allowed. All mooring buoys are private.

The most protected anchorage is between the fishing reef and the pier, in 5 to 10 fathoms. Protection is dubious here, as strong southwesterlies can funnel over the isthmus at Portage from Quartermaster Harbor.

Getting Ashore. Shore access is at the rocky beach near the fishing pier. About a half-mile south along the road is a country store. There are no other facilities within walking distance.

Des Moines Marina ★★★   1 (anchorage)   4 (marina) All Facilities

Charts: 18448, **18474**

The Des Moines Marina, which lies opposite Maury Island's Point Robinson, is the only full-service marina in this region other than Gig Harbor. The marina caters to every kind of boater, with permanent slips and boathouses, a large area for guest moorage, and a hoist and ample parking for trailerable boats. A park and fishing pier border the north side of the marina, and the commercial center of Des Moines is within walking distance.

Approaches. The marina is easily recognized by the sailboat masts and the flat boathouse roofs behind the dark line of its rock breakwater. Apartment buildings spread over the hill on both sides. From the south, prominent landmarks are the elevated, red-roofed water reservoir and the gabled Masonic retirement home. On this approach, stay 500 yards offshore to avoid the shoals that extend west from the beach. The buoy outside the breakwater,

The totem sign for the Des Moines Marina serves as a full-time perch for cormorants.

striped green, orange, and blue, marks a gas pipeline.

From the north, the long concrete fishing pier obscures the marina entrance. The round, light-blue water reservoir on the hill north of the marina is partially visible through the trees.

Moorings. The marina entrance is at the north end of the breakwater, just south of the fishing pier. Immediately inside the entrance is a float without cleats, used for loading and unloading only. South is a timber breakwater topped with a sign. Turn south at this breakwater; inside is a large hoist for trailerable boats, the fuel dock, and two guest moorage floats with finger floats attached.

Pull into an empty guest slip, or tie to the fuel dock to arrange a slip assignment; ring the service bell if no one is there. A pay box with envelopes is on the west side of the fuel dock hut. No overnight mooring is permitted at the fuel dock.

Expect to raft on busy weekends. There is no limit to your stay, but fees almost double after the first seven days. The Des Moines Marina does not take reservations for guest moorage. Anchoring is not recommended. A

cable area is outside the breakwater, and the waters north and south are exposed and deep.

For the Boat. The fuel dock is inside the marina, just south of the inner timber breakwater. A boatyard with marine supply and full repair facilities (including haulouts) is located toward the center of the marina.

For the Crew. Showers are in the small building next to the harbor office. There are a few groceries—and a great deal of fishing tackle—in the small store across the street. The closest supermarket is less than a half-mile southeast, up 227th. A marina laundry is planned; currently the nearest laundromat is northeast, up 218th; a supermarket is in the same strip mall.

Two waterfront restaurants are at the south end of the marina. More restaurants, as well as shops, banks, and a theater, are up the hill on Marine View Drive, less than a mile away.

Immediately north of the marina is Des Moines Beach Park, with picnic tables, play equipment, and stairs to the beach. Des Moines holds a Waterland Festival in late July, a five-day event with fireworks, parades, and an arts and crafts show.

Saltwater State Park ★★★

Charts: 18448, **18474**

The beach, campsites, and picnic areas of this park have long been popular with local residents. Saltwater State Park (shown on the chart as Salt Water State Park) surrounds a creek and steep ravine crossed by several bridges. Roads and trails connect the camping areas. A parking lot near the beach makes it easy for thousands of people to enjoy this park each year.

Campground facilities (including showers) are closed from Labor Day to Memorial Day.

Approaches. From the south, look for the notch of the ravine and the curved road leading down to the parking lot near the beach. The double arches of a concrete bridge are visible beyond. Toward the middle of the beach is a tan-and-green park building. Approaching, guard against drifting close to shore; a shoal that dries at low tide extends from the ravine. Stakes mark the boundary of the private tidelands.

From the north, look for the rock bulkhead beneath the wooded bluff, and the tan-and-green building on shore. The timber structure north of the park is a private staircase. A submerged rock is charted close to shore about a half-mile north of the ravine.

Anchorage, Moorings. Two white can buoys mark an artificial reef just north of the ravine. The park mooring buoys that flank this reef—one north and one south—are used primarily by scuba divers. Both buoys are in deep water. All other buoys are private.

If you anchor, watch for divers, and be prepared to set your hook in 10 fathoms or more; the underwater shelf is fairly steep.

Getting Ashore. The shoreline at Saltwater State Park is not easy to approach by water. At low tide the beach extends more than 100 yards into East Passage, warming the water deliciously in summer, but leaving skiffs high and dry.

For the Crew. Food is available in summer at the south end of the beach. Playground equipment is beyond the parking lot. Showers are in the campground on the other side of the bridge.

Redondo Waterfront Park ★★

Charts: 18448, **18474**

The beachfront community of Redondo hugs the "corner" of Poverty Bay. The county park here consists of a fishing pier, a launching ramp, and a thousand feet of shoreline. Floats next to the ramp are for loading and unloading only; these are removed in winter. North, on a separate pier, is a diving school operated by

Highline Community College, and a popular restaurant. Another restaurant is across the street. A small grocery next to a park and playground is a short distance east.

Approaches are clean, but keep a watch for scuba divers. Anchorage off this park is in 10 to 20 fathoms. All mooring buoys are private.

Dash Point State Park and Dash Point County Park ★★★

Charts: 18448, **18474**

East of Dash Point are two parks within a half-mile of each other. Both are difficult

to approach by boat.

Dash Point State Park is about halfway

between Dumas Bay and Dash Point. The park can be identified from the water by the absence of homes on its wooded bluffs, and by the tan-and-green building (restrooms) on the beach. Picnic tables, barbecues, and shelters are scattered inland. This is a fairly large park (almost 400 acres) with an extensive trail system; the campgrounds and showers are almost a mile uphill. Campground facilities are open year round.

Approaching Dash Point State Park, note that the beach extends west for nearly half a mile at low tide, a definite advantage to swimmers but a deterrent to landing a dinghy. If you anchor in less than 10 fathoms, take care that your swing won't put you aground.

Dash Point County Park is on the north side of Dash Point, where a long concrete fishing pier extends into deep water from a street end. Tie-ups are not permitted. Restrooms are in the blue-roofed shelter at the head of the pier. East is a small public beach, with picnic shelters and play equipment. A seafood restaurant is across the street from the fishing pier. Anchoring is tricky on the steep narrow shelf.

At both of these parks, the anchorage is too far away from shore to provide much protection from the north or south.

Browns Point ★★★

Charts: 18448, **18453**, 18474

The trimmed grounds of a Tacoma city park surround the square concrete lighthouse at Browns Point. This is a pleasant spot for a short visit, with picnic tables, restrooms, and a sloping beach. A marker at the foot of the white flagpole commemorates the 1792 Vancouver Expedition, which landed here to eat lunch before exploring Commencement Bay.

Approaches. From any direction, the square concrete lighthouse is visible at Browns Point, as well as the white flagpole and the tall antenna south of the red-roofed house. Large homes overlook the east beach. A shoal extends some 400 yards off both sides of the point.

Anchorage, Moorings. On the north side of the point are two park buoys in deep water. The west buoy is 5 feet deeper. Both appear to be on a narrow, 2- to 5-fathom shelf. If you anchor, you'll have better luck setting a hook in deeper water. Protection from moderate southerlies is fairly good; it'll be calm here when whitecaps are beginning to form on Commencement Bay. There is no protection from the north or from freighters in the commercial traffic lanes.

Getting Ashore. Use the park beach. The launching ramp at the street end south of the park is private, operated by the Browns Point Improvement Club. There are no facilities within walking distance.

Tacoma and Commencement Bay

Charts: 18448, **18453**, 18474

Tacoma spreads around the Puyallup River delta, encompassing all of Commencement Bay. Its residential and downtown areas on the southwest bluffs are not prominent from the water. What stands out instead are the broad industrial flats. The eight dredged commercial waterways of the Puyallup delta are lined with wharves, and as far as you can see upriver are manufacturing plants, warehouses, storage tanks and domes, cargo loading cranes, ships, tugs, and barges. A white haze rises from the tall steaming stacks.

Dwarfing all of this industry is the astonishing mass of Mount Rainier. Nowhere else in Puget Sound is this 14,410-foot peak so close and so completely visible. Tacoma took its name from the mountain, which the Indians called Tahoma. When it's "out" in Commencement Bay, Mt. Rainier is overwhelming, no matter how often you've seen it.

Tacoma is one of Puget Sound's oldest cities. It began as a sawmill in 1852, booming over a decade later with speculation of a railroad terminus. Two cities were laid out; one on the southwest shore of Commencement Bay (Old Town, shown on the chart as Old Tacoma), the other on the bluff above the Puyallup River, which then emptied roughly where the Thea Foss Waterway is today. When the Northern Pacific crossed the Cascade Mountains via Stampede Pass and terminated here in the late 1880s, Tacoma proudly declared itself the "City of Destiny." It prospered as a major coal and timber port, and was considered by many to be a harbor superior to Seattle. Buildings such as Old City Hall, with its square clock tower and elaborate cornices, and the fairy-tale French chateau of the Grand Hotel, are reminders of this optimistic time. The worldwide depression in 1893 abruptly halted Tacoma's growth; the hotel was abandoned in mid-construction (it eventually opened in 1906 as Stadium High School) and the population dropped by almost 25 percent.

Tacoma was dealt a second economic blow by the Klondike gold rush in 1897, which made Seattle, farther north and by then with its own railroad terminus, the embarkation point for the Yukon. Timber and cheap hydroelectric power eventually attracted investors and the city slowly rebounded, but it never regained its dominance in Puget Sound.

Though in second place as a commercial port, Tacoma is far ahead of Seattle in providing facilities for visiting boaters. At Browns Point, and from Old Town to Point Defiance, Tacoma welcomes pleasure craft to its parks.

Approaches. From East Passage, approaches are clean and deep. Your first view of the city past Browns Point will be the abandoned Asarco plant at Ruston (now being demolished) and the commercial wharves just west of downtown Tacoma. Approaching from the west, be prepared for tide rips in Dalco Passage, and watch for the ferry between Vashon Island and the mainland.

Commencement Bay is deep and steep-sided. Though surrounded by land, it is not as well-protected as you might think, especially from southerlies that track up through the Puyallup River delta. This bay is a favorite with sailors; on sunny, breezy days the blue water blossoms with sails and spinnakers, and the southeastern horizon is filled with the lordly presence of Mt. Rainier.

Northeast Tacoma ★

Charts: **18453**, 18474

Below the steep bluff of Northeast Tacoma is a barge storage area and general anchorage. Rusted hulls form a floating breakwater around two marinas. A green "1" on the end of a barge marks the entrance, which is about three-quarters of the way southeast along the breakwater. In a strong southerly, the hulls above you will heave in the swell of Commencement Bay.

The larger, west marina (Tyee) occasionally has guest moorage; call ahead—(206) 383-5321. Tyee Marina has a shower but no laundry. Boat repair is available at Sunnfjord, located between the two marinas. There are no other facilities within walking distance.

Hylebos Waterway ★ 5 💧 🎁 🔧 ⚓ 🧺 🚿

Charts: 18453

From the anchoring and booming area at its entrance to its final turning basin, the Hylebos Waterway is heavily industrial. Along its shores are shipping wharves for chemicals, petroleum products, logs, and scrap metal. Ships and tugs with tows come and go. Amid all this activity, the small-craft marinas tucked away here and there look out of place. The newest of these, Chinook Landing, has guest moorage for pleasure boats.

Approaches. Entering the Hylebos Waterway, look for the green "1" that marks a shoal on the northeast side. A privately maintained light is on the southwest pier. Two private marinas with rows of boathouses are just inside the waterway on the northeast shore. The next (third) marina, opposite the industrial building with the charted cupola, is Chinook Landing. Concrete octagonal pilings with pointed white caps secure its concrete floats. On shore is a two-story, wood sided marina office with dark green trim.

Moorings. Chinook Landing is owned and operated by the Puyallup Indian Tribe, one of several business ventures that followed a cash and land settlement in 1989 with city, state,

and federal agencies. Chinook Landing is a new facility, with concrete floats and pilings, and landscaped grounds—clearly built to last.

Officially, guest moorage is at the northwest end of the marina on "A" float. There is no power on "A," but permanent slips are often available; check with the marina office after tying up. All slips are set east-west. Inside slips are more protected from the wakes of commercial traffic, which is fairly steady in the waterway. Expect a constant industrial din as well. Chinook Landing welcomes inquiries about guest moorage—(206) 627-7676.

Anchoring is not permitted in the Hylebos Waterway.

For the Boat. A waste-oil receptacle is near the office. The nearest places for boat repair are at Ole and Charlie's Marina (just inside the entrance to the waterway), and south beyond the drawbridge at Hylebos Marina. Bridge clearance is charted at 21 feet.

For the Crew. Chinook Landing has restrooms with showers, a laundromat, and a small convenience store. A restaurant is about a half-mile south. There are no other facilities within walking distance.

Thea Foss Waterway ★ 4 💧 🎁 🔧 ⚓ 🛒

Charts: 18453

This westernmost waterway (also known as City Waterway) was named for the legendary founder of Foss Tug & Barge. The northeast shore is dominated by oil-handling wharves and storage tanks; on the opposite shore are Tacoma's downtown buildings. South, beyond the lift bridge, are small-craft marinas, a commercial fishing pier, several abandoned ware-

houses, and the copper dome of the restored Union Railroad Depot. The blue-and-gray Tacoma Dome rises from the head of the waterway.

The city has cleaned up and improved much of the southwest shore with pedestrian walkways. These connect the waterway to Union Station (now a federal courthouse) and to the site of the Washington State Historical Museum, scheduled to be built nearby. Currently, there are only a few facilities here for visiting boaters.

Approaches. The Thea Foss Waterway opens between the downtown office towers on the southwest shore, and the pulp mill and oil-storage tanks on the northeast. Stay north and west of the light that marks the northeast side of the entrance; piles and shoal water are charted between this light and the Middle Waterway. The *Coast Pilot* reports depths of 29 feet to the lift bridge, 22 to 19 feet from the bridge to the head of the waterway.

The lift bridge has a charted clearance of 64 feet. A gauge on the east pylon gives the actual clearance from the water.

Moorings. Totem Marina, located on the southwest shore north of the lift bridge, often has guest moorage. Tie to the outside float west of the hoist and inquire at the marina store. The fuel pumps are no longer in service. All slips have power and water, and the marina has showers and a laundromat. The marina store has ice, bait, and a few groceries. There is a restaurant to the west on Dock Street, and downtown is within reasonable walking distance to the south. Totem Marina does not take reservations for guest moorage, but encourages boaters to call ahead—(206) 272-4404 or (206) 627-8055.

Beyond the bridge, visitor moorage is available on the southwest shore beneath Johnny's

Seafood. This city float is used primarily by commercial fishing boats for offloading their catch. The float is about 100 feet long, with moorage limited to boats of 30 feet or less, and a maximum stay of 24 hours. Seaplanes have priority at the west end. A sign warns of shallow water at low tide. The ramp leads to a small parking area; stairs will take you over the highway to Union Station and downtown Tacoma. Next door is Johnny's Seafood, a popular market with fresh fish and shellfish in addition to seasonings and condiments. Protection here is good from weather, but the razor ribbon surrounding adjacent properties suggests a security problem.

The only other guest slip is across the waterway at Johnny's Dock, the restaurant side of the seafood operation at the city float. Moorage here is for restaurant patrons only. Talk to the manager about staying overnight.

Anchoring is not permitted in the Thea Foss Waterway.

For the Boat. Picks Cove, located on the northeast shore beyond Johnny's Dock, has a repair facility with a hoist, and a well-stocked marine store. To reach the store from the water, enter north of the boathouses and follow the "Haulout" signs. You can tie up to the float at the hoist while you arrange for repairs or go to the store. This float is about 30 feet long. Picks Cove has no guest moorage.

The nearest fuel is at Breakwater Marina, near Point Defiance Park.

Commencement Bay Waterfront Parks ★★★★

Charts: 18448, **18453**, 18474

Over the past couple of decades, the southwest shore of Commencement Bay has changed dramatically, from heavy industrial use (sawmills, log storage, and smelters) to recreation. A promenade connects a series of public beaches from Old Tacoma to Ruston, in effect creating a single, two-and-a-half-mile waterfront park that is enormously popular with local resi-

dents. Mooring buoys and floats make all of it accessible by boat.

Approaches, Moorings. From east to west, facilities for boats along this waterfront park are as follows:

Old Tacoma (locally known as Old Town) is the commercial center of a fine residential area. It has restaurants, shops, and a dock with floats for visiting boats. Approaching from Commencement Bay, look for a set of pilings topped with black cones. Four finger floats extend toward shore from the longer, outside float. Depths are good. Stays are limited to three nights; pay at the fee box on the pier. The floats are removed in winter. East of the floats are two mooring buoys in deep water. A seafood market is at the head of the pier. Stairs lead up from the beach to a grassy knoll and a metal sculpture. The main street of Old Town is a block away.

West of Old Town are three restaurants on pilings. Two of these have seasonal floats for patrons, but overnight moorage is not allowed.

West of the bright yellow fireboats is a long, T-shaped fishing pier, with shed-roofed shelters for rainy days. No mooring is allowed on this pier. An artificial reef lies offshore. Near the old red-and-white fireboat on shore is a takeout restaurant and a bait and tackle shop.

To the west of this fishing pier are seven mooring buoys, all in deep water. Shore access is via any of the small beaches. A 61-ton head-saw is displayed near the next public pier (no mooring), a reminder of the days when nine sawmills operated between here and Ruston. A restaurant is in one of the nearby buildings on pilings.

A little farther west is a second string of mooring buoys, with pocket-size beaches for shore access. All eight buoys are in deep water.

Anchorage. All of this Waterfront Park shore is fairly steep, rising quickly from 3 fathoms to less than 1 fathom. Expect to anchor in 50 feet or more in order to stay off the beach at low tide. Protection is generally good against southerlies, but you are completely exposed to northerlies.

WORKING THE WATER: THE VIEW FROM THE FERRY

The Washington State ferries are probably the most familiar commercial vessels in Puget Sound. On an average day the fleet makes over 500 departures, and totals some 2,500 back-and-forth miles. Their green-and-white cabin sides are symmetrical fore and aft, tiered like a wedding cake. It's easy to become casual in their lumbering presence.

The men and women working on the bridge of the ferry are rarely so casual about the recreational boater. Part of their job is figuring out what those who are on the water for fun are going to do. Will that sailboat tack out of the way, or keep coming? Does that skipper behind the genoa, or down below with the boat on autopilot, know where the ferry is? Will that speedboat cross the ferry's bow, thinking it can outrun a 20-knot, 2,000-ton vessel? The safest assumption is that boaters know nothing about the Rules of the Road. Captains and mates can't afford otherwise. "We're the ones with the license," they explain. "We're the ones who go before the Coast Guard board if anything happens."

Most of the time, ferries and recreational vessels are far apart, and a minor change in course eliminates a potential hazard. However, problems are common around ferry docks, where facilities such as marinas and fuel docks are often close by. The Point Defiance terminal is a good, if extreme, example: The ferry dock is between the Boathouse (with its busy small-boat rental business, fuel dock, and bait shop), and the equally busy marinas behind the peninsula (the park's Boathouse Marina floats, Breakwater Marina and fuel dock, and the Tacoma Yacht Club).

It's impossible to out-guess all the small boats, but most often their course is east-west, across the ferry route. "The fishing always seems to be better on the other side," explains one mate, as an open skiff skitters across the *Rhododendron*'s bow, and stops there.

Though most boaters have ridden the ferry as passengers, few have been in the wheelhouse. It's a different world up there. As expected, the visibility is good, but a blind spot exists along the guardrails; a small boat can't be seen when it's too close. On the older ferries, engine speed is telegraphed from the bridge to the engine room several decks below, where the engineer, ear-muffed against a deafening roar, adjusts diesels as big as boxcars. In new and upgraded vessels, control is direct from the pilothouse, with a telegraph backup. A toggle, rather than a wheel, is generally used for steering. *continued*

The Point Defiance ferry dock, through the wheelhouse windows of the Rhododendron.

continued from page 81

The work is in the landings. Ferries are tall and flat-sided, extremely vulnerable to crosswinds. Even a small ferry such as the *Rhododendron* draws 10 feet (the largest draw 18 feet) and currents are also an important factor. At the Point Defiance dock they are especially strong and unpredictable, making the landings here among the most difficult in the system. The captain begins the approach about a quarter-mile away, in bad weather as far away as a half-mile. At the landing, the wing-walls and ramp that tower over recreational boats are a small target when viewed from above the ferry's broad bow. Speed is critical; when a ferry has to slow down to avoid another boat, it loses the steerageway needed for a clean landing. Recovering gracefully in these cases requires skillful handling, and can be quite tricky. What's remarkable is not that the collision hazard is so great, but that so few collisions occur—there has never been a serious injury accident involving a Washington State ferry.

When boating near a ferry dock, a few simple courtesies will contribute to everyone's safety. If a ferry is at the dock, stay well out of the white water off its stern. Ferries arrive and depart at predictable times, and report their departures to Vessel Traffic on Channel 14 (on Channel 5A in the San Juans). One long blast is signaled when they leave the dock, one long and two shorts when arriving. Give way when you hear these.

When you are within a mile or so of a ferry dock, look around to see if a ferry is approaching. If so, give way (stop or go astern), and make it clear that you're doing so. Don't cut in front of the ferry even if you think you can outrun it; you cause needless anxiety in the wheelhouse when you do.

In open water, use common sense. Ferries monitor VHF Channel 13; if you're uncertain about what to do, give them a call.

Point Defiance Park ★★★★★

 (anchorage)   (marina)

Charts: 18448, **18453**, 18474

The jewel of the Tacoma waterfront is Point Defiance Park. This wooded 700 acres has many attractions: rental boats, trails, gardens, a reconstruction of old Fort Nisqually, a zoo, and an aquarium. For the boater, the park has provided public floats at Boathouse Marina, and a string of mooring buoys.

Approaches. The steep prominence of Point Defiance is unmistakable from any direction. From the west, be prepared for tide rips in Dalco Passage. From the east, the park begins at the breakwater peninsula; the low building on top is the Tacoma Yacht Club. This peninsula is bluish-purple with tailings from the for-

mer American Smelting and Refining Company (Asarco). The 562-foot Asarco stack at Ruston, still marked on the charts, was the tallest in the world when it was constructed in the early 1900s. It was demolished amid much fanfare in 1993.

Approaches are clean. Watch for the ferry, which makes frequent runs between Vashon and the terminal just north of the breakwater peninsula.

Moorings. The park's Boathouse Marina floats are just inside the breakwater peninsula, between the ferry dock and the three-lane launching ramp. The two 150-foot floats lie

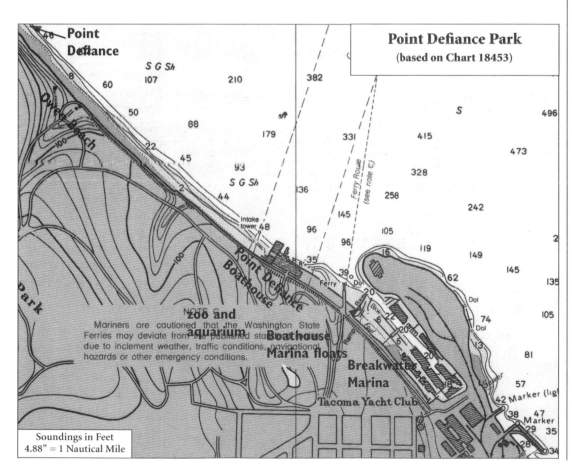

Point Defiance Park
(based on Chart 18453)

NOTE G
Mariners are cautioned that the Washington State Ferries may deviate from the published schedules due to inclement weather, traffic conditions, navigational hazards or other emergency conditions.

Zoo and aquarium

Point Defiance

Boathouse Marina floats

Breakwater Marina

Tacoma Yacht Club

Soundings in Feet
4.88" = 1 Nautical Mile

north-south, with dolphins on the west side that may make mooring difficult for larger boats. There is ample turning room between the floats. The end of the west float is reserved for sewage pumpout use. Stays are limited to three nights, with rafting permitted but not required. Register at the pay box or at the Boathouse Marina store on the other side of the ferry dock.

Guest moorage may also be available inside the breakwater at Breakwater Marina. Enter north of the timber wall. Continue past the Tacoma Yacht Club guest floats and boathouses to the fuel dock, where you can inquire about moorage. In summer it's a good idea to call ahead—(206) 752-6663.

About a half-mile west of the breakwater are eight buoys set off the park's Owen Beach. Though close to shore, all of these buoys are in deep water. Ashore there are picnic tables, barbecues, and restrooms; a snack concession operates in summer. The park trails and other attractions are a long walk uphill.

For the Boat. Gas is available at the Point Defiance Boathouse. This is a popular place to rent open boats for fishing the Narrows, and the hoist is always busy.

Both gas and diesel fuel are available at Breakwater Marina, inside the breakwater peninsula. Enter north of the timber wall, and continue past the Tacoma Yacht Club guest floats and boathouses to the fuel dock. There's good depth and turning room inside.

For the Crew. A few snack items are sold at the Boathouse Marina store, but the specialty here, for obvious reasons, is fishing tackle and bait. A restaurant is next door.

A laundromat is in Ruston, less than a half-mile uphill. Near the laundromat are several antique stores and cafés. A convenience grocery is another half-mile south on Pearl Street.

A city bus leaves from the parking lot west of the ferry terminal for downtown Tacoma.

Things to Do. If you're moored at the park floats or at Breakwater Marina, you don't have to go far to explore Point Defiance Park. Just inside the park entrance up the road are two gardens, one formal, the other native. A quarter-mile farther into the park is the zoo and aquarium, open every day except Thanksgiving and Christmas. The Rocky Shores exhibit alone is worth the walk and cost of admission. Ghostly white beluga whales with their beaked faces and small pointed teeth swim in one tank. In the other, among the seals and sea lions that seem to fly through the water, are two walrus—enormous, lumpy, and utterly mesmerizing.

For the energetic, trails beyond the zoo lead to other attractions: a rhododendron garden, a logging museum, the Never-Never-Land fantasy garden, and the Fort Nisqually Historic Site. The trails are a destination in themselves, a wilderness hike through thick forest and ancient evergreens.

Quartermaster Harbor

Charts: 18448, **18474**

This convoluted harbor more than makes up for Vashon's lack of other protected coves. It lies between Vashon and Maury, two islands effectively joined into one at the narrow isthmus at Portage. Four miles long, Quartermaster Harbor curves northeast and then west around the Burton peninsula, creating two exceptional anchorages.

Neither anchorage offers much on shore. Vashon Island has a rural flavor, with a population of less than 10,000. Almost all its shops and restaurants are in town, toward the center of the island. Here you'll feel far removed from the commercial activity of nearby Des Moines and Gig Harbor, and even farther away from the industry of Tacoma.

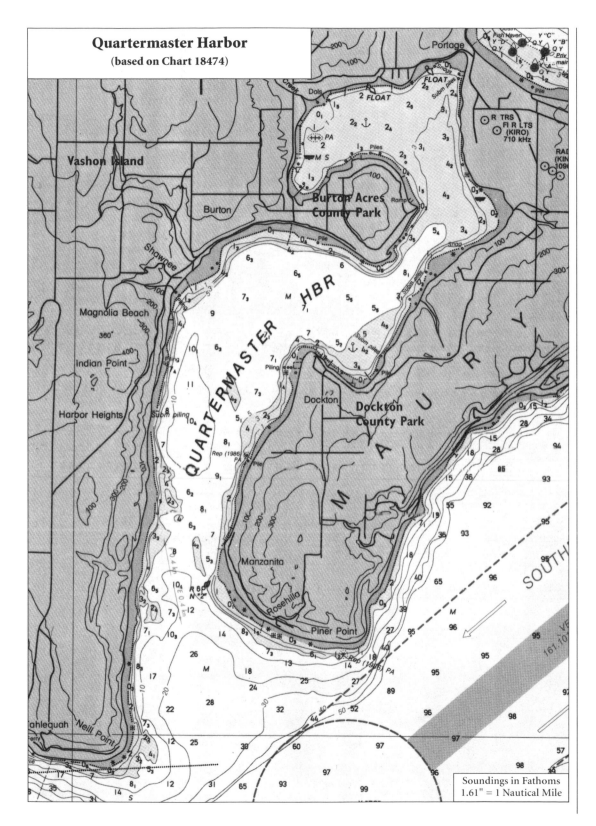

Quartermaster Harbor
(based on Chart 18474)

Vashon Island

Burton

Burton Acres
County Park

Shownee

Magnolia Beach

Indian Point

Harbor Heights

QUARTERMASTER HBR

Dockton

Dockton
County Park

Manzanita

Rosehilla

Piner Point

Neill Point

Soundings in Fathoms
1.61" = 1 Nautical Mile

Approaches. From the southeast, stay 500 yards off Maury Island between Piner Point and Manzanita. Stay a similar distance off Neill Point when approaching from the southwest. Watch for the ferry at Tahlequah, which shuttles between Vashon and Point Defiance Park.

Enter the harbor about mid-channel, west of red nun "2." This buoy marks a shoal that dries at low tide. North of "2" are shoals and pilings along both the east and west shores, and a couple of submerged rocks along the east shore, all unmarked. Stay at least 200 yards away.

Dockton County Park ★★★★

Charts: 18448, **18474**

The sleepy community of Dockton was once a busy shipyard, with the first dry dock in Puget Sound large enough for sailing schooners. As land travel became easier, and especially after the Navy built its own yard in Bremerton, the industry here began to fail. A smaller shipbuilding operation continued through World War I. Today nothing remains of these industries on the west shore except a few floats and piers used mostly by fishing vessels, and several rows of pilings. On top of the steep bluff, the wood-framed supervisors' homes—known locally as Piano Row—still oversee the long-gone shipyard.

The attraction for boaters and island residents is on the east side of this wide, V-shaped cove, at Dockton County Park. This 23-acre park has picnic tables, a large cook shelter, a bonfire pit, play equipment, and paths up the bluff. A swimming area and launching ramp are on the south side of the park's moorage floats.

Approaches. The dock pilings and the low gray park building on shore are visible after rounding the point of Dockton. As you head for the park, stay north of the anchored boats and the pilings, fish pens, and rafts that fill the south end of the harbor.

Anchorage, Moorings. The long, outside, park floats form a squared-off "J" that opens to the north. These concrete floats are braced with stout double pilings; inside are a fair number of concrete finger floats. Depth at the outside float is about 5 feet deeper than at the ramp.

A fee box is located at the restroom on the pier. Moorage is limited to three nights per week.

Anchorage is good in 3 to 5 fathoms, mud bottom. Protection is excellent from the south, but a strong northerly coming over the low isthmus at Portage can raise a good chop.

All mooring buoys are private.

Getting Ashore. Use the park floats. Stay clear of the swimming area south of the pier. Tidelands outside the park are private.

For the Crew. Showers are in the restrooms on shore. There's a pay phone and a bus stop at the road. The bus makes frequent runs north to the town of Vashon and on to the ferry terminal at the north end of the island.

About a half-mile up the road from the park is a post office. The country store is no longer in operation.

Burton ★★★

Charts: 18448, **18474**

The Burton Peninsula punches east into Quartermaster Harbor like a fist. At its pointed, east tip is a county park; to the northwest is a protected little anchorage and two marinas, one with occasional guest moorage.

A small private college operated in Burton at the turn of the 19th century. The college burned down in 1910, but some of the town buildings that briefly flourished with it remain.

Approaches, Anchorage, Moorings. Stay mid-channel between the peninsula and Maury Island. Shoals and pilings are charted off both shores.

Burton Acres County Park begins at the launching ramp, north of the peninsula's east point. As you approach, you'll see a few picnic tables beneath the twisted madronas. Anchor well offshore, in 1 to 3 fathoms; any closer, and you will go aground at low tide. All mooring buoys are private. Up from the beach are restrooms, and across the street is the rest of the park, an extraordinary, almost primeval forest laced with ungroomed trails. Your eyes will instantly relax in the filtered green light. The park is encircled by a road, and bordered at its south end by a private camp.

Northwest of the peninsula is the town of Burton, where there are two small marinas. The marina on the west shore is the Quarter-master Yacht Club, for members and reciprocal guests only. To the south is Quartermaster Marina, which occasionally has guest moorage by reservation—(206) 463-3624.

Many boats are anchored in this protected, fairly shallow cove (2 fathoms or less). Check the tides if your vessel is deep-draft. A wreck is charted north of the yacht club.

Getting Ashore. Check with the Quarter-master Marina office for permission to leave your skiff at the floats. The gate is locked after dark.

For the Boat, Crew. Quartermaster Marina does hull repairs and can arrange for engine repairs. A short walk south of the marina is a country store with hardware, some marine supplies, and groceries. The Back Bay Inn across the street serves dinners to the public Wednesdays through Saturdays; it's a good idea to make reservations—(206) 463-5355.

A bus stops at Burton, southbound on its way to the Tahlequah ferry, northbound on its way to the town of Vashon and the ferry terminal at the north end of the island.

REGION 4

BLAKE ISLAND TO

KINGSTON AND EDMONDS

The urban surroundings in this region don't necessarily detract from the scenery or wildlife. Here, a "spyhopping" orca whale scans Alki Beach and downtown Seattle.

(Paul Dudley photo)

INCLUDING PORT ORCHARD AND POULSBO

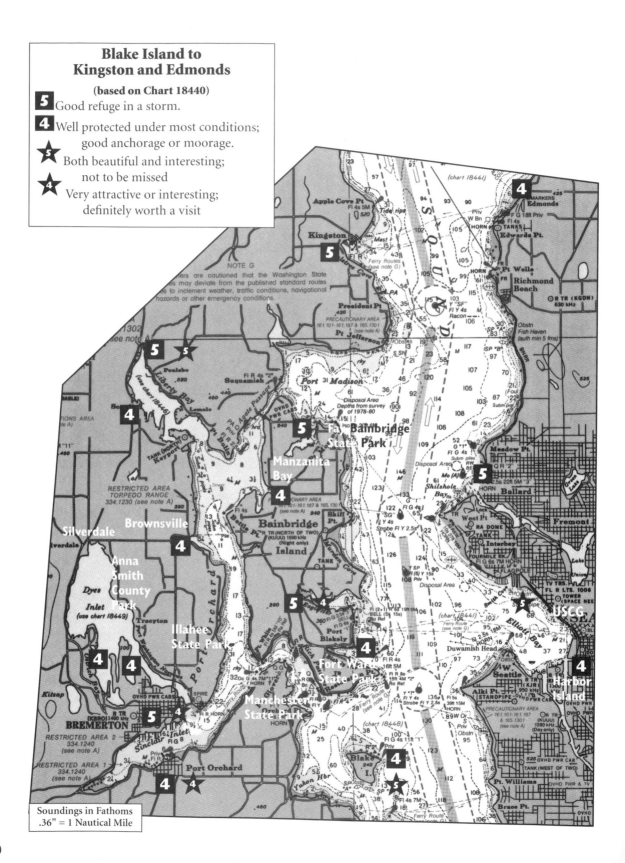

Blake Island to
Kingston and Edmonds

(based on Chart 18440)

5 Good refuge in a storm.

4 Well protected under most conditions;
good anchorage or moorage.

⭐**5** Both beautiful and interesting;
not to be missed

⭐**4** Very attractive or interesting;
definitely worth a visit

Soundings in Fathoms
.36" = 1 Nautical Mile

This region of Puget Sound is the most densely populated in the state. Seattle sprawls over the entire mainland shore, north and south of the high-rise towers in Elliott Bay. The homes that stand on almost every beach and bluff of Bainbridge Island and the Kitsap Peninsula radiate from several large towns. Not surprisingly, the public shores are often crowded.

Out on the water, there's always a freighter or a tug with tow in the commercial lanes of the traffic separation system, some passing on to Tacoma or Admiralty Inlet, many bound to and from Seattle or the Bremerton shipyards. Washington State ferries cross this area of the sound literally hundreds of times a day. On almost any weekend, recreational boats—from rough, wooden skiffs to chromed, polished yachts—take to the water. Despite all the busyness, the sense of "getting away" is real here, enhanced on a clear day when all the mountains are visible at once: the Olympics, Mount Baker, the Cascades, and Mount Rainier, a ring of blue-and-white peaks that seem to belong more to the sky than to the earth.

A word about weather: Don't let the developed shores fool you into thinking that the waters also have been tamed. Northeasterly and southwesterly gales can kick up high waves in the sound, and even on the west side of Bainbridge Island the seas can be serious. A cross-sound trip in the trough is uncomfortable at best, at times dangerous. This area is also the center of the Puget Sound Convergence Zone, a condition that occurs when a cold front off the Washington Coast splits at the Olympic Mountains. The front enters the sound both from the south (through the Chehalis Gap) and from the north (through the Strait of Juan de Fuca), colliding anywhere between Tacoma and Everett. The opposing winds force moist air up; clouds thicken, and the result is heavy rain—occasionally thunderstorms.

Nevertheless, boating is a year-round event here. There are many protected inlets with guest moorage and shoreside attractions, and several secure anchorages.

The first half of this chapter describes the coves and harbors in the main Puget Sound basin, beginning at Blake Island and moving clockwise north to Kingston and south to Alki. The second half describes those west of Bainbridge Island, from Rich Passage to Agate Passage.

Blake Island State Park ★★★★★ 3 (anchorage) 4 (marina)

Charts: 18448, **18449**, 18474

Only seven miles from downtown Seattle, Blake Island stands apart in this densely populated region of Puget Sound. All of its 475 acres are state park. Its only development is centered on Tillicum Village on the northeast point. The carved, decorated longhouse and totem poles seem to have emerged from the woods on their own, testimony to the island's heritage as campground of the Suquamish Indians. Visitors arrive by tour boat year round, for the salmon dinner, the traditional dances, and an all-too-brief glimpse of the island itself. The luckier ones enjoy longer stays on their own boats, tied to the dock of the snug harbor or to one of the park's many mooring buoys.

The facilities on Blake Island are open year round.

Approaches. From the north, Blake Island's low northeast point appears as a clump of trees; from the south, the sandy isthmus to the breakwater jetty, and the madronas off the campground are also visible. Approaches are clean and deep, except along the island's north-

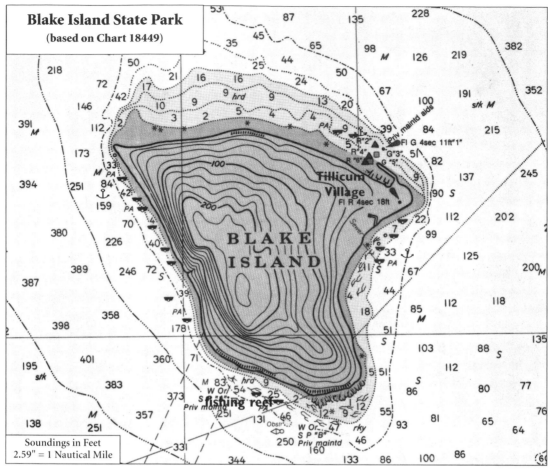

Blake Island State Park
(based on Chart 18449)

Tillicum Village

BLAKE ISLAND

fishing reef

Soundings in Feet
2.59" = 1 Nautical Mile

ern shore, where a considerable shoal extends almost 500 yards off the northwest corner of the island.

Anchorage, Moorings. A small-craft harbor with floats is tucked in behind the rock breakwater on the northeast point of the island. This breakwater is connected to the island by a low sandy isthmus. Enter northwest of the breakwater, between the three green and three red marks on pilings. Depths are steady, but you can easily go aground if you wander out of this narrow dredged channel. At green "5" make a sharp turn to port (southeast) into the harbor. Currents in the entrance channel can be strong, and generally run opposite to the current in Puget Sound, ebbing when the sound floods, flooding when it ebbs.

There are a number of floats inside the breakwater. The L-shaped float closest to the entrance is for commercial tour boats only. During winter, the north leg of the "L" is tied to dolphins further in. The pier with the small hoist, and its attached float, is for state park vessels.

Guest moorage is on the remaining floats. These are about 100 feet long, arranged in two wide "U" shapes open to the north. Each "U" is connected to the island by a ramp. Depths are good except on the south side of the floats, nearest the island. Fifty feet of the guest float, on the north side closest to the hoist, is reserved for 30-minute loading and unloading. A self-service pay station is on shore at the head of the ramps; fees are collected year round. Maximum stay on the floats is three days. On holiday weekends and throughout summer, this popular harbor is completely

Totems guard the entrance to Blake Island State Park marina.

filled with rafted boats. Protection is good in almost any weather, except when gales build up from the north.

Mooring buoys surround the island. Fees for these buoys are collected year round at any of three pay stations: off the west beach, the south beach, and near the ramp at Tillicum Village.

Immediately west of the harbor entrance is a string of seven buoys. The middle three are in slightly shallower water than the others here. All the buoys are on a fairly narrow shelf. If you anchor, note that the bottom is hard, with rocks and shoals charted off the Blake Island shore. The shoal widens northward at the northwest tip of the island. Protection is good from southerlies, but in any weather you are exposed to the ferry and freighter traffic of Puget Sound and Rich Passage.

Southwest of the harbor entrance, around the breakwater, are five mooring buoys. The three at the east end of this string are in deeper water (by 5 feet or more) than the other two.

The anchoring shelf around these buoys is fairly broad, but watch for kelp along the shore to the southwest. You are close to Tillicum Village here, and to the facilities in the main campground. This anchorage is partially protected from the north, but exposed to the south and to freighter traffic in the sound.

There are two mooring buoys off the south end of the island, close to shore in deep water. Both are inside (north) of the two white cans that mark the fishing reef. The beach is narrow and the bluff is steep. The hard kelpy bottom rises quickly.

Eight buoys are set on the west side of Blake Island. Depths at these buoys vary by as much as 15 feet, so check the tides; the deepest water is to the south. If you anchor, secure your hook on the narrow shelf in line with, or slightly west of, the buoys, and check that you won't drag into water too deep for your anchor line, or too shallow for your boat. Toward shore the bottom rises abruptly to a sandy beach, where there are picnic tables and firepits, campsites, and pit toilets. This side of the island seems farthest from Seattle and the busy comings and goings around Tillicum Village. Protection is good from the north, but open to southwesterlies. You may hear eerie underwater "pings" through your hull if sonar testing is taking place off Manchester.

Getting Ashore. The entire island is public.

For the Crew. Showers are in the restrooms south of Tillicum Village. Nearby are horseshoes and playground equipment, as well as picnic tables and barbecues. The nearest grocery store is two miles west of Blake Island, at Manchester.

Things to Do. Boaters are welcome to the salmon dinner and stage show held at the Tillicum Village longhouse. Both are worthwhile; this is one of the few places in Puget Sound where traditional Indian dances are routinely performed. In the darkened longhouse, amid the fragrance of alder-smoked salmon, you'll briefly touch a culture that thrived for more than two thousand years. Times and costs are posted at the pay station. Call ahead—(800) 426-1205—or make reservations at the longhouse an hour before dinner begins. You can skip the meal and pay for the show only.

Beyond Tillicum Village the island is all forest and beach, with trails that take you around, over the top, and through several campsites. The distance around the entire island is about four miles. A map is displayed near the harbor ramps. West of the longhouse is an interpretive loop trail, with markers that explain how the Indians used this lush vegetation for food, shelter, and clothing. Along this north side of Blake Island you can see the ordered Seattle skyline to the east. Or you can turn toward the island, where you face a gray-green forest woven with fern and salal. Cedar and fir lean against one another, and some of the younger trees seem to have climbed onto the enormous stumps left by loggers in the mid-1800s, as if determined to outgrow their ancestors.

Yukon Harbor

Charts: 18448, **18449**, 18474

Yukon Harbor opens north toward Blake Island. Much of it is shoal, but protection is better here from southerly wind and wave than on the west side of Blake Island. This may be an alternative when weather from the south threatens. Stay in water 20 feet or deeper to avoid the rocks and snags toward shore. All docks, mooring buoys, and tidelands are private, with the exception of a public fishing pier to the southeast at Harper. This pier was once a ferry landing; an old wing wall still stands at the end. There are rails all around, and no stairs from the beach. An outhouse and a pay phone are at the road.

A public launching ramp is about 500 yards southeast of this pier, at a low spot off the road in the shallow end of the bay. The backstop of a community ball park can be seen as you approach. This ramp is accessible only at high tide. There are no facilities within walking distance.

Manchester ★★

Charts: 18448, **18449**, 18474

Manchester, about a mile-and-a-half northwest of Blake Island, is handy for provisioning. A public float extends from a street-end park immediately south of a launching ramp. Approaches are clean on this steep beach, but the float itself is in shallow water; boats drawing more than 3 feet should avoid it at low tide. There is no overnight moorage here, but daytime visitors are welcome. At the nearby intersection is a grocery, restaurant, gas station, and post office.

Blakely Harbor ★★★ No Facilities

Charts: 18448, **18449**, 18474

Only a mile south of busy Eagle Harbor on Bainbridge Island, Blakely is its opposite, with soft wooded shores. All that remains of the lumbermill that once packed this harbor with timber schooners are abandoned pilings and the stone causeway of the old settling pond at the head of the bay.

Plans for an extensive residential community, currently struggling through the permit process, may change the character of this placid bay. For now it feels private and hidden, far from the city across the sound. Sunset reflects pink-and-gold in the glassed high-rises, and at night Seattle glitters like a distant fairyland.

Approaches. Give Blakely Rock a wide berth. Reefs extend off Restoration Point, and the point north of the entrance to Blakely Harbor. Inside, stay at least 100 yards off the south shore, which bares at low tide.

Anchorage. There's good depth throughout the middle of Blakely Harbor. The south shore is shoal, but has fewer homes. All mooring buoys are private. Take care that your swing doesn't put you aground at low tide. For many, the biggest concern is anchoring where the view of the Seattle skyline is best.

Protection in Blakely Harbor is fairly good from north and south, and the wakes of passing freighters are somewhat broken by Blakely Rock.

Getting Ashore. All floats and tidelands in Blakely Harbor are private.

An extra-low, minus-4 tide attracts a crowd to Blakely Rock on a sunny weekend. At high tide only the top of the marked rock is visible. (Paul Dudley photo)

Eagle Harbor ★★★★

Charts: 18441, 18448, **18449**, 18474

Eagle Harbor corkscrews its way into the east shore of Bainbridge Island. Inside is the town of Winslow, named after one of the owners of the large shipyard that operated here until the late 1950s. The abandoned creosote plant at the entrance is blamed for making Eagle Harbor one of the most polluted in Puget Sound, though clean-up efforts are making slow headway. The island was once known for its berry farms.

Today a repair facility for Washington State ferries operates west of the terminal, but Bainbridge is primarily a bedroom community. Many residents commute via ferry to jobs in Seattle; the early-morning runs are filled with walk-on passengers dressed in suits, toting briefcases and athletic bags. The condominiums and homes that ring Eagle Harbor reflect this development. The beauty it has nonetheless retained explains why so many live here and work "over there."

Approaches. From the south, watch for Blakely Rock, which is surrounded by rock, kelp, and shoal, especially on its north side. The stack of the old creosote plant is prominent on the south point of the entrance into Eagle Harbor.

From the north, look for the flagpole on Wing Point, then search south for red nun buoy "2." Keep this buoy to starboard. Just beyond is the buoy marking Tyee Shoal.

Enter Eagle Harbor west of red "2," either side of Tyee Shoal. As you round the point past the creosote plant, keep the green marks to port. The ferry navigates this twisting channel on its hourly runs between Winslow and Seattle; look around to see if it is approaching, and give it plenty of maneuvering room.

Moorings. Eagle Harbor offers several choices for moorage.

Past the ferry terminal and the repair yards is a waterfront park with a long concrete public float. Moor either side. Stays on this float are limited to 48 hours. The inner 50 feet is for dinghies; a yellow line painted on the float indicates where the shoreline bares at low tide. Donations for moorage help maintain this and other Bainbridge Island parks. This float has no water or power. The park has restrooms.

Winslow Wharf Marina, a little farther west, assigns vacant permanent slips to visitors. Call ahead—(206) 842-4202—or tie to the outside of "B" float. This float lies east-west, and has a small hut in the center. Report to the harbor office on shore or contact the after-hours manager as posted on the hut. The price of moorage includes power. On shore are restrooms, showers, and a laundry; access requires a key from the manager.

Harbor Marina, just west of Winslow Wharf Marina, sometimes has guest moorage. Check in advance by calling (206) 842-6502. Laundry and showers are up the stairs next to the pub restaurant. Dinghy space for pub patrons is inside, close to the bulkhead.

Guest moorage is also available, by reservation only, at Eagle Harbor Marina—(206) 842-4003—on the south shore. Though close to Winslow by skiff, there are no facilities within walking distance. The marina has showers, laundry, and a hot tub.

Anchorage. Depths are good until Eagle Harbor bends northwest beyond the marinas. You'll be well protected in the main basin, but anchoring takes care among the many boats and private mooring buoys. Soft spots are reported, so make sure you're firmly hooked before leaving your boat. The current has a tendency to flood along the north shore and ebb along the south; after a few days your line may be wrapped around your anchor.

The northwest end of Eagle Harbor is private, with anchorage for landowners only.

Getting Ashore. The main public shore access is at Waterfront Park. Winslow Wharf has a dinghy

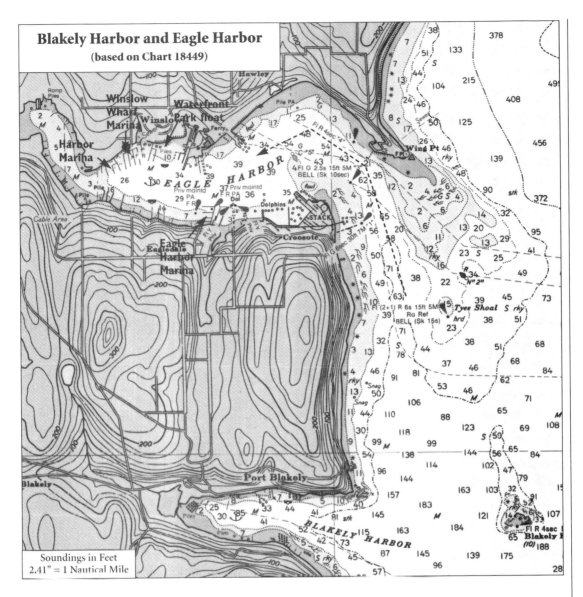

Blakely Harbor and Eagle Harbor
(based on Chart 18449)

Soundings in Feet
2.41" = 1 Nautical Mile

dock at the ramp for patrons of the restaurant and marine store, as does Harbor Marina for its pub patrons. Landing on the south shore is possible at several undeveloped street ends.

For the Boat. A well-stocked marine store is at Winslow Wharf Marina, and a boat repair yard lies between Waterfront Park and the ferry maintenance shipyard. The nearest fuel is in Seattle, at Elliott Bay Marina.

For the Crew. There are showers and laundries at the marinas, as described above. Boaters at anchor can use the laundromat a couple of blocks up the road from Winslow Wharf Marina, on Madison Avenue. A supermarket is a block west of Waterfront Park.

Things to Do. Eagle Harbor has enough attractions for many weekend visits. Winslow's main street is close by, lined with shops, bookstores, and restaurants. There's also a hardware store and library. Half-a-mile north on highway 305 is a winery and museum, open afternoons Wednesday through Sunday. Waterfront Park has playground equipment, picnic tables, tennis courts, and a bandstand shaped like a boat.

A row around the anchorage is fascinating in itself. Boats range from yachts to commercial fishing vessels to tiny houseboats. From the middle of the harbor you can look beyond the cranes of the shipyard to the highrises of Seattle.

Evening concerts are held in Waterfront Park in July and August, and a farmers' market through the summer at Winslow Green, a couple of blocks north of Winslow Wharf Marina, on the corner of Madison Avenue and Winslow Way.

Fay Bainbridge State Park ★★★

Charts: 18441, 18473, **18446**

This 17-acre park about a quarter-mile south of Point Monroe has picnic areas, play equipment, horseshoe pits, and a small campground with showers—all near the driftwood-strewn beach. In calm weather this is a pleasant stop for a few hours, and the panorama on clear days includes both Mount Baker and Mount Rainier.

Campground facilities (including showers) are closed from October through April.

Two public mooring buoys are set off the beach in 1 to 2 fathoms, the north buoy in slightly deeper water. The underwater shelf is narrow, with a steep drop-off; check your swing if you anchor.

Approaching, look for the pale green-and-yellow building (the park restrooms) on the low shore. Roads curve down the hill on either side. The mooring buoys are to the north. Shoals extend north and south about 100 yards off the beach.

All other mooring buoys and all adjoining tidelands are private, including those around the tidal lagoon to the south. There are no facilities within walking distance.

Port Madison—The Outer Bay

Charts: 18441, 18443, **18446**

The outer bay of Port Madison opens widely to the northeast, between Puget Sound and Agate Passage. Though too deep and exposed for anchoring, it branches north and south into two protected harbors, at Miller Bay and at inner Port Madison on Bainbridge Island.

Approaches. Approaches are clean from the northeast and southeast. Watch for sportfishing boats off Jefferson Head. From the southwest, pay attention to currents and shoal water in Agate Passage. A description of Agate Passage is given on page 122, under Approaches to Port Orchard Channel.

The charted mooring buoy is often used by tugs and barges waiting out rough conditions on the sound.

Port Madison—The Inner Harbor ★★★ No Facilities

Charts: 18441, 18473, **18446**

When local boaters talk about Port Madison, they are usually referring to the inlet on the

north end of Bainbridge Island. Tucked inside the zigzag of this little harbor, anchored firmly to its mud bottom, you're completely protected from almost any weather. The shores are lined with large homes set beneath tall trees on manicured lawns; most have private docks. The only marina is a yacht club outpost halfway into the harbor on the south shore. Private buoys are scattered everywhere in the quiet water. As a secure anchorage less than six miles from Shilshole and the Ballard Locks, Port Madison is popular with Seattle boaters.

This inlet was once a Suquamish Indian village site. In the mid-1800s the town—then larger than Seattle—was the county seat, with a timber mill that boasted the territory's first circular saw.

Approaches. From the east, look for the low sandy hook of Point Monroe. This point is crowded with homes, and encircles a shallow lagoon. It is marked with a flashing white light that's often difficult to distinguish from residential lights. The entrance to the inlet is about a half-mile west. A rock awash is charted about 100 yards off the bluff, east of the entrance.

The inlet is narrow and further constricted with shoals that dry at low tide. Enter at no-wake speed, favoring the east shore until the inlet widens. The piers and floats on both sides extend into deep water for the most part, but the area between goes dry at low tide; watch your drift.

Anchorage. The main anchoring basin is just inside, on the east side of the inlet. It is often crowded here, and you will need to set your hook carefully among the many anchored boats and private buoys to avoid swinging into them. There's room to anchor farther in, but check the tides or you may find yourself in the mud when the water drops.

Getting Ashore. All docks and tidelands are private. The closest public shore is a nature preserve about 600 yards northwest of the entrance to the inner harbor. However, there is no safe access to this park from the beach. A sign on top of the high, steep bank warns hikers to stay back.

Suquamish ★★★ 🖼 🎒 🛒 🍽

Charts. 18441, 18473, 18446

The community of Suquamish, north of Agate Passage, is an important historical site, known by most as the birthplace and burial ground of Chief Seattle. Suquamish Indians have lived here for more than two thousand years; their longhouse, the largest on Puget Sound (500 feet in length), once stood nearby on Agate Passage. It was burned in 1870 by federal agents in an effort to break up this ancient community. Ultimately the effort failed, and Suquamish is now a focal point for tribal activity, with a cultural center and museum south on the highway.

The town of Suquamish has a few small shops, a grocery and bakery, and a post office. Chief Seattle's grave is a short walk uphill from the launching ramp. From the beach, the panorama to the east includes Kulshan (Mount Baker), Tahoma (Mount Rainier), and all the Cascade Range in between. Nearby are the words of Chief Seattle, painted on a simple sign: LOVE THIS BEAUTIFUL LAND.

Suquamish is difficult to approach by water except in a beachable boat. The town is at the northern entrance to Agate Passage, where currents and heavy boat traffic discourage anchoring under most conditions. A public launching ramp is east of the charted fishing pier.

Chief Seattle Days are celebrated here in August, with canoe races, traditional Indian games and dances, and a salmon bake. The public is welcome.

Miller Bay

Charts: 18441, 18473, **18446**

This inlet at the northwest corner of Port Madison is too shallow for almost any boat to linger past high tide. The entrance is less than half-a-fathom deep and, once inside, even a runabout needs to take care. Much of the bay dries at low tide. Warm and protected, it is ideal for water-skiing, or paddling up its river-like head.

The only deep area in Miller Bay is along the north side of the spit that guards the entrance, roughly parallel to the charted dol-phin piles. The homes on the spit are close together, as are the floats, all of them private.

There are no public facilities in Miller Bay, and no public shore access. The charted launching ramp is private, but can be used for a fee.

Approaches. Stay roughly mid-course as you approach the entrance in order to avoid the mudflats that rise abruptly on both sides. Favor the spit as you enter.

Indianola ★★

Charts: 18441, 18473, **18446**

Indianola is located two miles west of Point Jefferson on the north shore of Port Madison. This small community was once served by ferry; its long, deepwater pier, rebuilt with local funds, is popular for fishing. A short float on the west side of the pier provides shore access, with visits limited to 30 minutes—enough time to walk up to the country store at the intersection for a few snacks. A post office and pay phone are across the street.

Approaching, stay in deep water, a good 500 yards off the beach on either side of the pier. Check the tides, as the float is on the edge of the underwater shelf, and may be too shallow for your boat.

All tidelands are private, including the small community beach on the west side of the pier.

Kingston ★★★ (anchorage) (marina) **All Facilities**

Charts: 18441, 18473, **18446**

Kingston is tucked inside the curl of Appletree Cove, eight miles northwest of Seattle's Shilshole Bay. Once dominated by a sawmill, the town is now a busy terminus for the cross-sound ferry from Edmonds. Small and easy to cover on foot, it caters to short-term visitors—many of them waiting for the ferry—and has a sizable marina.

Approaches. From the south, be prepared for crowds of anglers off "Jeff Head" (Point Jefferson) and President Point; the steep shelf makes for good fishing here, especially when salmon are running. This shelf continues into Appletree Cove, so stay offshore about 500 yards to avoid the charted shoals, rocks, and pilings. From the north, Apple Cove Point is distinctly pointy, with a marker offshore on a dolphin piling beneath the steep wooded bluff. Shoals, a wreck, and rocks lie between this point and Kingston. The biggest hazard from this direction is the ferry, which makes scheduled runs every 40 minutes or so. Look around to see if a ferry is approaching or leaving the dock, and stay out of its way.

Inside Appletree Cove, the ferry landing and passenger walkway may obscure the marina, which lies behind a rock jetty.

Moorings. The Kingston Marina is well protected inside its formidable breakwater. Enter west of the jetty, but don't cut too close (there are rocks beneath the surface on both sides) or drift too far west of the marked dredged area. A course about midway between the jetty and dredge mark is best.

Most of the slips in the Kingston Marina are for permanent moorage. Forty guest slips are on the east float, closest to the breakwater. The narrow approach to these slips soon widens; there's good turning room and depth inside. The shorter slips are to the south, the longest four slips (50 feet) are closest to the ramp and fuel dock.

Pull into any slip that does not display an "Occupied" sign; these have been paid for by boaters who are out sailing or fishing. Pay at the drop box at the top of the ramp, or report to the port office, west near the hoist. The office is open seven days a week. All slips have power. Stays of two hours or less are free. Maximum stay at the guest floats is 14 days.

Boats may tie to the east side of the guest float at their own risk. There is usually enough depth for shallow-draft boats, but check the tides, as the rocks of the breakwater are quite close.

No mooring is allowed at the fuel dock.

The port office does not take guest moorage reservations.

Anchorage. Appletree Cove is shallow and over half is filled in with mud. The remaining area for anchoring is exposed to weather and freighter wakes. Set your hook south of the breakwater. The bottom is grass, and lightweight anchors may not hold well. Make sure your swing won't put you aground at low tide. Shore access is via the Kingston Marina guest floats.

For the Boat. The fuel dock is at the north end of the guest floats, just inside the breakwater. There's enough turning room and depth, but on busy weekends you may feel more comfortable waiting your turn outside the breakwater. A repair shop that works on marine engines (gas and diesel) is close by on the main road. A marine store is across the street. A map on the pier above the guest floats can help you locate these. The port has a tidal grid that can be used for minor repairs.

For the Crew. Restrooms and a laundry are in the building at the head of the ramp. Get the entrance code from the port office. A supermarket is less than a half-mile up the main road; you'll pass a convenience grocery on the way.

Kingston has restaurants, shops, and a few galleries. Small as it is, it's difficult to get through town without an ice cream cone attaching itself to your hand.

Through Fourth of July weekend, Kingston celebrates Seafest, with fireworks, food, and crafts.

Edmonds ★★★ ☐1 (anchorage) ☐4 (marina)

Charts: 18441, 18473, **18446**

In growing from a small town to a large suburban city, Edmonds has managed to retain an inviting waterfront and downtown area. The marina has guest moorage and is flanked by two public beach parks. On shore are restaurants and boat facilities. Uphill beyond the railroad tracks is Old Town Edmonds.

Approaches. The long pier extending from the fuel tanks at Edwards Point is a prominent landmark. From the south, stay well offshore between Point Wells and Edwards Point in order to avoid the shoals there. From the north, watch for the ferries, which leave the Edmonds dock for Kingston every 40 minutes or so.

Moorings. The marina is on the north side of Edwards Point. A public walkway and fishing pier run parallel to the outside of the north jetty wall, extending from a low cluster of buildings on shore. The entrance to the marina is in the center of the rock breakwater, marked with a green "1" and a red "2." Approaching from the south, green "1" is visible first.

Entering, you'll head squarely into a timber breakwater, with signs pointing south (starboard) to the fuel dock and guest moorage. Guest moorage is on the floats between the travel lift and the fuel dock. All other slips are permanent moorage.

Report to the Marine Services office after tying up. A fee box with envelopes is outside the office for late arrivals. All slips have power. Stays of four hours or less are free; maximum stay is seven days.

The Port of Edmonds does not take reservations. Boaters are encouraged to call on VHF Channel 69 about a half-hour before arrival to inquire about guest moorage. During summer, vacant permanent slips can be assigned to visitors, so there is usually room.

There is no protected anchorage off the Edmonds waterfront. The area north of the ferry terminal is a popular underwater park and, for the safety of scuba divers, it should not be used for boating.

For the Boat. The fuel dock is just inside the marina, south of the inner timber breakwater. The float is set north-south. The Port of Edmonds has a public launching ramp, dry-land storage with a travel lift, and a boatyard. Repairs and marine supplies are also available.

For the Crew. Showers are in the Marine Services building at the head of the fuel dock ramp. A laundromat is fairly close, in the mall on the other side of the railroad tracks, between James Street and Dayton Street. Ice is available at the Marine Services office, and there is a bait store and a fish market nearby. A supermarket is about a mile uphill, on 5th Avenue.

Several restaurants and gift shops overlook the marina. Old Town Edmonds is a mile north and east. Here you'll find more shops and restaurants, many antique stores, a bakery, a movie theater, a hardware store, and a post office.

The marina is bordered by two beach parks. Edmonds Marina Beach to the south has picnic tables, play equipment, a volleyball net, and a lovely stretch of sand and driftwood. North of the marina is Olympic Beach. This pocket-size park adjoins the public walkway and fishing pier. Here a bronze family stands motionless on the grass, watching a family of bronze sea lions.

North of the ferry terminal is Edmonds Underwater Park, a marine sanctuary popular with scuba divers.

Special events in Edmonds include the Waterfront Festival in mid-May, the Edmonds Art Festival in mid-June, and Taste of Edmonds in mid-August. The Fourth of July is celebrated with a parade and fireworks.

Shilshole Bay Marina ★★★

Charts: 18441, 18473, **18446**, 18447

Shilshole Bay Marina is the largest facility in Seattle for pleasure craft. It sits under a bluff north of the Ballard Locks, protected by a rock breakwater, so full of sailboats that from a distance it resembles a white-toothed comb. To the north is Golden Gardens Park, to the south are restaurants and the Ballard Locks. Nearby are a complete range of marine supply and repair facilities, including a full-service boatyard.

Approaches. Shilshole Bay is generally a busy place. Sportfishing boats drift around the channel buoys and off the breakwater, ships

Shilshole Bay Marina. Guest slips and the fuel dock are near the central marina building. The anchorage area is in the crook of the rock breakwater. (U.S. Army Corps of Engineers)

and vessels of all sizes come and go through the locks, and sailboat regattas seem to take place here every weekend.

From the south, keep the red buoys north of West Point to starboard. These mark the entrance to the Ballard Locks, which is dredged through a broad shoal that lies between West Point and the marina. From the north, stay well off Meadow Point (marked with green buoy "1") and well off the Golden Gardens Park beach. Watch for sailboarders and scuba divers close to shore.

From any direction, stay alert for traffic in and out of the locks.

Moorings. Enter the marina from either the north or south end of the breakwater. At the north end, watch for activity around the wide launching ramp next to the blue hoist.

Guest moorage is available at several locations and clearly marked. The main guest floats ("J" and "I") are at the center of the marina, near the large Port of Seattle building with its distinctive square tower. "J" has 60-foot berths set north-south along its full length on both sides. These may be shared as long as there is no overhang into the main waterway. During winter, some of these slips are assigned, and others are used year round for charter; these are marked with "Reserved" signs. More guest floats are on "I," inshore (east) of the fuel dock. These floats are more than 200 feet long, set east-west around both sides of the central pier.

103

Rafting of up to five vessels is permitted here—a common occurrence during weekend regattas. Boats of 35 feet or less also have the option of "W" dock, where guest moorage is available in slips 1 through 11.

No overnight mooring is permitted on the fuel dock.

Turning room is generous in all the waterways. The marina reports minimum depths of 10 feet between floats and 15 feet in the channel along the breakwater.

Pay at the fee box located at the head of "I" dock, or report to the marina office in the port building. A fee box is also at the head of "W" dock. Stays of four hours or less are free.

Power is included in the moorage fee. Water is available on all floats; on "I" you'll need to drape your hose down from the central pier.

Shilshole Bay Marina does not take reservations for guest moorage. Boaters are encouraged to call ahead from outside the breakwater on VHF Channel 17, especially those with vessels over 60 feet.

When the harbor is full, boats may be directed to anchor at the south end of the marina, inside the crook of the breakwater. Take care to leave the main channel clear. Boats anchored here are charged the same fee as those tied to the floats.

For the Boat. Fuel is available at the end of "I" dock, which extends from the tower of the port building. The small store here sells a few marine supplies. On shore is a full range of boat services: repair and supply, a yard with a travel lift, sailmakers, and yacht riggers. If you need something that's not here, there are even more choices in Ballard, a mile-and-a-half away.

For the Crew. Showers and laundry are in the low gray building at the head of "J" dock. Get the lock code from the marina office. There are a couple of restaurants in the port building, and many more nearby. Ice and snack items are available at the fuel dock store. The nearest supermarket is in Ballard, a mile-and-a-half south and east on Shilshole Avenue.

Things to Do. In addition to several restaurants, some with live entertainment, the nearest recreation is at Golden Gardens Park, a half-mile walk north. The broad sandy beach, picnic areas, and trails inland draw visitors from all over the city. This is one of the premier saltwater sunbathing beaches in Seattle, much used in summer. A little over a mile south and west are the Ballard Locks, where there is an arboretum, a natural amphitheater for watching the boat traffic, a fish ladder for migrating salmon, and a visitor center. It's another half-mile east to the shops, banks, post office, and movie theater in downtown Ballard. Ballard has a lively nighttime music scene.

A city bus stops on Shilshole Avenue north of the Marina Office, and travels east into Ballard, with connections to downtown Seattle.

Elliott Bay

Charts: 18449, **18450**, 18474

When Captain Vancouver first saw Elliott Bay in 1792, he remarked on its "pleasing landscape," its "serenity of climate," and its "abundant fertility." In his view, all it lacked was "the industry of man . . . to render it the most lovely country that can be imagined." It's hard to say what he would think of the vista now: layer upon layer of office towers standing at attention above the wharves, bracketed to the north by the wasp-waisted, saucer-topped Space Needle and to the south by the squat gray beanie of the Kingdome. Very likely he would recognize only Mount Rainier to the southeast, which despite all the "industry of man" remains the most impressive object on the horizon.

Seattle's white settlers spent their first winter on Alki Point in 1851, moving the next year to the present downtown area where the harbor was more suited for loading timber. They named the town after the gracious chief of the Suquamish tribe. From the beginning, Seattle tirelessly competed with Tacoma, which had the advantage of being closer to the Chehalis Gap and Fort Vancouver on the Columbia River, then the entryway into Puget Sound for most settlers.

A certain talent for adapting and exploiting circumstances soon emerged; when Seattle lost the bid for the Northern Pacific railroad terminus in 1880, it organized to construct one of its own. The 1889 fire, which consumed 58 city blocks in a single day, was taken as a sign to rebuild to more greatness, this time exclusively in brick, stone, and metal. Even the worldwide depression in the late 1800s was relatively short-lived; the discovery of gold in the Yukon led to Seattle's cornering the Alaska market in a trade partnership that continues to thrive, and the Pacific war led to naval activity and ship-building that is still important to the economy of Puget Sound.

Before the 1900s, Elliot Bay was twice its present size, lapping against First Avenue (east of the present stacked Viaduct highway), curving south beyond today's chart margins to the foot of Beacon Hill. The Duwamish River was all broad tideland. In order to make land transportation easier and to promote growth, many of the city's steeper grades were leveled—including one entire hill. The sixteen million cubic yards of dirt that were removed provided enough fill to push the Seattle waterfront several hundred yards west. Later efforts filled in the Duwamish flats.

Today, Elliott Bay throbs with the life of this largest city in the Pacific Northwest. A major port, it attracts commercial shipping from all over the world, especially the Pacific Rim. Seattle's city limits extend far north, south, and east, encompassing a population of half-a-million. A street map of the land around Elliott Bay reveals a city densely scored with streets, checkered green here and there with parks, veined with blue waterways.

A chart of the waters is equally full. Anchorage areas used by commercial ships are marked from Fourmile Rock off Magnolia Bluff to Pier 66 on the north shore, and from Duwamish Head east past Harbor Island on the south shore. What open water remains is given over to cable area and ferry routes. It's difficult for pleasure boaters to find a place in all this activity, but it can also be difficult to resist. Fortunately, after so many decades of building for commerce, the waterfront is beginning to open itself to boaters.

Approaches. From the south, the towers and cranes of Seattle are hidden behind the hill of West Seattle until past Alki Point. Stay in deep water (5 fathoms or more) around this point. Shoals lie on both sides, and the underwater shelf rises abruptly, especially on the north side. Your first view of the city will be the white side-by-side silos of the grain terminal on Pier 86, and the Space Needle.

From the north, you can see a few of the downtown office towers protruding over Magnolia Bluff, and the orange cranes of Harbor Island beyond the lighthouse at West Point; on a clear day the cranes and radio towers seem to touch the base of Mt. Rainier.

Stay west of green buoy "1," which is west of West Point, and well offshore (about 1,000 yards) until past Fourmile Rock. There's enough depth to the east, but seas pile up in this area when the sound's 100-plus fathoms collide with the less than 5-fathom shelf, then bounce back. In even a moderate gale, expect rough seas here; the smoother ride is farther from shore. The tideflats below Magnolia Bluff are so broad they were platted into streets during the earth-moving frenzy that occurred early in the century; some road maps still show these streets.

Downtown Seattle is spectacular from the water. Following a spell of sunny weather it may be obscured by smog, but after a rain and a brisk wind it appears cleanly scoured, each building standing in sharp relief. You can orient yourself by any number of landmarks. A few of these, from north to south, are: the Space Needle; the red neon "E" of the Edgewater Hotel at Pier 67; the dark gray, 50-story Seafirst Building (nicknamed before it was completed as "the box the Space Needle came in"); the cream-colored Smith Tower with its steep, peaked roof; the Kingdome sports sta-dium; and the web of cranes south toward Harbor Island. The Coast Guard station is on Pier 36, a short distance south of the King-dome.

Elliott Bay Marina ★★★ All Facilities

Charts: 18449, **18450**, 18474

This sparkling new marina sits below Magnolia Bluff, immediately west of the Smith Cove wharves. The view from the cupola-topped building on shore and from the platform on the breakwater encompasses the Cascade Mountains, the Seattle skyline, Mount Rainier, and the Olympic Range across the sound. This is the largest privately owned marina in Seattle, one of the few with guest moorage, and the only one available to the general public that features hotel-like, luxury accommodations.

Approaches. The Elliot Bay Marina is protected on its south side by a rock breakwater, and on its west side by a breakwater wall of concrete and steel. There are two entrance channels, one east and one west.

The east channel is between the breakwa-ter and green "3." Approaching from the south, look for the grain elevator west of the Space Needle, then farther west to the wharves in Smith Cove. Head for Smith Cove until you can pick out the entrance on the east end of the breakwater.

Approaching the west channel from the north, stay 1,000 yards off the Magnolia Bluff shore until you are past Fourmile Rock. The marina lies between you and the Seattle sky-line. Continue to stay in deep water as you head for the south end of the rock breakwater, which wraps north at a right angle around the whitish, concrete-and-steel wall on the mari-na's west side. Enter between the two, and be ready to make a sharp turn to port, south of the steel-and-concrete wall.

Moorings. Floats inside the breakwater are marked from west to east as "A" through "N."

Guest moorage is on "A." Pull into an empty slip on "A," or check in at the fuel dock, which is located on the south end of the center float, opposite the breakwater viewing platform. Check in with the harbormaster in the marina complex after tying up. The marina encourages boaters to call ahead for reservations, either by phone—(206) 285-4817—or on VHF Channel 78.

All floats except the fuel dock are set east-west. In strong southwesterlies, you'll be beam-on to the wind—a vulnerable position for most boats that's made worse at high tide when the breakwater is less protective. Turning room between the floats is somewhat tight. Prepare your lines and fenders accordingly. Fortunately, the marina provides dockhands to take your lines; call on Channel 78 a few minutes before you enter the breakwater and they'll be there to help you as a free service.

All slips have power, water, and cable-TV hookups. Short-term moorage is free (three hours or so) for restaurant patrons; call ahead on Channel 78 to arrange for a slip.

For the Boat. The fuel dock is located at the south end of the middle float, opposite the breakwater viewing platform. The small store on the dock has a fair variety of marine sup-plies. Marine repair is available; there is no haulout facility on site.

For the Crew. A few groceries are sold in the fuel dock store. Restrooms, showers, and laun-dry are on both sides of the marina; an inter-com system controls access. There's a café on the ground floor of the marina complex, and a fine restaurant with outdoor dining on the sec-ond floor.

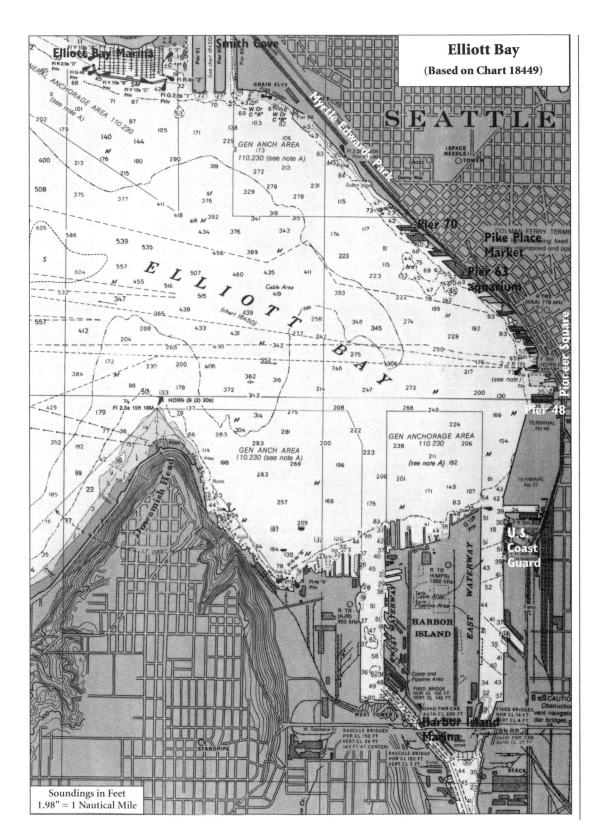

Elliott Bay
(Based on Chart 18449)

Soundings in Feet
1.98" = 1 Nautical Mile

Things to Do. The marina provides a free shuttle boat service, upon request, to and from the breakwater viewing platform every day during daylight hours. The shuttle leaves from the fuel dock. A pocket-size park with picnic tables is east of the marina. Elliott Bay Marina has a concierge to help with land transportation, and restaurant and hotel reservations.

The Seattle waterfront is more than two miles away. The energetic can get there on foot or bicycle via the promenade of Myrtle Edwards Park, which joins Pier 70. From Elliott Bay Marina, use the overpass to get to the other side (east) of Smith Cove; follow the bike path signs on Elliott Avenue to pick up the promenade.

A description of Myrtle Edwards Park and of Seattle's waterfront attractions is given in the next entry.

Seattle Waterfront ★★★★★

Charts: 18449, **18450**, 18474

Once crammed with the commerce of shipping and fishing, Seattle's downtown waterfront piers are now a tourist Mecca. Colorful maps—available in almost every store—show an unbroken series of attractions from the grain elevators to the ferry terminal.

At the northern end, beginning at Pier 70, is the promenade of Myrtle Edwards Park. This popular park follows the shoreline past the grain terminal to a public fishing pier. Along the groomed paths are exercise areas and interpretive signs.

About a mile south of Pier 70 is the Seattle Aquarium; among its many exhibits are touch-tanks, an irresistible family of sea otters, and an underwater viewing dome where you look out and up like a diver from the bottom of Puget Sound. The aquarium is open every day. Uphill from the aquarium is the Pike Place Market, renowned for its bakeries, its farm-fresh produce, and its seafood—the best market anywhere.

From the aquarium south to the ferry terminal, the sidewalks are more crowded, the restaurants and shops closer together and the atmosphere more carnival-like, especially on sunny days. At any time you can stroll east under the Viaduct to explore even more stores and restaurants, the Seattle Art Museum, and the financial district; buses fan out to the rest of the city. Boats offer tours of the harbor and trips through the Ballard Locks or across the sound to Blake Island. The Washington State ferries make scheduled runs to Bremerton, Vashon Island, and Bainbridge Island from Pier 52, and a passenger ferry departs for Victoria, British Columbia, from Pier 69, north of the aquarium. East of the Washington State ferry terminal is Pioneer Square, with shops and galleries in the brick buildings that were erected after the 1889 Seattle fire.

The entire waterfront is served by streetcars, from Pier 70 south to Pioneer Square and east to the International District.

Spring through fall, the Seattle waterfront seems to be in a state of perpetual celebration. A notable event occurs during Maritime Week in mid-May, when the bay froths white with tugboat races.

Few tourists arrive here in their own boats. The renovation of the Seattle waterfront over the past decades, and the expansion of the ferry terminal to include passenger-only ferries, has overlooked downtown access for visiting pleasure boaters. Plans are underway for such moorage, but meanwhile the choices are far from ideal.

Approaches, Anchorage. The old visitors' floats can still be found between Pier 48 and the Washington State ferry terminal. Moorage is limited to vessels of less than 35 feet, and length of stay is restricted to 10 hours. The gold letters on the riveted iron gazebo read VISITORS WELCOME, but the floats themselves are not hospitable. Ferry and other traffic is constant here,

WORKING THE WATER: THE VIEW FROM THE VESSEL TRAFFIC CENTER

It's a fine day for boating in Puget Sound. As you pull out of your marina, a freighter bound for Tacoma enters the Strait of Juan de Fuca. An oil tanker with its escort heads west from the refinery in Anacortes. A tug with a log tow creeps toward Everett as a barge laden with liquid chlorine is moved upriver from Elliott Bay. A few minutes later, a tour boat departs for Blake Island, the Bainbridge ferry leaves Seattle, and a Navy destroyer leaves Bremerton.

A quarter of a million commercial transits occur in Puget Sound every year. Tracking them all with radar and VHF is the job of the Vessel Traffic Service, known as "Seattle Traffic" or simply "Traffic."

This Coast Guard entity has been operating since 1972, one of seven in the U.S. helping ships safely navigate crowded waters, advising and informing like air traffic controllers. Their work is critical; a single collision or grounding could have disastrous consequences, not only to passengers, crew, and cargo, but to the environment as well.

The Puget Sound Vessel Traffic Service consists of three elements: a traffic separation scheme (explained in the introductory chapter), radio communication, and radar coverage. These elements converge at the Vessel Traffic Center in Seattle, in a windowless, dimly-lit room. Against the walls surrounding the watch supervisor's station are ten radar screens. These screens are grouped into three sectors: Strait (Cape Flattery to New Dungeness), North (the San Juan Islands, Rosario Strait, inside Whidbey Island, and south of Port Townsend to Marrowstone Point), and South (Marrowstone Point south to Olympia and Shelton). Above each group of screens is a back-lit chart covered with plastic film.

In the green-and-yellow glow of instruments, the room seems submerged, far removed from the realities of water and wind, the rhythms of daylight and darkness. Twenty-four hours a day, every day in three shifts, six operators stand watch before huge, Cyclopean eyes that blink with the circular sweep of radar. These watchstanders are highly trained at reading the screens, and can identify most of the blips almost at a glance: A grain of rice is a container ship; a pale shadow behind an oval spot is a log boom trailing a tug; the "measles" around Point No Point are sport fishing boats. The actual radar transmitters are located at eleven strategic sites, from Cape Flattery north to Lummi Island and south to Point Defiance. In calm seas almost every vessel with a reflector is detectable.

Radar sweeps only the busiest areas, however, leaving the system with significant blind spots. As important as the system's radar eyes are its ears—VHF Channels 14 and 5A. Watchstanders communicate steadily with the vessels in their sectors, their professional radio shorthand punctuated with a polite "Good morning" or "Thank you, Captain." The voices on the other side of the transmission are calm; these are people in the routine of their workday, not at play, announcing simply who and where they are, what they intend to do. .

Virtually every large ship—as well as smaller vessels engaged in towing or carrying more than six passengers for hire—is required to report its movements to Seattle Traffic. When a vessel calls, it is often advised of other commercial traffic in its path. The watchstander makes notes on a small card, which is then time-stamped and placed on a sill near the relevant screen. If the vessel moves from one sector to another, its card moves with it, to the next screen and watchstander.

Some of this work has been computerized, most notably in the busy South Sector, which also uses video camera views of Elliott Bay and the Duwamish waterway. Most of it is done manually. Vessel activity that occurs in areas not covered by radar, such as Rich Passage, Hood Canal, or Olympia, is tracked with grease pencil on the back-lit charts leaning over each station. Thus each watchstander monitors his or her sector, matching radar blips with names and types of vessels, confirming everything by radio.

Seattle Traffic encourages recreational boaters to monitor its VHF radio channels—5A north of Marrowstone Point, 14 everywhere else. You'll overhear only a fraction of the communication taking place in this room, probably in your immediate area only. What you hear is especially useful in a busy harbor, crossing a traffic lane, or near a ferry dock. Not only will you know the movements of commercial vessels, you'll be advised with them of high-tide conditions, regattas or commercial fishing that may be taking place, and any lights or buoys that are off-station.

With their far-seeing eyes and acute hearing, Seattle Traffic is often the first to know about search-and-rescue operations, sudden changes in weather, and other navigational hazards. As a service, they will relay distress calls and may assist disoriented mariners.

If you need to call Seattle Traffic, take a cue from commercial skippers. Keep your initial communication short, giving your boat's name without call sign, for example: "Seattle Traffic, this is *Eagle*, over." Always use low power when transmitting, as high power tends to cover communication that is occurring elsewhere. Wait patiently for a response; at any time Seattle Traffic may be handling many vessels. When Traffic answers, state your boat's name again, the type of boat (power or sail), where you are in relation to a buoy or point of land (not latitude or longitude), and what information or help you need.

Visitors are welcome at the Vessel Traffic Center on Pier 36 in Seattle, weekdays from 8 A.M. to 6 P.M.

109

and the surge makes for a rocky stay. This location is additionally insecure due to its proximity to Pioneer Square, a lively district—rather too lively for some. Boaters should not leave their vessels unattended.

Outdoor concerts are held in summer on Pier 63, between the aquarium and the Edgewater Hotel's red "E." Pleasure boats often anchor north of Pier 63 to hear the show. The water is quieter than at Pier 48. Depths are 6 to 10 fathoms. The only shore access is via the ladders descending from the pier. With a tidal range of up to 18 feet, securing a dinghy while you explore the city can be a challenge.

To remedy the lack of small-craft facilities on the waterfront, the Port of Seattle has recently approved plans for a small marina as part of a commercial development on the west side of the waterfront, between Pier 63 and 66. The plans call for a maritime museum, a conference center, shops, restaurants, and a public plaza. The marina will offer visitors' moorage (48 hours maximum), restrooms with showers, and power and water on all slips. A harbormaster will be on duty.

Harbor Island Marina ★

Charts: 18449, **18450**, 18474

From Pier 48 south into the Duwamish River, Seattle is heavily industrial. There are a few small-craft marinas, but little to draw pleasure craft toward them. Only Harbor Island Marina has facilities for visiting boaters.

At the time Harbor Island was created, this flat-iron shape of landfill was the largest man-made island in the world. Wedged into the Duwamish River delta, it is surrounded on all sides by wharves and cranes, and studded with storage tanks. On its north face are the enormous dry docks of Todd Shipyard. Above are radio towers, slim and delicate among the massive equipment.

Approaches. Harbor Island Marina is at the blunt southeast point of Harbor Island, at the juncture of the West and East Waterways. The close-set pilings and low vertical clearance of the fixed bridge in the East Waterway (4 feet) makes the West Waterway the preferred approach.

The entrance to the West Waterway lies between the two tallest radio towers. Todd Shipyard is east of the entrance; a row of orange cranes for container handling is upriver on the west shore. The waterway is dredged for deep-draft ships; it's a good idea to listen to Vessel Traffic on Channel 14 so you'll know if one of these large ships is en route here.

You'll feel the pull of the river current soon after you enter, especially when the tide is ebbing. You may also feel as though you're heading into a dead end. At the Fisher Flour mill the waterway narrows, making a turn to the east toward the swing bridge, and the arches of the freeway high above it come into view. The swing bridge has a vertical clearance of 55 feet; when it opens it swings apart, each half pivoting on its thick circular pedestal. It takes from six to seven minutes to open this bridge; call ahead when you're about a quarter-mile away. The whistle signal is one long and three short blasts.

Harbor Island Marina is south of the swing bridge, around the bend to the east.

Moorings. Note the current before you approach the fuel dock, which is set east-west, broadside to the river flow. Tie up and inquire at the office about visitor moorage, which is usually available. This is a relatively new marina, with concrete floats and well-maintained facilities. All slips have power and water.

For the Boat, Crew. The fuel dock sells a few marine supplies, ice, snack foods, and bait. The marina restrooms have showers. Nearby is a deli, open weekdays.

Duwamish Head to Alki Point ★

Charts: 18449, **18450**, 18474

The public tidelands of Alki Beach Park stretch from Duwamish Head southwest to Alki Point. A monument at this park commemorates the landing of the Denny party in 1852, "the little colony that became Seattle." This is one of the most popular beaches in the city. In summer, sunbathers, joggers, and walkers crowd the shore and fill the fast-food restaurants across the street, and traffic slows to a crawl as drivers "cruise" the scene.

None of this activity is readily accessible by boat, because of Seattle City ordinances that do not permit landing on its park beaches. Boaters who wish to cruise the lively scene by water should take care to stay in at least 10 fathoms; the bottom rises abruptly, especially toward Alki Point.

Anchorage. An anchorage area is about two miles away, on the southeast side of Duwamish head—one of the few in Seattle where you can legally drop your hook inside the city limits.

The shoreline here is not particularly scenic, but the view of Seattle is one of the best anywhere. The panorama includes Mount Rainier, rising behind the container cranes on Harbor Island. You're protected from southerlies but completely exposed to the north and to freighter and ferry wakes. This anchorage is used by ships and barges and is quite deep. Toward shore you should be able to find a shelf 5 to 10 fathoms deep.

On shore is a public fishing pier, with a small gravel beach to the south. The boathouse at the pier sells snacks and bait. A restaurant is a short walk south. About a quarter-mile north of the fishing pier is a public launching ramp, with floats that are removed in winter. A pocket of gravel beach is on either side, where it's possible to land a skiff between high tides. A take-out restaurant is across the street, but there are no other facilities within walking distance.

Rich Passage

Charts: 18448, **18449**, 18474

South of Bainbridge Island, Rich Passage twists northwest and south, with a sharp turn at its west end. Bainbridge Reef and Orchard Rocks constrict the eastern approach. Currents are often strong in this passage, especially in the vicinity of Point White. The *Coast Pilot* describes at length the many eddies and countercurrents that occur on the ebb and which tend to decrease the "effective width" and increase current velocities. Despite these warnings, Rich Passage presents no unusual difficulties when visibility is good.

Traffic is the real challenge of Rich Passage. Washington State ferries make 10 or more runs every day between Seattle and Bremerton.

Navy vessels of all sizes and tugs with tows pass through on their way to and from the Bremerton shipyard. Pleasure and sportfishing boats contribute to the congestion. It's no wonder the *Coast Pilot* describes the collision hazard here as "considerable."

Approaches. From any approach, depths are good and the passage is well marked. Westbound, its a good idea to stay north, out of the ferry route whenever possible; eastbound, stay south. Look behind periodically for oncoming ships; deep-draft vessels need all the maneuvering room they can get when negotiating Rich Passage, especially off Point Glover. Ships are advised to sound a long blast within half-a-mile of this point—the blind spot in the passage—to warn vessels approaching from the opposite direction. Pay attention if you hear this blast and maneuver accordingly.

Take special care in Rich Passage when fog is thick; even experienced captains on routine runs have run into trouble here.

Clam Bay

Charts: 18448, **18449**, 18474

Clam Bay, located between Orchard Point and Middle Point on the south side of Rich Passage, does not welcome pleasure craft. Most of the bay is filled with fish pens—itself a sign of considerable current here. The long pier south of Middle Point is a Navy fuel dock. Signs warn boaters away from these government properties. All other tidelands are private.

Manchester State Park ★★★

Charts: 18448, **18449**, 18474

This state park on the north side of Middle Point was once a military fortification. Like Fort Ward on the opposite shore, it was built before World War I to protect the Bremerton Naval Shipyards. The most impressive structure remaining from that time is the brick torpedo storehouse that overlooks the beach, now used as a picnic shelter. Along the west beach are more picnic areas. Trails lead east to an abandoned gun battery and overlook. Inland are more trails and the main campground.

This park is closed from Labor Day to Memorial Day.

Approaches, Anchorage. The beach of Manchester State Park is located in the "corner" of the cove between Middle Point and Point Glover. This is not a good anchorage. The cove is shallow, and the bottom fairly rocky. There are extensive eddies and countercurrents here on the ebb, and you are exposed to the wakes of traffic. What's more, most of the beach is rocky and hard, with rock ledges that make landing a dinghy unpleasant.

From the southwest, watch for the reef and kelp off Middle Point. Reefs extend north as well.

For the Crew. Near the beach is a pay phone, picnic shelters, barbecues, and a bathhouse. Showers are in the upland campground.

Fort Ward State Park ★★★

Charts: 18448, **18449**, 18474

Fort Ward State Park is on the Bainbridge Island (north) side of Rich Passage, across from Middle Point. Like Manchester State Park across the passage, this day-use park was formerly a military base for the protection of the Bremerton Naval Shipyard, with residences for officers and enlisted personnel, gun batteries, and—during World War II—a submarine net that stretched across to Middle Point. The guns, most of the homes, and all of the vigilance is gone. Wild roses and blackberries obscure the old sidewalks and crowd the batteries. The haphazard pattern of the mown picnic clearings defies any semblance of military order. Blinds along the beach invite you to watch, not for enemy subs, but for cormorant and other birds.

This park has picnic tables, barbecues, and restrooms near the beach. A loop trail takes you up into the woods and another picnic area.

Approaches. Look for the park's launching ramp about a quarter-mile southeast of Pleasant Beach. A guard rail is immediately east of this ramp. The low white building to the southeast is the park ranger's residence.

Approaching from the south, stay clear of Orchard Rocks and the fish pens between them and the Bainbridge shore. The pier east of Orchard Rocks is part of this commercial operation. From any direction, stay in deep water (20 feet or more) to avoid rocks and kelp. Expect swift current.

Anchorage, Moorings. Two mooring buoys lie in deep water northwest of the launching ramp, just off the underwater shelf. The water at the south buoy is slightly shallower than that at the north buoy. Seaweed streams behind them. There's enough depth between the buoys for anchoring, but it is not advised; the current is swift and the bottom is hard. The traffic in Rich Passage will keep you rocking.

Getting Ashore. The park beach is rocky, with some sandy patches. All adjacent tidelands are private. There are no facilities within walking distance.

Sinclair Inlet

Charts: 18448, **18449**, 18474

More than a hundred years ago the Wilkes Expedition described this inlet as "perfectly protected." The U.S. Navy found it defensible as well, and chose it as the site of a shipbuilding operation that has grown since the 1890s to encompass almost the entire north shore. Mammoth gray warships pack the wharves, and sleek black submarines raft together like resting whales. An enormous, T-shaped "hammerhead" crane stands over the shipyard like a watchful giant.

Despite these almost overwhelming military-industrial views, neither Bremerton, nor Port Orchard south across the inlet, are large cities. The shoreline is developed, not with high-rise apartments, but with low, 1950s-style homes built right on the bank and surrounded by trim lawns. At sunset the square plant buildings and the silhouettes of ship antennas and conning towers are backed by the incomparable Olympic Mountains.

In summer, jellyfish are thick here, the inlet coated with their translucent globular bodies. According to Indian legend, these jellyfish are the transformed pieces of the ogress Snail Woman, who was pushed into a fire by children she intended to devour.

Approaches. From Rich Passage, the hammerhead crane of the shipyard is visible after rounding Point Glover. Approaches are clean from this direction and from the Port Washington Narrows. At night especially, watch for unlit Navy mooring buoys and anchored ships.

Public Piers on the Southeast Shore ★

Charts: 18448, **18449**, 18474

On the southeast shore of Sinclair Inlet are two public piers. The first is a fishing pier at Waterman, a little more than a mile south of Point Glover (and south of Waterman Point). Railings around the pier discourage boat access. Only the end of the pier is in deep

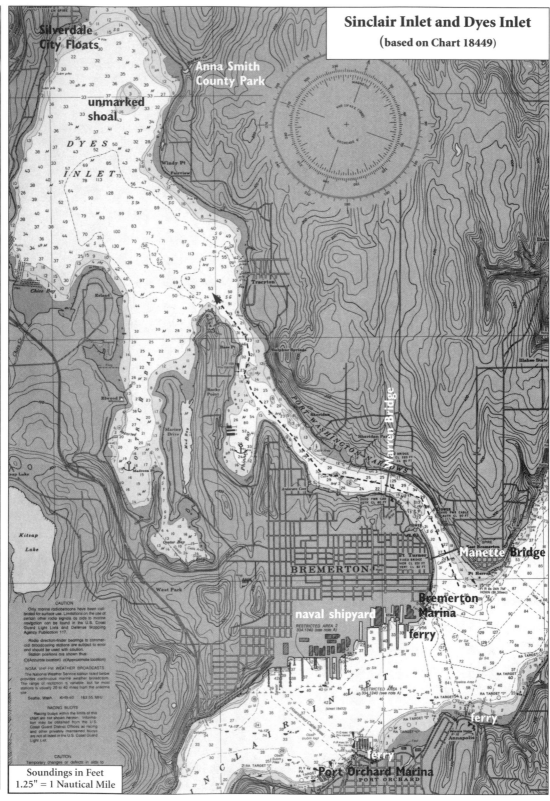

Sinclair Inlet and Dyes Inlet
(based on Chart 18449)

Silverdale City Floats

Anna Smith County Park

unmarked shoal

DYES INLET

Windy Pt

Chico Bay

Tracyton

Sulphur Springs

Rocky Point

Elwood Pt

POULSBO BAY

Marine Drive

Phinney Bay

PORT WASHINGTON NARROWS

Sheridan

Sheridan Pt

Warren Bridge

Manette Bridge

Kitsap Lake

Oyster Bay

Anderson Cove

Pt Turner

BREMERTON

West Park

Pt Herron

Bremerton Marina

naval shipyard

RESTRICTED AREA 2
334.1240 (see note A)

ferry

RESTRICTED AREA
334.1240 (see note A)

SINCLAIR INLET

ferry

Annapolis

ferry

Port Orchard Marina
PORT ORCHARD

Soundings in Feet
1.25" = 1 Nautical Mile

water; the sides are shoal. There are stairs to the beach on the north side, with a pay phone and portable toilet on shore. There are no facilities within walking distance.

Farther south at Annapolis is a stout pier west of a public launching ramp. The concrete float is used by the passenger ferry that makes regular runs between here and Bremerton. As with the Waterman pier, the end is in deep water, the sides dry at low tide. There are no facilities other than a restaurant at the road. The large building on the hill above this rocky public beach is the Veterans Home.

Port Orchard ★★★★ 3 (anchorage) 4 (marina)

Charts: 18448, **18449**, 18474

In full view of the Bremerton shipyards, Port Orchard is a distinct contrast to its industrial neighbor across the inlet. The town has a deliberate old-fashioned look, with covered sidewalks, antique shops, and murals that depict life here 100 years ago. The waterfront, devoted almost entirely to public and retail use, includes a city park and a large marina that welcomes visitors. Port Orchard has earned its favorable reputation among Puget Sound boaters.

Approaches. The boathouses and sailboat masts in the Port Orchard Marina make it a prominent feature on the waterfront. From the northeast, stay 500 yards or more offshore to avoid the broad shoal between Annapolis and the marina. Watch for the passenger ferry that operates east of the breakwater.

Almost a half-mile of floating breakwater surrounds the marina on its east and north sides. The entrance is at the far west end.

Moorings. Guest moorage is on both sides of the breakwater, on the east float inside the breakwater, and on the outside of the west (fuel dock) float. All guest moorage areas are clearly marked. Turning room is generous and depths are fine, about twice as deep at the breakwater as at the floats close to shore. The breakwater is a necessity, as even a moderate north wind builds up a roll. It's noticeably bouncier if you're moored on the outside.

After tying up, report to the harbormaster's office located on shore about the center of the marina. Power is available on all guest floats. The Port Orchard Marina takes reservations by phone at (360) 876-5535.

The marina to the west is the Port Orchard Yacht Club. All slips are private.

Anchorage. It's OK to anchor west of the yacht club, north of the charted red TARGET mark on pilings. You're close to the main highway here, and directly in front of a fuel oil distributor. If an oil barge is making a delivery, it'll be noisy and smelly. Protection is good from the south, but you'll be exposed to the north.

Anchoring is not recommended east of the Port Orchard Marina, where it is shallow and busy with passenger ferries.

Getting Ashore. Use the marina guest floats or the park beach east of the passenger ferry dock. A good portion of the park beach is dry at low water, so check tides before landing there.

For the Boat. The fuel dock is to starboard as you enter the marina, at the south end of the float toward shore (the squat cylindrical tank is the sewer plant). Moor on either side.

The nearest boat supplies are a block west of the parking lot, on the main road. A mile farther west is a repair yard with a hoist that allows boaters to do their own work; this yard also has a small marine store.

For the Crew. Showers and laundry are near the harbormaster's office. Restaurants and shops are a block away in town. A convenience grocery across the parking lot sells snack food;

115

Port Orchard Marina, looking west. The fuel dock is just inside the breakwater entrance, toward shore.

real groceries are more than a mile away, east along the busy main road.

Things to Do. Port Orchard's main street has covered sidewalks that encourage window-shopping on even the rainiest days. Here you'll find numerous antique shops, a couple of bookstores, restaurants, galleries, and a movie theater. Murals depicting early days in Port Orchard are ingeniously painted to blend into each building's construction; it's easy to be fooled about what's real and what's not. The waterfront park east of the marina has stairs to the beach and a seating gallery for summer stage shows and concerts. A farmers' market, with fresh produce and local crafts, is held here every Saturday from early May to late October.

There are special events in Port Orchard almost every month. These include the Opening Day of Yachting and the In the Water Boat Show in early May, Fathoms o' Fun Fireworks on the Fourth of July, and a Chris-Craft rendezvous in mid-July. Of particular interest to maritime history buffs is the Mosquito Fleet Days celebration in late September, which commemorates the passenger ferries that were once the major mode of transportation between Puget Sound cities and towns.

A passenger ferry leaves for Bremerton every 30 minutes from the east side of the Port Orchard Marina.

Coves at the Head of Sinclair Inlet ★

Charts: 18448, **18449**, 18474

The head of Sinclair Inlet is shallower than charted, and exposed not only to wind from the north and south, but to the busy highway that skirts the perimeter of the inlet. A wedge of public shoreline is at the prominent point about a mile west of Port Orchard; some protection from the north might be possible west of this point, but stay alert for the charted pilings, some of which are submerged.

The wreck east of the point is a double-ended lifeboat. Farther west is a small-craft marina in shallow water, with no guest moorage. The shop on the pier does haulouts and repairs, and also sells marine supplies. There is another marine repair facility to the west, along the road.

Bremerton ★★★★

Charts: 18448, **18449**, 18474

For many years the Bremerton waterfront neither attracted nor welcomed pleasure craft. Boaters headed south to Port Orchard, discouraged by the blank square buildings of the shipyard, the dull gray hulls of warships and submarines, and the numerous yellow signs warning them to stay 300 feet away. In recent years, Bremerton has renovated its waterfront east of the shipyard's main gate, with a promenade and a marina designed specifically for visiting boats. The downtown area, once tired and abandoned-looking, seems to have squared its shoulders and put out the welcome mat for waterborne tourists.

Approaches. The prominent landmarks of the Bremerton waterfront are, from east to west, the Navy destroyer *Turner Joy*, the state ferry terminal, and the T shaped "hammerhead" crane looming above the shipyard. The marina lies between the *Turner Joy* and the ferry terminal. It is protected by an L-shaped floating concrete breakwater that opens to the northeast, and is marked with a red light on the north end. The outside of the breakwater is railed for public fishing.

Approaches are clean. Watch for ferry traffic, and for tour boats leaving from the float at the *Turner Joy*.

Moorings. The Bremerton Marina has 45 slips for boats 40 feet or less. Larger vessels may be moored inside, along the breakwater. Depth at the innermost float is about 20 feet shallower than at the breakwater. All slips (including those on the breakwater) have power and water.

Report to the marina office at the head of the ramp. The security code number is displayed underneath a hinged board inside the gate; this code is changed several times a week. Boaters moored at the breakwater are outside this security system, but are given the code number when moorage fees are paid in order to unlock the marina restrooms, showers, and laundry. The Bremerton Marina takes reservations by phone—(360) 373-1035. Short-term tie-ups are free.

Anchoring north of the marina slips is not encouraged by the port authority.

About a half-mile north, on the northeast side of the Manette Bridge, is a restaurant on pilings with a 40-foot float for customers arriving by boat. Depths are good on both sides of the float, but currents are strong.

For the Boat. A fair-sized marine and sport-fishing supply store faces the Bremerton Marina. The nearest repair and fuel facilities are across the inlet at Port Orchard.

For the Crew. A laundry and showers are situated in the blue roofed complex southwest of the marina office, across the promenade. These buildings are surrounded by a chain-link fence; use the entrance code to get in. The only store within walking distance where you can buy groceries is on Second and Washington, a beer-and-cigarettes kind of place with a few snack foods. Fresh produce and local crafts are sold at the farmers' market Sundays on the promenade, April through October. Restaurants and shops are downtown, two blocks north.

Things to Do. A visit to Bremerton is an unusual opportunity to see up-close the U.S.

Navy presence in Puget Sound. The naval ship-yard has operated here for 100 years, at one time building—now primarily repairing and overhauling—ships and submarines for the entire U.S. fleet. The shipyard hosts a fairly extensive "mothball" fleet, and is also the home port for four active vessels, including the nuclear aircraft carrier *Nimitz*. Though all ships and facilities, including the shipyard, are off-limits to the public, there are many ways visitors can experience this very different sea-faring world.

A good way to begin is to visit the Naval Museum, just a block away on Washington Street. Here equipment and artifacts are crammed side-by-side, identified for the most part with hand-lettered signs: a Korean cannon dating back to 1377, made of wood and bamboo that had the tensile strength of spun steel; a Japanese torpedo, cut away to expose the steam engine inside that powered it; steel plates almost an inch thick that were ripped by shells and removed for repair at the shipyard. Power-ful in its simplicity, this museum also displays letters written home by Navy men and women, a sobering list of vessels lost in World War II, and intricate ship models.

At the north end of the promenade is the retired Navy destroyer *Turner Joy*, now main-tained by the Bremerton Historic Ships Association and open for self-guided tours. Harbor tour boats sharing this same pier take visitors southwest to view the Navy shipyard, and north to Poulsbo and the Naval Undersea Museum in Keyport.

Those who are not Navy history buffs may enjoy the galleries and shops close by in town.

The bronze man and boy examine their ship model at Bremerton's Waterfront Park.

A walking map of Bremerton is available at the marina office. The passenger ferry to Port Orchard leaves every 30 minutes from the south side of the breakwater.

Special events on Waterfront Park include Thursday night concerts in July and August, and the Blackberry Festival on Labor Day weekend.

Dyes Inlet and the Port Washington Narrows

Charts: **18449**, 18474

Dyes Inlet branches northwest from its junc-tion with Sinclair Inlet. At its south end it is convoluted, and developed with Bremerton residential neighborhoods. At the north end of the inlet is the town of Silverdale.

Though rich in shellfish, Dyes Inlet is closed permanently to harvesting because of septic drainfield pollution. Jellyfish thrive here in summer.

Approaches. The Port Washington Narrows has a navigable width of about 500 yards for most of its three-mile length. Two fixed bridges span the narrows; the south (Manette) bridge has a clearance of 82 feet, the north (Warren) bridge a clearance of 80 feet. Between them is a power cable with a charted clearance of 90 feet. Of more concern to most boaters are currents, which can attain speeds of more than 4 knots. It's important to check current tables before navigating this busy passage.

The Port Washington Narrows has an irregular bottom that may discourage those with deep-draft vessels. From the south, the deepest water is in mid-channel. Once past the overhead power cable between the two bridges, favor the north shore to the second bridge.

From there, head slightly north of Anderson Cove in order to avoid the unmarked shoal that dries at low tide on the opposite (north) shore.

From Anderson Cove, stay in mid-channel to the entrance of Phinney Bay, then make a soft curve north past Bass Point, and northwest past Rocky Point. (Note that Rocky Point is also the name of a community on the peninsula.) The charted mark south of Bass Point is now gone; take care to stay 100 yards off the west shore. Expect tide rips around Rocky Point. Throughout the channel, expect heavy boat traffic as well.

In clear weather, the reward for navigating this winding channel is the surprise of the Olympic Mountains, which give Dyes Inlet the appearance, at first, of a high mountain lake.

Anderson Cove ★★ (anchorage) (marina)

Charts: **18449**, 18474

Anderson Cove is a small bight a little more than a half-mile west of the second (north) Narrows Bridge. The cove is shallow. The Port Washington Marina is on the south shore, to the west of a row of cylindrical tanks. This marina has limited guest moorage; call ahead—(360) 479-3037.

The "corner" of this cove dries at low tide. Be prepared for strong currents, which, along with traffic, discourage anchoring.

Phinney Bay ★★★ No Facilities

Charts: **18449**, 18474

Phinney Bay is a welcome escape from the busy waters of the Port Washington Narrows. The shores are wooded, and the overall effect is a tranquil one. The only noticeable development is the Bremerton Yacht Club on the west side of the bay. It is difficult to believe that all the industry of the naval shipyard is less than two miles away by land.

Approaches. From the south, the entrance to Phinney Bay is visible after passing under the north (Warren) bridge. Be mindful of the reef, submerged rock, and kelp charted southeast of the unnamed point at the entrance to the bay.

From the north, the boathouses and masts of the yacht club are visible past Bass Point. Head slightly east as you enter the bay; a charted shoal and rocks extend from the west shore.

Anchorage. There's good anchoring depth almost all the way into Phinney Bay, especially toward the east shore. A submerged piling is charted half-way down, less than 500 yards off this shore. The bottom is mud.

The marina on the west shore is the Bremerton Yacht Club. Moorage and other facilities, including fuel and repairs, are restricted to members and reciprocal guests only.

All tidelands in Phinney Bay are private.

Ostrich Bay ★★★ No Facilities

Charts: **18449**, 18474

Ostrich Bay branches south from Dyes Inlet. The east shore is crowded with waterfront homes. On the west shore is a large Navy hospital and park. Protected, warm in summer, and with no shore access, this is a fine "do-nothing" anchorage. The ambitious water-ski, or explore Oyster Bay.

Approaches. Keep in mid-channel when entering. North of Elwood Point is a flagpole and the large, monolithic structure of the Navy Hospital. Also on this west shore is Jackson Park; its fishing pier, playfields, beach, and picnic area are for use by active and retired military personnel. This area and the pier south of Elwood Point are the former site of a Naval ammunition depot. Shoals and submerged obstructions are reported along this shore.

Anchorage. There's good anchoring through-out Ostrich Bay, but the most protected and lovely is to the southwest, toward the wooded, undeveloped shore. If you set your hook south and slightly west of the abandoned ammunition pier, you'll be protected from northerlies. The major concern boaters seem to have here is calculating how far offshore to anchor in order to capture the afternoon sun.

Getting Ashore. All tidelands are private. The undeveloped woods and beach are U.S. government property, posted with NO TRESPASSING signs.

The nearest shore access is at Tracyton, at the northeast end of the Narrows, and at Chico, northwest of Erland. Both have public launching ramps. A gas station and convenience grocery are four short blocks uphill from the Tracyton launching ramp.

Oyster Bay

Charts: **18449**, 18474

As much as anything, Oyster Bay resembles a private pond. Its entrance is narrow and shallow—a fathom or less—and its basin slightly deeper. Beachfront homes and apartments completely enclose this bay; their large windows gaze, unblinking, at every boat that enters and leaves. You'll be in everyone's front yard if you anchor here. All tidelands are private.

Chico Bay ★★ No Facilities

Charts: **18449**, 18474

This open bay at the southwest end of Dyes Inlet is almost entirely foul with pilings and tideflats. North of the charted pilings (a former shellfish farm) there is depth and a soft mud bottom for anchoring, and better protection from southerlies than in Silverdale. A public launching ramp at a street end on the west shore is the only place to land. There are no facilities within walking distance.

Silverdale ★★★

Charts: **18449**, 18474

As if to attract boaters to this far northern end of Dyes Inlet, the town of Silverdale has sub-stantially renovated its waterfront. Stout wooden floats attached to steel-and-concrete pilings extend into deep water from a tidy park. Silverdale's charming Old Town is a block away, a sleepy reminder of the days when this was a logging and poultry-producing area.

Approaches. Past Windy Point, favor the west shore to avoid the unmarked shoal in the east half of the inlet; this shoal bares at low tide. Look for the row of pilings topped with white cones—these support the city float—and the pitched-roof shelter and flagpoles of the waterfront park. The charted spire of the church in Silverdale is obscured by trees and surrounding structures.

Immediately east of the city floats are abandoned pilings that mark the boundary of the dredged channel. The water to the north and east is shallow.

Anchorage, Moorings. The outside float is set roughly north-south, with fingers running toward the shore. Depths are steady all around, about 10 feet deeper than the depth shown on the gauge near the launching ramp. Maximum stay is three days, with fees collected at the self-service pay box near the road.

Anchoring depths are good southeast of the floats. Anchored or moored, don't expect protection from serious southerlies. A sign at the ramp warns that sudden and severe dock movement during storms and high winds can be hazardous.

Getting Ashore. Use the public floats or the park beach.

For the Boat. The nearest marine facilities are in Sinclair Inlet. The hardware store across the highway, a half-mile northwest, has only a few boating items. There is a gas station on the highway, and several automobile repair shops.

For the Crew. Old Town Silverdale has a few shops, a pub, and a bakery. A supermarket is across the highway, a half-mile's walk northwest. A laundromat is in this same strip mall; the sign inside (DO NOT WASH: GREASY CLOTHES, COMMERCIAL MOPS, HORSE BLANKETS) says a lot about the non-boating orientation of this community. Restaurants are also nearby. An enormous shopping mall is a mile away, at the head of the inlet.

Things to Do. The chief attraction in Silverdale is Waterfront Park. Activities begin early, when local residents—mostly kids—fish from the floats. The park itself has colorful, ingenious play equipment, a large picnic shelter, and enough room to throw a frisbee. The twisted paths are inset with rock and etched with shore creatures, tinted with watery color that makes the concrete appear almost fluid. In clear weather, the top of Mount Rainier is visible to the south. Within a block of the park is the Kitsap County Museum, a wood-framed former bank. The museum is open Tuesday through Saturday.

Special events at the park include a Saturday farmers' market April through October, and a Whaling Days celebration with limited hydroplane races on the last weekend of July.

Anna Smith County Park ★★★ [2] No Facilities

Charts: **18449**, 18474

On the northeast side of Dyes Inlet, south of Barker Creek, is an exquisite county park built by community volunteers. A trail leads up the bank through cedar and fir to a children's garden of extraordinary variety. The raised beds, numbered and hand-labeled, are planted with everything from corn to kiwi fruit. One bed is devoted entirely to heather, others to lilies, roses, berries, and dahlias. A teepee is covered with varieties of beans. After the pungent salt smells of Dyes Inlet, the flowers and herbs of this garden exude a powerful perfume, and the colors—red, gold, bright pink—are dazzling.

Anna Smith Park also has picnic tables, restrooms, and an amphitheater that overlooks the inlet.

121

Approaches, Anchorage. From the water, Anna Smith County Park is not immediately distinguishable from surrounding beaches. Look for the crumbling concrete bulkhead south of Barker Creek, with the brick-and-rock fireplace above it. The beach is gravel, and just over 600 feet long. All adjacent tidelands are private.

Approaching from a westerly direction, take care to avoid the large shoal in the east half of the inlet, about 1,000 yards off the park beach. This shoal bares at low water.

Anchorage is good for the short term off the park beach, in 3 fathoms or more.

Port Orchard Channel

Charts: 18441, **18446**, **18449**, 18474

The channel of Port Orchard (also the name of a town in nearby Sinclair Inlet) is on the west side of Bainbridge Island. This waterway connects with the rest of Puget Sound via Rich Passage at its south end and Agate Passage at its north end. Port Orchard channel is easily navigated, with few obstructions and a tidal current that the *Coast Pilot* describes as "weak."

The north half of the channel between Brownsville and Keyport is a torpedo testing area. When testing is in progress a red light flashes on a float opposite Battle Point and on the south dock at Keyport. Avoid the testing area at these times by hugging the Bainbridge shore.

Approaches. From the south, approaches are clean once clear of Rich Passage. A description of Rich Passage is given earlier in this chapter, on page 111.

From the northeast, the approach is through Agate Passage. The navigable portion of this steep-sided pass is only about 200 yards wide. As charted, both sides of the channel are shoal and lined with kelp. Currents are swift—up to 6 knots—setting southwest on the flood and northeast on the ebb. The fixed Agate Passage Bridge has a charted vertical clearance of 75 feet. All these factors make for a somewhat claustrophobic approach, but with good visibility and a near-slack current this passage is straightforward.

From Port Madison, stay well off the shoals north of Agate Point and southeast of Suquamish. Look for red nun buoy "2A" in the middle of the channel and stay east, entering midway between it and Agate Point. Slightly favor the southeast shore until you've cleared the bridge, then stay in midchannel past red "4." Take care to stay east of red "6" on pilings, which marks an extensive shoal about a quarter-mile south of Sandy Hook. Red "6" is so far from shore that it fools many boaters. A rock is charted about 500 yards northwest of this mark.

The charted pier at the spit near Sandy Hook is private, for use by Kiana Lodge guests only. A fish pen is north of the spit.

Illahee State Park ★★★

Charts: 18441, **18449**, 18474

This park in the southwest portion of Port Orchard channel has a sandy beach, a fishing pier and float, and mooring buoys set beneath a steep bluff. Trails lead up the bluff to a campground in old-growth cedar and fir. Near the campground is a playground and a ball field. With a beach that's reachable by car, Illahee State Park is a popular picnic site. The steep

Divers on the south side of the Illahee State Park pier. The park mooring buoys are farther south, out of view in this picture.

drop-off to deep water makes it a favorite for divers, anglers, and crabbers as well.

The campground is open year round.

Approaches. The high sandy bluff of the park is prominent from any approach. The parking lot bulkhead, penetrated by a launching ramp, is at the park's north boundary. Slightly south are restrooms and a bathhouse.

From the south, approaches are clean, provided you stay in deep water 100 yards or so off the bluff. From the north, watch for the low, detached floating breakwater (set east-west) to the north of the park dock, and stay east of it. Despite its reflective uprights, from a distance this breakwater seems to be part of the dock itself.

Anchorage, Moorings. The park float is set north-south. Depths are good, about 10 feet shallower on the inside. You'll rock and roll here, abeam to the pleasure-boat traffic in Port Orchard channel, which is often heavy.

Five park mooring buoys are south of the float. The south and the middle buoy are about 5 feet shallower than the others.

Anchoring is OK north of the breakwater, in 3 fathoms or more. South, toward the park, the bottom rises more steeply; take care that your swing doesn't put you aground.

The worst weather in this exposed anchorage is reported to come from the north. Best protection is inside the park float, behind the low floating breakwater. The closest real shelter is Bremerton Marina.

Getting Ashore. Use the beach or the park float. Watch for divers on the south side of the pier.

For the Crew. Cold showers are near the beach, outside the bathhouse. Hot showers are in the campground, a mile's hike up a steep trail.

Illahee ★★   2 

Charts: 18441, **18449**, 18474

A long fishing pier extends from a street end at the town of Illahee. Two 30-foot floats are on the north side of this pier, in shallow water. Stays are limited to three days, but exposure to boat traffic and weather makes this most suit-able as a short-term grocery stop. Approach this float from the north to avoid the fish haven off the end of the pier. A small grocery and gas station are across the road. There are no other facilities within walking distance.

Brownsville ★★★   3 (anchorage)   4 (marina)

Charts: 18441, **18446**, **18449**, 18474

Brownsville sits in a valley beside the Burke Bay lagoon. The town consists of little more than a small grocery and a fire station—no restaurants, no gift shops, no bustle. The chief attraction for boaters here is the marina and fuel dock.

Approaches, Moorings. From the south, the boathouses and masts of the marina are visible past University Point. The marina is protected by a floating breakwater to the east, and by the long guest float to the north.

The marina has two areas for guest moorage. The largest is on the long float just north of the marina, with its own pier to the land and bright blue power boxes all along its 400 feet of length. This float is set east-west. Approach from the north side of the floating breakwater. Check the tides if your vessel's draft is deep.

Additional guest moorage is inside the marina, west of the fuel dock. Slips here are 24 feet long. Enter south of the floating breakwater. A sign warns of shallow water at minus tides; if your boat is deep-draft, enter close to high tide. Watch for boats off the launching ramp west of the marina floats.

Report to the port office at the head of the ramp after mooring. Use the fee box there after hours. All slips have power. Stays of two hours or less are free.

Anchorage. The anchoring basin is south of the marina, but check tides; depths are less than 2 fathoms. The best protection is from the south.

Getting Ashore. Use the marina guest floats. Surrounding tidelands are private.

For the Boat. The fuel dock is at the southern end of the marina's innermost float. Enter south of the floating breakwater, near high tide if your boat draws more than 6 feet. The fuel dock is set east-west. Turning room is tight but adequate. Watch for boats coming and going from the launching ramp.

For the Crew. Showers and laundry are near the port office building. Next door is a deli, with fast food and a few groceries. A small, fairly well-stocked grocery with some fresh produce is at the intersection, a block west.

A small park is on the bluff behind the port office; another, with beach access, is along the parking lot overlooking the bay. The wildlife preserve at Burke Bay can be explored at high tide in non-motorized craft.

Fletcher Bay

Charts: 18441, **18449**, 18474

This bay across from Brownsville on the west shore of Bainbridge Island is small, ringed by homes and private floats. The entrance to this lagoon dries at low tide; according to Indian legend, a monster lived here that preyed on those who tried to walk across it.

All tidelands in and around Fletcher Bay are private.

Manzanita Bay ★★ No Facilities

Charts: 18441, **18446**

This bay on the northwest side of Bainbridge Island is shaped like a high-heeled shoe. Its shoreline is crowded with fine homes, most with private docks. Manzanita Bay has no public facilities, but is a good alternate anchorage for those who don't want to make the long run into Liberty Bay, or who need to wait out the current in Agate Passage.

Approaches, Anchorage. Approaches are clean. From the west, Manzanita Bay is a little difficult to make out against the wooded shore. As you get closer, the steep, almost perpendicular rise of Arrow Point should become clear; the charted piles are just inside.

There's good anchoring depth almost all the way in. In a northerly, expect a chop from Agate Passage.

Getting Ashore. A public street end at the little knob just north of the "heel" of Manzanita Bay provides shore access. All other tidelands are private. There are no facilities within walking distance.

Liberty Bay

Charts: 18441, **18446**

Liberty Bay is one of the most popular year-round cruising destinations in Puget Sound. Past Keyport the bay has a soft rural feel, with tidy, almost reclusive homes along the shore and the picturesque Scandinavian town of Poulsbo at its head. The Olympic Mountains stand tall to the west. Though close to Seattle and other population centers, Liberty Bay seems far away. Off-season and mid-week, when the crowds are gone, you may feel you've escaped into a quieter time.

Like its neighbors to the south, Dyes Inlet and Sinclair Inlet, Liberty Bay blooms with red algae and thickens with jellyfish in summer. Year round, its shallows create estuaries for herons, cormorants, and grebes. A family of harbor seals has made the Poulsbo Marina breakwater its home.

This area also supports a large human population, whose chief employers are the Naval Shipyard in Bremerton, the Trident Submarine Base on Hood Canal, and the Naval Undersea Warfare Engineering Station at Keyport.

Approaches. From the south, watch for the red light opposite Battle Point. If it is flashing, stay

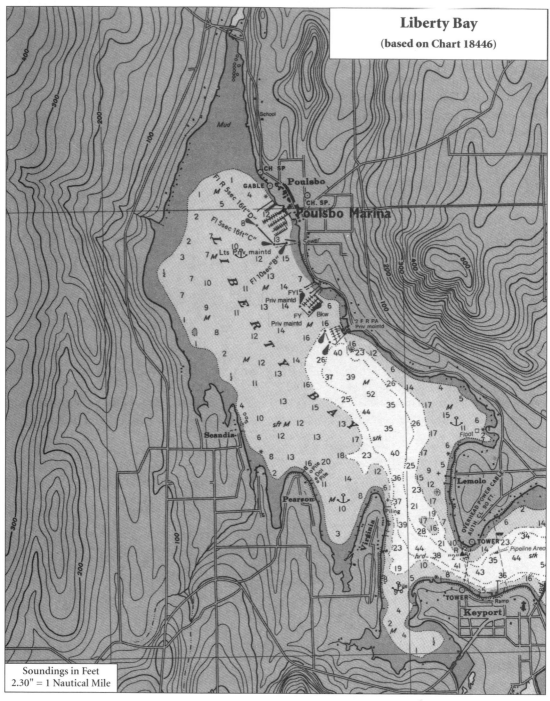

Liberty Bay

(based on Chart 18446)

Soundings in Feet
2.30" = 1 Nautical Mile

out of the torpedo testing area along the west shore.

From the east, keep a respectful distance off Point Bolin to avoid the shoals around it.

After entering Liberty Bay, follow a mid-channel, S-shaped course.

Most boaters head for Poulsbo, but a few other anchorages are also available.

Keyport ★★ 3 🔧 ⚓ 🛒 🍽

Charts: 18441, **18446**

The entrance to Liberty Bay is dominated by the square, blank structures of the Naval Undersea Warfare Engineering Station at Keyport. This is not a new facility; torpedo testing has been conducted here since 1910, and continues still. A flashing red light on the end of the south dock warns boaters to reduce speed, and to keep out of the test area along the west shore that stretches south to Brownsville.

Approaches, Moorings. West of the Undersea Warfare Station are two small marinas. Keyport Marine Service, east of the boathouses, has good depths and some guest moorage. Call ahead—(360) 779-4360—or inquire at the office on shore after tying up. The marina with the boathouses, operated by the Port of Keyport, has no guest moorage. Short-term visitors occasionally tie up on either side of the east boathouse; the north side is reserved for tour boats. A public launching ramp is tucked away behind this marina. Both marinas are exposed to the wake of boat traffic.

The anchorage to the north across the channel, in 1 to 2 fathoms, is exposed to southerlies and boat traffic.

For the Boat, Crew. East of the boathouses is a marine repair shop with a hoist. A small grocery and a café are close by. The Naval Undersea Museum is a short walk south on Stiles Road, past the church. This museum takes you under the surface; you "descend" through each exhibit to learn about submarines, undersea weapons, exploration, salvage, and rescue. The museum is open Tuesday through Sunday in summer, Tuesday through Saturday in winter.

A tour boat leaves Keyport several times a day in summer, with stops at Poulsbo and Bremerton.

Coves on the West Side of Liberty Bay ★★ 4 No Facilities

Charts: 18441, **18446**

Immediately west of Keyport are two small coves. Both are surrounded by homes, with a scattering of private mooring buoys and floats.

The first cove is somewhat L-shaped. It has good depth at the entrance, but is shallow inside. Oyster beds fill the head of this cove. Protection is good from both north and south.

The second cove is slightly deeper than its neighbor, but less protected. Depth is steady to about a third of the way in; beyond that, it is too shallow for most vessels.

All tidelands surrounding these coves are private. The nearest shore access is the launching ramp behind the marina at Keyport.

Cove on the East Side of Liberty Bay ★★ 4 No Facilities

Charts: 18441, **18446**

A wide cove north of Lemolo opens to the west. Protection from southerlies is better here than at the head of the bay near Poulsbo; bottom and anchoring depths are about the same. The

floats off the private docks go aground during minus tides. All surrounding tidelands and mooring buoys are private.

Approaching from the south, note the charted submerged rocks off Lemolo.

Poulsbo ★★★★★ (anchorage) (marina) All Facilities

Charts: 18441, **18446**

The chief attraction in Liberty Bay is Poulsbo, a European-looking town renovated to preserve the heritage of its Scandinavian settlers. For the first half of this century one of the largest fish processing plants in the Pacific Northwest operated here, salting cod from the Bering Sea for a bustling world market. Poulsbo was home port to the three-masted *Thayer*, the last sail-powered cod-fishing vessel on the west coast, now a National Parks museum in San Francisco harbor.

In the early 1960s, the "Little Norway" theme was adopted by the community to attract tourists, and the waterfront was improved for pleasure craft. This move has been enormously successful. Despite the population growth and sprawl that accompanied development of the Trident Submarine Base on Hood Canal, Poulsbo has retained a downtown and waterfront that entices and embraces visitors.

Approaches. Past Lemolo, head toward Poulsbo, with its prominent church spire on the hill. The first two marinas on the east shore are private: Liberty Bay Marina (no transient moorage) and the Poulsbo Yacht Club north of it (members and reciprocal yacht clubs only). The Poulsbo Marina is next, behind the timber breakwater.

North of the yacht club, the bay gets increasingly shallow; deepest water is in the east half. Check the tides if your boat is deep-draft.

Moorings. The Poulsbo Marina is protected south and west by a marked timber breakwater open to the north. The posted speed limit is 3 miles per hour.

Slips on the four floats immediately behind the breakwater ("A" through "D") are assigned to permanent moorage. The last two floats north ("E" and "F") are guest moorage. Guard against drifting much north of "F" float, where it is seriously shallow. Slips 24 through 56 (south) on "E" are 40 feet long; all others are 30 feet. Boats moored at a 40-foot slip are charged for its full length. The end slips on both floats can accommodate boats more than 50 feet in length.

Pull into any open slip and check in with the port office at the head of the ramp. Pay the next morning if you arrive after working hours. Power is available on all slips. The main business office for the port is to the southeast, on the upper floor of the Marine Science Center, overlooking the launching ramp.

The Port of Poulsbo does not take reservations for guest moorage.

Anchorage. Anchorage is good south and west of the Poulsbo Marina, in about 2 fathoms. The sloping bottom is mud, with deepest water in the east half of the bay. Do not anchor beyond the line of "F" (the northmost) float, as the tideflats extend farther south than charted.

Protection is generally good here, but strong southerlies often turn into Liberty Bay, making it rougher than expected.

Getting Ashore. Motor or row around the north side of "F" float to the dinghy dock. The park beach north of the Poulsbo Marina is public, but rock and mud make it unpleasant for landing a skiff.

The public launching ramp is behind the permanent moorage floats, and approached inside the timber breakwater, south of "A" float.

For the Boat. The fuel dock is located in front of the old tidal grid. A mud bar is reported just

Low tide reveals the mudflats northwest of the Poulsbo Marina. The boardwalk connects Liberty Bay Park to American Legion Park.

south of the fuel dock; choose a rising tide if your vessel is deep-draft. Enter between "D" and "E" floats. South of the guest float, across the parking lot, is a well-stocked marine supply store.

A marine railway and boat repair yard lie just southeast of the Marine Science Center; other facilities operate at Liberty Bay Marina. Repairs can also be arranged through a local mobile marine service. The Port of Poulsbo's tidal grid is available for minor repairs (no hull cleaning or painting); check with the harbormaster.

For the Crew. Showers and a laundry are near the port office, at the top of the guest float ramp. Entry requires a key combination, obtainable from the harbormaster. A deli grocery is across the parking lot. The closest supermarket is in the commercial area on the highway, a half-mile walk uphill on Hostmark Street.

Things to Do. Open and grassy Liberty Bay Park borders the shoreline near the guest floats, with walking paths, picnic tables, and a stage pavilion. The 35-ton boulder displayed on the grounds was deposited in the bay during the last ice age; once a hazard to boats, it was pulled onto land and is now a climbing challenge for kids.

Liberty Bay Park is linked to American Legion Park by an elevated boardwalk, which begins at Grieg Hall and leads to a natural arboretum and grassed play area.

Front Street, less than 50 yards from the harbor, is crowded with shops and restaurants. The bakery is famous for its Scandinavian pastries, and reason enough for most boaters to overnight here. The drugstore features an old-fashioned soda fountain. Other shops, banks, and the post office are a short distance north on Jensen Way.

South of the marina is the Marine Science Center. This educational facility is open to the public every day. In summer, a tour boat leaves from the waterfront every two hours, with stops at the Naval Undersea Museum in Keyport and Waterfront Park in Bremerton.

Ambitious walkers might want to head southeast along the bay toward the playground and tennis courts of Lions Club Park on Fjord Drive, or up the hill to the cemetery next to the Lutheran Church.

Community events, many with a Norwegian theme, are held almost weekly from mid-May (Viking Fest) to mid-December (Parade of Boats). A Boat Rendezvous for 16-foot and 18-foot launches is held in late July.

129

REGION 5

INSIDE THE LOCKS

Lake Union, looking south toward downtown Seattle from the knoll on Gasworks Park.

INCLUDING LAKE UNION AND LAKE WASHINGTON

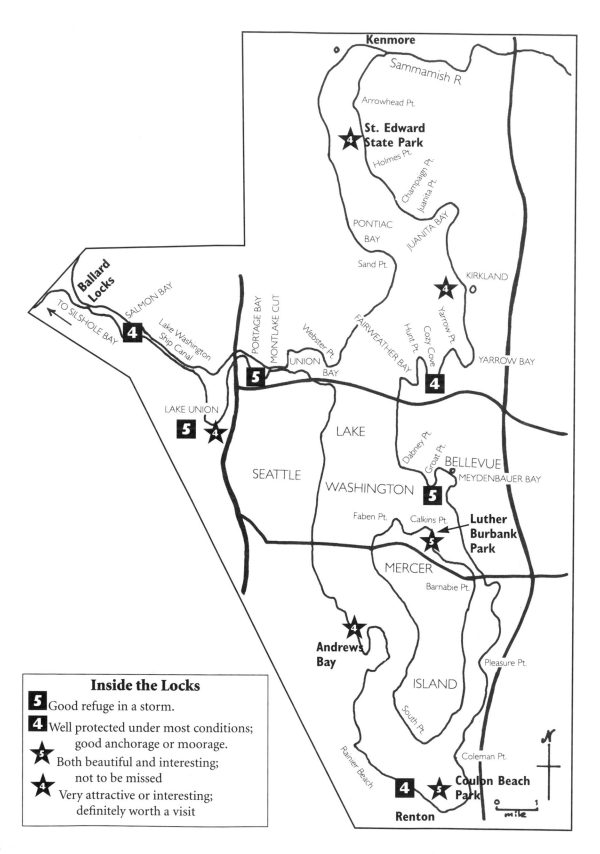

Kenmore

Sammamish R

Arrowhead Pt.

**St. Edward
State Park**

Holmes Pt.

Champaign Pt.

Juanita Pt.

JUANITA BAY

PONTIAC
BAY

KIRKLAND

Sand Pt.

**Ballard
Locks**

SALMON BAY

Lake Washington
Ship Canal

TO SILSHOLE BAY

PORTAGE BAY

MONTLAKE CUT

Webster Pt.

FAIRWEATHER BAY

Hunt Pt.

Cozy Cove

Yarrow Pt.

YARROW BAY

UNION
BAY

LAKE UNION

SEATTLE

LAKE

WASHINGTON

Dabney Pt.

Groat Pt.

BELLEVUE

MEYDENBAUER BAY

Faben Pt.

Calkins Pt.

**Luther
Burbank
Park**

MERCER

Barnabie Pt.

Pleasure Pt.

**Andrews
Bay**

ISLAND

South Pt.

Rainier Beach

Coleman Pt.

**Coulon Beach
Park**

Renton

Inside the Locks

5 Good refuge in a storm.

4 Well protected under most conditions;
good anchorage or moorage.

★ Both beautiful and interesting;
not to be missed

★ Very attractive or interesting;
definitely worth a visit

The freshwater cruising grounds inside Seattle's locks, so enjoyed by local boaters, are an unusual destination for saltwater cruisers. It's true that, from here, the natural beauty and solitude of Puget Sound is as remote as the salt air. It's also true that the locks are a deterrent; the patience and close maneuvering required for them is generally more of an annoyance than an adventure.

Nonetheless, this is an area worth visiting. You'll get a different view of Seattle from the inside, and of Lake Washington's communities as well. An immediate benefit for your boat is the fresh water itself, which kills saltwater growth. If you don't like crowds, visit sometime from mid-fall to early spring, when guest moorage is more plentiful and anchorages emptier. At any time of year, the air is warmer here than on Puget Sound, and the waters are more protected. Motoring the channels and lakes, exploring the neighborhoods and parks, you'll soon understand why Seattle is considered one of the country's most beautiful and livable cities.

Seattle, a major seaport of half-a-million people, claims the largest per-capita boat ownership in the U.S. Thousands of private slips line the shores from the locks to both ends of Lake Washington. Maritime services are in abundance; propellers, engines, electronics—entire ships—are not merely available for purchase but are manufactured here. Many vessels come here specifically for repair, refit, and supply.

The major areas inside the locks are the Ship Canal, Lake Union, the Montlake Cut, and Lake Washington.

A Few Pointers. Inside the locks you can set aside your tide and current tables, but don't set aside your vigilance. Besides the increased boat traffic, watch for:

- Navigation buoys. Dredged channels are charted and should be respected. There are no tides to help you out if you run aground.
- Unmarked shoals. Chart 18447 will help you locate these. **Note that soundings are in feet.**
- Speed buoys and markers. The speed limit is 7 knots from Salmon Bay to Webster Point at the entrance to Lake Washington. Lower speed limits are posted in some areas. East of the Montlake Bridge and around the perimeter of Lake Washington, small white can buoys mark areas of reduced speed. Keep your wake to a minimum.
- Bridge clearances. Four bascule drawbridges span the waterway from the Ballard Locks to Lake Washington, and two floating bridges lie within the lake itself. Vertical clearances are charted, and noted on each bridge. If your boat has a mast, know how high it is from water level.

In addition to chart 18447, a road map of the area is useful for identifying landmarks, neighborhoods, and streets.

The Ballard Locks

Charts: 18446, **18447**

Tourists are fascinated by them. Some boaters view them with minor annoyance, others with dread. The Ballard Locks, officially named after engineer Hiram M. Chittenden but locally called "the Locks," are navigated each year by more than 100,000 commercial and pleasure

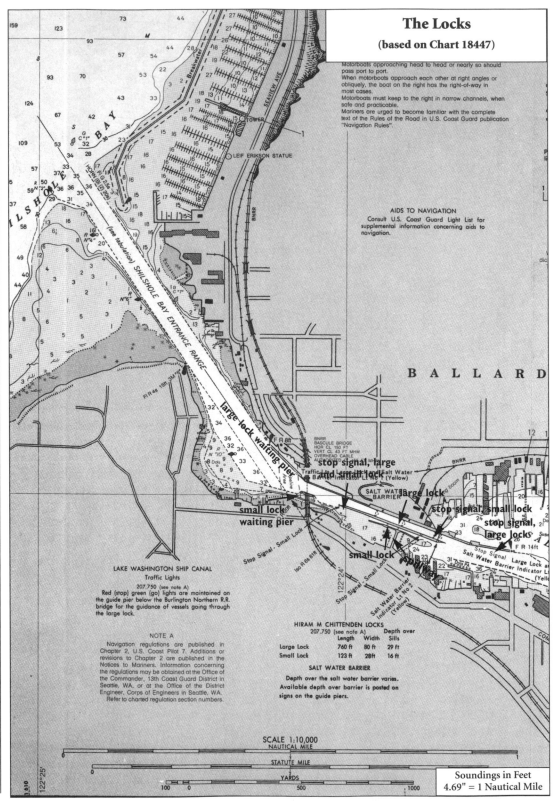

The Locks
(based on Chart 18447)

Motorboats approaching head to head or nearly so should pass port to port.

When motorboats approach each other at right angles or obliquely, the boat on the right has the right-of-way in most cases.

Motorboats must keep to the right in narrow channels, when safe and practicable.

Mariners are urged to become familiar with the complete text of the Rules of the Road in U.S. Coast Guard publication "Navigation Rules".

AIDS TO NAVIGATION

Consult U.S. Coast Guard Light List for supplemental information concerning aids to navigation.

B A L L A R D

stop signal, large and small lock

large lock

stop signal, small lock

stop signal, large locks

large lock waiting pier

small lock waiting pier

small lock waiting pier

LAKE WASHINGTON SHIP CANAL
Traffic Lights
207.750 (see note A)

Red (stop) green (go) lights are maintained on the guide pier below the Burlington Northern R.R. bridge for the guidance of vessels going through the large lock.

NOTE A

Navigation regulations are published in Chapter 2, U.S. Coast Pilot 7. Additions or revisions to Chapter 2 are published in the Notices to Mariners. Information concerning the regulations may be obtained at the Office of the Commander, 13th Coast Guard District in Seattle, WA, or at the Office of the District Engineer, Corps of Engineers in Seattle, WA. Refer to charted regulation section numbers.

HIRAM M CHITTENDEN LOCKS
207.750 (see note A)

	Length	Width	Depth over Sills
Large Lock	760 ft	80 ft	29 ft
Small Lock	123 ft	28ft	16 ft

SALT WATER BARRIER

Depth over the salt water barrier varies. Available depth over barrier is posted on signs on the guide piers.

SCALE 1:10,000
NAUTICAL MILE

STATUTE MILE

YARDS

Soundings in Feet
4.69" = 1 Nautical Mile

The Hiram M. Chittenden Locks, looking east toward Ballard and the fresh water of Salmon Bay. Note the turbulence below the spillway to the right of the small lock. In this picture, two of the three miter gates in the large lock are closed. The Burlington Northern railroad bridge, bottom left, is open. (U.S. Army Corps of Engineers)

craft. Since 1916, boats have been raised and lowered anywhere from 6 to 26 feet within the steep concrete walls—the difference, depending on the tide, between the water level in Puget Sound and the higher, freshwater level inside.

The two parallel locks are distinguished by their size and the method of their use. The large, north lock is 825 feet long and 80 feet wide; boats are secured to large mooring bollards (referred to as *buttons*) along the top of the lock walls. The small south lock is 150 feet long and 28 feet wide, with mooring buttons along floating steel guide walls. Both locks fill and drain by gravity, via underwater culverts. Each lock carries traffic in both directions, alternately raising eastbound traffic and lowering westbound traffic. Both locks are used for pleasure craft.

The Locks operate 24 hours a day, every day of the year.

Preparation. Before your arrive, preview this section to understand the basics. If possible, talk to other boaters with vessels like yours, and visit the Locks by land. You'll learn a lot from watching the process when you're not distracted by handling your own boat. A brochure for boaters is available from the Visitor Center.

Once you know the basics, explain them to those on board who will assist you. Be sure they know how to use a cleat, and how to secure a line with figure-eight turns around the cleat, rather than with half hitches or other knots. Position your helpers so you can all communicate with each other.

You'll need two 50-foot lines of adequate

size for your boat, each with an eye on one end. Coil the lines so they'll pay out smoothly, working out the tangles, and place them at bow and stern for a port or starboard tie (you may not know which until the last minute). Place fenders on both sides of your boat, and have a boathook ready. Your engine, and especially the reverse gear, should be in working order. All the standard equipment (life jackets, fire extinguishers, and so on) should also be on board.

Turn off your radar for the safety of those standing and working along the lock walls.

Children and nonswimmers should wear life jackets or stay inside the boat. If you have a pet, secure it. Lockwall attendants tell of people who have fallen overboard, and pets that have jumped ship.

Approaches. From the west, stay within the channel. Entrance buoys begin west of the Shilshole breakwater. Use the range markers to keep on course. Areas outside the channel are shallow, with mudflats and rocks extending from the south bluffs. During fishing season, commercial gill nets attached to shore are anchored toward the channel. At night the offshore ends of these nets are lighted, but may be difficult to locate.

Burlington Northern's railroad bridge has a charted vertical clearance of 43 feet. Signal for an opening (one long and one short blast), or if necessary call "Bridge 4" on VHF Channel 13. Beyond the bridge, where the channel narrows, expect to feel a strong current. Rushing water from the spillway south of the small lock flows swiftly, like a river, especially at low tide. You can be pushed sideways easily and unpredictably.

Approaching the Locks from the east, watch for a current pulling you toward the spillway south of the small lock. If one of the locks is emptying of traffic, be prepared for boats heading toward you.

Traffic lights are on the north wall and on the separation wall between the large and small lock. If either of these is green, proceed to the indicated lock.

Waiting. When the lock traffic lights are red, you need to wait. Your presence at a waiting pier or wall is a clear sign to the lockmaster that you wish to lock through.

Eastbound into the Ship Canal: For the large lock, there's a traffic light northwest of the Burlington Northern Bridge, and another at the west tip of the concrete wall that separates the large and small locks. The traffic light for the eastbound small lock is also on the tip of this separation wall.

Ships and other large vessels requiring the large lock wait at the timber pier that angles northwest from the railroad bridge. Except on busy weekends, pleasure boats generally wait at the opposite pier that extends east and west under the bridge, on the south side of the channel. Approaching this pier, be prepared for strong current off the spillway that may push you toward the center bridge support. All timbers are rough and creosote-soaked, and the mooring buttons are often missing.

Westbound into Puget Sound: For the large lock, the traffic signal light is on the north wall. Wait east of the turn in this wall. For the small lock, the light is on the concrete wall that separates the two locks. Wait east of this light.

Yellow lights are at both east and west ends of the large lock. When on, these lights indicate that the submerged saltwater barrier is in the upright position. This barrier is at the freshwater end of the large lock to help prevent heavier salt water from entering the Ship Canal. If your vessel draws more than 14 feet, signal the lockmaster (one long and two short blasts) to lower the barrier.

In crowded conditions, some boaters choose to drift rather than to tie to a waiting pier or wall. If so, it's important to stay out of the way of boats leaving the Locks, and be aware of currents. Don't crowd in front of boats that have arrived before you—unless instructed otherwise, the general order is first come, first served. Rafting to boats on the waiting piers or walls is customary, but take care not to congest the channels.

Be patient. Sometimes you'll get the green light almost as soon as you tie to the pier or wall, but most often you'll wait a while. On busy weekends and during special events, the

A fleet of gillnetters fills the small lock, eastbound from Puget Sound. Their bow and stern lines are looped around buttons on the floating steel guide walls. A lockwall attendant stands by with coiled line as the water rises.

wait can be three hours or more. During summers with water restrictions, the wait can extend another hour in order to make most efficient use of each locking.

It's impossible to predict when the Locks will not be busy. However, on Friday evenings westbound traffic is generally heavy, and on Sunday afternoons, eastbound. Try to avoid these times.

Entering. A green light, often accompanied by an announcement on the public address system, signals that boats may approach the large or small lock. Approach the announced lock slowly, at about 2.5 knots, and leave room for others to maneuver. Defer to boats that have been waiting ahead of you, and to larger vessels that need more room and will generally be waved in first. A lockwall attendant may call a boat from behind you in order to make best use of space.

Sometimes the signal will remain red while priority vessels are called in. Government vessels, commercial passenger vessels on scheduled trips, and freighters, fishing vessels, and tow boats may be locked through ahead of pleasure craft.

Securing. As you enter the lock chamber, a lockwall attendant will gesture or call out where you are to tie up. It will help the attendants if you clearly confirm their instruction.

For the small lock, secure the eye-ends of your bow and stern lines to their respective cleats on board. Eastbound, loop the line (stern line first) around the button the lockwall attendant tells you to try for. The buttons are numbered. If you hold a section of the line like a jump rope and swing it over with the right amount of slack, you might get the button on the first try. Pull the boat to the wall, and secure both lines to your cleats with unhitched figure-eights.

137

A raft of boats in the large lock chamber, eastbound to Salmon Bay. Lines from the fishing boat are secured to buttons on top of the concrete wall. These lines will need to be taken up by the crew as the lock fills to freshwater level. Note the typical rafting order: largest to smallest vessel, with the largest on the wall.

Westbound in the small lock, the lockwall attendant will take your line and loop it around the button for you.

Eastbound in the large lock, the lockwall attendant will throw a line down to you, with unexpected accuracy ("It's all in the coiling," they explain). Use a simple bend to attach the eye-end of your line to the attendant's. He or she will pull up your line and loop the eye over the button on top of the lock wall. Take up the slack and cleat off with figure-eights.

Westbound in the large lock, the lockwall attendant will ask you to hand over or heave the eye-end of your line, and will then loop the eye over the button.

Once you're made fast to the lock wall, be ready to help another boat to raft outboard, or to squeeze in next to you.

If your boat is rafting, secure the eye-end of the line, and ask the person on the other boat to loop your line over a cleat or windlass and pass the rest back to you. This way you'll stay in control of your own line.

Inside the lock, keep your engine on or off as you prefer. During full lockings, the atmosphere can become foul with exhaust gases, but it's important that you be able to move under power safely and quickly.

Filling a lock, especially during crowded weekends, takes ingenuity on the part of the lockwall attendants, and patience on the part of boaters. Each locking is like fitting a jigsaw puzzle, with pieces that are never the same. The skills of boat operators vary widely and can slow down the process. Lockwall attendants quickly learn that this skill doesn't depend on the size or type of boat. They recognize from a distance the anxious looks of inexperienced skippers and crew.

Raising and Lowering. When all boats are secured and the miter gates begin to close, you'll be reminded to stand by your lines. In the small lock, this is mainly a precaution against a mooring float hanging up on the wall. Against the wall in the large lock you've got work to do, either taking up or letting out line as the water level rises or falls, generally trying to keep your boat parallel to the wall. This will be easier if your rudder is centered.

In the large lock, raising and lowering is controlled by the lockmaster in the square, central tower. The small lock is generally controlled from the nearby, rounded operating house. The gravity transfer of millions of gallons of water takes surprisingly little time, about 10 minutes for the full length of the large lock, five minutes for the small. Turbulence is common, so stay alert even if you're rafted to another boat.

When raising or lowering is complete, you'll be told to tie down your lines; do so as before with figure-eights. Opening the gates creates about a 3-knot current. If your boat weaves excessively, you may have better luck straightening it out by using your rudder than by scrambling for fenders and lines.

Leaving. Emptying the lock of boats is a fairly quick, methodical process controlled by the lockwall attendants. Don't release your lines until directed. Motor away slowly. If you're westbound and need the railroad bridge raised, it may be OK to remain in the lock chamber until you're sure of a bridge opening; ask the lockwall attendant. The bridge answers Channel 13. Be mindful of the current from the spillway south of the small lock.

About VHF Channel 13. Commercial vessels are required to call the Locks on Channel 13 with length, width, draft, and type of cargo. If yours is a pleasure boat, it's a good idea to monitor Channel 13 for a general sense of what's happening. However, if you call the Locks yourself the lockmaster won't be able to tell you when you can lock through or where you will tie up, as these decisions are made— often necessarily at the last minute—by the lockwall attendants.

The primary purpose of Channel 13 is to provide instant communications between large vessels in a passing or collision situation. Before transmitting on this channel, make sure your communication is really necessary.

Salmon Bay

Charts: 18447

The Ballard Locks open east into heavily industrial Salmon Bay. Water-related businesses solidly line both shores with boatyards, shipyards, marinas, and working wharfs. From here to Lake Union you'll feel the press of a city that still earns a living from the sea: dry-docked ships illuminated by welding flash, tramp steamers tended by screeching cranes, piles of bed-sized crab pots. The only visual relief is the poplar-lined cut between the Ballard and Fremont bridges.

In this setting, it's no surprise that there are only two public moorings, neither of them for overnight use.

24th Avenue Landing ★★★

Charts: 18447

The community of Ballard maintains a public pier and pocket-size beach at the foot of 24th Avenue. The pier is a pleasant stop in itself, a chance to stretch your legs and regroup after clearing the Locks. Its location in the heart of Ballard—a town with a Scandinavian flavor, formerly separate from Seattle—puts you within walking distance of some of the best marine supply and repair facilities in the Pacific Northwest.

It's only a block north to the commercial district on Market Street, with its shops, supermarkets, and restaurants. There's a laundromat nearby, up 24th Avenue, beyond Market. Two commercial fuel docks sell to pleasure boats: Ballard Oil is about 200 yards west, Covich-Williams about a quarter-mile east.

The 24th Avenue Landing is for boats less than 40 feet long. No mooring is permitted between 2 A.M. and 5 A.M.

Approaches. As soon as you enter through the Locks, scan the north shore for the large PACIFIC FISHERMEN'S INC. sign and shipyard. The 24th Avenue Landing is the second dock east (just west of the gray restaurant). The wooden pier itself is marked with a small sign. Tie either side, or across the end. Depth to about halfway along the pier is 15 to 20 feet.

The 24th Avenue Landing was constructed—and is maintained—by volunteers. Donations are much appreciated. A tall metal sculpture of Rusty the Donation Bird stands near shore to accept your contribution.

Fishermen's Terminal ★★★

Charts: 18447

Fishermen's Terminal is an extensive marine facility that has been operated by the Port of Seattle since 1918 for commercial fishing vessels. A renovation in 1988 added administrative buildings, restaurants, and retail shops, but it remains a working port crowded with robust trawlers and seiners. One large area is devoted to net mending, others to gear storage. The outer, northwest pier was built in 1988 for factory (fishing and processing) ships that now tower over the inner harbor.

Fishermen's Terminal provides a fascinating glimpse into the fishing industry. However, it is first and foremost a working harbor, not a tourist attraction. Pleasure boats are welcome to visit and enjoy, but not to stay.

Approaches. From any direction, Fishermen's Terminal is easily found southwest of the Ballard Bridge. The fuel dock is prominent, though it may be obscured by boats. To reach the visitors' float between Docks 9 and 10, motor east between the inner harbor docks and the factory-ship pier; the docks are numbered. The 80-foot concrete float for visitors is set east-west. Maneuvering room is tight, with deepest water off the west end of the dock.

Moorage at the float, though free, is limited to four hours.

Commercial vessels seeking temporary moorage can call the harbormaster directly on VHF Channel 17. There is no overnight moorage available for pleasure craft.

For the Boat. The fuel dock is at the north end of Dock 4. Marine supplies and repair facilities on shore cater to commercial fishing: stout line and rigging, lots of galvanized fittings, and rain gear that works. Captain's Nautical Supplies is the jewel here, with a complete selection of charts and nautical books covering Pacific Northwest and Alaskan waters. The marine ways that flank the bridge do not ordinarily accommodate pleasure craft. If you need to haul your boat out, make arrangements with the yards on the north side of Salmon Bay and the Ship Canal, or those in Lake Union.

For the Crew. The remodeled terminal building has restrooms and several restaurants. Showers and laundromat are for commercial fishers only. Some groceries are available in the small convenience store east of the terminal tower. The nearest supermarket is a mile south, on Dravus Street.

SHIP CANAL DRAWBRIDGES

Sailboats and other vessels with masts may need as many as four bridge openings between the Ballard Locks and Lake Washington. Vessel—not road—traffic has priority on navigable waterways such as the Ship Canal, hence these bascule drawbridges. All the bridges operate similarly, their steel roadway structure balanced against a counterweight of several hundred tons, like an enormous seesaw.

Clearance. All vertical clearances are charted and posted on each bridge. These clearances are:

- Ballard Bridge—45 feet;
- Fremont Bridge—30 feet;
- University Bridge—44 feet at the center of the span;
- Montlake Bridge—46 feet at the center of the span.

Know the actual height of your mast or antennas from the water level. You may not need an opening at all.

Bridge Opening Restrictions. Check the time of day before you request an opening. Bridges open on demand, but as a consideration for rush-hour auto traffic, they remain closed to vessels during certain periods:

- Ballard, Fremont, and University bridges remain closed to vessels during weekdays from 7 A.M. to 9 A.M. and from 4 P.M. to 6 P.M., except on national holidays. It's OK to tie to the protection piers through these closed periods.
- The Montlake Bridge is closed to vessels during weekdays from 7 A.M. to 9 A.M. and from 3:30 P.M. to 6 P.M., except on national holidays. In addition, on weekday afternoons the Montlake Bridge opens for vessels on demand only on the hour and half-hour. This means weekday afternoon openings are possible at 12:30, 1:00, 1:30, 2:00, 2:30, 3:00, 3:30, 6:00, and 6:30.

Exceptions to the above restrictions are ships of 1,000 gross tons or more, or vessels towing more than 1,000 gross tons.

- All Bridges. Between 11 P.M. and 7 A.M., one bridge operator is responsible for all four bridges. Openings must be scheduled an hour in advance so that he or she can efficiently group boats and limit the time required to drive from bridge to bridge. To schedule an opening during these hours, call the Bridge Shop on VHF Channel 13, or telephone (206) 386-4251. (Telephones for this purpose are located near the bridge signs on the west side of the Ballard Bridge and on the east side of the Montlake Bridge.) In either case, make your call after 11

P.M., as bridge operators on shift before this time cannot take these appointments.

Traffic Signals. Red and green traffic signals are located on the west side of the Ballard Bridge, the east side of the Fremont Bridge, and 1,000 feet east and west of the Montlake Bridge. These "block lights" apply to vessels of 300 gross tons or more and to vessels with tows. All other vessels may ignore these signals, but if the light is red, be alert—something big is passing through.

Requesting an Opening. Request an opening when you are within 100 yards of the bridge. For the Montlake Bridge, you must be at the mouth of the Cut on either end, or closer.

Signal (one long and one short blast) or if necessary call on Channel 13. If you use Channel 13, put your radio on low power and keep your communication short: the bridge name, your vessel type (commercial or sail), and the direction in which you are traveling. Your vessel's name and call letters are not needed. Once you initiate radio contact, continue to monitor Channel 13 until you are through the bridge.

If there are already boats waiting, you probably don't need to call the bridge yourself. Don't signal or call if you have heard someone else do so.

Be Patient. If the signal or call isn't answered immediately, wait a few minutes. The bridge operator could be busy at the controls or in the bathroom, or your boat could be in a dead spot. Look behind you. Other boats with masts may be approaching, in which case the bridge operator will wait for them.

Keep your boat visible from the tower (operating towers are at the southeast end of each bridge). At dusk or dark, turn on your masthead light. Bridge operators have no radar, and depend on seeing you with their own eyes.

Before committing to an opening, bridge operators look for natural breaks in auto traffic on the main and feeder roads. Pedestrians, bicyclists, emergency vehicles, buses—all figure in the decision. Most waits are short, though the Coast Guard allows vessels to be held up for as long as 10 minutes.

Passing Through. When the operator is ready to open the bridge he or she will usually signal one long and one short blast. The auto barriers drop across the road, gongs sound, and lights flash as a warning to drivers. The clank of the bridge's center-lock indicates that opening has begun.

Pass under the bridge as soon as it is safe to do so. Motorists appreciate short openings. It is not necessary to signal when you have cleared. All bridge openings are logged, as well as the number of vessels per opening.

continued

A bridge operator at the controls of the Fremont Bridge. His is a busy job; in fall of 1991, this bridge opened for the half-millionth time.

continued from page 141

The bridge closes fairly quickly except for the last 7 degrees of travel. This deliberate slowdown ("creep" speed) drives the pistons through air cylinders to buffer the final drop and prevent damage to the bridge itself. Don't misinterpret this slowdown as a decision to keep the bridge open—it is definitely closing.

Openings and closings take about four minutes on average, from the time auto traffic stops until it starts again. Traffic back-ups take about 10 minutes to recover.

Lake Union ★★★★

Charts: 18447

Lake Union is a totally urban lake. Its shoreline is a jumble of marinas, boatyards, shipyards, restaurants, condominiums, and a unique community of floating homes. The north shore is heavily industrial; even the park on the tongue of land protruding south into the lake is dominated by the giant tanks and pipes that once converted coal and oil into household gas. Opposite, to the south, is a fleet of ships used by the National Oceanic and Atmospheric Administration (NOAA), a nest of private moorages, yacht brokers, restaurants, shops, a U.S. Navy Reserve Center, and a seaplane base. Beyond are the Space Needle and Seattle's downtown high-rises.

There's a din and activity on Lake Union that cruisers from outside the Ballard Locks may find overwhelming. On a sunny day at any

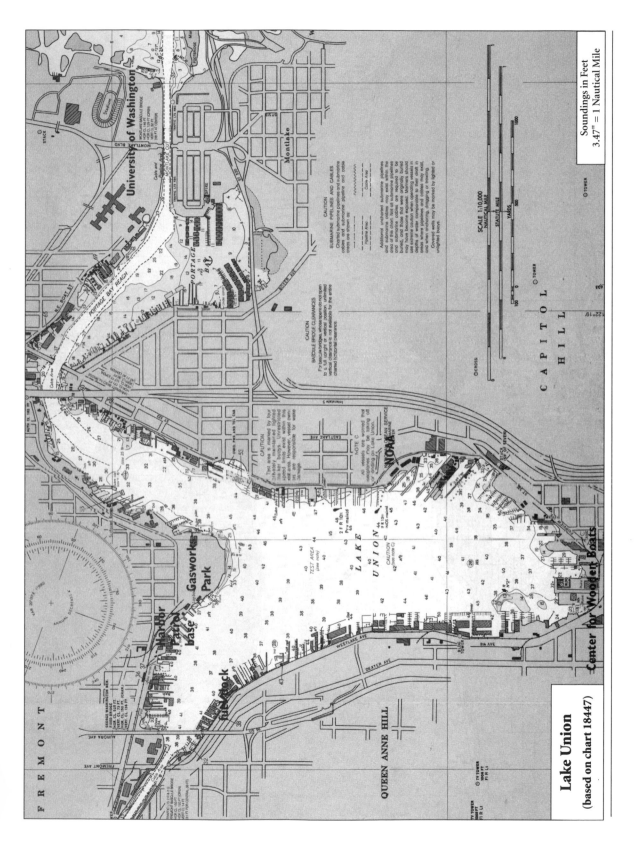

Lake Union
(based on chart 18447)

Soundings in Feet
3.47" = 1 Nautical Mile

time of year the lake is filled with boats circumnavigating and criss-crossing aimlessly, some powering full-throttle between the four white buoys in the northern half of the lake that mark the only speed run. The noise of seaplanes taking off is loud enough to interrupt conversation. Traffic on the interstate freeway that parallels the east shore adds its roar.

Anchorage, Moorings. Anchoring is not permitted anywhere in Lake Union. Docks for visiting boats are concentrated at the south end of the lake, amid the sleek yachts and glass-fronted restaurants whose pitched, pale-green metal roofs are prominent. Stays are limited to three hours. Expect many of the docks to be reserved for tour boats. In summer, this end of the lake is a congested circus. Overnight berths may be secured by prior arrangement: telephone (206) 292-0513 or (206) 624-6534.

Getting Ashore. Small boats may be tempted to beach at Gas Works Park or at one of the many pocket-size parks around the lake. Be aware that the Seattle Park code prohibits this, even for craft without motors. There is one small floating dock off the tiny park that's just north of the NOAA ships moored on the east shore. The dock has cleats that seem to invite a tie-up, but the depth is 4 feet or less.

For the Boat, Crew. The only fuel dock on Lake Union is on the west shore, less than a quarter-mile southeast of the Fremont Bridge. A few marine supplies, as well as groceries and ice, are available at the fuel-dock store. A grocery with a wider range of stock is situated a couple blocks north of the tiny park mentioned above, at Lynn Street and Fairview Avenue.

Many of the dozen or so lakeside restaurants provide short-term berths for diners. For the most part, these are well marked, but space is generally limited and maneuvering is tight. It's a good idea to telephone ahead for information if you have a particular restaurant in mind.

Things to Do. For a cruising pleasure boat, Lake Union is sometimes crowded, but it's always a fascinating place to visit. Tuesday evenings, from early May to Labor Day, it's filled with sailboats of every description competing at close quarters in the informal Duck Dodge sailing race; the winner tows a duck decoy during the next week's race. Summer evenings, Lake Union is perfect for drifting, for enjoying this remarkable open space in the heart of a major city, for watching the setting sunlight emblazon the glassy towers of downtown Seattle. Midwinter, the lake is empty and peaceful.

The chief attraction is at the south end. It's worth the search for moorage here not only to eat and shop, but especially to visit the Center for Wooden Boats. Located immediately east of the Navy Reserve Center and marked by the masts of the tall ship *Wawona*, the Center for Wooden Boats is a living museum that invites you to experience maritime history firsthand. The Center's lovely, working craft—sharpies, catboats, dories, canoes—comprise the largest active small-boat fleet on the West Coast. You're welcome to rent any of them, or watch the volunteers in the workshop as they varnish, paint, and splice. Marine skills workshops are offered year round, as are monthly evening presentations by local and visiting shipwrights and sailors. The Center hosts the annual Lake Union Wooden Boat Festival in early July.

Portage Bay ★★ 5 No Facilities

Charts: 18447

Though extremely shallow in places and constricted by private marinas, Portage Bay deserves mention as the only permitted freshwater anchorage inside Seattle's city limits. You must be south of an imaginary extension of the Montlake Cut channel line, and take care not to

WORKING THE WATER: THE VIEW FROM THE HARBOR PATROL

It may not be the first thing you notice that's different about cruising inside the Ballard Locks, but it'll strike you soon enough: Inside the city limits, the Seattle Police Department, not the Coast Guard, routinely patrols the water. There are eight boats, all specially equipped and prominently painted, all unmistakably police vessels. What, exactly, are they doing out here?

There doesn't have to be a specific reason for a police boat to pull away from the Harbor Patrol base, a tidy cluster of blue-roofed buildings west of Gasworks Park. Something will present itself: Is that plume of smoke across the lake a fire, or just a smoky exhaust? Has that oil slick been reported to the Coast Guard? There's a large piece of plywood floating in the middle of the channel; better haul that aboard. The two officers on each boat are always watching, seemingly wandering, open to a wide range of tasks.

Harbor Patrol work leans heavily toward service rather than enforcement. "Out here, people wave at us with all their fingers," explained one officer. If your boat is sinking, they'll pump the water out at 230 gallons a minute, a common task after a thaw, when seacocks often fail. Reversed, the same pump works to put out fires. If your boat is out of fuel or otherwise disabled, the Harbor Patrol can tow it to the nearest fuel dock.

Other calls come in: A suicide jumps from the Aurora Bridge; a propane stove explodes aboard a boat at its dock; a burglary is reported in progress on one of the houseboats. These are the serious calls—along with fires and sinkings—that turn on the sirens and blue lights, and cause the tremendous wake as the patrol boat races to the scene.

Getting Pulled Over. What concerns most boaters, of course, is what concerns motorists at the sight of a police car: What am I doing that I can be ticketed for? A common violation is lack of registration. All local pleasure vessels must display a current Washington State registration sticker near the bow. Unless federally documented, they must also display registration numbers. Don't expect to get away with the excuse that you "just pulled into town" unless it's true. There are only 18 officers in the Harbor Unit, turnover is low, and, like you, they enjoy looking at boats and have a pretty good memory for them. The fine is stiff—currently $200. Seattle Harbor officers do not enforce federal registration. Speeding is also a common reason to pull over a boat. From the Ballard Locks to Webster Point at the entrance to Lake Washington, the speed

limit is 7 knots—basically a "no wake" speed. There are only two exceptions: the test area between the buoys at the north end of Lake Union, and the center of Union Bay. From the vantage of a patrol boat, a speeder isn't difficult to spot. No speed traps are set or needed. A violation will cost up to $50, but won't be reported to the Department of Motor Vehicles.

If speeding or unsafe behavior is associated with alcohol, you may be cited for driving while intoxicated (DWI). This is not to say that you can't drink while boating; no need to furtively hide that can of beer from the Harbor Patrol. It's the amount of alcohol consumed, and how it affects you, that counts here. As with a speeding ticket, a DWI won't be reported to the Department of Motor Vehicles, but it is a criminal offense with a mandatory court appearance. Your boat may be impounded if you're too drunk to handle it safely.

The Harbor Patrol doesn't do routine safety inspections, but if you're stopped for speeding or any other violation they'll ask to see your life jackets and fire extinguisher. Officers admit to enforcing safety standards "without mercy" when children are on board. "We're the ones who have to dive for those kids when there's a drowning," they explain. It's a part of the job they hate, and don't much want to talk about. Their eyes flash with impatience when they describe boaters who allow kids to sit on the bow, legs dangling, without a lifeline or a life jacket. "What do they think will happen if one falls in? The boat won't just STOP."

Getting Help. Chances are you'll never be pulled over by the Harbor Patrol. Instead, you'll want to call them for assistance. There are three ways to do so:

- Call the Harbor Patrol on Channel 16; they'll ask you to switch to Channel 10, a working frequency they use but don't generally monitor.
- Telephone the Harbor Patrol office—(206) 684-4071. The boats themselves do not have cellular phones, but radio contact between boats and office is swift and smooth.
- Telephone 911. This may be the slowest way to get help, as you will be put in priority order with all emergency calls in the city, and 911 operators may not be familiar with boat-related problems, or how to locate you on the water.

On Lake Washington, outside Seattle's city limits, contact King County Harbor Patrol on Channel 16.

The Montlake Bridge, looking west through the Cut.

obstruct marina access. Anchored here, you will be surrounded by yacht clubs and houseboats. The traffic on Highway 520 roars endlessly. South of the highway is Montlake's community playground. Across the channel are the medical complexes of the University of Washington.

The closest shore access for this anchorage is a public launching ramp across the channel at the foot of Brooklyn Avenue, about a quarter-mile northwest. From here it's about a 20-minute walk north to the University's commercial district.

Expect a visit from the Harbor Patrol if you're anchored here. Depending on the length of your stay, you may be asked to apply for an anchoring permit.

On the first weekend in May, Portage Bay is completely taken over by Seattle's Opening Day celebration. More than 200,000 spectators and 5,000 boats converge to mark the official kick-off of the yachting season. Portage Bay is closed to all but official and decorated parade boats during this colorful, crowded event.

Union Bay

Charts: 18447

The east end of the Montlake Cut widens into Union Bay Reach; these two dredged channels are collectively referred to as "the Cut." To the north is shoal and shallow Union Bay. During fair weather, this bay is busy with jet-skiers and water-skiers, and with small boats rented from

the University of Washington's boathouse. Canoeists often paddle south across the Cut to explore the marshlands around Foster Island—part of the University of Washington Arboretum.

As with most Seattle bays and waterways, anchoring is not permitted. There are exceptions: During football games, tour and pleasure boats commonly anchor near the canoe house and docks southeast of the stadium. The area north of the Cut and west of can buoy "29" is University of Washington property. During Opening Day celebrations on the first weekend of May, anchoring is also permitted. However, the best view of the Saturday rowing shell races and parade is from the log boom placed on both sides of the Cut for the occasion.

Take special care when entering Union Bay, as the bottom shoals unpredictably.

The speed limit is 7 knots within 200 yards of all shores, and 200 yards north and south of the Cut to Webster Point. The small, white can buoys, with the speed limit circled in red, are frequent reminders of this.

Lake Washington

Charts: 18447

East of the Montlake Bridge and Union Bay, the urban feel of Lake Union gives way to the suburban, at times park-like feel of Lake Washington. This is a huge, deep lake, long and serpentine, enclosing Mercer Island in its southern half and spanned by two floating freeway bridges. In clear weather, the setting here is spectacular, Mt. Baker visible to the north, Mt. Rainier to the south; it's enough, sometimes, to slow commuter traffic.

Lake Washington seems tame. It's often smooth and luminous, or ruffled with light winds that make for steady sailing. The air temperature is as much as 10 degrees warmer than on Puget Sound, the water clean and actually swimmable. But mariners should guard against complacency: fresh water is lighter than salt, and in heavy winds the waves are steep and dangerous. In addition, there are no tides. In spring, the lake does gradually rise about 2 feet from snow melt, but this is an annual, not twice-a-day, event. By late fall, the water level is low. If you run aground—and there are many places to do so—you may be stuck.

For the most part, the Lake Washington shoreline is the preserve of the wealthy. Dramatically designed homes rise from manicured lawns that drop undisturbed to tidy private docks showcasing impeccably maintained yachts. Only toward the extreme ends of Lake Washington—Kenmore to the north and Renton to the south—does commercial and industrial use resume.

More than a dozen municipalities border the lake, and most provide beach access for their residents. These—as well as several state and county parks—are heavily used; however, all but a handful are designed for the landbound. In most cases, not only is the park shore unsuited for anchoring, city ordinance prohibits it. Most parks do not permit beaching of any watercraft.

Nevertheless, there are fine anchorages and moorings open to boaters in Lake Washington. The following are those where depth, public shore access, and protection combine to create good cruising destinations.

Kenmore ★★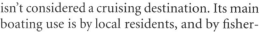

Charts: 18447

Out of the way for most boaters, at the far northern end of Lake Washington, Kenmore isn't considered a cruising destination. Its main boating use is by local residents, and by fisher-

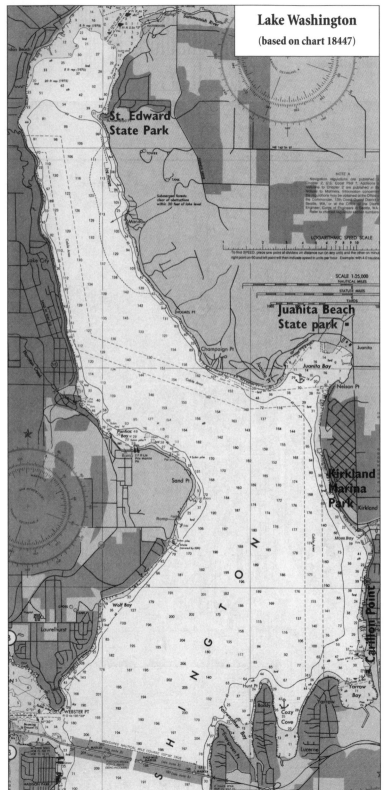

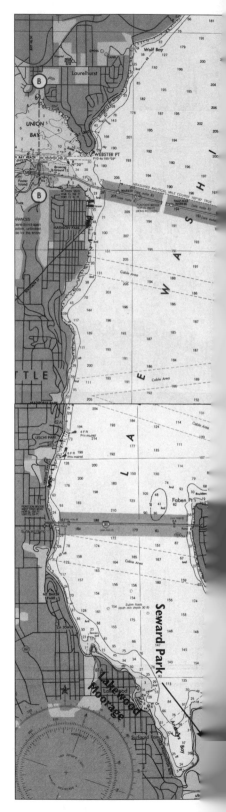

Lake Washington

(based on chart 18447)

Soundings in Feet
1.12" = 1 Nautical Mile

men in pursuit of Sammamish River salmon.

The mariner's view of Kenmore is heavily industrial. Tugs regularly deliver mountains of sand and gravel to the concrete plant at the end of the dredged waterway; the silos and elevators are a prominent landmark. Barges often lie at anchor outside the harbor. Seaplanes use the waterway for takeoffs and landings. The harbor was once jammed with logging activity as well; today the booming area to the west is a King County park. The Sammamish River, flowing from the low marsh on the east shore, fills this end of Lake Washington with enough silt to discourage all but the shallowest-draft vessels from wandering out of the channel.

Approaches. It's important to enter the harbor within the dredged channel. A large mooring buoy is on the left side of the channel entrance. Two red buoys, "2" and "4," mark the channel's east side; each is topped with a triangle. Don't be confused by the narrow, uncharted red and green cans that mark the entrance to the Sammamish River. Watch your depth sounder, and favor the river side of the channel. The charted depth in 1989 was 13 feet 6 inches.

Anchorage, Moorings. Harbor Village Marina, west of the channel, is a private condominium moorage with both covered and uncovered slips. Visitors are welcome at the breakwater pier during daylight hours only—no overnight stays. The first three hours are free. The marina tries to maintain a depth of 10 feet along the breakwater. If your keel is deep, approach as close to the breakwater as you can; the charted depth just south of the breakwater is 5 feet.

Daytime moorage is also available to the west at Logboom Park's public pier. Fewer than a dozen 20-foot finger piers extend east from the main dock for boating use. Depths are a fathom or less.

Boats may anchor for as long as 72 hours south of Logboom Park, where there is deeper water. Watch for shoals in this area. You can go ashore either at the park dock, or at the Harbor Village marina breakwater. There's also a launching ramp up the Sammamish River slough that's used year round by sport fishers.

For the Boat. The fuel dock is located east of the condominium moorage; counting from the west, it is between the fourth and fifth covered slips. Turning room adjacent to the fueling area is more generous than it appears when you first approach, but the depth—a fathom or less—will discourage deep-draft vessels. Near the fuel dock is a small marine lift, a marine repair shop, and marine supplies.

At the east end of the Harbor Village breakwater pier is a water hose for public use.

For the Crew. There's a restaurant at Harbor Village Marina, and others along the main highway. A deli and grocery is in the strip mall just across the street from Logboom Park. A supermarket is a half-mile east along Bothell Way, at the next major intersection.

Harbor Village has no facilities for visiting boats other than restrooms, but its walkway leads to Logboom Park, where there are picnic tables and a play area. The park paths link with the paved Burke Gilman trail; from here it is possible to walk or bicycle 13 miles southwest to the Ship Canal, or five miles east to the town of Woodinville.

St. Edward State Park ★★★★ No Facilities

Charts: 18447

At 316 acres, St. Edward State Park is the largest undeveloped area remaining on Lake Washington, as well as its largest public park. It is located a little over a mile south of Kenmore, between Arrowhead Point and Manitou. The land was once private; from the late 1920s to 1970s it was owned by the Seattle Catholic Diocese for use as a seminary. The magnificent seminary building is now maintained by the state park system, near the public pool and gym. A small portion

TRANSFORMED BY THE LOCKS: SEATTLE'S LAKES AND WATERWAYS

The imprint of human habitation and industry is visible everywhere inside the Locks, most especially—though perhaps most subtly—in the shape and course of the waterways themselves. When Seattle was first settled by white Americans, the two principal inland lakes were separate. Lake Washington drained to the south through the Black and Duwamish Rivers into Elliot Bay. Lake Union drained west through a small stream into the salt water of Salmon Bay, which was nearly dry at low tide. Though boats did travel upriver from Elliot Bay to Lake Washington, no direct navigable connection existed between Puget Sound, Lake Union, and Lake Washington.

In the mid 1800s, a canal and lock system linking these waters was proposed; Congress authorized the project in the early 1900s. The Montlake Cut between Lake Washington and Portage Bay was dredged and widened (it had been dug by hand in the previous century to float logs) and the Ship Canal dug between Lake Union and Salmon Bay. When the Locks were complete and the Montlake Cut opened in 1917, Lake Washington dropped nine feet to the level of Lake Union. Salmon Bay, dammed by the Locks, filled with fresh water. The Black River at the south end of Lake Washington, deprived of its source, dried up completely, and the Cedar River, which had flowed into the Black, was diverted to flow into the lake.

Today, it's difficult to imagine Seattle without its connected lakes and waterways, or to speculate how the city would have developed without them.

---

of the park, the St. Thomas Conference Center, is still owned by the Diocese for religious retreats and other non-profit uses. The state park grounds, heavily wooded and criss-crossed with trails, give visitors a sense of what Lake Washington was like before logging and development took place.

Approaches, Anchorage. From Lake Washington, St. Edward State Park appears as a steep, wooded hillside. The southern border is marked inland by an elevated water tower that you can see if you approach from the west side of the lake. More apparent from other directions is the abrupt interruption of housing tracts. Look for hiking trails that touch the half-mile of park shore, and the small state park sign.

The underwater terrain makes for tricky anchoring: The hard bottom descends gradually to about 30 feet, then drops off abruptly to 100 feet. The sloping ledge is narrow and doesn't afford much swinging room between the beach and the drop-off, though there is a slightly wider portion of this ledge near the state park sign. If you intend to spend the night here, anchoring in deep water is probably safest, as the holding ground is better and the distance to shore greater. Watch out for crayfish pots.

Getting Ashore. You can put ashore anywhere along the park. There's no beach to speak of, so you'll need to tie your dinghy to a tree or snag.

Things to Do. The hiking trails are extensive, steep, and energizing. All trails eventually lead up ravines and gullies to the former seminary building and the public gym and pool. Here also are facilities for tennis, handball, racketball, soccer, and volleyball.

St. Edward State Park is for day use only—no overnight camping.

If you walk east to the main highway, Juanita Drive, then walk about a half-mile farther south, you'll find a supermarket and gas station—a considerable distance from the beach.

O. O. Denny Park ★★★ No Facilities

Charts: 18447

Midway between Holmes Point and Champaign Point is Camp O. O. Denny, a park owned by the City of Seattle and managed by King County. This day-use park is well-groomed and grassy, with a low-bank gravel beach, picnic shelters, and trails.

Approaches, Anchorage. The north end of the park is marked with a flagpole. The parking lot and road beyond are visible from the water. As with the anchorage off St. Edward State Park, the underwater terrain at O. O. Denny descends gradually for a short distance and then drops off abruptly to 90 feet. You're in deep water—more than 50 feet—quite close to shore. Be sure your swing won't put you on the beach. Anchoring is limited to 72 hours.

Getting Ashore. You can beach your skiff anywhere on shore.

Juanita Bay ★★★

Charts: 18447

Juanita Bay is broad, westward-facing, with a gradually sloping bottom that's perfect for anchoring. During summer, when prevailing winds are from the north, the bay offers quiet water and enough room to drop and raise your hook under sail. Swimming from your boat is a pleasure here, but don't stray far; the bay is also full of tireless water-skiers.

Approaches, Anchorage. The outer third of the bay is deep, about 30 to 40 feet. Respect both shorelines as you enter; sighting on the broad white complex of apartments and condominiums will keep you fairly well centered. A white marker on a piling off the southeast shore indicates a sandbar and rock. North of this mark, depths are less than 20 feet. The area east of the mark is shallow.

Getting Ashore. Shore access is via Juanita Beach Park, at the north end of the bay, west of the building complex. The large swimming beach of this King County Park is enclosed by a U-shaped, concrete walking pier; no boarding or landing of boats is permitted at this pier. Beach your skiff on the sandy beach to the west, where a stream outfall marks the park border. This is an active park, with picnic areas, playing fields, restrooms, and a concession stand. Restaurants are a short walk away, east along the road.

Juanita Bay Park, located to the southeast and maintained by the city of Kirkland, is designed for more passive use. This extensive area is a wildlife conservancy zone, with an elevated wetland trail. Although kayaks and canoes without motors are welcome to explore quietly, the beaching of watercraft is discouraged.

Kirkland Marina Park ★★★★

Charts: 18447

Marina Park in Kirkland's Moss Bay is one of the most satisfying destinations in Lake Washington. Moorage for visitors is convenient and plentiful, except during the busiest weekends. The grounds are beautifully maintained, there's a tiny beach park nearby, and you're only a half-block away from the shops, restaurants, and art galleries of pedestrian-friendly downtown Kirkland.

Approaches. From the north, look past the series of private homes and docks until you spot the launching ramp. Marina Park is immediately south. Approaching from the south, you'll pass a grassy stretch of park, then a private marina crowded with large yachts and fishing boats; the park is immediately north. A distinguishing feature of Marina Park from any direction is the large round electric light globes on the dock pilings.

Moorings. Three piers extend north from the main dock. The southwest end of the main dock is for commercial tour boats only; all other slips are for visitors. There's no charge if your stay is brief. For an overnight stay, pay at the drop box on shore. Moorage is limited to 72 hours per week. Depths are 10 to 20 feet.

Although the piers are stout, take note that Moss Bay is completely exposed to the north and south.

For the Boat. There's fresh water on the piers (two faucets only), but nothing else for boats. The nearest fuel is south, at Yarrow Bay Marina.

For the Crew. The nearest supermarket is a half-mile up Kirkland Avenue, east of Marina Park. There are deli markets closer. To find the laundromat, walk north (left) on Lake Street for a half-block, then east (right) on Park Lane. The laundromat is at the end of the block, on the north side.

The Kirkland waterfront is the site of the "Day on the Lake" festival in mid-August.

Yarrow Bay ★★★

Charts: 18447

Yarrow Bay, square and shallow, opens north. Its east shore is busy and developed, with crisply designed condominiums, shops, and office buildings, and two private marinas. Its west shore is more stately and residential. To the south is low, wooded wetland—an undeveloped park.

Approaches, Anchorage. The approach to the anchorage is clean from the north and west. A round buoy marks the pipeline area. The bay offers shelter from the south, but its protective area is shallow, 10 feet and less south of the mooring buoy. Most boaters prefer the nearby—and deeper—Cozy Cove. Watch for milfoil, which grows dense by late summer and can foul your prop and plug your cooling system.

Temporary berthing—up to two hours—is available at Carillon Point, a luxurious office, hotel, and shopping complex overlooking the private marina on the east shore. The marina is protected by a concrete breakwater; north of this breakwater a public pier with a flagpole at its western tip extends from the hotel. Tie up on either side, but don't go too close to shore if your keel is deep.

Getting Ashore. The only shore access in Yarrow Bay is the public pier at Carillon Point. The wetland is a wildlife conservancy area that can be explored by non-motorized craft, but there is no hard shoreline. As with Juanita Bay Park, landing of watercraft is discouraged. The dredged channel shown on the chart is obstructed by a sand bar.

The small park on the southwest shore, adjacent to the wetland, is for the private use of Yarrow Point residents only.

For the Boat. The fuel dock is located south of the Carillon Point breakwater, at Yarrow Bay Marina. You'll see the sign toward shore, beyond the covered moorage. Depth at the fuel dock is a fathom or less. Water, ice, repairs, and marine supplies are available.

For the Crew. The restaurants and shops are at Carillon Point. Canoes and paddle boats can be rented at the base of the public pier. The nearest supermarket is about a mile north and a quarter-mile east up the hill from Carillon Point, across the highway and just beyond the railroad overpass.

Cozy Cove ★★★ [4] No Facilities

Charts: 18447

Cozy Cove is well named, with good protection from all but a rare northeasterly. This is a popular spot for an overnight anchorage. Some of the most expensive real estate in the Pacific Northwest is located here. The large homes that ring the shore look down and across the water; don't expect much privacy.

Approaches, Anchorage. The entrance and the cove itself is clean, shallowing gradually from 60 to 10 feet, from hard to soft bottom. Anchor well away from the docks. All mooring buoys are private.

Getting Ashore. All shoreline in Cozy Cove is private.

Fairweather Bay ★★ [2] No Facilities

Charts: 18447

Unlike its neighbor, Cozy Cove, Fairweather Bay opens in a "V" north and west that exposes it to prevailing winds. It's narrower and the water is also shallower than that in Cozy Cove. The homes are equally luxurious.

Approaches, Anchorage. Approaches are clean. Overnight anchorage is on the Evergreen Point side only, as private property lines on the east side extend halfway into the bay.

Getting Ashore. All shoreline in Fairweather Bay is private.

Meydenbauer Bay ★★★ [5] No Facilities

Charts: 18447

Foot-shaped Meydenbauer Bay is a perfect anchorage. It is also a dramatic one, in an urban sense. Opulent, landscaped homes dominate the entrance. Two small parks are set like jewels against the northeast shore. Private marinas line the "toe" of the bay's Whaler Cove. Beyond are the Oz-like, reflective glass high-rises of Bellevue, Washington's fourth largest city.

During the early part of the century, Meydenbauer Bay was the winter home of the American Pacific Whaling fleet. While crews repaired the vessels' topsides, the fresh water killed the hull's barnacles and worms.

Approaches, Anchorage. The approaches are clean and deep. The most protected anchorage is east in Whaler Cove, with depths of about 30 to 40 feet. Private docks and the yacht club restrict swinging room. Anchoring is limited to 24 hours.

Getting Ashore. Two Bellevue City parks provide shore access for non-motorized craft only. Clyde Beach Park, located in the northwest "heel" of the bay, can be approached year round. The park is tiny; during summer months stay outside the L-shaped dock to avoid swimmers. Meydenbauer Beach Park, to the east and closest to Whaler Cove, is open to watercraft without motors from fall to late spring only, roughly during the period between

LAKE WASHINGTON'S FLOATING BRIDGES

For commuters, the concrete pontoon bridges across Lake Washington are a necessity. For pleasure boaters they can be a blessing: There is always calm water on the lee side. They can also be a hindrance. Boats with masts taller than 57 feet—the charted vertical clearance at the east end of the 520 bridge—may not be able to pass without an opening.

There are two floating bridges. The 520 bridge spans the lake from Montlake to Evergreen Point. The I-90 bridge stretches across Mercer Island, from Seattle to the east side of the lake.

Numbers at water level on the bridge pilings indicate the actual, not charted, clearance. Since the lake level varies, in the fall the actual clearance under the east span of the 520 bridge (charted at 57 feet) may be as much as 65 feet. Similar markings are on the piling of the I-90 bridge, whose charted vertical clearance on the east span is 71 feet.

Only the 520 bridge opens. Vessels that require an opening must telephone 24 hours in advance:

(206) 764-4100. Because this bridge is used heavily by commuters, openings are scheduled for the middle of the night, roughly between 11 P.M. and 2 A.M. Floating bridge openings bear little resemblance to the swift routines of the bascule bridges along the Ship Canal. Since 1989, when the span accidentally lifted and killed a motorist, floating bridge openings are carefully supervised, requiring the work of three to seven persons. The opening itself takes an average of 10 minutes.

It was Lake Washington's unusual depth—more than 200 feet—that led to the construction of the first of these unusual bridges. Built where the I-90 bridge is today, it was the longest of its type in the world when it opened in 1939. Two more followed: the 520 highway bridge from Montlake to Evergreen Point in the 1960s, and a parallel span to Mercer Island. While under repair—its side hatches open—the original flooded and sank during a severe storm in 1990. It has since been rebuilt.

Labor Day and Memorial Day. This park, marked with a flagpole, has picnic tables, playground equipment, and a swimming beach.

Things to Do. A mile's walk will take you to the downtown core of Bellevue, with its shopping malls, restaurants, art museum, and office buildings. From Clyde Beach Park, walk north up 92nd Avenue, then turn east (right) on N.E. 8th Street. From Meydenbauer Beach Park it's a slightly shorter walk, north up 98th Avenue, then east on N.E. 8th Street. The two-lane residential streets change to four lanes or more, full of traffic, bordered by concrete sidewalks and parking lots—a bit of a shock after the relative seclusion of Meydenbauer Bay.

Luther Burbank Waterfront Park ★★★★★

Charts: 18447

This King County park is a fine destination for Lake Washington boaters, and certainly one of the best for a cruising family. The park grounds—72 acres in all, 50 on the water—begin at Calkins Point on the northeast end of Mercer Island and extend south to a swimming beach and marshland.

Luther Burbank Park, originally a homestead, served for many years as a parental boys' school. The school was totally self-contained, with orchard and farmland. The brick stack and building on shore was a coal-fired power house; the stately brick buildings upland are what remain of the school itself. King County acquired the land after the school closed in the late 1960s; it was officially established as a waterfront park in 1984.

Approaches. From the north and west, the park is first seen as wooded Calkins Point, where the waterfront homes of Mercer Island stop. Tall poplars on the point are prominent. As you head south, the brick stack at the park docks will gradually emerge from the trees.

The north branch of the visitors' dock at Luther Burbank Waterfront Park.

When approaching from the south, look for the stack about the middle of the wooded shore, north of the white floats that encircle the swimming area. With the exception of a charted submerged piling at the tip of Calkins Point, all approaches are clean.

Anchorage, Moorings. The concrete park dock extends from the power house, branching into three main docks. Short finger piers radiate from the main branches; these piers are ideal for boats 20 feet in length or less. Only the north side of the north branch can accommodate larger vessels. These piers are for day moorage only, not overnight. Depths at the outer docks are good, 10 to 20 feet. Anchoring off the park is permitted, but holding ground is poor.

The single dock south of the power house is a fishing pier, not for boating use.

Getting Ashore. Use the park docks for landing and securing your skiff.

Things to Do. Directly up the short, steep trail from the docks is a restroom, a large playground area, and several tennis courts. Trails to the north lead to the foundations of a dairy barn and a viewpoint at Calkins Point. Other trails lead south to a swimming area and marsh.

Luther Burbank Park is named for the American naturalist and plant breeder, and the grounds are abundant with a wondrous variety of trees, shrubs, and flowers. Many of these plants, as well as the wildlife, are described in the park brochure's self-guided tour. Beginning in mid-July and continuing through the remainder of summer, the park hosts free Sunday afternoon concerts in the amphitheater west of the Parks Department building.

Newport Shores ★ (gas only)

Charts: 18447

Newport Shores is located in the broad bay east of Mercer Island's Barnabie Point, south of the I-90 freeway bridge. All slips in the yacht basin are private. The fuel dock is easy to spot. As you approach, watch for the low breakwater floats between the dolphins and pilings; these are parallel to the fuel dock. The entrance north of the fuel dock is shallower.

The fuel dock also sells a few marine supplies. There's an ice machine on land.

South of the yacht basin the shoals continue. A development of tightly packed homes lines the dredged channels; the private community discourages non-residents from exploring this area.

Coulon Beach Park ★★★★★ 3 (anchorage) 4 (marina)

Charts: 18447

The city of Renton at the south end of Lake Washington, like Kenmore at the north end, is heavily industrial along the waterfront. Here, much of the industry is masked by the massive block of dull gray buildings that contains one of Boeing's jet aircraft manufacturing plants. Inside, 727s and 737s are produced around the clock. When complete, aircraft are rolled out for engine testing and takeoff at Renton Airport west of the Cedar River. Boeing office buildings sprawl south into the city of Renton itself, and beyond to business parks that seem to touch the base of Mt. Rainier.

Beside all this industry, Renton has developed the Gene Coulon Memorial Beach Park, an extensive waterfront park along the east shore that offers an amazing variety of activities as well as overnight moorage.

Approaches. The gray hangars of the Boeing plant are visible from the south end of Mercer Island. Head toward them, and as soon as you can, pick out the three stacks to the east. These will help you locate the tiny island at the park's western end. Beware of snags and shallows in the Cedar River delta area, and along the entire south shore.

The park docks are along the east shore, beneath the glass-roofed viewing tower. Entrance to the harbor basin is slightly to the south.

Anchorage, Moorings. There are 12 berths in the harbor alongside concrete floats. Each float is about 25 feet long. Depths inside the harbor are reported at 20 to 30 feet, with a steep drop off from about 12 feet. You can moor for up to four hours without charge between 8 A.M. and 6 P.M.; for longer, or overnight stays, pay at the fee box. Moorage is limited to 24 hours.

It's OK to tie up to the wall in front of the viewing tower for a couple of hours, but it's considerably shallower there, especially to the south.

Anchoring is permitted outside the harbor for up to three days. If you plan to anchor for this period, the Parks Department—(206) 235-2568—would appreciate being notified in advance.

Getting Ashore. Row or motor to the visitor floats. A small dock to the north, at about the middle of the park, is used to launch canoes. Farther north is a fishing pier; keep your distance.

Things to Do. Coulon Beach Park is about a mile long, tip-to-tip. Shore walks and jogging trails extend north and south from the harbor; the many trees and shrubs are identified with small plaques to create an interpretive walk. Beneath the viewing tower are picnic shelters. More benches and picnic tables are scattered throughout the park, with some "picnic floats" attached to the walkway that extends into the lake north of the harbor. During the summer, rowing shells, rowboats, and pedal boats can be rented at the main building. There's a six-lane launching ramp and a large swimming beach to the south; a log boom protects swimmers from boating activity. South of the swimming beach is a concession stand, playground area, and tennis courts. Walking farther west will take you to the Nature Island Sanctuary.

The restaurant near the harbor sells take-out food.

Close proximity to a major airport has led to some interesting restrictions: no model airplanes, no metal detectors, and no kite flying.

The special summer event is Renton River Days, held every year in early August.

Boaters won't find much to attract them outside the park. Railroad tracks parallel the length of the park, and downtown Renton is a mile-and-a-half south.

Cove Between Rainier Beach and Atlantic City

Charts: 18447

The cove on the southwest shore of Lake Washington, between Rainier Beach and Atlantic City, is half-filled with marinas, all of them private. A fuel dock once operated here beneath the apartment complex; this facility is no longer operating.

Anchoring is not permitted off the public park and launching ramp at the north end of the cove.

Andrews Bay ★★★★

Charts: 18447

Technically not a permitted anchorage, Andrews Bay is nonetheless frequently used as such, especially on summer weekends. The bay is bordered on the west by fine homes set back from Lake Washington Boulevard, and on the east by Seattle's Seward Park, which occupies all of wooded Bailey Peninsula. Andrews Bay is well protected from southwesterlies, though totally exposed to the north.

Approaches. Hazards to watch for are on the west shore near the marina, where a daymark on a piling indicates a rock and shoal. There are unmarked rocks and shoals north of Ohlers Island as well. When entering Andrews Bay it's best to favor the clean east shore.

Anchorage, Moorings. Holding ground is good in 20 to 50 feet, in a soft bottom that slopes gradually to the head of the bay. There's a steep drop-off on the Bailey Peninsula side. You may be slightly more protected from northerlies in the southeast portion of the bay.

Lakewood Moorage at the entrance is a public marina with some guest moorage. Telephone ahead—(206) 722-3887—to reserve a spot.

Getting Ashore. Probably the only drawback to this anchorage is the lack of a dinghy landing. Seattle Park Code prohibits beaching even non-motorized craft, especially near swimming areas, or tying up to a fishing dock. The only designated landing area in Andrews Bay is at the launching ramp on the west shore; however, there is no convenient way to secure your dinghy if you wish to explore the park.

For the Boat, Crew. A few marine supplies and groceries are available at the Lakewood Moorage marina store. The nearest fuel dock is north at Leschi.

Things to Do. From early morning on, and in any season, Seward Park is a popular area for walking and jogging. Trails encircle and traverse the kidney-shaped peninsula. There's an amphitheater inside the park, and a salmon hatchery on the east side of the peninsula.

On the east shore of the bay itself is a small fishing dock; at the head is a large swimming beach. The large brick building, a former bathhouse, is now a Parks Department art studio offering classes for adults and kids. On the isthmus beyond the swimming beach is a playground and tennis courts; on a clear day the view of Mt. Rainier is astonishing.

This peaceful bay is transformed each year on the last week of July and first weekend of August, during Seattle's Seafair celebration. For days, thundering hydroplanes circle the racecourse nearby to the north, hoping to qualify for Sunday's race. Vessels of every size crowd the log boom that's placed around the course. Boats anchor everywhere. Screaming jets perform aerobatics on the final weekend. Stay away if you're not in a party mood.

Leschi Park ★★   (gas only)

Charts: 18447

Leschi Park is about three-quarters of a mile north of the I-90 floating bridge, on the west side of Lake Washington. The park is named for the Nisqually chief who reputedly landed here to lead the attack on Seattle during the 1856 Indian War. At the turn of the century, a ferry crossed regularly from this site to Meydenbauer Bay on the east side of Lake Washington.

Leschi is now a park and commercial area, with private and public moorage. The marina between the two restaurants sometimes has overnight guest moorage; telephone ahead—(206) 328-4456—to reserve a space. Short-term docking is provided by the two waterfront restaurants, for diners only.

When approaching from the east, Leschi can be seen directly beneath the high-rise towers of Seattle that pop up over the hill.

The fuel dock is located in the center of Leschi's commercial complex, behind a short, timber breakwater. Enter either side. The fuel dock is closed from Labor Day to Memorial Day. A grocery store is across Lakeside Avenue.

REGION 6

HOOD CANAL

The Olympic Range, from the south end of Hood Canal.
The headland is Ayres Point.

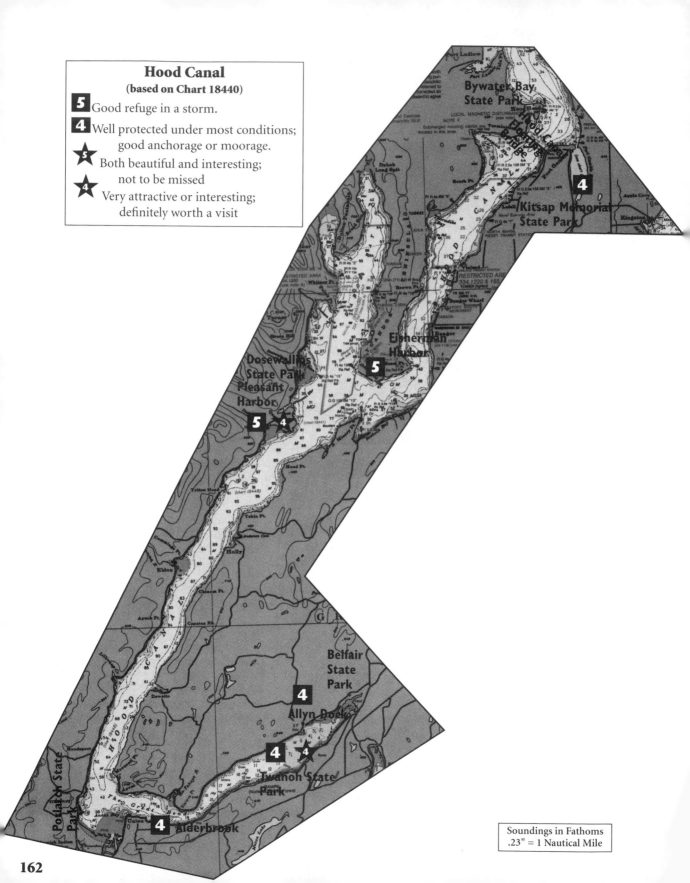

Hood Canal
(based on Chart 18440)

5 Good refuge in a storm.

4 Well protected under most conditions; good anchorage or moorage.

⭐**5** Both beautiful and interesting; not to be missed

⭐**4** Very attractive or interesting; definitely worth a visit

Soundings in Fathoms
.23" = 1 Nautical Mile

162

Hood Canal is shaped like a hairpin, and spanned at its entrance by a floating bridge. It's a canal to nowhere, ending in tideflats that almost—but not quite—connect to South Puget Sound's Case Inlet. Though relatively close to Everett, Seattle, and Tacoma, it seems far removed from these metropolitan areas. There are developed shores around the floating bridge, at the Navy base near Bangor, and in the Great Bend, but no towns of any size. Most of the canal's 50-mile length is still as it was described by Vancouver's explorers in 1792, empty and silent: ". . . only now and then interrupted by the croaking of a raven, the breathing of a seal, or the scream of an eagle."

All the peace disappears during shrimp season in May, when thousands of small boats descend upon the canal like flocks of gulls. From Dabob Bay to the Great Bend, trailers line up at the launching ramps, and boats loaded with gear crowd the harbors and marinas. It's an event those who live here describe as "crazy." The "season" begins on the third Saturday in May and lasts several days; the State Department of Fisheries opens additional seasons depending on the catch.

The dominant geographic feature in Hood Canal is the Olympic Mountain Range. These mountains have many faces: They rise craggy, crisp, and white above the forested foothills, or turn shades of lavender against the evening sky, or fade and disappear into low cloud. At times they are so close you need to crook your neck to see their jagged peaks, over 6,000 feet above you.

Visible or not, the Olympics are a powerful presence here, funneling weather from north or south, increasing the speed of wind and the height of wave. The steepness overhead continues below. Throughout most of the canal, high tide almost touches the evergreens that line the shores, and low tide reveals broad mud flats rich in clams and oysters. These mud flats typically—and quickly—drop to 60 feet and more.

Hood Canal has few protected anchorages and only a few isolated resorts or marine facilities. It's no surprise that most of the boats here are small, shallow-draft, and trailerable.

The North Arm

Charts: 18441, **18458**, **18476**, 18477

From Foulweather Bluff, Hood Canal bends southeast, then southwest to Seabeck Bay. The north end of this arm is spanned by a floating highway bridge (U.S. 101) that connects the Kitsap and Olympic peninsulas. There are many homes along the east shore, where residents are within comfortable commuting distance of the submarine base at Bangor, the Navy shipyard at Bremerton, and the torpedo station at Keyport. The west shore is less populated and more wooded.

Active Navy operations center on Bangor. North and south of it there are several bays and harbors for recreational boaters.

Coon Bay

Charts: 18441, **18477**

This shallow bay, about two miles south of Foulweather Bluff on the east shore, is surrounded by the waterfront and hillside homes of a private community. Shoals choke the narrow dredged entrance, which is protected on both sides by wide jetties. On a minus tide, the private, orange-striped entry buoys lie over on the sand, and the channel itself is dry.

All floats and tidelands in Coon Bay are private. There are no facilities for visiting boaters.

Bywater Bay State Park ★★★ No Facilities

Charts: 18441, 18476, **18477**

Bywater Bay is tucked in south of the "chin" of Hood Head. In settled weather this bay is a pleasant, undeveloped alternative to Port Ludlow. Here, homes are small and cabin-like. The tidelands from the bridge to the lagoon are public, with good clamming and crabbing along the shore. Around the lagoon is an undeveloped state park. Moss hangs from trees that grow right down to the opaque water, and herons fish the shallows. This is a place to sit still, to listen and watch in a setting that has all but disappeared from Puget Sound.

Approaches. From the north, stay east of Point Hannon. The flashing "2" mark is inland of the tip of the point; a shoal that dries at low tide extends east another 100 yards. Beyond Point Hannon, resist the impulse to round the south end of Hood Head into Bywater Bay, especially if your boat draws more than a couple of feet and the tide is out; a charted rock (shown as "Rk") lies some 400 yards south of the head, 4 feet beneath the surface at zero tide—a nasty surprise. To avoid this submerged rock, head for the west tower of the bridge until you are clearly south of Hood Head. Then head toward the west span, near shore, until Foulweather Bluff is visible across the isthmus that connects Hood Head to the mainland.

Approaching from the south, head for the dark line of the isthmus that connects Hood Head to the mainland.

Heading into Bywater Bay, note that the west shore is shoal, as is the head of the bay.

Anchorage. There is good holding ground just inside the bay, in 2 to 5 fathoms. Stay out of the cable area near the boat launch and campground. The floating bridge gives some protection from the south. Hood Head and its isthmus will protect you somewhat from a northerly fetch, but not from a northerly wind.

Getting Ashore. Landing is possible at the launching ramp at the campground near the bridge, and at a street end inside the bay on the west shore. There are no facilities within walking distance.

Tidelands are public from the bridge north, around the lagoon and east around Point Hannon.

Port Gamble ★★★ No Facilities

Charts: 18441, 18476, **18477**

Its Indian name was Teekalet—"brightness of the noonday sun"—and this wide, long bay with its green, wooded shores does seem to gather all the sky's light into itself. The sawmill at the entrance—the oldest operating in North America—was established in 1853, and the tiny New England–style community that grew around it is still managed by the Pope & Talbot timber company. Despite its quaint restored appearance, Port Gamble is a working mill town, not a tourist attraction. Visitors who arrive by land are welcome to walk the self-guided tour, to admire the 1880s heirlooms in the Historical Museum, and spend time in the

Country Store, whose upper floors contain an extraordinary display of seashells.

Visitors who arrive by water, however, have no way to reach these attractions; there is no public shore access anywhere in the bay, not even at the town itself. Perhaps this factor more than any other accounts for the absence of pleasure boats here. This may be a benefit in disguise, however, for beyond the industrial harbor entrance is something rare in Hood Canal: good holding ground and protection, a peaceful spot to swing on the hook away from the crowds.

Approaches. The church spire and the buildings of the lumber mill are visible from the north as you approach Hood Head, and from the south after rounding Salsbury Point. The *Coast Pilot* warns that the entrance is "quite constricted by shoals" requiring "careful, precise piloting"—critical advice for a tug with a log tow. Heed this advice, but note also that the entrance is well marked, deep (24 feet reported in 1981), and unobstructed.

The channel is east of the mill, bordered by two green square marks on pilings. When approaching from the west, avoid the shoals on the west side of the channel by first heading north of north mark "1." As you turn into Port Gamble, look behind to check that you're lined up with the range markers on shore; these are about a mile north of the entrance. Don't get too close to the green marks as the pilings are set in the shoal, not in the deep water of the channel. Past "3," favor the mill side of the channel to avoid the shoals north and south of Point Julia.

Anchorage. Anchorage is good anywhere in the bay. The bottom is mud and slopes gradually. Perhaps the best protection is at the south end, where the bay hooks slightly east. Modest homes surround this quiet cove, and the mill activity seems distant. If you anchor south of the mill toward the west shore, watch for deadheads and submerged pilings. These are booming grounds, and you may be awakened by a tug arriving with a tow. Here also is a curious relic, a section of the original floating Hood Canal Bridge.

Getting Ashore. Surprisingly, there is no authorized shore access to the picturesque town of Port Gamble anywhere in the bay. The county park and launching ramp outside the bay, at Salsbury Point near the Hood Canal Bridge, is a mile-and-a-half walk from the town.

The northeast shore around Little Boston is part of the Port Gamble Indian Reservation.

Squamish Harbor ★★ No Facilities

Charts: 18441, 18476, **18477**

Squamish Harbor is triangle-shaped, with a lagoon and marsh at its head. Mile-long Case Shoal fills much of its western half. The harbor offers scant protection and no more than a launching ramp for shore access. It would probably be overlooked as a boating destination but for the public "beach" of Case Shoal, where clamming is splendid at minus tides, and blue herons are numerous at almost any time.

Approaches. From the north, stay well off-shore south of the bridge to avoid several unmarked submerged rocks. Watch also for the Sisters, two rocks 200 yards apart, the south rock marked with a red "4" on pilings. If approaching from the south, don't count on the privately maintained buoys to mark Case Shoal; look for red "6" on pilings before turning into the harbor. The north end of the shoal is marked by a white daymark.

Anchorage. The best protection in Squamish Harbor is at its head, in 3 to 6 fathoms. The bottom is charted as mud and clay.

Getting Ashore. A county park is at the

THE HOOD CANAL BRIDGE

Like its cousins on Lake Washington, the Hood Canal Bridge floats on a string of hollow concrete pontoons that are joined to fixed spans at each end. The bridge lies between Termination Point and Salsbury Point, about four miles south of Foulweather Bluff. A mile-and-a-half long, it is a major highway linking the Olympic and Kitsap peninsulas.

For most pleasure boaters, this bridge isn't a deterrent to exploring Hood Canal. The major hazards are the shoals off both shores. Avoid these shoals by navigating between the pontoon and the pylon, where depths are 5 to 10 fathoms. At the west span, stay clear of the Sisters rocks south of the bridge, and another rock (shown as "Rk") west of the Sisters charted 3 feet beneath the surface at zero tide. At either span, pay attention to currents, which can be strong. These currents make for good fishing, and the platform under the east span, accessible by land, is a popular spot.

Clearance shown on the chart is 35 feet on the west span, 55 feet on the east; however, notices posted on the spans themselves give the clearance as one foot less in each case (34 feet and 54 feet). For boats that need more, arranging for the bridge to open requires a little planning. Bridgetenders are on duty weekdays from 6:30 A.M. to 5:00 P.M., but they are usually performing maintenance tasks and are not in the tower to respond to VHF radio. Openings must be arranged ahead by telephone: (206) 593-2285. This number calls the Hylebos Bridge in Tacoma; the operator there will ask if you need a 300-foot opening or a 600-foot opening, and alert the Hood Canal Bridge. After hours, and on weekends and holidays, openings must be arranged at least an hour ahead. Two bridgetenders are dispatched to the Hood Canal Bridge, and will be ready to open it at your estimated time of arrival.

Bridgetenders monitor VHF Channel 16 and work on Channel 13. When you arrive, identify yourself by radio if you like. The bridge signals when it is ready to open.

When the bridge opens for vessel traffic, one (or both, in the case of a 600-foot opening) of the pontoons retracts into the side, where the bridge bulges below the towers. The entire process, from the time highway traffic stops and resumes, can take as little as 10 minutes.

The Hood Canal Bridge began operation in 1961. In 1979 a severe February storm, with winds clocked at 100 miles per hour, forced open an inspection manhole in one of pontoons. The western half of the bridge sank, some of the portions breaking free. During the four years it took to rebuild, a ferry ran between Lofall and South Point. To ease wind and water pressure, the bridge now closes to auto traffic during stormy weather, and the center spans are opened.

The Hood Canal Bridge opens for a Navy ship bound for Bangor.

launching ramp on the north shore, about a mile west of Termination Point. This park is little more than a street end, with a picnic table, a tire-rim firepit, and a toilet. Adjacent beaches are private. A bed-and-breakfast inn is about 500 yards west on the road above the ramp.

There is no shore access on the west side of Squamish Harbor. Behind the rock-and-tim-ber spit crowded with homes that extends north of Bridgehaven is a private marina, and many private floats. The narrow entrance is marked, and about 5 feet shallower than the inlet itself. The community of Bridgehaven, a former ferry landing south of this inlet, has no public shore access.

Kitsap Memorial State Park ★★★

Charts: 18458, 18476, **18477**

The only developed state park in this portion of Hood Canal is Kitsap Memorial. This park is located north of Lofall on the east side of the canal, about two-and-a-half miles south of the floating bridge. Most of it is inland, where there are picnic tables, barbecues, play equipment, and a ball field. A log shelter and meeting hall are in a thick stand of fir.

Campground facilities are open year round.

The park has only two mooring buoys, but the bight is big enough to accommodate a few more boats at anchor.

Approaches, Anchorage, Moorings. Look for the park's concrete bulkhead and rock terrace north of Lofall (a former ferry landing) and south of the green "5" mark on pilings. Two park buoys are set toward the south end of the beach; water at the south buoy is about 10 feet deeper than at the north buoy. If you anchor, make sure you won't drag off the shelf or swing onto the beach.

Getting Ashore. Land your skiff at the rocky park beach. Expect company during shellfish seasons; this is a popular spot with local residents. A short trail connects the beach to the picnic area. The old ferry pier north of Lofall is now private, and moorage at the attached float is for community members only.

For the Crew. Showers are across the ball field in the campground restrooms.

Thorndyke Bay

Charts: 18441, 18458, 18476, **18477**

This bay on the west shore south of Squamish Harbor is not recommended. Much of it is marsh, and the area deep enough for anchoring is unprotected. An emergency explosives anchorage is in the south portion. All tidelands are private.

Approaching from the north, stay east of red "8" on pilings.

Fisherman Harbor ★★★ 5 No Facilities

Charts: 18441, **18458**, 18476

Fisherman Harbor, between Oak Head and Hazel Point, is narrow and shallow, with a tricky entrance that dries at low tide. Inside, the shores are thickly wooded, the water green with the reflection of the tall trees, and Hood Canal seems far away. This secure little harbor

167

THE TRIDENT SUBMARINE BASE

Most of Hood Canal is so relatively undeveloped that the Navy's Trident Submarine Base, located between the communities of Vinland and Bangor, comes as something of a shock. The base was constructed in the early 1970s, designed specifically for Trident-class submarines. It spreads inland over some 7,100 acres, and includes housing for Navy personnel, training simulators, refit facilities, and arsenals for nuclear weapons. Some 10,000 military and civilian employees work here, among them a full-time Fish and Wildlife Department biologist who monitors environmental health; the base is also home to about 700 deer, as well as coyotes, fox, and many other animals.

The Trident submarines that inspired all this are 560 feet long, nuclear powered, and carry in their enormous bellies a forest of nuclear missiles. Most of the time they are on patrol in the Pacific, totally submerged for 70 to 90 days. Crews are rotated when the sub comes into port, and the sub itself is completely overhauled. The facilities along the shore, with their blinking towers and sober faces, are used for many of these refit tasks.

The northmost facility is a little over a mile south of Vinland. Its most striking feature is a double wall of tall pilings, which appear on the chart as a square-shaped wharf marked with a lighted tower. This is the Magnetic Silencing Facility. Any large object made of steel carries a magnetic field almost as unique as a fingerprint. Whenever a sub is in port, it is positioned between the pilings and its magnetic signature is degaussed—neutralized or reduced—so it cannot be identified from the air.

South of the silencing facility is the Explosive Handling Wharf. Here nuclear weapons are loaded and unloaded, as well as serviced. This white square structure looks like an enormous, open-ended box, totally out of place amid the rounded contours of Hood Canal. It is marked with a 500-foot tower.

A few thousand feet south of the Explosive Handling Wharf is Delta Pier. This triangular dry dock was designed to replicate naturally occurring points of land in order to promote the salmon runs along shore, rather than inhibit them, as square piers tend to do. It is the only one of its kind in the world. Submarines are moored outside the pier, their smooth black bodies encircled by bright yellow oil containment booms.

On the inland side of the pier is the dry dock itself, built parallel to shore. When a sub is in dry dock, 65 million gallons of seawater are pumped out of the dry dock chamber; this water goes through a filtration system before it is returned to the canal. The tower on top of the Delta Pier is used for surveillance.

On the chart, broad purple lines mark the Navy Operating Area west and south of the base. This area is periodically used for submarine maneuvers, which mainly consist of diving and surfacing. Patrol boats flash their lights when this area is active. You can still use the canal by staying on the west side, along the Toandos Peninsula. Most of the time, vessels can navigate without restriction provided they stay west of the boundary marked by yellow buoys "A" and "B." The base monitors Channel 16, responds to distress calls, and conducts search and rescue in cooperation with the Coast Guard.

Like commercial vessels, submarines participate in the Vessel Traffic System and use the traffic lanes. At night, they display a distinctive flashing yellow light.

If you see a submarine anywhere in Puget Sound, don't try to get close. Think of it as a moving iceberg, mesmerizing, potentially dangerous, most of it below the surface. The conning "sail" of a Trident sub is about 200 feet aft of the bow, 300 feet forward of the stern. Less than a third of the sub, which draws 36 feet, is visible. The danger to boaters lies in its wake: an enormous, smooth-sided hole that the sea rushes to fill.

is best visited by boats that draw 4 feet or less.

Approaches. Fisherman Harbor is protected by a narrow spit that extends off the west shore. The underwater shelf outside the entrance is steep, rising from 50 to almost zero fathoms in less than 300 yards. The tidal mudflat extends 100 yards south (outside) the spit and a good 200 yards inside. Even a shallow-draft vessel should enter on a rising tide.

An L-shaped course will keep you in the deepest water. Past the spit, make a sharp turn west, staying close to the spit for most of its full length. Then turn sharply north, favoring the west shore until you reach deep water. The center of the harbor is about 20 feet deeper than the entrance.

Anchorage. Anchoring is good anywhere in the middle of Fisherman Harbor. All floats and mooring buoys are private, including the Coyle community floats on the northeast shore.

Getting Ashore. There is no public shore access in Fisherman Harbor. The tidelands just outside the entrance on the northeast side are public.

Seabeck Bay ★★★    (gas only)

Charts: 18441, **18458**, 18476

The only community in this portion of Hood Canal with water access, Seabeck is busy with sportfishing and shrimping in spring and summer. The town was once the site of a large timbermill. Now it consists of a scattering of homes, a cluster of commercial buildings near the marina, and a conference center across the road.

Approaches. From the north and east, watch for green "11A" on pilings that marks the shoals off Big Beef Harbor; "11A" is farther out into the canal than you might expect. From the south and west, stay 500 yards off Misery Point to avoid the obstructions and shoals there. Approaches are clean inside Seabeck Bay.

Anchorage, Moorings. The marina is on the east shore toward the head of the bay, minimally protected from the north by a string of large round breakwater buoys. Enter west of these buoys. Guest moorage is on the north

Seabeck Marina, from the east shore. Note the breakwater buoys at the far right beyond the sailboat.

floats of the marina. The floats do not have power. There's good anchoring in line with the marina. Don't go in too far, as the inner third of the bay dries at low tide.

Seabeck Bay is a good harbor in a southerly, but poor when wind and wave build from the north. The breakwater buoys are a reminder of this; of the original 250, fewer than 50 remain. In 1990 the entire marina was knocked out by a winter storm. There are plans for a "real" breakwater, but meanwhile any boat in the bay is vulnerable to northerlies. When these pipe up, the only protection—such as it is—is along the west shore toward Misery Point.

Getting Ashore. Use the marina guest floats. All other floats and tidelands are private.

For the Boat. Fuel (gas only) is on the float at the west end of the marina pier. The nearest diesel is across the canal in Pleasant Harbor. Minor repairs can be arranged through the marina office.

For the Crew. A fair variety of groceries and sundries is available in the country store on the road just south of the marina pier. This store also sells fast food. Small as it is, Seabeck serves as a kind of town square for this region. Locals gather around the coffee pot inside the store, check their mail at the tiny post office next door, or hang out—in good weather—at the picnic tables outside. In early evening the take-out pizza on the north side of the pier serves a steady stream of customers.

Things to Do. There is little to explore close by. The conference grounds and buildings are for guests only. Scenic Beach State Park, on the west side of Misery Point, is two miles away. In good weather and with a shallow-draft boat, the trip around the point to the park is worthwhile. This 90-acre park has campsites, picnic areas, and a bathhouse on the beach. There is also playground equipment, several volleyball nets, and horseshoe pits. The view west across the canal lives up to the park's name. A public launching ramp is north of the park beach. Campground facilities (including showers) are closed from Labor Day to Memorial Day.

Dabob Bay

Charts: 18441, **18458**, 18476

Dabob Bay is the largest inlet in Hood Canal. Broad and deep at its entrance, its north end forks around the Bolton Peninsula, terminating eventually in mud flats. At its center is the deepest water in all of Hood Canal, more than 100 fathoms. To the northwest is Mount Walker, 2,800 feet high, close and green. The entire west shore is steep, and against the backdrop of the Olympic Range seems powerful and wild.

This topography intensifies winds from the north or south. Combined with a steep underwater shelf that discourages anchoring, Dabob Bay has few cruising destinations. Another discouragement is the fact that almost all of Dabob Bay is a Navy Operating Area. The depth and emptiness of the bay are ideal for testing torpedoes and other equipment. Navy ships, submarines, and helicopters are a common sight here. The little white huts on shore flash green lights when these operations require caution, and red lights when the area is closed to navigation. Stay at least a mile away from Navy vessels unless directed otherwise.

Approaches. From the southwest, approaches are clean past Quatsap Point, and from the southeast past Tskutsko Point. Along the west shore, give a wide berth to the Dosewallips Flats, whose eastern edge is marked with a green "15" on pilings.

Pleasant Harbor ★★★★

Charts: 18441, **18458**, 18476

This perfectly named cove has ample guest moorage, a state park float, and enough room for anchoring. Not only is this the most protected harbor in Hood Canal with the most marine facilities, it is beautiful besides. Even the crowds of summer do not detract from its wooded shores and calm waters.

Approaches. From the south, Pleasant Harbor is hidden completely behind Quatsap Point. From the north and west, the entrance appears as a distinctive slot. Approaches are clean.

The entrance, though narrow and somewhat shallow, is straightforward. Depths are good on both sides of the white speed-limit buoy just outside the entrance channel. Past this buoy, stay in mid-channel, especially through the narrowest portion. The shallowest area in the channel is about 100 yards northeast of the spit that extends from the north shore. Deeper water is beyond.

Anchorage, Moorings. The state park float is on the north shore just inside the entrance. Depths are good on either side of the 100-foot float. There are no facilities here. Maximum stay is 36 hours. Fees are collected at the self-service pay station at the head of the ramp, from May 1 through September 30.

Visitor moorage is also available at Pleasant Harbor Marina, beyond the state park float and the smaller, private marina. All slips at Pleasant Harbor Marina have electricity and water. Reservations can be made by telephone—(360) 796-4611—or VHF; the marina monitors Channel 16 and 9. If you arrive after hours, moor at the fuel dock and check the list of vacant slips posted there. A self-service pay box is outside the marina office.

All other floats and mooring buoys in

Pleasant Harbor Marina, looking north toward the entrance.

Pleasant Harbor are private.

Anchoring is good almost anywhere in the harbor, in 4 to 7 fathoms.

Getting Ashore. Use the state park float or the Pleasant Harbor Marina floats. The marina charges a dinghy landing fee that gives boaters who anchor out full use of their facilities (see below). All other floats are private.

For the Boat. The marina has gas and diesel fuel. Repairs can be arranged through the marina office.

For the Crew. The marina store has a few groceries and a small deli. If you stay at the marina, you can use the covered barbecue deck and picnic area, the swimming pool and hot tub, as well as showers and laundromat. Except on holiday weekends and during shrimp season in early May, boaters at anchor (not at the state park float) may use these facilities if they pay a dinghy landing fee; check at the marina office.

There are no facilities at the state park float.

Things to Do. Major activities in Pleasant Harbor are at the marina. If you have a skiff and the tide is rising, head north about a mile to Dosewallips State Park; upriver you can pick up a tidal trail. Maps are posted on information boards throughout the park, which has more than 400 acres and over 5,000 feet of shoreline. It's a good idea to take along rubber boots, as most of the shoreline is river delta and mud flat. Watch the time or you may be stranded until the next high tide. Coming and going by water, stay away from the raft east of the river, an important resting spot for a large group of harbor seals. A fence keeps them, and their shellfish-contaminating feces, out of the river delta.

Dosewallips State Park has picnic areas, more than 150 campsites, and restrooms with showers. Distance by road from Pleasant Harbor is 2 miles.

Jackson Cove ★★

Charts: 18441, **18458**, 18476

Jackson Cove opens widely to the south, as does its neighbor, a small bight to the west. The setting is dramatic, with Mount Walker rising above and the rustic buildings of Boy Scout Camp Parsons centered on shore. Pulali Point is steep rock.

Approaches, Anchorage. Approaches are clean and depths are good. This cove is recommended only in settled weather, as it is utterly exposed to the full southern length of Hood Canal and less protected from northerlies than you'd expect. The surrounding mountains are

2,000 to 3,000 feet high, and a north wind often funnels down Walker Pass, or williwaws down the steep sides of the bay. You'll need to anchor close to the north shore in order to be protected from these unpredictable gusts.

Getting Ashore. A private, gravel launching ramp in the cove west of Wawa Point can be used for a fee.

For the Crew. At the highway near the launching ramp is a grocery and hardware store that sells fishing and shrimping gear, and everything else from socks to soda pop.

Quilcene Bay ★★★

Charts: 18441, **18458**, 18476

Quilcene Bay branches northwest off Dabob like a fat thumb. Its upper third is shallow,

filled with silt from the Big Quilcene River and other creeks. Once a logging area, the bay is now famous for its oysters. The hatchery here began with oysters imported from Japan, and is now the largest in the world. Understandably, Quilcene Bay pays more attention to its aquaculture than to the occasional visiting boater. Nevertheless, there are facilities for those who wander in this direction.

Approaches. Approaches are clean from the south and east. Watch for crab pots off Fisherman's Point, and oyster rafts north.

Moorings. Quilcene Boat Haven is about halfway up the bay on the west shore. The marina is tucked in between a rock jetty and timber breakwater that protects it from southerlies, and a shorter jetty that protects it from the north. Approaching from the south, you'll see the low white buildings and tanks of the oyster hatchery on the marina's north shore. The large orange buoy northeast of the marina is the intake siphon for the hatchery.

Depths are steady as you enter, about 8 feet shallower off the timber breakwater. The entrance itself is short and tight. A few boulders spill from the north rock jetty; take care not to swing too close.

The Quilcene Boat Haven is well named: tidy and small, with flower boxes along the pier. Two main floats—with finger floats attached—form a U that opens to the east. Officially, guest moorage is on the 100-foot float set east-west across from the fuel dock. Tie to the fuel dock for a slip assignment, or better yet call ahead—(360) 765-3131. The marina office is across the parking lot.

This marina is not as quiet as you might expect. The hatchery tanks circulate all night, and the boom trucks and other machinery are busy almost every day.

Anchorage. Holding ground is good southeast of the Boat Haven, but protection is not. If wind is from the north, your best bet is south of the breakwater, away from the swimming area. Southerly protection is best at the south end of Quilcene Bay, west of Whitney Point.

Getting Ashore. Use the marina floats. The float at the Point Whitney Shellfish Lab is for loading and unloading.

For the Boat. The Quilcene fuel dock is just inside the entrance of the Boat Haven; this 50-foot float is set north-south. Gas and diesel are available, but no other marine supplies. A gas station in town may have engine parts.

For the Crew. Showers are across the parking lot, in the restrooms surrounded by a chain-link fence. A grassy area with a picnic table is nearby. Ice, groceries, and a small laundromat are in town, a one-and-a-half mile walk north on Linger Longer Road. A family restaurant is a short walk west of town on the highway.

Things to Do. Even if you don't need anything in town, take the walk north on Linger Longer Road; you'll soon realize how it got its name. The abandoned trestle to the west was built for a mining railroad that never materialized.

The Whitney Point Shellfish Lab welcomes visitors on weekdays during working hours. A window display and interpretive center explain the development of oysters, clams, and mussels. Use the float, or beach your skiff near the gravel launching ramp. State Fisheries boats enter the lagoon behind the lab on a 10-foot tide.

As everywhere in Hood Canal, the busiest time on Quilcene Bay is shrimp season, which usually begins the third Saturday in May. A community fair and parade are held the second Saturday in September.

Coves on the East Side of Dabob Bay

Charts: 18441, **18458**, 18476

The east arm of Dabob Bay doesn't offer much in the way of anchorages. The most protected area is north of Broad Spit. All tidelands here are posted as private, and the pens and floats of a commercial oyster operation north of the spit occupy the shallows. The underwater shelf is steep; take care that your swing won't put you on the beach as the tide goes out.

On the southeast shore are two bights between Tabook Point and Zelatched Point. Anchoring depths are fair but there is no protection. At times, Navy operations restrict boating activity in this area. All tidelands are private.

The Long Reach

Charts: 18441, 18448, **18476**

South of Dabob Bay, Hood Canal heads resolutely south. This reach is 20 miles long and, for most of this distance, only about a mile wide—possibly the most spectacular run in all of Puget Sound. With the exception of a few settlements along its wooded margins, both east and west shores are undeveloped. In clear weather your gaze will be drawn westward and up toward the Olympic Range, whose peaks tower from 6,000 to almost 8,000 feet, so close you'll feel like you're cruising through a mountain pass.

Even a large vessel looks small in this setting. The pristine forests of the Olympic National Park are only six miles away. Beyond the shorn new growth of the foothills stand some of the world's largest cedars, firs, and hemlocks. From this empty reach of the canal the wilderness is palpable. You have to cruise a long distance, to northern British Columbia or Southeast Alaska, to experience scenery like this from the water.

Navigation may seem straightforward here, but a few cautions are in order. Pay attention to where you are, as there are no navigational markers in this reach. This alertness is especially important where river deltas extend into the canal; near Eldon, for example, the bottom rises from 10 fathoms to nothing in less than 50 feet. Most of the points and spits on the chart are not distinctive from the water, and you are so closed in by mountains that it may be difficult to use land forms to take bearings.

Weather is a serious consideration here as well. Pacific gales track straight up the reach from Grays Harbor through the Skokomish River flats, or down from the Strait of Juan de Fuca via Discovery Bay and Admiralty Inlet. The steep sides of the canal, both above and below water, magnify wind and wave. There's virtually no refuge anywhere; check the forecast before making this run.

Approaches. Approaches are clean past Misery Point and the Dosewallips Flats. Southeast from the Great Bend, favor Ayres Point to avoid the extensive tideflats of the Skokomish River in Annas Bay. Stay 500 yards off the beach south of Musqueti Point, whose lesser flats are easy to overlook while rounding the Great Bend.

A tour boat motors north in the long reach of Hood Canal, beneath the 6,800-foot peak of the Brothers. (Paul Dudley photo)

Triton Cove ★★ ☐3 No Facilities

Charts: 18441, **18476**

V-shaped Triton Cove, narrow and deep, provides the best southerly protection in this region of Hood Canal. It is located four miles south of Quatsap Point, behind a low headland. A tiny state park is at the bottom of the curved road on the west shore, with a short float in shallow water for loading and unloading. The float is removed in winter. North of the park is a community launching ramp, and north of that a shellfish farm that sells fresh seafood.

The park has a picnic area and toilets, but no other facilities.

Approaches. From the north, stay some 500 yards offshore until past the tideflats off Fulton Creek. From the south, you'll first see the white hoist and the private community beach on the south side of Triton Head, across the Canal from Tekiu Point. As you enter the cove from either direction, watch for the rock about 100 yards off the flagpole on the north tip of Triton Head, marked with a flagged stake; there are other charted rocks to the southwest and southeast that are unmarked, so keep a respectful distance.

Anchorage. Set your hook in deep water, 10 fathoms or more. The underwater shelf is steep, and the beach dries at low tide along the Triton Head side of the cove. Expect no protection from the north. Mooring at the state park float is limited to 30 minutes.

Getting Ashore. Use the state park float. All other tidelands are private. There are no facilities within walking distance.

Coves South of Triton Head

Charts: 18448, 18476

Between Triton Head and Hoodsport are several coves, but none of them is recommended.

Anderson Cove is a cove in name only. Entirely filled in with silt, at low tide its shallows extend into the canal itself. South, off the community of Holly, is a bight that may give slight protection. Watch for rocks, one awash, at the north end of this bight. All mooring buoys and tidelands here are private.

Frenchman's Cove to the north and Dewatto Bay to the south are, like Anderson Cove, dry at low tide. Neither provides any protection on the narrow anchoring shelf. Dewatto Bay has several small public tideland areas accessible by boat at high tide.

The public tidelands south of the entrance to Lilliwaup Bay are popular for gathering clams and oysters, but the bay itself is too shallow for anchoring. The steep underwater shelf rises abruptly at the entrance from 5 to zero fathoms. A small community is at the highway bridge, with a country store and gas station.

The small, family-style resorts on the west shore cater to RVs and trailerable boats. Mike's, north of Eldon, has a launching ramp north of its narrow pier. The buoys to the south are private. On shore are rental cabins, a laundromat, and a store that sells mostly candy and ice cream. The Rest-A-While is south of Lilliwaup, at a metal building on the pier. This resort has an RV park and a yard for small-boat storage and repair. A store and restaurant are across the street. Holiday Beach and Glen Ayr resorts to the south have similar facilities.

Approach these resorts with caution if your boat is deep-draft, as the underwater shelf rises quickly.

Hoodsport ★★★ 🖼️ 🎁 🔧 ⚓ 🛒 🍽️

Charts: 18448, **18476**

Hoodsport is oriented toward the water, with facilities for visiting boaters and tourists. A state-managed salmon hatchery operates off the creek north of the docks, and a winery is nearby. In town are cafés, a few shops, a couple of grocery stores, and gas stations. There's more activity here than you'll find anywhere south of Quilcene and Seabeck.

Approaches, Moorings. The pier, hoist, and low blue-roofed buildings of the private marina are visible from the north or south. From the north, stay well offshore until past the staked (but otherwise unmarked) shoal that extends from the creek.

Hoodsport has two marinas, the south one private, the north one operated by the Port. They are close together and may be confusing to separate from a distance.

The floats of the private marina are just north of the blue hoist. Slips are generally filled from May through September; overnight moorage can occasionally be arranged. Call ahead by phone—(360) 877-9657.

The pier north of the private marina, managed by the Port of Hoodsport, has visitor moorage for small craft (30 feet or less). The three floats are approached from the north. Depths are good on the outside float, 10 feet shallower at the ramp. Moorage is free.

Visits to Hoodsport are recommended in calm conditions only. The floats pound and heave in the chop whenever the wind kicks up. On the port dock, the pilings are severely worn, and many of the cleats are twisted, loose, or missing altogether.

For the Boat, Crew. Outboard and small-craft repairs are available south on the highway. The closest fuel dock (gas only) and marine supply store are three miles south, at Union.

Hoodsport has two small groceries and several cafés. Visitors are welcome at the salmon hatchery, a short distance north of the floats. The Hoodsport Winery is a half-mile south on the highway, open for wine-tasting from 10 A.M. to 6 P.M. every day. Hoodsport celebrates the Fourth of July with a children's parade, a street fair, a dance, and fireworks.

The Great Bend

Charts: 18448, **18476**

The south end of Hood Canal crooks to the northeast like a bent pin. Here the land softens and lowers, going flat altogether at Annas Bay and at the terminus of Lynch Cove. By canal standards this entire area is fairly shallow—less than 30 fathoms—and although the underwater shelf retains its characteristic steepness, there are more opportunities for anchoring.

After the remote feel of the long reach down, the Great Bend will seem tame. Daylight lingers here in summer. Small beach cabins crowd the shoreline, and the many private docks, marinas, and beach clubs give this entire area the appearance of a lake resort. Having come so far by water, you'll find you've circled back; Bremerton and Tacoma are close by land, and less than two miles of low isthmus separates Lynch Cove from South Sound's Case Inlet.

Approaches. Give the tideflats south of Musqueti Point a wide berth. Favor Ayres Point to avoid the extensive tideflats of the Skokomish River in Annas Bay.

Potlatch State Park ★★★

Charts: 18448, **18476**

Potlatch State Park occupies a bump of land at the "elbow" of the Great Bend, on the west shore of Annas Bay. Immediately to the north is the standpipe for Tacoma City Light's hydro-electric generating plant; powerlines run from here to the Narrows. The dominant sounds are the rush of water and the whoosh of highway traffic. The Skokomish Indians, whose reservation lands are to the south, once used the area for their elaborate potlatches. It's easy to see why; the unbroken vistas north, south, and east have the power to make almost anyone feel wealthy and expansive. Campground facilities (including showers) are closed November through February.

Approaches. The most prominent landmark is the standpipe, which appears as a silver tank with flumes above the steep west shore. From the north, stay well offshore until 500 yards or so past the standpipe in order to avoid the shoal between it and the park. Approaching from the east, favor Ayres Point to avoid the unmarked tideflats of the Skokomish River, then head south of the standpipe to avoid the shoal between it and the park. Guard against drifting south into the tideflats.

The beach of Potlatch State Park surrounds a low grassy area that is bounded on the north by a stand of evergreens. North of the ever-greens is a private RV park.

Anchorage, Moorings. Five park mooring buoys are set off the beach at the edge of the underwater shelf. The deepest water is at the middle buoy; the two buoys south are in slightly deeper water than the two buoys farther north, but have less swinging room. Watch the tides.

The anchoring shelf is somewhat broader to the north than to the south, but take care not to foul the private buoys. The pier and float north of the park are posted NO TRESPASSING.

There is no protection here from the north or south.

Getting Ashore. Land your skiff on the park beach. All surrounding floats are private.

For the Crew. Showers are in the campground restrooms across the highway. There are picnic tables, shelters, barbecues and firepits near the beach, as well as playground equipment. The RV park across the highway has a laundromat and sells ice and beverages.

About a half-mile to the north at the hydro-electric plant is the Hood Canal Recreational Park, where there is a launching ramp, picnic tables, and a display of old generator parts. The beach here is rocky.

Union ★★  (gas only)

Charts: 18448, **18476**

Union sits east of Annas Bay, on the edge of the Skokomish River tideflats. This town—little more than a few commercial buildings and a small-craft marina—boomed briefly in the early 1800s, in the proud expectation of a railroad terminus that never materialized. Today Union is important to boaters as a gas and grocery stop.

Approaches. Stay north until abeam of the marina to avoid the unmarked tideflats that spread north and west.

177

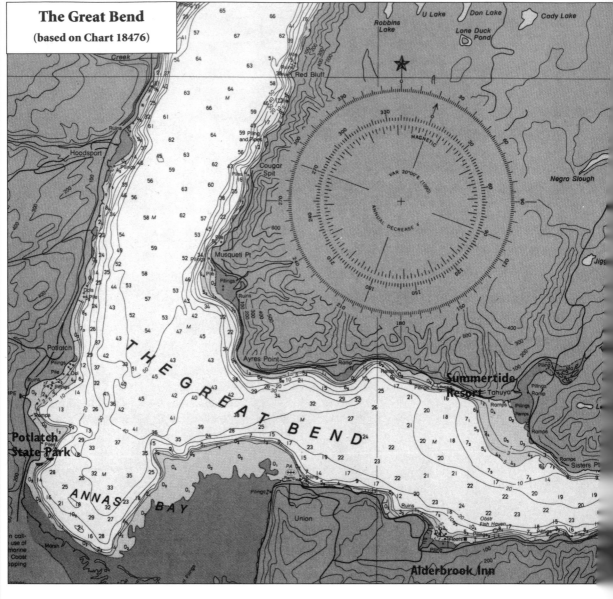

The Great Bend
(based on Chart 18476)

Anchorage, Moorings. The slips of the Hood Canal Marina are attached to an L-shaped float that points east. This float appears to have been T-shaped at one time, as pilings extend in a line to the west. The gas dock is at the bend in the "L." Some moorage is available for visitors, especially in winter when residents pull their boats into dry storage. May through September it's a good idea to call ahead—(360) 898-2252.

Anchorage is possible to the east, in line with the marina's outer float. Watch for private buoys.

The floats of the former marina to the east have been removed; only the pilings remain.

Getting Ashore. A public launching ramp is on the west side of the Hood Canal Marina.

For the Boat. The gas dock is on the marina's outside float. Depths are good, but the dock itself is short, only about 15 feet. The gas dock is closed Sundays and Mondays. The nearest diesel fuel is in Pleasant Harbor, some 20 miles north. Repairs and a few supplies are available at the marina office, the

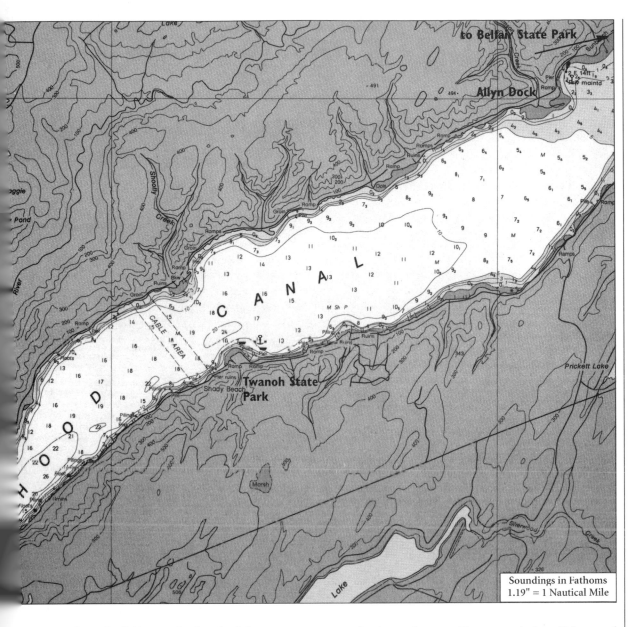

Soundings in Fathoms
1.19" = 1 Nautical Mile

large building at the head of the ramp.

For the Crew. The Union Country Store across the street has a surprising variety of dry goods, fresh produce, and homemade hot dishes and desserts. A café is on the water side of the road, just east of the marina.

Alderbrook ★★★

Charts: 18448, **18476**

A mile east of Union, across the canal from Tahuya, is a small bight that is probably the best anchorage in this entire area. V-shaped, it has a sloping bottom and gives fair protection

179

from north and south. Though tucked inside the Great Bend, you remain in view of the Olympic Range.

The stream that empties into this V-shaped cove powered one of the first hydroelectric plants on Hood Canal. The wooden water-wheel, built in 1923 by a local resident and maintained by his son, still turns tirelessly spring through fall, though it now generates nothing but admiring smiles.

The chief attractions here for boaters are the facilities and ample guest moorage of the Alderbrook Inn Resort and Conference Center.

Approaches. The Alderbrook Inn, with its glassed-in pool and spa, is prominent from the water. Approaches are clean. Watch for private buoys and crab pots.

Anchorage, Moorings. Guest moorage is on either side of the inn's long outside float; the east end of this float is about 10 feet deeper than the west. Watch for the unlit piling located north of the center of this float, in front of the hut. A swimming area is cordoned off inside the west arm of the "T."

Anchoring is good in 3 to 5 fathoms. Don't go too far into the bight, as much of it dries at low tide. The same distance out as the long resort float is about right.

Getting Ashore. The resort floats are officially for paying guests only, and for patrons of the restaurant. All other floats and tidelands are private.

For the Boat. The nearest gas dock is about a mile west at Union; the nearest diesel fuel is more than 20 miles north in Pleasant Harbor.

For the Crew. The Alderbrook Inn has a swimming pool and spa with showers. Use of these is included when you pay for power and water. A playground and volleyball court are near the guest cottages, just west of the resort's main building. Fishing equipment, crab pots, and a variety of small boats can be rented from the hut on the dock. If you want to play golf or tennis, you'll have to go more than a mile uphill.

The resort has a restaurant; others are on the road toward Union. The nearest laundromat is a half-mile west past the post office, in the Robin Hood R.V. Trailer Park. A liquor store here sells ice. The nearest groceries are at the Country Store in Union, about a mile-and-a-half west on the road.

Tahuya ★★

Charts: 18448, **18476**

A small community is at the mouth of the Tahuya River on the north side of the Great Bend. The inlet dries, and the tideflats outside are fairly broad. A pier extends from a private community park. About a half-mile to the west, at a cluster of aquamarine buildings, is the Summertide Resort. This resort rents rooms and RV space, and has mooring floats for small craft. The entire operation is a kind of throwback to the family resorts that existed all over Puget Sound in the 1950s: linoleum floors, naugahyde furniture, unmatched bathroom towels. There are showers and a laundromat up the ramp, and an office store that sells bait, ice, and snacks.

As you approach, watch for the shoal off Tahuya. Depths are OK on the outside float. Protection is good from the north, but you're exposed to southerlies from the Skokomish River delta. All ramps, floats, and tidelands in this area are private.

Twanoh State Park ★★★★

Charts: 18448, **18476**

An interpretive display at this park describes the Twana Indians as a group that "produced wealth beyond their needs." Some of that wealth seems to have been left behind in this exquisite park. There's more to enjoy than you'd expect on and around this squared-off knuckle of land. Twanoh State Park—with its swimming beach, its trails, and its rustic Civilian Conservation Corp (CCC) structures—is the prize at the end of Hood Canal.

This park is closed from Labor Day to Memorial Day.

Approaches. From any direction, the most prominent feature of this park is the detached pump-out float off the northwest shore, supported by stout dolphin pilings. A two-lane launching ramp and parking lot is on the west side of the point; a stone bulkhead that continues around to the sandy beach is on the east side. Mooring buoys and the park float are off this beach.

Anchorage, Moorings. Seven mooring buoys are set in two rows on the east side of the point. The outer (northern) three are approximately 5 feet deeper than their counterparts closer to shore. The nearby swimming area is enclosed with a string of small orange floats. The anchorage is north and east of the mooring buoys, in 5 to 10 fathoms. The shelf is relatively narrow, so set your hook carefully or, better yet, anchor in deeper water.

The 60-foot park float is for shallow-draft

Ingenious stonework characterizes the shelters at Twanoh State Park.

vessels only; a sign at the head of the ramp warns that boats may go aground at low tide. Depth at the ramp is about 4 feet shallower than at the end of the float. There is currently no charge for the park float or buoys.

Getting Ashore. The park beach is sloping gravel. Private tidelands are marked at the park boundaries.

The long dock and float about a half-mile to the east is a private beach club.

For the Boat, Crew. Water is available at the head of the park float. Ice can be bought at the snack concession near the swimming area during summer. Showers are in the campground across the road.

Things to Do. On the beach side of the road are picnic areas and barbecues, tennis courts, and playground equipment. The beach itself is described as one of the finest saltwater swimming areas in the state, with a wading lagoon for children. Interpretive signs describe the geologic history of the canal, the Twana Indians who once roamed this area, and the CCC work in the 1930s and 40s. Many of the log-and-stone structures, with their peek-a-boo views of stream and beach through small mullioned windows, seem to have been constructed especially to spark fairy-tale imaginations.

On the south side of the road are another 150 acres of park and more, with campgrounds among the cedars and two loop trails up the wooded ridge.

Port of Allyn Dock ★★

Charts: 18448, **18476**

The Port of Allyn maintains a public launching ramp and float on the north side of the Great Bend, in a small bight east of Simpson Creek. Guest moorage is usually available for small craft. Pay at the fee box; day-use is free. The floats have power, but no water.

The town of Allyn is on Case Inlet, some seven miles away by land.

Approaches, Anchorage, Moorings. From the west, wait until you're 300 yards past the spit that extends from the west shore before turning toward the pier. To stay in deepest water, approach the pier head-on. The floats are arranged in a U-shape, open to the south. Deep-draft vessels should anchor to the southeast, in 2 to 5 fathoms. You'll be reasonably protected from north and south winds.

Getting Ashore. All tidelands except the launching ramp southwest of the float are private. The facilities of Belfair State Park, including the deli grocery at the entrance, are about a mile northeast. Midway between the park and the Allyn dock is a family restaurant.

Belfair State Park

Charts: 18448, **18476**

This park is popular, especially with RV campers, but is difficult if not impossible to reach by water. Lynch Cove dries totally at low tide, and the beach at Belfair State Park is often tideflat for almost half-a-mile. Even a speedboat is left aground on a 5-foot tide.

There are many facilities here: showers, picnic tables, barbecues, playground equipment, horseshoes, and a deli grocery at the entrance. The best way for a boater to reach them is via the Allyn Dock a mile to the southwest. With lovely Twanoh so accessible by water, even this may not be worth the effort.

Belfair State Park's clam and oyster beds have been contaminated by septic systems, and are now closed permanently to shellfish gathering.

Campground facilities are open all year.

REGION 7

ADMIRALTY INLET

A schooner sails across Port Townsend bay, reaching toward Point Wilson and the bluffs of Whidbey Island.

FROM PORT LUDLOW TO PORT TOWNSEND

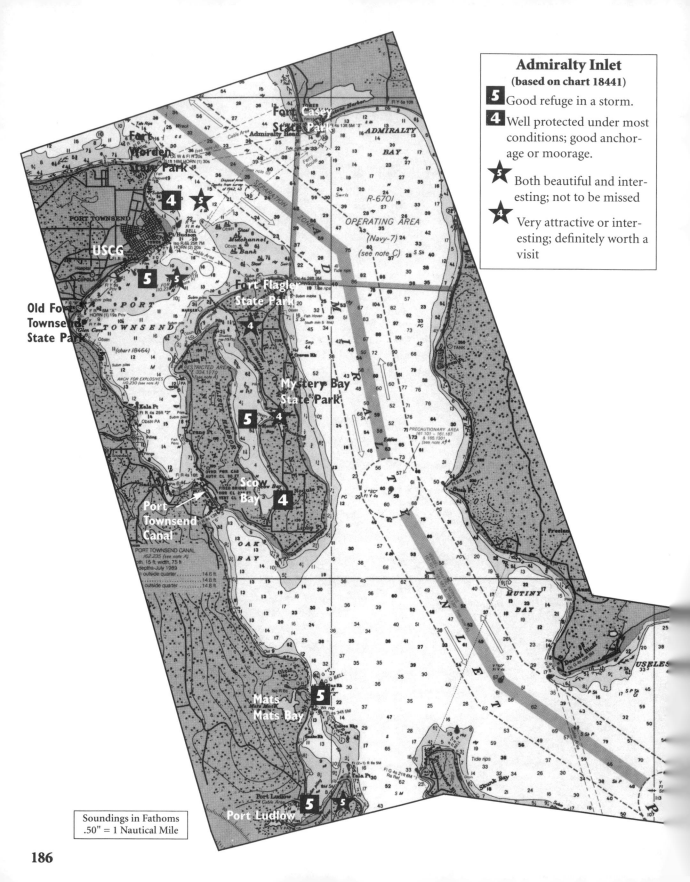

Admiralty Inlet connects central Puget Sound with the Strait of Juan de Fuca. It is bounded on the south by Point No Point and the tip of Whidbey Island, and on the north by Point Wilson and Admiralty Head. Shipping traffic is heavy through these waters, not only to and from the port cities of Tacoma, Seattle, and Everett, but to and from the Navy ports in Bremerton and Hood Canal.

For pleasure boaters, Admiralty Inlet is both a highway and a destination, with several fine anchorages. Sailing is good and fishing often excellent—it's not unusual to see small boats clustered thickly around Point No Point, Possession Point, and the north end of Marrowstone Island, or sailboats taking advantage of afternoon westerlies and a favorable current. This is a relatively dry area. Port Townsend averages only 18 inches of rain per year (half the Seattle average), making these waters popular year-round.

If there is a drawback to Admiralty Inlet, it is the fog. In late summer and early fall, when cold ocean air off the Strait meets the warm land around Puget Sound, a thick bank may persist all day. It can be rough here as well, from the north and south. Foulweather Bluff is well-named.

In clear weather, the mountain views from Admiralty Inlet are among the most spectacular anywhere in Puget Sound: Mount Baker to Mount Rainier, the Cascade range to the east, the Olympics and their foothills layered lavender and blue to the west.

Point No Point and Hansville

Charts: 18441, 18473, **18477**

Between Point No Point and Foulweather Bluff are two seasonal resorts for sport fishing. The resort west of Point No Point has boat rentals, bait tanks, and fishing gear; the laundromat is for guests using the cabins or RV park. The boat rental at the small community of Hansville sells bait and a few supplies. A small grocery is across the street. There are no facilities for visiting boats at either resort, and anchoring in this exposed area is not recommended.

Port Ludlow ★★★★★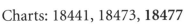

Charts: 18441, 18473, **18477**

In almost every way, Port Ludlow is one of the best anchorages in Puget Sound. It's only about 24 miles from the large marinas of Seattle and Everett, even closer to Edmonds or Kingston—a perfect cruising destination or stop en route. The harbor is deep, with a mud bottom and an easy entrance, big enough to accommodate many boats, small enough to protect from any weather that may roar off nearby Foulweather Bluff.

Although some boaters speak nostalgically of the days when Port Ludlow was pristine and undeveloped, in fact this harbor has been a busy one for more than 100 years. During the mid- to late-1800s it was a major lumber port, filled with timber schooners and log booms,

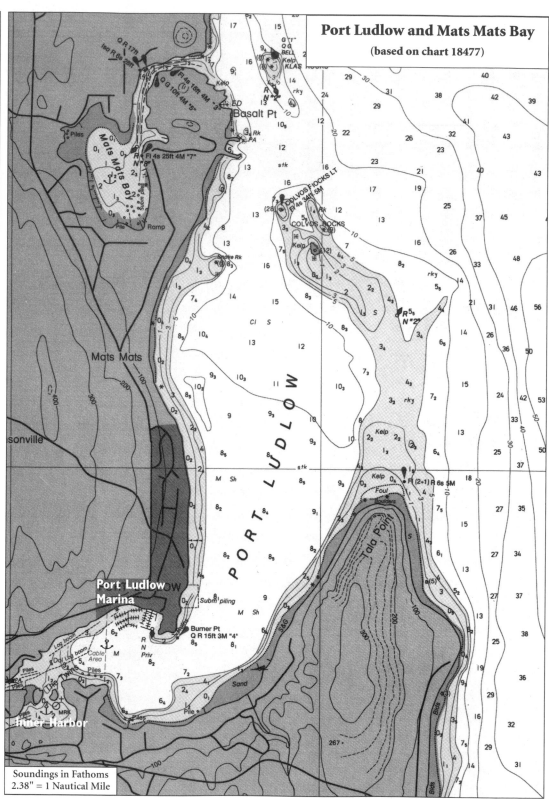

Port Ludlow and Mats Mats Bay
(based on chart 18477)

Soundings in Fathoms
2.38" = 1 Nautical Mile

the air thick with the smoke and smell of the Pope and Talbot sawmill. This industry survived, through boom and bust, until World War II, when the mill was permanently shut down and dismantled. In the 1960s, Pope and Talbot—speculating on a different market—built a resort community at the old town site on the northeast shore, with a marina, golf course, swimming pool, and tennis courts. Today, condominiums spread north, and a hotel stands on the point at the harbor entrance. A large residential development faces the resort from the south. Two Seattle-area yacht clubs maintain marinas on the south shore, and more will probably follow. The once silent and wooded inner harbor, behind The Twins islands, is now surrounded by private homes.

Approaches. From the south or east, the major hazards are off Tala Point. Note that the triangular red-and-green mark on pilings is inside the kelp and shoals. Stay well north of this mark; it's a good idea to favor red nun "2," though this may seem to take you out of your way. Every year the shoal off Tala Point snags the inattentive or impatient, especially during fog.

From the north, pick your course around Klas and Colvos rocks—these are well-marked. If you choose to pass between Colvos and the west shore, watch for unmarked Snake Rock, which covers at 6 feet, and another rock awash south of it. Both of these are charted.

The north point of the harbor entrance itself is well marked. Watch for slow-moving traffic coming around this point from the fuel dock and marina.

Anchorage, Moorings. Port Ludlow Marina is immediately inside the north point of the harbor entrance. Though it has 100 overnight slips, demand often exceeds supply. It's best to make reservations: telephone (360) 437-0513. The marina is often booked a year in advance for three-day weekends.

A raft of boats at anchor in Port Ludlow's inner harbor. The entrance is between The Twins islands.

If you arrive without a reservation, tie to the fuel dock and check in there or at the marina office for a slip assignment. After hours, pull into an open spot on "A" float, the long outside float south of the fuel dock; use the pay envelopes outside the office or on the fuel dock. If "A" float is full, you'll have to anchor. All slips have electricity and water.

All other docks and floats in Port Ludlow are private.

Anchorage anywhere inside Port Ludlow is good. Entrance to the inner harbor is between The Twins islands; a white can marks a shoal off the west island. If your draft is deep, you'll be more comfortable entering and leaving this area on a rising tide. During winter cold snaps, this inner harbor often sheets over with ice.

Getting Ashore. The only public shore access in Port Ludlow is at the marina.

For the Boat. The fuel dock is on the east side of the marina, with tie-ups on either side. At low tide, favor the marina floats when approaching the fuel dock. The marina office has a small store with supplies. There are no repair facilities, but the office will call in a mechanic for you.

For the Crew. A few groceries are sold in the marina store. A larger store is about a mile west on the highway. Laundry and showers are on the east side of the building, off the breezeway. The restaurant is across the pond in the main building, with a small pub downstairs.

If you stay at the marina you also have access to the tennis courts and the 18-hole golf course; a van service is provided to these facilities. Runabouts and small sailboats may be rented at the fuel dock.

Mats Mats Bay ★★★ No Facilities

Charts: 18441, 18473, **18477**

This nearly landlocked bay is an excellent anchorage. The shoreline is low and mostly wooded, without the dense development of nearby Port Ludlow. Although a commercial rock quarry operates at the inlet on the northeast side of the bay, it is hidden from view, and Mats Mats seems almost pastoral.

Approaches. Klas Rocks lie about 500 feet east of the entrance to Mats Mats Bay. If you're approaching from the southwest, the rock jetty and timber structures of the quarry, with its private harbor and large cylindrical buoys, are prominent off Basalt Point.

The entrance itself is well marked, but narrow and shallow. At the mouth of the entrance, there are reefs off the north shore, and considerable kelp off the south shore. Boaters with deep-draft vessels should choose a rising tide when entering.

Enter mid-channel. Just beyond green "3" is a navigational range. The range piling is set in shallow water at the turn in the channel,

northeast of a large squarish rock. After you make the turn at green "5," favor the east shore, setting a straight course past red nun buoy "6" and on between lighted green "7" and red nun "8." Expect depths to decrease through this last leg of the channel; between red "6" and red "8," the channel is from 2 to 5 feet shallower than at the entrance. South of "8," depths are about the same as at the entrance.

Anchorage. The anchoring basin is in the south half of the bay, in about 2 fathoms. Much of this area is taken by boats on private buoys, however, so anchor with care, especially during periods of minus tides. The northern half of Mats Mats Bay is charted at a fathom or less.

Getting Ashore. A public launching ramp and float is at the southeast end of the bay. Ashore there is a small, grassy area with parking and a portable toilet. There are no facilities within walking distance. All other docks and tidelands are private.

The public float and launching ramp in Mats Mats bay.

Oak Bay ★★ 2 No Facilities

Charts: 18441, **18464**, 18473, 18477

Oak Bay, located just south of the Port Townsend Canal, is more of a shortcut than an anchorage, an area pretty much ignored by cruisers taking the shortest route between Port Townsend and the rest of Admiralty Inlet. The bay is deep, but currents are strong and the shoreline extremely shoal. The parks on each side of the canal are best approached by land, or by small, beachable craft. Lower Oak Bay County Park on the west has a launching ramp and rustic campsites around the lagoon; South Indian Island County Park on the east has picnic sites only. Both have salt marshes and smooth beaches that are excellent for clam digging and crabbing.

Approaches, Anchorage. From the south, head for the canal entrance. If your destination is South Indian Island Park, turn toward the park about a mile northwest of the Kinney Point buoy, where the bottom slopes more gradually. Even here you'll need to anchor well offshore to stay out of the tideflats. If your destination is Lower Oak Bay Park, head southwest of the canal entrance. The launching ramp is at the end of a rock jetty.

Deep-draft vessels approaching from the Port Townsend Canal should resist the temptation to hug either shore; stay in mid-channel.

Port Townsend Bay

Charts: 18441, **18464**, 18471

This large bay at the northwestern end of Admiralty Inlet deserves its many superlatives. The *Coast Pilot* describes it as "excellent" and easily entered. Local sailors enjoy its steady afternoon winds, and cruisers from all over Puget Sound appreciate its state parks and marinas. Together with Kilisut Harbor between Indian and Marrowstone islands, this entire area offers over a week's worth of cruising and exploration, and a lifetime of return visits.

Approaches. There are two entrances to Port Townsend bay, the man-made canal at its south end, and the wide mouth at the north.

The Port Townsend Canal, once a tidal portage between Indian Island and the mainland, was dredged for shipping in the early 1900s. Note that ebb and flood do not occur here at the same time as in Admiralty Inlet. Approaching from the south, the entrance is well-marked, but the colors may be confusing at first—the green "7" to the east is kept to starboard, the red "6" on pilings is kept to port. The controlling depth inside the channel is 14 feet 6 inches, with the shallowest area reported about 200 yards south of the bridge. The fixed bridge has a vertical clearance of 58 feet; pay attention to tides if your boat has a tall mast. At the northern end of the channel, continue several hundred yards past red "4," as shoals extend beyond it from both shores. You're free of the channel about 100 yards north of the timber cribbing on the east shore.

The northern approach to Port Townsend bay is wide and deep, but there are several factors to watch for. From the Strait of Juan de Fuca, the lighthouse on Point Wilson appears well east of the bluffs. In fog or haze, it will seem to float offshore. Look for red nun buoy "6" a half-mile northwest of the point; this marks a shoal and tide rips. Look around for ships in the shipping lanes—these lanes pass close to Point Wilson—and stay out of their way. Don't be surprised if some of this traffic turns toward Port Townsend, as military vessels frequent the Indian Island ammunition depot, off-loading before entering Puget Sound, reversing the process when leaving. Be prepared also for strong currents; on the ebb, all of Puget Sound empties against you, and an underwater ridge here creates extra turbulence.

Boaters approaching from the south should also heed shipping traffic and current. North of Marrowstone Point, Midchannel Bank is expansive and shoal. The water here dances, and on the ebb in a strong westerly wind it can be quite rough. Sportfishing is popular here, and the entire area is often crowded with boats of all sizes.

A prominent feature of Port Townsend bay, visible well out into Admiralty Inlet, is the whitish smoke from the pulp mill in Glen Cove on the west side of the bay. The direction of this smoke is a handy indicator of strong westerlies on the Strait.

Port Hadlock ★★★

Charts: 18441, **18464**, 18471

Port Hadlock is at the south end of Port Townsend bay, just inside the canal. What was once a busy timber town is now a cluster of white buildings and weathered pilings on the west shore. The main community is up the hill, oriented toward the highway. At the water's edge, Port Hadlock is sleepy and surprisingly undeveloped.

Southeast of Skunk Island are the large concrete structures of a plant built in the early

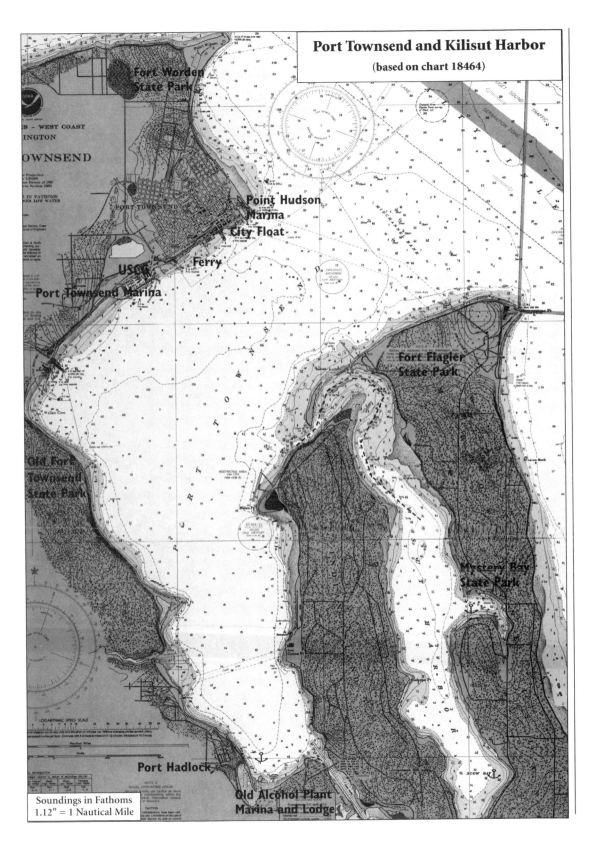

Port Townsend and Kilisut Harbor

(based on chart 18464)

Fort Worden
State Park

Point Hudson
Marina
City Float

Ferry

USCG
Port Townsend Marina

Old Fort
Townsend
State Park

Fort Flagler
State Park

Mystery Bay
State Park

Port Hadlock

Old Alcohol Plant
Marina and Lodge

Soundings in Fathoms
1.12" = 1 Nautical Mile

At anchor northeast of Skunk Island, near Port Hadlock. The Old Alcohol Plant marina is to the left (east) of the lodge.

1900s to convert sawdust to fuel alcohol—a venture that never got beyond its experimental batches. The plant now houses a restaurant and lodge with a small marina.

Approaches. The old alcohol plant, remodeled with white stucco and red tile roofs, is visible from the north end of the bay. Approaches are clean. From the south, take care to clear the Port Townsend Canal (at least 200 yards north of red "4") before heading toward Port Hadlock.

Anchorage, Moorings. The town of Port Hadlock maintains a small float and a launching ramp at the street-end south of the waterfront buildings. Mooring is free and depths are good. The *Coast Pilot* warns of submerged pilings in the vicinity of this float; the wreck south of it is obvious.

The Old Alcohol Plant Lodge and Marina has guest moorage inside its timber breakwater. Enter from either end, staying on the out-side float if your draft is deep. Pull into an empty slip and follow the signs to the harbormaster's office. It's OK to tie to the north side of the concrete float.

Anchorage is good anywhere in the crook of the bay, but stay north of Skunk Island; the surrounding area and the lagoon created by a low sandspit dries at low tide. The Port Hadlock Yacht Club mooring buoys, set between the Old Alcohol Plant and the launching ramp, can be used for a fee. All other mooring buoys are private.

Port Hadlock is not as calm as it seems. Generally, you are protected from prevailing westerly winds, but when these turn to northerlies you are exposed to the full reach of Port Townsend bay. An extreme case occurred in 1990, when a severe winter storm destroyed the marina, and many boats were lost. Even in quiet weather you'll feel the wake of boats hurrying through the Port Townsend Canal.

Getting Ashore. Use the Port Hadlock float, or

the Old Alcohol Plant marina if you're visiting the restaurant and lodge. All other tidelands are private.

For the Boat. The nearest fuel dock and repair facilities are in Port Townsend. There is a gas station about a half-mile up the hill.

For the Crew. One of the best restaurants in the area is right on the waterfront. The town of Port Hadlock is about a half-mile up the hill. There you'll find a good-sized grocery store, a laundromat, cafés, a bak-ery, and several antique stores.

The Old Alcohol Plant Lodge and Marina has a large restaurant that's also a local favorite. If you pay to moor, you may use the lodge showers, laundry, and exercise room. The structure of these buildings alone is worth a visit; the massive walls are original, reinforced with twisted bars that were forged in nearby Irondale.

Port Hadlock holds an annual celebration that includes a parade and clam-feed on the second weekend of June.

Kala Point

Charts: 18441, **18464**

Kala Point, on the west shore of Port Townsend bay, is a privately developed community. The dock and buoys north of the point and the sur-rounding recreation area are for members and their guests only.

Old Fort Townsend State Park ★★★

Charts: 18441, **18464**, 18471

The wooded bluffs of Old Fort Townsend State Park rise from the beach south of Glen Cove, about halfway between the Pulp Mill and Kala Point. The park is the site of a fort built in the mid-1800s to soothe the anxieties of white set-tlers after the Indian Wars. None of the original buildings remain. An information board near the old parade ground displays photographs of the fort as it once was, and signs along one of the park's many trails invite you to imagine a military rigor that now seems incongruous amid the cedar, madrona, and salal.

The park is closed from late September to mid-April.

Approaches. Old Fort Townsend is somewhat difficult to locate, as there are no distinctive state park signs on the beach. Look for an undeveloped wooded hillside and a steep sand bluff about a mile north of Kala Point. Near the park's northern boundary are a rock bulkhead and a row of pilings extending into the water. These pilings once supported the fort pier.

Anchorage, Moorings. Four mooring buoys parallel the beach south of the pilings. The south buoy is almost 10 feet deeper than its opposite near the pilings. Anchorage is south or east, as the shelf between the buoys and the beach is narrow and shallow, and the area north of the pilings dries at low tide.

This anchorage is exposed to weather from all directions and to freighter wakes from Admiralty Inlet.

Getting Ashore. The public beach extends only about a half-mile south of the pilings. All adjacent tidelands are private.

For the Crew. The broad trail that begins at the stone bulkhead takes you up to the old fort's parade ground. Nearby are horseshoes, play equipment, and picnic tables. There is a pay phone beyond the information board. Rest-rooms with showers are in the campgrounds.

Port Townsend ★★★★★ [2] (anchorage) [5] (marina) **All Facilities**

Charts: 18441, **18464**, 18471

Port Townsend opens its arms to visiting boaters, with a marina at each end of its waterfront. Brick downtown buildings and a ferry landing are in between, embellished Victorian homes set primly above. The town itself is relatively small—only about 7,000 in population—with a "big city" look from the 19th century that's human-scaled and inviting.

During the age of sail, Port Townsend was a major West Coast shipping port, on its way to becoming the commercial hub of Puget Sound—another San Francisco. Speculative booms in the 1800s were fueled by rumors of a railroad terminus; during this period many stately buildings and homes were constructed. The railroad never came, steam replaced sail—making the runs to Seattle and Tacoma profitable for shipping—and Port Townsend was left behind.

Today, some of the prosperity that eluded Port Townsend is brought in by tourists, many of them boaters. They fill the restaurants, shops, and galleries, and the quaint bed-and-breakfast inns. The waterfront is the city's major attraction, and its Wooden Boat Festival in early September is renowned throughout the West Coast. Seeing the town rise jewel-like from the bay, walking the lively streets, you may feel some of the hope its founders felt, believe a little of their inflated promise. Certainly you will be glad, not disappointed as they were, that Port Townsend remained small and lovely.

Port Townsend is served by a highway from the south and a ferry that makes several runs a day from the west side of Whidbey Island.

Approaches. Once inside the bay, the approach to Port Townsend is clean. Precise headings depend on whether you're going to moor or anchor, as described below.

Moorings. There are two harbors for visiting boaters: the marina operated by the Port of Port Townsend—usually referred to as Port Townsend marina—at the southwest end of town, and Point Hudson Marina at the northeast end of the waterfront.

The Port Townsend marina consists of two basins separated by a jetty and surrounded by an L-shaped stone breakwater that opens to the east. All the slips in this large marina are permanently assigned; in the tenant's absence these are rented to visiting boats. Approaching, head west of the ferry dock and the clock tower on the high bluff. The marina entrance is at the eastern end of the breakwater, with a reported controlling depth of 10 to 12 feet inside. Slightly favor the marina side of the channel to avoid a ledge of rock near the jetty. As you enter, the commercial basin will be to starboard; immediately in front of you is the Coast Guard station on the jetty. Motor past the commercial basin and the jetty, then make a turn to starboard for the fuel dock. Tie to the fuel dock and report to the marina office for a slip assignment. After hours, report to the pay station on the east side of the harbormaster's office, where you can choose from a list of available slips (this list is updated daily). Do not pull into an empty slip before checking with the office or pay station. No overnight mooring is permitted at the fuel dock. The Port Townsend marina does not take reservations.

Point Hudson Marina is a large rectangular basin leased by the port to a private company. Although more expensive than the Port Townsend marina, it is close to town and all its attractions, and is popular with visiting boaters. Approaching from any direction, the fuel tanks west of the entrance are prominent, as is the tall square tower with its pitched roof. The entrance itself is marked but narrow, inside a timber breakwater that takes a turn to starboard. At low tide, the entrance passage will feel especially tight. A long guest float for boats over 40 feet is on the west side of the basin. There are other slips to the north, and fingers for smaller vessels to the east. Pull into

The west float in Point Hudson Marina.

any empty slip except one with an "Occupied" sign; these slips have been paid for by boaters who are out sailing or fishing and who plan to return for the night. Report to the office on the east shore, at the south end of the complex of white clapboard buildings, which once housed the Coast Guard and quarantine station. After-hours, use the pay envelopes and fee box on the office door. Point Hudson Marina does not take reservations. Berthing fees are halved for guests staying at the nearby motel or RV park.

A 50-foot city float lies between the Port Townsend and Point Hudson marinas, just east of the old ferry dock. Officially, this float is for loading and unloading only. At the northern end of the float, near shore, the water shallows dramatically, and piling stubs lie beneath the surface. A sign at the southern end of the pier warns against using the float when winds exceed 35 knots.

Anchorage. Anchoring in front of Port Townsend is popular in the summer, but can be tricky. In order to be close to town, many

boaters drop their hooks between the piers east of the ferry dock. These areas are shallow, however, and the bottom is rock and clay. Many report dragging through kelp, and on almost any holiday weekend a carelessly anchored boat will drift out into the bay or be left aground by an outgoing tide. Anchor in deeper water, 5 fathoms or more, south of the pilings and piers, and off the ferry route. You'll be exposed, but with adequate scope you'll be more securely hooked.

Getting Ashore. Many of the street-ends in front of the town are public. A marine park with a sandy beach is east of the city float. If you need to secure your skiff, your best bet is the city float.

For the Boat. Fuel is sold at the Port Townsend marina only. Extensive haulout and repair facilities are near both marinas, as are hardware and supply stores. Since the 1970s, Port Townsend has been a Mecca for wooden boats; shipwrights take pride in their craft, as do sailmakers, riggers, and others who have been attracted to the area by their shared love of boats. Their skills, and the fact that Port Townsend is only half as rainy as Seattle, draw boats in for repair from all over Puget Sound.

For the Crew. Both marinas have restrooms, showers, and laundromats. Point Hudson has a small grocery in its marina office. In town are restaurants of almost every description, and a number of delis. A small, old-fashioned grocery is downtown. The closest supermarket is about a half-mile west of the Port Townsend marina, on Sims Way—a good mile-and-a-half from Point Hudson.

Bicycles may be borrowed during summer from the stand at the Port Townsend marina; other bicycle stands are located around town; one is just two blocks west of Point Hudson. This service is currently in transition from "free wheels" to a nominal fee. Port Townsend also has bus service.

Things to Do. Port Townsend seems laid out specially for visiting boaters. Everything is within the square mile between the two marinas: shops, restaurants, a waterfront park, a restored movie theater, and a museum in the old City Hall. Historic markers and information boards are everywhere. The commercial district is mostly at sea level, along Water and Washington streets; more than 40 of these buildings are on the National Register of Historic Places. Proud Victorian-style homes overlook the harbor from the steep bluff. Most of these are private residences, though some have been converted to bed-and-breakfast establishments open to the public. A walking-tour map published by the Chamber of Commerce is available at the visitors' information center across the street from the Port Townsend marina, at the museum, and almost everywhere else.

If the town seems too crowded for your taste, visit Chetzamoka Park, a 10-minute walk northwest of Point Hudson. This small park has an ingenious series of gardens and pathways, as well as picnic tables, shelters, and play equipment that includes a first-rate tire swing. A trail leads down to the beach. Chetzamoka Park, named after the Indian chief who was known as a "friend to pioneers," is a good place to check on fog conditions at Point Wilson.

If you're moored at the Port Townsend marina, Kah Tai Lagoon Park is just across Sims Way. Named for the Indian phrase "pass through," this park has picnic shelters, a play area, open fields, and trails around the lagoon. Farther north is the municipal golf course.

Fort Worden State Park, north of the Port Townsend waterfront at Point Wilson, is itself a historic district, with floats and mooring buoys. This area and its attractions are described in the next entry.

The downtown ferry runs to Fort Casey State Park on Whidbey Island.

Among Port Townsend's numerous special events are a summer farmers' market on Saturday mornings next to the police station, a Rhododendron Festival and Arts and Crafts Fair in early May, and a Jazz Festival in July. The Wooden Boat Festival at Point Hudson occurs on the weekend after Labor Day. First held in 1977 to attract master craftsmen from around the country, this three-day event now draws almost 20,000 visitors, and an extraordinary array of power and sailing vessels.

Fort Worden State Park ★★★★★  (anchorage) (marina)

Charts: 18441, **18464**, 18471

Fort Worden State Park occupies all but the very tip of Point Wilson. When the Vancouver Expedition came upon it 100 years ago, it was a place "where solitude-rich pasture and rural prospect prevailed," its only possessors "a few gigantic cranes who stride over the lawn with a lordly step."

By the early 1900s, U.S. Coast Artillerymen

The float and launching ramp inside the pier at Fort Worden.

were marching on the parade ground and drilling at the gun batteries that had been built—along with nearby Fort Flagler and Fort Casey—to defend Puget Sound from enemy invasion. Today the 400-plus acres are a National Historic District and park, open year-round with campsites, hiking trails and other attractions. The officers' homes are rented to tourists, and many of the buildings are leased by Centrum, a non-profit arts organization that hosts jazz, blues, and classical music concerts, as well as drama, dance, and variety shows. On sunny weekends, the sandy beaches off Fort Worden are especially lovely, with wide views of Admiralty Inlet and the Strait of Juan de Fuca, of Mt. Rainier, Mt. Baker, and the Cascade Range.

For many boaters, Fort Worden is too exposed to be comfortable, but the area is so interesting that it is worth a stop, if only during a settled afternoon.

Approaches. From Admiralty Inlet, a good approach is to head for the saddle between the two hills west of low, flat Point Wilson. The pilings of the park pier are east of a prominent white building on shore. The building on the pier is the Marine Science Center. Inside the L-shaped pier is a launching ramp and float for small craft, and around the pier are mooring buoys.

From Port Townsend, be sure to pass east of red buoy "2" in order to avoid the shoals north of Point Hudson. Boaters arriving from the Strait of Juan de Fuca can hug the shore south of Point Wilson, as the beach is quite steep.

The approach to Fort Worden from the northwestern (Strait of Juan de Fuca) side of Point Wilson is foul with kelp and rock, and is subject to tide rips. It is not recommended.

Anchorage, Moorings. Inside the L-shaped pier is a single float, about 80 feet long, suitable for small craft with shallow draft. Entrance is from the east. A fee box is at the head of the ramp. Fees are collected year round.

Five mooring buoys are placed north of the pier, close to shore. Depths vary by as much as

BRIGHT BEACONS: THE LIGHTHOUSES OF ADMIRALTY INLET

Fog, shoals, rocky headlands, and heavy traffic on a zig-zag course: all these elements combine in Admiralty Inlet. Aids to navigation and especially lighthouses are plentiful here; there are as many lighthouses in this 20-mile stretch of Puget Sound as in all the regions south of them. Before these bright beacons and their fog signals existed, ships often waited out the darkness at anchor, or groped their way with dead reckoning. In thick fog a vessel risked running aground on one shore trying to avoid hazards off another.

The jewel of every lighthouse is its lens. All the lighthouses in Admiralty Inlet once boasted a "fourth-order" Fresnel lens, though only the Point Wilson lens remains in operation. The order of the lens (first through sixth) refers to its inside diameter, with the lowest number assigned to the largest diameter. The Fresnel lens consists of many separate hand-polished glass prisms, curved and shaped like segments of a giant crystal orange. These are mounted horizontally into a heavy brass frame, above and below rounded glass bulls-eyes that are also prisms. The result is a hollow, many-paneled, egg-shaped lens surrounding a single lamp, as beautifully faceted as a diamond. The light from the lamp is refracted toward the bulls-eyes, intensified outward in a horizonal beam. Fully assembled, a first-order lens is about 12 feet high and weighs around four tons. The fourth-order lens said to be from the Admiralty Head lighthouse is three feet high, with 72 prisms arranged in six panels. It rotated on bearings and was wound like a grandfather clock by cranking up weights. From a single oil lamp flame it origi-

nally projected 180,000 candlepower, visible on a clear night for 12 miles. Today the lens is displayed at the Coast Guard Museum on Seattle's pier 36, lighted with a 25-watt bulb that makes you squint; anything more would be blinding.

The four lighthouses in Admiralty Inlet were built in the late 1800s, funded by Congress in response to increased shipping, collisions, and groundings. The first was constructed at Admiralty Head on Whidbey Island in 1861. Originally made of wood, the lighthouse stood on the 90-foot bluff overlooking the east side of the entrance to Admiralty Inlet. When Fort Casey was built for military defense some 40 years later, the light was moved to a new stucco structure with a round tower and a graceful arched entry. Over the next two decades steam and diesel replaced sail. The favored route through Admiralty Inlet changed, from east-west tacks that had been necessary for catching prevailing winds, to the more direct north-south. No longer useful as a navigational aid, the Admiralty Head light was extinguished in 1922. Today the lighthouse is a museum, dazzling white and surrounded by a low picket fence on the grounds of Fort Casey State Park. Once so vital to shipping, from the water it is now barely visible through the trees on the bluff.

The lighthouse that remained to mark the entrance of Admiralty Inlet is at Point Wilson. It began operation in 1879, the lens mounted on a square tower along with a 12-inch steam fog whistle. Twenty-five years later the masonry structure that stands today was built nearer the spit, its 51-foot tower octagonally shaped to ease wind pressure. The

15 feet, with the deepest at either end. The three buoys south of the pier are in shallower water. If you anchor north of the pier, do so on the 5-to-10 fathom shelf, and stay clear of the charted fish haven used by divers as an underwater park.

Unless you are inside the breakwater of the pier, you are completely exposed here. The westerly wind off the Strait rounds the bluffs above Point Wilson, and currents are strong. Wind-driven swells add to the wakes from ferries and freighters. If you choose to stay overnight, expect to roll, even in calm weather.

Getting Ashore. Beach your skiff on the sand or tie to the float inside the pier.

For the Crew. A small but fairly well-stocked store, open in summer, is across the road from the pier. This store also sells snacks. Inland, close to the park office, is a restaurant and laundromat. A commercial bakery is across the street from the theater.

Showers are in the nearby restrooms. An outdoor shower is just off the beach.

Things to Do. Make time to visit the Marine Science Center on the pier. The aquarium at the entrance entices you inside, where waist-high "touch" tanks and enthusiastic staff are sure to open your eyes to something new about

Point Wilson light, now automated, is a prominent landmark and major turning point for shipping. The nearby radar monitors the entrance for the Coast Guard's Vessel Traffic Center in Seattle. The former keeper's home is shoreside housing for the crew of the Coast Guard cutter moored in Port Townsend. Inland are the abandoned bunkers and restored officers quarters of Fort Worden State Park.

The Point No Point lighthouse was also commissioned in 1879, but had to wait several months for its lens; it began operation with a household kerosene lantern. This lighthouse was built low and square, its cupola tower only 27 feet high. A fog horn replaced the original bell in 1900. This is also a radar site for the Vessel Traffic Center. Though the lighthouse is now automated, Coast Guard personnel still reside here, and visitors are welcome.

The last lighthouse built in Admiralty Inlet was at Marrowstone Point in 1888, after those at West Point and Alki Point were in service. For many years the station consisted of a low, fixed red lantern on a post, and a fog bell that mariners claimed was largely inaudible. By 1918 a foghorn with three trumpets was in operation, and a new light structure added. True to its humble beginnings, the Marrowstone lighthouse remains square and plain. It has no distinctive cupola tower, and from the water looks like a simple white box. The keeper's house is now a U.S. Fish and Wildlife Service laboratory, and the surrounding land is Fort Flagler State Park.

Cleaning soot from the prisms and the tower windows, rewinding the rotation mechanism, filling the oil reservoirs—these and other maintenance tasks made lighthouse keeping a full-time job. Technological improvements inevitably led to cost-

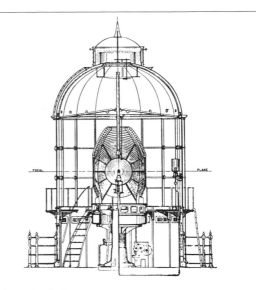

A major light. (U.S. Coast Guard Aids to Navigation Manual)

saving automation in the 1960s and 70s. Electric lights have replaced all the oil lamps, and electric motors the clockwork weights that rotated them. Today photocells turn the lights on and off, and light beams sense the need to activate the fog signal. Generators stand by in case of power failure, and monitoring systems alert off-site Coast Guard Aids to Navigation teams when anything is amiss. Yet empty as they are, the lighthouses in Puget Sound continue to reassure. "You have arrived at this point," each seems to say. "May you continue safely to the next."

the marine environment. Stare down through the clear water and watch the graceful, feather-like feelers of barnacles, or watch shrimp rub their delicate, striped legs. The octopus in its tank seems to breathe with its entire head, soft and vulnerable against the glass walls. The Center conducts interpretive beach walks on summer Saturdays and Sundays, as well as short courses and workshops.

Near the beach are picnic tables and shelters, abandoned gun emplacements, and a trail to Point Wilson, past the cable house—a former radio relay station—and the searchlight tower.

The interior of the park is large but walk-able. Follow the road that runs south and west of the pier to the park office for maps and information about special events. The Coast Artillery Museum next to the park office commemorates the regiments who were once stationed here. The Commanding Officer's quarters, across the parade ground on "Officers' Row," has been restored and is open for tours in summer. Tennis courts are located at the west end of the parade ground.

Downtown Port Townsend is about two miles from the pier. A bus runs into town from the park entrance on Cherry Street.

Kilisut Harbor

Charts: 18441, **18464**, 18471

Kilisut Harbor is a long, narrow inlet between Indian and Marrowstone Islands, south of Port Townsend. The two islands are joined by a low marsh at their southern ends, and the slender sandspit of Marrowstone almost connects them at the north. This area has long been inhabited; evidence of Native American settlement has been found here that traces back 3,000 years. Today Indian Island, which appears deserted, is an active Naval weapons depot. Most of the waterfront homes on Marrowstone are south of Mystery Bay. Two state parks, with mooring buoys and floats, make this harbor well worth the effort it takes to navigate its shallow, serpentine entrance.

Approaches. Kilisut Harbor must be approached from the southwest. If you're coming from the north, keep at least 500 yards off Marrowstone Island, and especially from the spit that overlaps the tip of Indian Island. Look for the outermost buoy, red nun "2." This buoy will be farther south than you expect. Then look a bit north for green "3." Don't confuse "3" with "5,"

which is off the tip of the spit—there's a shoal between them that dries at low tide.

Once you're centered between entrance buoys "2" and "3," head into the harbor, favoring Indian Island. At green "5," the channel follows a curled, question mark–shaped course. Hold fast to the "red-right-returning" rule and pay attention to the ascending numbers on the marks. You'll be a lot more relaxed if the tide is rising.

Make your course from buoy to buoy curved rather than straight. For example, don't motor straight from red "8" to red "10"—which will put you right on a sandbar—but instead curve northward toward green "9." From red "6" to green "13," strongly favor the Marrowstone shore, then favor Indian Island until past "15." Expect a shallow zone between green "13" and "15," and between "15" and red "16."

If your destination is Fort Flagler State Park, you will need to navigate only the upper half of the entrance course.

Fort Flagler State Park ★★★★

Charts: 18441, **18464**, 18471

Fort Flagler State Park comprises almost 800 acres at the north end of Marrowstone Island. The east portion of the park is wind-swept sandbar, the interior wooded, the north, south, and west shores steep bluff. Like its companions across Port Townsend bay and Admiralty Inlet, this park was once a gun emplacement for the defense of Puget Sound. The old gun batteries still stand, as do many of the buildings now remodeled into park offices, residences, a hostel, and a museum and learning center.

Fort Flagler is heavily used by campers who arrive by land, but also has facilities for visiting boaters. Campground facilities (including

showers) are closed from early November through February.

Approaches. Once past green buoy "9," head for the park float or for the mooring buoys. Stay in the channel, as the shore is shoal. There is a launching ramp just east of the dock.

Moorings. The park float is on the edge of the shoal that extends from shore, best suited for shallow-draft boats. On a minus tide, depths are less than 10 feet. Six buoys are set in deep water below the bluff, along the edge of the entrance channel.

Anchoring is not recommended. The currents are strong during full ebb and flood, the channel is narrow, and the buoys are set close together.

Keep in mind that prevailing winds here are from the west. The sandspit provides no protection from these westerlies, and during extreme high tides it provides no protection from wind-driven waves.

Getting Ashore. All shoreline in the park is public, including the sandspit.

For the Crew. A concession stand operates during summer near the top of the ramp. In addition to a few groceries and snack foods, you'll find an exceptional variety of toys and candy priced for a kid's budget. A pay phone, picnic tables, and barbecues are also nearby, as

well as a covered area with running water for cleaning fish and crab. The closest shower is in the restroom in the lower campground. The upper and lower camp areas provide more than 100 campsites.

Things to Do. Superb clamming and kite-flying are the major activities near shore at Fort Flagler. It's a long walk—about two miles—to the Admiralty Inlet side of the park, where the ranger station, museum, learning center, and youth hostel are located. The chart shows the main roads through the park, but it's more pleasant to branch off on the trails, to follow them out past the old gun emplacements and interpretive markers.

Mystery Bay ★★★★

Charts: 18441, **18464**, 18471

This small bay halfway down the west side of Marrowstone Island is a secure, cozy alternative to the crowds and activity of Fort Flagler. Most visiting boats gather around the park float; the southern end of the harbor is shallow, and its navigable portion largely full of boats on private buoys. The land around Mystery Bay is low and soft, with farm-like homes surrounded by pasture and orchard.

Mystery Bay State Park is open year round.

Approaches. After the winding course into Kilisut Harbor, the entrance to Mystery Bay will seem simple and clean. However, note that at low tide the shoreline is shoal, especially to the south. Stay in mid-channel and watch for the concrete blocks some 20 to 30 feet off the east end of the state park float.

Anchorage, Moorings. The state park float is more than 200 feet long, with fair depths on both sides. Check the tides, as deep-draft boats sometimes find themselves aground here at low water. Fees are collected year round.

There are seven state park mooring buoys strewn among the private buoys. Anchorage

is good in the mud bottom.

Getting Ashore. Use the state park float. The Nordland Grocery maintains a small float for customers; check the tides if you take anything bigger than a skiff to this float.

For the Boat. Mystery Bay has no fuel dock. Gas is available at the pump on the road in front of the grocery store.

For the Crew. The Nordland Grocery is a country store with some fresh produce, a post office, and pay phone. Picnic tables and public toilets are at the state park.

Things to Do. Mystery Bay State Park is little more than an open field with picnic tables and a launching ramp. The park extends west to the lagoon, and its borders are clearly marked. From the park you can walk southeast to Nordland. The road branches east about three-quarters of a mile across the island to East Beach County Park. This undeveloped park has a picnic shelter and sweeping views of Admiralty Inlet. The entrance to Fort Flagler State Park is more than two miles north.

203

Mystery Bay State Park, on Marrowstone Island. Many of the boats are moored to park buoys.

Scow Bay ★★ 4 No Facilities

Charts: 18441, **18464**, 18471

The south end of Kilisut Harbor, Scow Bay, ends in a low marsh that connects the two islands. The Marrowstone side is lined with private homes and docks. The Indian Island side is wooded and quiet. This is a fairly good anchorage, and would probably be more popular but for nearby—and more protected—Mystery Bay.

Approaches, Anchorage. Favor the Marrowstone side to avoid the shoal off Bishops Point. Anchorage is best toward the southeast, in 2 to 3 fathoms. All mooring buoys are private.

Getting Ashore. All tidelands are private. Indian Island is federal property and is posted with KEEP OUT signs.

Keystone Harbor ★★ 2

Charts: 18441, **18464**, 18471

Tiny Keystone Harbor tucks itself under Admiralty Head, as if hiding from the Strait of Juan de Fuca. It is shaped like a keyhole, with an entrance about 150 feet wide opening to a small, rounded basin. Much of the harbor is occupied by the ferry landing and its dolphin pilings. On the east shore is a launching ramp and a small float. Little room or depth is available for anchoring.

Keystone Harbor is surrounded by Fort Casey State Park. Along with Fort Worden and Fort Flagler across Admiralty Inlet, this was once part of the coastal artillery defense system of Puget Sound. The old gun batteries on the bluffs north of the harbor now serve as viewpoints for visitors, and in summer the lighthouse is open as a museum. The former quartermaster's dock east of the entrance is now an underwater park. Fort Casey State Park is open year round.

Approaches. From the north, the barracks of Fort Casey are visible north of the lighthouse on the overgrown bluff of Admiralty Head (the lighthouse is no longer functioning). The rock jetty on the south side of the harbor entrance, with its red marker, comes into view as you round the head. From the south, Admiralty Head is distinctive against the horizon of the Strait, a low finger of land reaching toward Point Wilson.

Before heading into the harbor, look around to see if a ferry is approaching from Port Townsend or is about to leave the Keystone dock. The narrow entrance and strong current make this run the most challenging in the ferry system, and skippers need all of the channel clear in order to maneuver safely.

Enter mid-channel. Be prepared for strong currents, especially on the ebb. The *Coast Pilot* reports a controlling depth of 18 feet at the entrance to Keystone Harbor.

Anchorage. Anchoring is possible on the west side of Keystone Harbor, clear of the channel and of the area around the ferry landing. This is not a peaceful anchorage in any way. Ferries come and go hourly, the launching ramp is busy during fishing season, and a popular campground crowds the west shore. In a southerly, the wind funnels into the harbor, making this an uncomfortable—if not dangerous—place in a blow.

Getting Ashore. All of the shoreline in Keystone Harbor is public.

For the Crew. Showers are in the campground restrooms on the west shore, and on the east shore beyond the launching ramp, where there is also an outside shower for divers. The restaurant across the street from the ferry landing is no longer in operation.

Bays on the West Side of Whidbey Island

Charts: 18441, **18471**, 18473

The west side of Whidbey Island is wind-torn, with high bluffs eroding slowly into Admiralty Inlet. Even the houses here seem threatened, as if they were dragging anchor. Fishing along the shelf is popular.

There are four bays on this side of Whidbey, and not one of them is a good anchorage. All are exposed to weather, current, and the wakes of freighters.

Admiralty Bay is suggested only as a brief stop in calm weather, an alternative to Keystone Harbor for larger vessels.

Mutiny Bay has a public launching ramp, but few boaters linger there. The *Coast Pilot* warns of strong tide rips, "at times dangerous to small craft."

Useless Bay is perfectly named. Its western shore is foul, and the eastern half is treacherously and unpredictably shoal. The head of the bay toward Deer Lagoon is densely developed with private homes. There are private mooring buoys here, but the only anchorage is in water more than 20 fathoms deep.

Cultus Bay, on the southern tip of Whidbey, has a private mooring basin on its east side that may be entered at high tide. This bay dries at low tide. The area outside the bay, exposed and shoal, is a dangerous place in a southerly blow. The name of this bay is taken from the Chinook word for "useless."

REGION 8

EVERETT TO

ANACORTES

Motoring south in Skagit Bay. Mount Baker is visible beyond Ika Island.

INCLUDING DECEPTION PASS AND LA CONNER

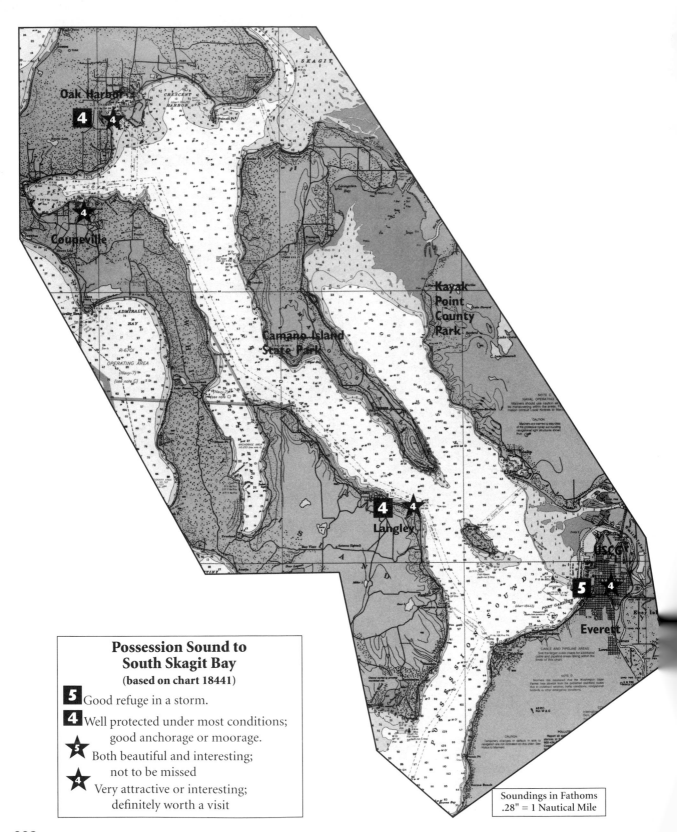

**Possession Sound to
South Skagit Bay**
(based on chart 18441)

5 Good refuge in a storm.

4 Well protected under most conditions;
good anchorage or moorage.

★**5** Both beautiful and interesting;
not to be missed

★**4** Very attractive or interesting;
definitely worth a visit

Soundings in Fathoms
.28" = 1 Nautical Mile

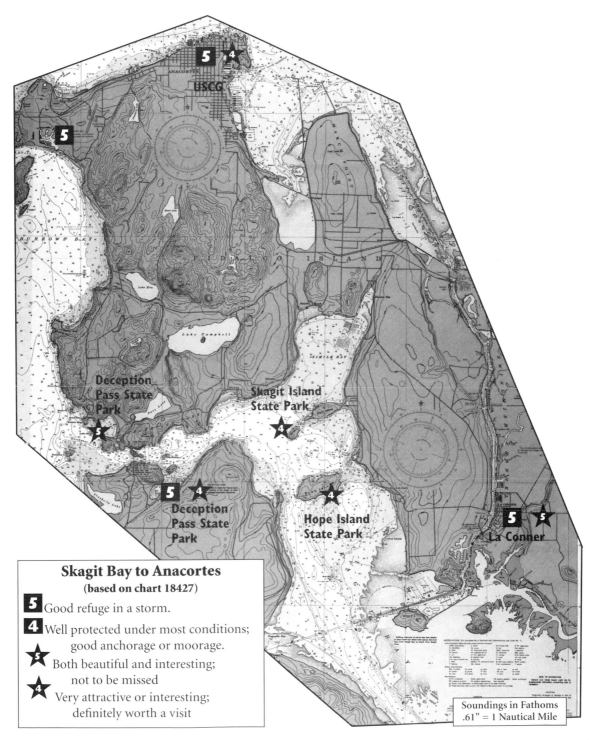

Skagit Bay to Anacortes
(based on chart 18427)

5 Good refuge in a storm.

4 Well protected under most conditions;
good anchorage or moorage.

⭐**5** Both beautiful and interesting;
not to be missed

⭐**4** Very attractive or interesting;
definitely worth a visit

Soundings in Fathoms
.61" = 1 Nautical Mile

USCG

Deception
Pass State
Park

Skagit Island
State Park

Deception
Pass State
Park

Hope Island
State Park

La Conner

The most popular route between mid-Puget Sound and the San Juan Islands is "inside" Whidbey Island. This route avoids exposure to the Strait of Juan de Fuca and, though longer (Whidbey is considered the longest island in the nation), in many ways is far more interesting. Channels widen and narrow along Whidbey's convoluted shores, and Mt. Baker rises above the marshes and rolling hills, peeking around sand bluffs and wooded islands. The scenery might still be described in the words used by Vancouver's botanist 200 years ago: "softer beauties of landscape harmoniously blended in majestic grandeur," so varied that the traveler is "eagerly occupied every moment on new objects."

This is a cruising area in its own right, with many intriguing anchorages and some of the finest moorage facilities anywhere in Puget Sound.

Though protected from the Strait of Juan de Fuca, these inside waters are not immune to its weather. Stiff winds from the strait often funnel over the narrow lowlands of Whidbey; depending on where you are, the same wind can blow from the north, the south, or the west. At times, wind speed is also exaggerated by the surrounding channels and bluffs, so while there may be less than 5 knots at Mukilteo, there may be 15 knots in Saratoga Passage.

In addition to the usual cautions about current (with special attention to Deception Pass and Swinomish Channel) be aware that several rivers empty from the east. Among them is the Skagit—the second-largest river in the western United States. More than 20 percent of all the fresh water in Puget Sound flows from the Skagit, and its influence on current, bottom characteristics, wildlife, and even weather, can be considerable.

This region includes not only the waters "inside" Whidbey, but also around Fidalgo Island, and through both Deception Pass and Swinomish Channel.

Possession Sound

Charts: 18441, **18443**, 18473

Possession Sound branches northeast from Puget Sound, widening to surround Gedney Island (known locally as Hat Island). On a clear day, Mt. Baker is centered north above these waters, and to the east the foothills of the North Cascades rise behind the city of Everett.

Navigating Possession Sound west of Gedney Island is straightforward. However, the waters to the east are complicated by the Snohomish River delta and a shoal on the south side of Gedney. As with most of the area inside Whidbey Island, prevailing winds are from the west or southwest, and, despite the appearance of protection, can be quite strong.

During fishing season, the south entrance to Possession Sound is active with sportfishing boats and commercial boats. Watch for nets and cross-traffic in this area.

Mukilteo

Charts: 18441, 18443

Although its name means "good camping," the community of Mukilteo at Elliot Point is a poor anchorage. The beach is steep and the entire area exposed. Kite fliers often take advantage of the steady winds here. South of the lighthouse is Mukilteo State Park and a three-lane launching ramp; north is a public fishing pier. The long wharf north of the ferry dock is a railroad siding for the fuel tank farm. The state ferry runs every half hour between here and Columbia Beach (Clinton) on Whidbey Island.

Mukilteo is the site of the 1855 Elliot Point Treaty, in which the Lummi, Skagit, Snohomish, Snoqualmie, Suquamish, and Duwamish tribes ceded all of their lands to the United States government. The tribes were relocated to the current Lummi, Snohomish, Tulalip, and Port Madison reservations.

Everett ★★★★ ☐ 5 All Facilities

Charts: 18441, 18443, **18444**

Once proudly described as "the city of smoke-stacks," from Possession Sound Everett still shows an industrial face. The city spreads over the west bank of the Snohomish River, which encircles it from the south. The deep south basin of Port Gardner is crowded with wharfs, log storage, cranes, a pulp mill, and the awaited home port of the U.S. Navy's Pacific Fleet. The large silver dome currently stores refined bauxite from Australia, used in the production of aluminum. Upriver are more cranes and log storage. Inland is a railroad yard and highway.

In the midst of all this industry is one of the largest small-craft marinas on the West Coast. The Everett Marina fills the middle basin, accommodating over 2,000 permanently moored vessels. Upgraded facilities, nearby shops and restaurants, and ample guest moorage make it attractive and convenient for visiting boaters.

Approaches. From the south, the stacks and towers of Everett are clearly visible after rounding Elliot Point. Head for the silver dome until you spot green entrance buoy "3."

From the northwest, the approach is more complicated. If you're east of Gedney (Hat) Island, it's important to find the black-and-white mark on pilings that indicates the western edge of the extensive Snohomish River delta. Stay well west of this mark. Look also for the green can buoy about a half-mile east of

Gedney Island, and stay east to avoid the shoals there. A conservative heading will aim you south of the silver dome until you spot green buoy "1," about a mile west of the harbor entrance.

If approaching from the west side of Gedney, watch your drift. The southwest shore is foul with kelp and rock. It is also shoal, ideal for fishing but dangerous in a stiff southerly.

The yellow buoy west of the harbor entrance is in deep water and marks the center of the commercial anchorage.

The Everett marina is protected from the west by man-made Jetty Island and a timber seawall. Green entrance buoy "3" is more than 500 yards south of the seawall. Once past "3," use the range marks on the east shore if you need to stay centered in the deepest part of the entrance channel. This channel is wide, and often busy.

You've just entered the Snohomish River, so expect to feel the current, especially on an outgoing tide. Entrance to the marina is between the two guest floats, just north of the restaurant with the red "lighthouse" top.

Moorings. Guest docks lie on either side of the two outside floats that form the entrance to the marina. These floats are held in place by braced pilings. The south float is closer to the harbor facilities, restaurants, and shops of Marina Village; the restaurant with its red "lighthouse" top is a prominent landmark. The north float is

211

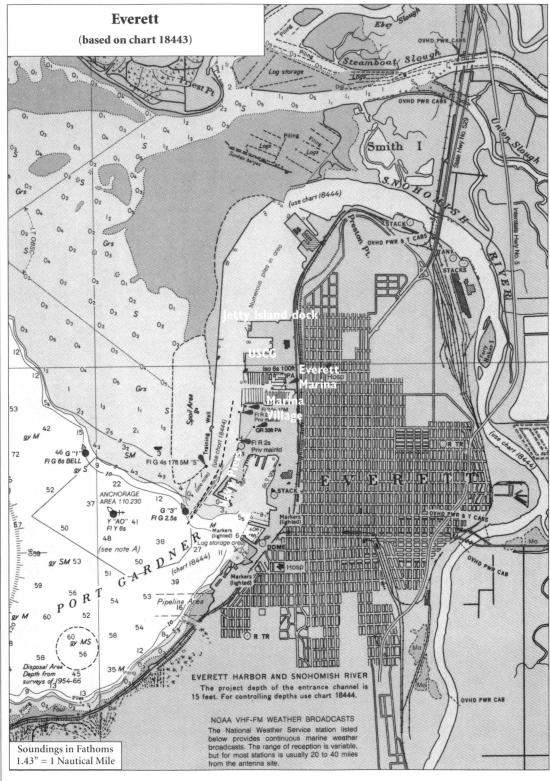

Everett
(based on chart 18443)

Ebey Slough

OVHD PWR CABS

Steamboat Slough

Priest Pt

Log storage

Logs

OVHD PWR CABS

Piling

Piling

Logs

Logs

Smith I

Sunken barges

S N O H O M I S H

State Hwy No 529

Union Slough

Interstate Hwy No 5

Grs

(use chart 18444)

Numerous piles in area

Preston Pt

STACK

OVHD PWR & T CABS

TANK

STACKS

Grs

Grs

Jetty Island dock

USCG

Iso 6s 100ft PA

Everett Marina

Hosp

Spoil Area

Marina Village

Fl R 2s

Fl R 2s Priv maintd

Training Wall

QR 33ft PA

(use chart 18444)

Fl R 2s Priv maintd

(see note)

Fl G 4s 17ft 5M "5"

46 G "1"
Fl G 6s BELL

gy M 42

15

gy S

SM

12

22

STACK

E V E R E T T

R TR

OVHD PWR & T CABS

(use chart 18444)

52

ANCHORAGE AREA 110.230

37

G "3"
Fl G 2.5s

Y "AO"
Fl Y 6s

(see note A)

Markers (lighted)

50

48

gy SM 53

(chart 18444)

Log storage area

Markers (lighted)

DOME

Hosp

P O R T   G A R D N E R

59

56

gy M 60

52

Pipeline Area

R TR

OVHD PWR CAB

gy MS

Disposal Area
Depth from
surveys of 1954-66

Piling

Piles

Foul

Dol

OVHD PWR CAB

EVERETT HARBOR AND SNOHOMISH RIVER
The project depth of the entrance channel is
15 feet. For controlling depths use chart 18444.

NOAA VHF-FM WEATHER BROADCASTS
The National Weather Service station listed
below provides continuous marine weather
broadcasts. The range of reception is variable,
but for most stations is usually 20 to 40 miles
from the antenna site.

Soundings in Fathoms
1.43" = 1 Nautical Mile

closer to the fuel dock, yacht club, and to marine supply stores and repair facilities. At either float, note the current when docking and pulling away.

Pay for moorage at the fee box located at the head of either ramp. The harbor office is east of the shop-and-restaurant complex on the south shore of the marina basin. Slip reservations can be made from Memorial Day to Labor Day—telephone (360) 259-6001; from Seattle, (206) 243-3164.

The guest floats are noisy. If you're moored on the outside, you'll hear the rush of the current against your hull in addition to the crash of trains shunting in the nearby railroad yard and the sounds of birds and sea lions on Jetty Island. Every boat going in and out of the marina passes by the south guest float: commercial crabbers, shrimpers, and sportfishing boats. The traffic often begins quite early in the morning.

An alternate moorage (one night only) is at the Jetty Island floats, upriver about a quarter-mile and across the channel from the 13-lane launching area. Depth at the floats is a few feet less than at the marina guest floats.

There is no suitable anchorage for pleasure craft in Everett.

For the Boat. The fuel dock is just inside the marina entrance, to the north, in water about 3 feet shallower than at the guest floats. A number of marine repair and supply shops are also located on this side of the harbor, toward the highway and north toward the launching ramps. A marine hoist and railway are on the northeast shore.

The brick-enclosed garbage collection areas on the south shore have waste-oil receptacles.

For the Crew. Marina Village, on the south shore, has a variety of restaurants and shops. Showers and a laundromat are on the main floor of the harbor office, east of the retail complex. The closest groceries are at either of two small delis, one on each side of the marina; a supermarket is more than a mile away on Everett Avenue and Broadway. A bus leaves for town from near the harbor office.

Things to Do. You're a long way from town, but there are many attractions nearby. Beyond the shops and restaurants of Marina Village, toward the highway, is the Chamber of Commerce office. Originally built to illustrate the versatility of local timber, this ornate building now displays many historic photographs of the area; unfortunately, it is closed on weekends. North of the marina basin is a Firefighter Museum.

A quick escape from the industry of Everett is provided by the Jetty Island ferry, which leaves Marina Village every half-hour from July through September. This free ferry takes you across the river to the island's park and wildlife preserve. A short trail leads to a sandy, two-mile beach with long, wide tideflats. There are guided walks and special events, but most visitors prefer to simply sit on the driftwood among the bold gulls and gaze across Possession Sound to the Olympic Mountains, or to wade the tideflats. If you take your own boat or skiff to the Jetty Island dock, be prepared for strong river current.

Gedney Island

Charts: 18441, **18443**, 18473

Gedney Island, locally called Hat Island, is about four miles west of Everett harbor. There is a small private marina on the northeast shore, but no facilities for visiting boats. All of the island is private. A private

ferry serves residents.

Anchorage is possible in settled weather, north of the island. The bank here is steep, and all tidelands are private. Watch for kelp.

Tulalip Bay ★★★

Charts: 18441, **18443**

This nearly landlocked bay north of Everett has been occupied by the Snohomish Indians for over 2,000 years. The old village was the site of elaborate potlatches, and the spit at the end of Mission Beach was a sacred burial place. In its more recent history, Tulalip was known for the boarding school operated here by the federal government to "assimilate" Indian youth from all over Puget Sound into white culture; any reference to Native language or customs was punished, and parents who resisted sending their children to this school often were jailed. The school was closed in 1935. The clapboard building still stands, its overgrown orchards and grounds part of an interpretive loop trail with displays written in both the Snohomish language (Lushootseed) and English.

Among their many business enterprises today, the Tulalip tribes (which also include the Skykomish and Snoqualmie Indians) operate a small-craft marina for tribal fishing boats and the occasional visitor. The bay itself has many unmarked shoals and submerged hazards. Now, as in ancient times, it is best suited for shallow-draft vessels.

Approaches. The approach to the Tulalip marina requires a winding course. Boaters without experience in this bay should choose a rising tide. Enter from the south, where there is deepest water. Red nun buoy "2" marks an extensive shoal northwest of the Mission Beach peninsula. About 500 yards northeast of "2," head toward the charted water tank behind the old school; this should keep you clear of the submerged wreck in the center of the entrance and of the shoals in the middle of the bay. The marina is east, in front of the pitched steeple of the mission church, but stay on this northerly heading until about 100 yards from shore. Then make a soft turn toward the timber breakwater.

Anchorage, Moorings. The marina entrance is south of the breakwater; the north side is blocked by floating logs. A sign on pilings and a red light on a rock keep you in the narrow channel. Don't cut too close to the breakwater.

Tie to the fuel dock at the northwest end of the marina. This float is about 20 feet long, with depth about the same as at the marina entrance. Check in at the marina store and café across the street for a slip assignment. Moorage is usually available January through August; from September through December the marina is busy with tribal fishing boats.

A small anchoring basin is west of the old school toward Hermosa Point, in a fathom or less. Watch for pilings.

Except for the marina, all docks and mooring buoys in Tulalip Bay are private.

Getting Ashore. Use the marina fuel dock. All other tidelands are private.

For the Boat, Crew. Gas and diesel are sold at the fuel dock, and some marine supplies at the store directly across the street. A few grocery items are also here. A café operates next door.

Port Susan

Charts: 18441

Port Susan lies between Camano Island and the mainland, connecting with Skagit Bay at its northern end via a narrow slough. Only about half of Port Susan is navigable; the northern portion soon shallows into the broad mudflats of the Stillaguamish River.

A dead-end bay with only a few anchorages and no facilities, Port Susan doesn't attract many outside cruisers. Almost all the boats here are local runabouts and skiffs used for water-skiing and for fishing, shrimping, and crabbing. The shores of Port Susan are steep and wooded, with homes crowded together around private community beaches.

Approaches. From the south, Camano Head is steep and rounded. Keep green buoy "1" to port if you enter along the west shore. Ahead of you in the distance are the lowlands connecting Camano Island with the mainland. As Port Susan widens past Kayak Point, the silos of the farming community of Stanwood appear on the horizon, and South Pass looks like a clear channel to Skagit Bay.

Take care north of Kayak Point. The Camano side shoals irregularly, and the tide-flats of the Stillaguamish are closer than you may think. Don't count on the charted, privately maintained light to mark the edge of the flats. The broad expanse of Port Susan is deceptive; it's easy to understand how one of Vancouver's ships ran aground "almost immediately" here in 1792, so abruptly does the bottom rise.

Cavalaro Park ★★ No Facilities

Charts: 18441, **18473**

The best anchorage on the west side of Port Susan is off a small county park about a mile-and-a-half south of Triangle Cove. This day-use park has a cobble beach, a few picnic tables and barbecues, portable toilets, and a launching ramp at its northern boundary. There are no facilities within walking distance.

Approaches, Anchorage. From the west side of Port Susan, head for the radio tower charted southwest of Triangle Cove. Look for a point of land crowded with homes that spread around a lagoon and up the hill. At the south end of this development is a cook shelter for the Camano Country Club; to the north is the main clubhouse. Beyond is the upended-log bulkhead of Cavalaro Park, beneath a sand bluff. The launching ramp is at the northern end of the park.

A small-craft anchorage is south of the ramp, in 2 to 5 fathoms, mud bottom. All tidelands outside the park are private.

Kayak Point ★★★ No Facilities

Charts: 18441

The best anchorage in all of Port Susan is off the county park at Kayak Point. This park is a popular destination by land, and for good reasons: western exposure, numerous picnic shelters above a sloping gravel beach, firepits, a fishing pier, a launching ramp, trails, and inland campsites. The grassed play area off the beach is large enough for a game of volleyball and touch football and Frisbee, all at the same time. In fall and winter, the stiff winds of Port Susan attract many board sailors to Kayak Point.

Approaches, Anchorage. From the south, Kayak Point is distinctively "pointy," its long fishing pier extending into deep water. From the northwest, look for the face of the pier and the shed-roofed gray park buildings.

Anchor north or south of the point. The charted mooring buoys north of the pier no longer exist, and the shelf is steep and narrow. Take care that you won't swing onto the beach, or drag into deep water. Anchorage is slightly better south of the point, but the 6-fathom shelf is narrower than charted; take care anchoring here as well.

Saratoga Passage

Charts: 18441

This narrow passage between Whidbey and Camano islands connects Possession Sound to Skagit Bay. It is primarily a highway to and from Deception Pass or Swinomish Channel; boats plow along the Whidbey shore in its southern half, near the Camano shore in its northern half. There are only a couple of stop-offs, both of them popular destinations by land, one with facilities for boaters.

Getting Ashore. Beach your skiff anywhere in the park, keeping the launching ramp clear. Do not tie to the fishing pier. This entire area of the park closes at dusk. All surrounding tidelands are private.

For the Boat, Crew. There are no facilities nearby. The closest restaurant is more than two miles away in the Kayak Point Golf Course, across the highway and up the hill.

Langley ★★★★ | 2 | (anchorage) | 4 | (marina) (gas only)

Charts: 18441, **18473**

Langley is northwest of Sandy Point, a cozy little Whidbey Island town that enthusiastically welcomes tourists. The main street is crowded with shops and restaurants, with park benches along the narrow sidewalks and flower boxes blooming at almost every door. The small marina is a short walk from these attractions, and is operated exclusively for visiting boats.

Approaches. The town of Langley is on top of a low bluff, with a promenade along the beach and a marina to the south. From a distance, three major elements on the waterfront blend together: the timber breakwater of the marina, the hoist and gas float north of it, and another private pier north of the gas float. Approaches to the marina from the south are fairly straightforward. From the north, stay well off the Whidbey shore to avoid the charted rocks and shoals. A spit north of Langley is privately marked with a flagged stick that's visible at half-tide.

Anchorage, Moorings. The Langley small-boat harbor is inside a hook-shaped, timber breakwater and is entered from the south. A sign on the breakwater, shaped like an arrow, directs boats into the marina. There's good depth inside, though it shallows briefly at the southeast end of the breakwater. Turn sharply into the marina, close to the outside (west) floats; 200 feet west of these you'll run out of water at low tide.

This is a tight marina, with limited turning room. Slips are labeled for boats over and under 30 feet, and boats on the outside (west) floats should be prepared to raft. The stout breakwater looks and feels like a stockade,

Langley's small-boat harbor and anchorage, looking southeast. The entrance to the marina is southwest of the breakwater.

especially at low tide. Stays are limited to three nights in a seven-day period. A fee box is at the head of the ramp. Daytime moorage is free. The marina does not take reservations.

Anchorage is south and west of the breakwater, in good depth and holding ground. Expect to roll, both from weather and from the wakes of passing boats. Only shallow-draft vessels should anchor inside the breakwater, taking care to stay out of the marina entrance channel and launching ramp area.

Getting Ashore. The marina has floats designated for dinghies.

For the Boat. The gas dock is between the marina breakwater and the hoist, beneath the orange-and-white striped building on the pier. There are two floats, each about 50 feet long and very bouncy; the wear on the pilings is impressive, and indicative of the wave action that's common here. The depth at these floats is about 5 feet shallower than it is inside the marina. The nearest diesel fuel is in Everett.

Immediately north of the marina is a marine store with basic hardware and service for outboards and small boats.

For the Crew. The marine store has a few grocery items, but real shopping is in town, a short walk uphill. The supermarket's main entrance and parking lot are on 2nd Street.

Showers are in the marina restrooms, across the road from the launching ramp. The closest laundromat is about three-quarters of a mile north along 2nd Street, near the brewery.

Things to Do. You'll find plenty of restaurants, gift shops, and bookstores in town, as well as a bakery and several bed-and-breakfast inns. Galleries feature fine arts and crafts. Halfway down 1st Street are stairs that lead to a promenade and public beach. The bronze sculpture of a boy and his dog overlooks the beach, the boy's shoulder and the dog's head brightly polished by the hands of their many admirers.

Langley hosts a Choochokam Festival of the Arts in mid-July.

Camano Island State Park ★★★

Charts: 18441

At the turn in Camano Island at Lowell Point is Camano Island State Park. The park's beach stretches north beneath a 150-foot bluff, almost to the navigational light. A launching ramp is at the northern end of the picnic area. Cars can be driven right down to this beach, making it especially attractive for group and family picnics. There are two large campgrounds in the upper woods and hiking trails everywhere.

Despite these amenities, this park is not a good overnight cruising destination. The west beach is too steep for anchoring, and while there is better holding in Elger Bay, the southwest exposure there is uncomfortable; even in good weather you'll feel the wake of every passing boat on Saratoga Passage. This park is best suited for beachable and trailerable craft, especially for boaters who want to launch close to the good fishing off the shelf of Camano.

Approaches, Anchorage. Watch for the charted rocks along the shore east and west of Lowell Point. The dock with floats east of the bluff in Elger Bay is private. If you anchor near here, keep in mind that even a northerly wind can reach you from over the low marsh at the head of the bay.

Getting Ashore. The tidelands outside the park are private. The south beach of the park is cobble, the north beach gravel.

For the Crew. Showers in the bathhouse on the beach are not always functional. Better showers are at the campground, about a half-mile away. To reach these, take the trail uphill from the south parking lot. Water fountains and spigots are at the beach parking lots.

There are no other facilities within walking distance.

Holmes Harbor

Charts: 18441

Holmes Harbor branches south from Saratoga Passage, cutting Whidbey Island almost in two. The harbor is clean, deep, and wide enough for a sailboat to tack in or out. There are a few residential areas along shore, but no town of any size except Freeland, at the southern toe of the harbor.

Anchorage is possible, but not recommended, on the east side of Holmes Harbor, where exposure to the north and south is considerable, and in many places the shelf is narrow. The best anchorages are to the west.

Approaches. The main hazard to watch for when approaching Holmes Harbor is the spit and rock around Baby Island (also known as Hackney Island) on the east side of the entrance. This tiny flat-topped island, connected to land at low tide, was once a favorite clamming and picnic area for the Tulalip tribes. Weather, and failed bulkhead, have shaped it into a lop-sided cake.

From the south, you'll first see the clutch of homes beneath the bluff on East Point; as you come abeam of this point, Baby Island emerges well off Rocky Point. Look for green can "1" about that same distance north of Baby Island. From the north, expect Baby Island to merge somewhat with the land behind.

Freeland ★★★ ⬛3 🎁 🛒 🧴 🐚 🍽️

Charts: 18441

This small Whidbey town has no facilities for visiting boats. It's friendly and quiet, geared to the lives of the people who live and work here rather than to the short-term comings and goings of visitors. Freeland was established at the turn of the century as a Utopian socialist community. It is now slated to become the urban business center of Whidbey Island.

Approaches. Approaches are clean to the ruins of the former marina, about a mile north of Freeland on the west shore. From here, the harbor appears to divide into two coves separated by a wooded knoll. A county park and launching ramp is in the eastern cove, the shipyard with its pale green cranes and buildings is in the western cove.

Anchorage. Anchor in the west cove, south of the ruins of the abandoned marina. Take care to stay north of the road that descends almost to the water on the west shore. South of this road the bottom shallows rapidly. This west side of the harbor affords better protection from the north; there's enough rise in the land to protect somewhat from the south as well.

This anchorage is used by the shipbuilding company. All mooring buoys and docks are private. The developers of the nearby golf course plan to rebuild the ruined marina.

Getting Ashore. Freeland County Park tidelands begin east of the launching ramp and extend west around the wooded knoll, which is part of the park. Unless the tide is high and your visit is brief, beach your skiff well west of the launching ramp. On the east side, groundwater creates a quicksand effect; you'll easily sink to your knees in the muck. Watch for boulders west of the launching ramp, especially off the wooded knoll.

All other tidelands are private.

For the Boat. The hardware store, about a half-mile up the road at the main intersection, has a few marine items in its sporting goods section. A nearby commercial station sells diesel and gas on weekdays; a block farther south is a gas station.

For the Crew. The park has picnic tables, barbecues, and play equipment. Clamming is good at minus tides. Uphill about a half-mile is a supermarket, variety store, post office, library, laundromat, and café.

Honeymoon Bay ★★ ⬛3 No Facilities

Charts: 18441

Triangular Honeymoon Bay is a little over halfway down the west side of Holmes Harbor, south of Dines Point. Modest homes are scattered over the wooded hills and bluffs. At the head of the bay is a small man-made lake, part of a private community center.

Approaches, Anchorage. Approaches are clean. Anchor southwest of the concrete pier and other pilings on the north shore of the bay, inside the 10-fathom line. The shelf is wide and holding ground is good. Protection from the southwest is better here than at Freeland.

All mooring buoys are private, as are the surrounding tidelands.

Coves North of Honeymoon Bay ★ ☐ 1 No Facilities

Charts: 18441

North of Honeymoon Bay are two indentations in the shore used as seasonal anchorage by residents. One is north of Dines Point, off a sandy beach crowded with summer cabins. The other is off Greenbank, north of the row of charted pilings. Neither of these areas is well-protected. All docks, mooring buoys, and surrounding tidelands are private.

Penn Cove

Charts: 18441

Penn Cove creases the northeast shore of Whidbey so deeply it seems to fold the island over on itself. Less than a mile-and-a-half of land separates the head of the cove from the Strait of Juan de Fuca; at times westerlies are quite stiff here.

Like much of Whidbey Island, the land around Penn Cove is low and gentle. In 1792, Vancouver found it "a delightful prospect" with "beautiful pastures, bordering on an expansive sheet of water." These were the primary lands of the Skagit tribe, who raised crops on the naturally occurring prairies and built a fortified village near the cove's entrance against marauding Haida Indians. Today, all of Penn Cove is part of Ebey's Landing National Historic Reserve, which incorporates public and private lands to maintain their natural beauty, historic interest, and present economic importance. Local brochures and guidebooks invite you to imagine the area as it was 100 years ago. Arriving by water on a pearl-gray Northwest day, you may easily find yourself imagining farther back than that.

Penn Cove supports a rich aquaculture, with mussel-rearing pens in the southwest quadrant of the cove.

Approaches. Respect the navigational marks off Forbes Point (north) and Snatelum Point (south). A barely submerged wreck lies north of Snatelum Point, east of the mark.

Coupeville ★★★★ ☐ 3

Charts: 18441

The brightly colored wharf of Coupeville reaches out into Penn Cove, inviting boaters to this small New England-style town. Coupeville attracts many visitors; on weekends, Front Street is often crowded with people of all ages wandering between the restaurants and gift shops, most of them licking ice cream cones. Large parking areas, public restrooms, and benches for the footsore make this an especially comfortable stop for those arriving by land. Dockside facilities make it attractive for boaters as well.

Despite its historic veneer, Coupeville is a real town, the Island County seat serving both Whidbey and Camano Islands. The courthouse and county agencies are located up the hill, where the restored homes and bed-and-breakfast inns thin out.

Approaches. From any direction, the large red

The Harbor Store pier and fuel dock at Coupeville, approaching from the north. Moorage is to the east (left).

building on the pier—the Harbor Store—is a prominent landmark. If approaching from the west, watch out for the mussel pens, and stay north of them. From the east, stay clear of the charted rocks off Lovejoy Point.

Anchorage, Moorings. Two floats, each about 50 feet long, are arranged in a staggered pattern east of the Harbor Store pier. Current at the floats can be surprisingly strong. A drawing at the head of the ramp shows the depth at zero tide: as little as 4 feet 9 inches at the southwest end of the float, with a maximum of 7 feet at the northeast end. The fee box is next to the drawing. You may also pay at the harbormaster's office on the north side of the building.

If you need more water under your keel, anchor in the basin to the east, more or less in line with the moorage floats.

An alternate, but shallow, anchorage is farther east, off Captain Thomas Coupe Park. A launching ramp and float connect to a small beach and picnic area, with restrooms and RV pumpout toward the road.

Getting Ashore. Use the floats, or beach your skiff on either side of the pier.

For the Boat. The fuel dock is on the north side of the pier. The nearest marine supply and repair facilities are in Oak Harbor.

For the Crew. Restrooms and a shower are on the Harbor Store pier, behind the harbormaster's office. Get a key when you check in. The Harbor Store has a deli, but real groceries—including meat and produce—are about a half-mile up the hill on Main Street. Front Street has numerous restaurants and gift shops. The closest laundromat is in Oak Harbor.

Things to Do. Coupeville is set up for walking and ideal for boaters. Pick up a walking-tour map at the museum just beyond the head of the pier, adjacent to the blockhouse and dugout canoe. From here you can guide yourself through the town past colorfully restored homes, most of them private residences. The museum displays artifacts of early Coupeville, and celebrates its maritime origins.

Immediately west of the pier, on top of the steep bluff, is a large town park, with play-ground equipment, a tennis court, picnic areas, and an enormous slice of an ancient tree. A steep trail descends to the beach.

Coupeville hosts a Water Festival in late May, and an arts and crafts fair in mid-August

Head of Penn Cove ★★★

Charts: 18441

At the head of Penn Cove, on the knob of land south of the community of Coveland, is the Captain Whidbey Inn. Constructed of madrona logs in 1907, today the inn's rustic accommodations and tasty food draw patrons from all over western Washington. Accommodations for boaters are rustic as well—little more than a seasonal float and a few mooring buoys—but enough to make you feel welcome.

Approaches, Anchorage, Moorings. At the head of the cove, look for the restaurant's large peaked roof covered with weathered shingles. The gazebo of the outdoor dining area is in front and slightly to the south. A dock, festooned in summer with small flags, extends straight out into the cove, with a seasonal T-shaped float at the end. Four buoys are scattered east of the float, in water roughly 3 feet

Tending mussels in Penn Cove. The shellfish are suspended in long bundles from the floats.

222

deeper than at the float itself. Maximum stay is one night, unless you are a guest of the inn.

Anchorage is good around the buoys, in mud bottom. Though you may feel protected, keep in mind that the full length of the Strait of Juan de Fuca is only a mile-and-a-half away, on the other side of the relatively low "waist" of Whidbey Island. If a storm is brewing out there, you may be in for a rough night. Slightly better protection may be found south of the restaurant anchorage, closer to shore in a small bight used by local residents. All mooring buoys and tidelands here are private.

Getting Ashore. The Captain Whidbey Inn buoys, floats, and beach are for patrons only.

All other tidelands are private.

For the Crew. The restaurant is small and does not take reservations unless you are staying at the inn; expect to wait for an empty table.

If you want to stretch your legs, walk northwest on Madrona Way and then west on Libby Road, toward Point Partridge and Fort Ebey State Park. It's a long walk—more than two miles each way—but your reward will be the county park at Libby Beach. On a windy day the crash of surf is truly impressive here, and you can almost watch the bluffs eroding away under the force of waves from the Strait of Juan de Fuca.

Monroe's Landing County Park ★★★ No Facilities

Charts: 18441

An undeveloped day-use county park occupies a street end on the north shore of Penn Cove, about a mile-and-a-half southwest of Blowers Bluff. A sewer outfall is indicated on the chart here. The small bight is deep and exposed. The beach is empty and lovely, curving east and north, bordered with driftwood and beach grass. An interpretive sign shows a photo of the potlatch house that stood on this site until 1910, and a photo of the Skagit Chief Snakelum and his wife. Their calm, lined faces seem to

invite you to enjoy their ancient home.

Approaches, Anchorage. Stay at least a quarter-mile from shore when approaching from the east in order to avoid the shoals. Turn in when you're in line with the street that ends at the launching ramp. Anchor slightly west of the street end. Check your depth and swing.

Getting Ashore. The beach east of the launching ramp is public. All other tidelands are private.

Oak Harbor ★★★★

Charts: **18428, 18441**

The original Indian name translates to "Closed Mouth," an apt description of Oak Harbor, curled behind the peninsula of Maylor and Forbes points. The harbor offers protection from southerly winds off Saratoga Passage, but little from westerlies blowing across Whidbey from the Strait of Juan de Fuca.

Oak Harbor is a military town, home to the Whidbey Island Naval Air Station. All of the

peninsula and most of the land east of the marina is Naval Reservation. To the north are the long runways used for training fighter pilots; the screaming engines of their low-flying aircraft (described on billboards as "The Sound of Freedom") are heard throughout the area.

Approaches. The large buildings of the old

Navy seaplane base and the white aeronautical sphere on the peninsula ("Aero" on the chart) make Oak Harbor easy to spot from a distance. The channel to the marina is clearly marked, but may be confusing at first. Especially when approaching from the northeast, take care to round Forbes and Maylor points south of red buoy "2." This will line you up for the entrance channel and keep you off the shoals and the rocks, often dangerously awash, scattered between the buoy and the Forbes Point peninsula.

Much of Oak Harbor is dry at low tide, or nearly so, and it is important to stay in the channel that slightly favors the peninsula, red buoys and daymarks to starboard, green to port. The confusion comes at green "11," which is lined up almost perfectly with a traffic signal on shore. Observe this flashing six-second light carefully; if it turns yellow or red, it's the traffic signal, not the navigation light. Inattention and miscalculation has put many a boat on the mud to wait out the tide.

Between green "11" and flashing red "12," you'll be in the shallowest portion of the channel. The entire harbor is slowly silting up since the seaplane base was de-activated in the 1940s and the Army Corps stopped dredging. Past red "12," head for the marina.

Moorings. Guest moorage is just inside the breakwater. Enter between the marks at the south end. It's a sharp turn to port once you're inside, and another into the slips (the first few are reserved for reciprocal yacht club members only). In a blow, these maneuvers will put you broadside to the wind, and docking may be a scramble. If you need more than 50 feet of dock space, continue on to the float at the north end of this moorage basin.

Additional guest moorage is on the north side of the main float that connects to the harbor office, north of the boat houses. To reach this float, head north of the breakwater. Stay south of the buoys that mark the edge of the dredged channel.

To take the guesswork out of docking, you can call the harbormaster on VHF Channel 16. Reservations can be made ahead by phone: (360) 679-2628. Fee boxes with envelopes and

gate keys are located on the guest floats and at the harbor office. Electricity is included in the fee.

Anchorage. Anchorage is west of the breakwater, in about 2 fathoms, mud bottom. Check your swing, as the mudflats are fairly close.

Getting Ashore. Use the marina guest float.

For the Boat. The fuel dock is toward shore, east of the boathouses. Here also is a marine repair facility and lift, and an enormous launching ramp (the former seaplane ramp). There's a marine store on shore.

For the Crew. The marina has restrooms and showers, and a park with sand volleyball courts, horseshoe pits, barbecues, and a large firepit. The main street of Oak Harbor is close by, about a half-mile west. Groceries are a mile-and-a-half from the marina, in the shopping mall at the highway intersection. A large laundromat is near the supermarket, on 300th Avenue. The laundromat across the street from the marina is for Navy personnel only.

Things to Do. A highlight on nearby Pioneer Way is the Five-and-Dime, where you can find everything from yard goods and Halloween makeup to a complete assortment of cribbage boards. City Beach is farther west, on the water off 70th, marked by a large windmill commemorating Oak Harbor's Dutch settlers. Here is a wading pool, play equipment, and picnic tables. The walk along the water is pleasant, with views across the harbor.

If you have only a short time in Oak Harbor, climb the stairs to the harbormaster's office and admire the old photos and the intricate knotwork displayed there.

Special events in Oak Harbor are the Holland Happening in April and the Olde Fashioned Fourth of July Parade. By far the biggest event in the marina is Race Week in mid-July, which jams the harbor and fills nearby Saratoga Passage with sailboats competing in a range of classes. Race Week sponsors include Oak Harbor Yacht Club and Seattle Yacht Club.

In August, Oak Harbor hosts a Dixieland Jazz Festival and a Metal Boat Festival.

Crescent Harbor ★★ ☐2 No Facilities

Charts: **18428**, 18441

Crescent Harbor is large and completely open to Saratoga Passage. All of the shoreline is Naval Reservation, including Polnell Point, a demolition and ordnance disposal area. This side of the isthmus was part of the old float-plane base, and is now a small-craft marina for the Navy. The rest of the beach is undeveloped.

Approaches, Anchorage. From the east, stay a couple of hundred yards south of Polnell Point; from the west, stay a half-mile east of Forbes Point. Anchorage is fair north of the rock jetty and pier, on the west side of the harbor. Docks and mooring buoys are for Navy personnel only. The nearest shore access is on the other side of the peninsula, in Oak Harbor.

Skagit Bay

Charts: 18421, **18427**, 18441

Bounded by Camano, Whidbey, and Fidalgo islands, Skagit Bay appears wide, especially to the east where it meets the rich agricultural lowlands and rises gently to the North Cascade mountains. This extensive wetland area is noted among birdwatchers for the clouds of snow geese that pass through each winter. However, the navigable portion of Skagit Bay is only a narrow channel on the margin of the Skagit River mudflats. Buoys and marks are carefully observed, and by the time boaters reach the north end of the bay, where depths permit exploring and anchoring, they are usually in a hurry to continue on to Deception Pass or Swinomish Channel. Relatively few linger.

Utsalady ★★ ☐3 No Facilities

Charts: 18441

A fairly good anchorage is in the cove at the north end of Camano Island, between Utsalady and Brown points. The shore is developed, with many homes and numerous flagpoles. Little is left of the forest that supported a sawmill here 150 years ago.

Approaches. From the southwest, Utsalady Point is not as obvious as from other directions. East of Rocky Point is a launching ramp and street-end park, but anchorage here is not good. Continue on past Utsalady Point, where there is also a launching ramp (no park). From the north, wait until you're south of red nun buoy "2" before turning toward the cove. From any direction watch for crab pots.

Anchorage. There's good depth in the west half of the cove, just east of the spit and parallel to shore. The private buoys are scattered around the 3-fathom line. As the cove rounds northeast toward Brown Point, it becomes shallower, and the number of crab pots increases.

You'll be reasonably protected from prevailing westerlies here, but exposed to the north.

Getting Ashore. The launching ramp on the west side of the cove is the only public access here.

For the Boat, Crew. There are no facilities for boaters in Utsalady. A mile-and-a-half walk uphill and east will take you to a country store.

The town of Stanwood is six miles away and not easily accessible by water.

Hope Island State Park ★★★★

Charts: 18421, **18427**

Steep-sided and thickly wooded, Hope Island has a beach only at low tide, and only one small cove on its north shore. The southeast point appears as a separate islet and is surrounded by reef. The entire island seems perched on the edge of the river delta; the waters south and east are shallow, the waters west and north drop from a narrow shelf. This marine park is relatively undeveloped. Winter storms have obscured the trails, but have not toppled the impressive stand of trees in the center of the island. Here the cedars tower straight and thick, living columns rising into the filtered green light.

Approaches, Anchorage, Moorings. Hope Island has two anchorages. In the north cove, four mooring buoys are set inside the 5-fathom shelf. If these are full, set your hook east of them; the bottom shallows rapidly between the buoys and shore. This anchorage gives protection from the south, though wind still skitters around the point and funnels through Deception Pass. Current can be strong.

South of the island there is good holding ground and depth, in a pocket 2 to 5 fathoms deep about midway along the shore.

Approaching from the south, head for the red mark on the western tip of the island, but wait until you're within a quarter-mile of this mark before turning east. Stay about 500 feet from shore to avoid the charted ¼-fathom shelf and shoal. You're exposed here, not only to southerlies but also to the beam swell of boats transiting Swinomish Channel.

The east side of Hope Island is foul, and the current through the narrow channel there is swift. Anchoring is not recommended.

Getting Ashore. All of the island is public, but beaches disappear at high tide. The best landing is in the north cove.

For the Crew. A few picnic tables and pit toilets are on shore above the north cove. Crabbing is good south of the island. Less than a mile away, on Snee-oosh Point, is a restaurant that welcomes boaters. Use the seasonal float, or beach your skiff just south of the restaurant. This restaurant is open seven months a year, beginning in late March. The development on Lone Tree Point is a Thousand Trails camp for members only.

Skagit Island State Park ★★★★

Charts: 18421, **18427**

This small, sheer-sided island is surrounded by a steep and narrow gravel beach. Off its north shore are rocks and reefs—hardly an inviting anchorage. However, if you can hook a buoy, a visit here is worthwhile. An overgrown game trail skirts the perimeter of the island, through salal and madrona. From the grassy knoll on the southwest tip, you can look over the channel toward Deception Pass and watch other boats hurrying on their way to somewhere while you luxuriate in the peace you've already found.

Approaches. Approaches are clean from the south and west. Avoid passing between Skagit and Kiket Islands, as the entire channel there is foul.

The footpath around Skagit Island.

Anchorage, Moorings. Two state park mooring buoys are on the northwest side, within 100 feet of the sheer rock face. The west buoy is about 15 feet deeper. Possible anchorage is east of the buoys, in 3 to 5 fathoms.

Getting Ashore. The steep shore relaxes into a pocket-size beach on the northeast tip. Beaches are flatter, but rockier, as you proceed around this tip.

Nearby Kiket Island is privately owned, as are the docks and mooring buoys in the open bay to the south.

Similk Bay ★ 2 No Facilities

Charts: 18421, **18427**

Similk Bay, located north of Skagit Bay, is open and shallow. The northwest quarter is littered with pilings. This area was once a railhead for timber, and log booms are still assembled here. The east shore is Swinomish Indian Reservation land; to the north and west are private homes and beaches.

Approaches. Slightly favor Skagit Island to avoid the shallow area off the Gibraltar (west) shore. Past Skagit Island watch your depth and be alert for crab pots and submerged pilings halfway into the bay.

Anchorage, Moorings. Anchorage is possible north and east of Kiket Island, in less than 2 fathoms, mud bottom. Don't expect much protection here. All docks and mooring buoys are private.

Getting Ashore. The only public access is at the end of Thompson Road, west of the log booming area. There are no facilities within walking distance.

Deception Pass/Deception Pass State Park

Charts: 18421, **18427**, 18429

The Deception Pass area is steep, rugged, and dramatic. The land north and south of the high bridge that spans the pass—a total of more than 2,000 acres and 14 miles of shoreline—is a state park, the most heavily used in Puget Sound. Visitors who arrive by land are attracted to its camping and picnic areas, its extensive trail system, and its lakes and beaches. You can fish in salt water or cast your line into freshwater lakes, explore rocky tidepools or grassy sand dunes, watch boats navigate the swirling, narrow pass, or gaze across

the vastness of the Strait of Juan de Fuca. Visitors who arrive by boat can enjoy many of these activities as well, thanks to marine facilities on both sides of the pass.

Approaches. Descriptions of Deception Pass always include extreme words or phrases. Vancouver, who mistook the narrow entrance for an isthmus connecting Whidbey Island to the mainland, gave the pass its present cautionary name. The *Coast Pilot* uses the words "impressive," "challenging," and "prohibitive."

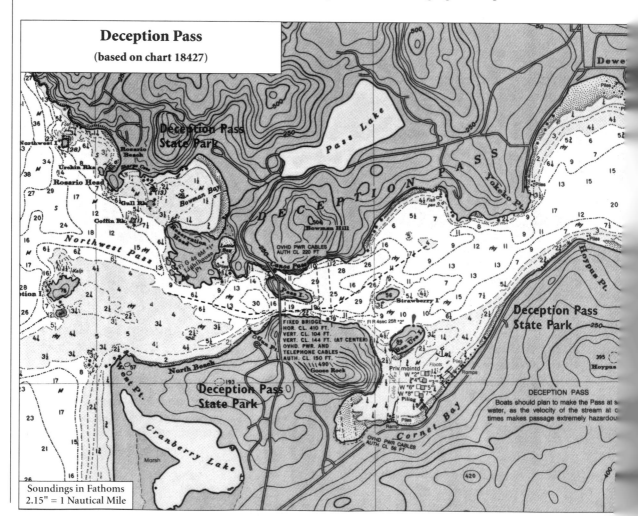

Deception Pass
(based on chart 18427)

Soundings in Fathoms
2.15" = 1 Nautical Mile

Deception Pass from the west. South of Pass Island—the preferred route—the bridge has a vertical clearance of 144 feet at the center of the span.

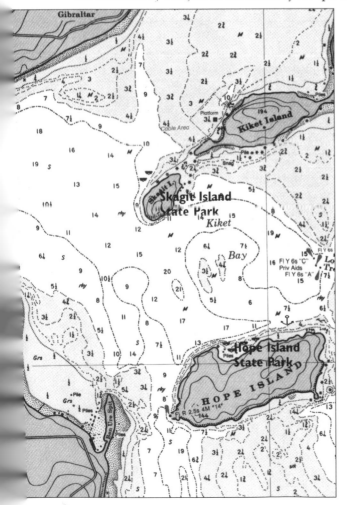

The Indians knew it, simply and accurately, as "Dangerous." Currents exceed 8 knots at times, and in a westerly with a heavy swell off the Strait of Juan de Fuca, this pass is treacherous for any boat.

If Deception Pass were anywhere else, it would probably be avoided. Instead, it is favored. Boaters heading for, or returning from, the San Juan Islands prefer it to the "outside" route across the Strait of Juan de Fuca, or the longer route through Swinomish Channel. Even in fog, and especially in stormy weather, this narrow pass—barely 200 feet wide—is surprisingly crowded.

One of the major reasons boaters choose Deception Pass is that, unlike the strait, the waters are predictable. Determining slack water—the optimal time to transit the pass—is easy; a current table is published specifically for this area, and no calculation is required. Those with small, fast boats who know how to negotiate the whirlpools often ignore the currents, but most boaters time their arrival carefully. The timing pays off; with slack water, chart 18427, and reasonable visibility, navigating Deception Pass is straightforward. The biggest challenge is to pay attention to the channel, resisting the temptation to gape, open-mouthed, at the canyon-like beauty above and around you.

229

From the east, take a mid-channel course between Yokeko Point and Hoypus Point, then either side of Strawberry Island. A reef marked by kelp extends south of Strawberry Island. Head for the channel south of Pass Island, slightly favoring the island in order to avoid the pinnacle rocks and ledges along the Whidbey Island shore. Once past the bridge, the cleanest route is to the northwest.

From the west, all the above applies, in reverse. After the open waters of Rosario Strait and the Strait of Juan de Fuca, take care to stay well off Deception Island, which is foul with shoals, reef, and kelp, especially on its north and south sides. The waters south of Deception Island are shoal; if there's a swell running in the strait, the seas will be steeper here.

From either approach expect to feel current, even at slack.

Cornet Bay ★★★★

Charts: 18421, 18427

So close to the rush of current and traffic in Deception Pass, Cornet Bay can feel like a refuge of quiet water, despite the summer crowds. The navigable portion is deceptively small—almost a third of the bay dries at low tide—but the state park facilities make creative use of the deep water, and there is room for anchoring.

The park facilities at Cornet Bay are open year round.

Approaches. From the east, favor the south shore after rounding Hoypus Point. Boats approaching from the west should enter east of Ben Ure Island. The shoal east of the island can be avoided by staying 500 yards off Ben Ure and turning into the bay along the Whidbey shore. Watch for crab pots.

Avoid the passage west of Ben Ure, which dries at a minus tide.

Moorings. The state park floats are west of the three launching ramps. Two detached floats, each about 100 feet long, are set parallel to the main float and ramp. There's a fee for these floats year round; pay at the head of the ramp. There are water spigots on land, but none on the state floats.

Cornet Bay Marina, west of the state park floats, has no overnight moorage.

The county float west of the Cornet Bay Marina also has no overnight moorage. This float goes dry at low tide.

Anchorage. The anchoring basin is northeast of the state park floats, between Ben Ure Island and Whidbey Island. Westerlies funnel from the strait over Whidbey, and currents can be strong—take time to set your hook well.

Getting Ashore. The best shore access is at the marina or at the state park float. The west end of Cornet Bay dries at low tide, and is not recommended. Ben Ure Island tidelands are private.

For the Boat. The fuel dock is west of the state floats, beyond the boathouses at Cornet Bay Marina. This marina maintains a dredged channel. Enter between the marked pilings, then turn to port and tie up in front of the marina store and office. Some marine supplies are available at the store. A nearby shop does small repair, but the five-ton hoist is no longer used for hauling boats.

For the Crew. Restrooms with showers are at the head of the state park float. Groceries and ice are available at the marina store, a short walk west along the road, where there's also a pay phone. The nearest laundromat is on the highway, a mile-and-a-half up the hill. A café is farther north.

Things to Do. This south side of Deception Pass State Park has more variety than you can experience in a weekend. Walk east to Hoypus Point, where concrete ruins are all that remain of the old Fidalgo Island ferry dock, or pick up the trail that circles Hoypus Hill—about a four-mile round trip.

West along the road, at the head of Cornet Bay, is an Environmental Learning Center (ELC), which the park rents out for group activities; access to this area is restricted. A trail that skirts the west edge of the ELC leads to the summit of Goose Rock, around the perimeter to the bridge, and across the highway to more trails and to Cranberry Lake, a total distance of almost three miles each way. The lake has a fishing dock, swimming beach, and bathhouse. A large camping area—more than 250 sites—is north of the lake. West on the beach is a seasonal concession stand and another trail, this one through sand dunes and marsh. The Haida Bear monument at West Point is a reminder of the northern clans who frequently raided the local Samish Indians.

There's lots more state park north across the bridge, described below in the Bowman Bay entry.

Lottie Bay

Charts: 18421, **18427**, 18429

Lottie Bay indents the north shore of Deception Pass, west of Pass Island. The bay is tiny and shallow, with rocks on both sides of its entrance and charted piles inside the 1-fathom line. Almost half of Lottie Bay goes dry at low tide. Even for a small boat it is not a good anchorage, as it is exposed to the turbulence of both the pass itself and the wakes of boats hurrying by.

The bight east of Lottie Bay is alive with the current, an even worse choice of anchorage.

Bowman Bay ★★★★★

Charts: 18421, **18427**, 18429

Bowman Bay faces the Strait of Juan de Fuca on the northwest side of Deception Pass, guarded by reef, rock, and the curl of Reservation Head. For an offshore cruiser accustomed to ocean swell, this bay will seem comfortable enough. For boaters who prefer calm inland waters, it may be too exposed.

This exposure is part of what makes Bowman Bay so beautiful. The beach is a crescent of sand, the headlands wind-torn, rocky, and steep. The view west toward the strait is a limitless horizon. Sunsets can be spectacular. Deception Pass State Park is more accessible from here than from Cornet Bay. On shore is an interpretive center, trails leading to cliff overviews, and a freshwater lake.

The campground facilities at Bowman Bay are open year round.

Approaches. From Deception Pass or Rosario Strait, the cleanest approach is via Northwest Pass. Stay south of Coffin Rock. Past Gull Rock, favor Reservation Head, watching for kelp that spreads north and east of the head. There is enough depth between Gull and Coffin rocks, but you will have to pay close attention if you use this route. At low tide it's obvious that Coffin Rock is aptly named.

Anchorage, Moorings. North and east of Reservation Head, Bowman Bay begins to shallow. Five mooring buoys are set across the bay, the one farthest from shore in water almost twice as deep as those closer to shore. Anchoring is good in mud bottom. Almost any weather turns in from the west here, so be prepared for a night of rocking. In calm conditions the swells of commercial vessels may affect you. Shallow-draft boats may be more protected east of the hook of Reservation Head. No mooring is permitted at the fishing pier.

Getting Ashore. All shoreline is public.

For the Crew. There are restrooms with showers north of the fishing pier.

Things to Do. On shore are picnic tables and shelters, and a fishing pier. The timber-and-stone shelters and other park structures were built in 1930 by the Civilian Conservation Corps (CCC). Perfectly suited to their surroundings, they seem to have grown by themselves from the rocks and trees. The interpretive center here is open in the summer, staffed by CCC alumni.

The trails from Bowman Bay are some of the most popular in the park. Hike south to climb Reservation Head, north to Pass Lake, or west to Rosario Head. At Rosario Head stands the Maiden of Deception Pass, a wooden story pole that commemorates the Samish princess who saved the land and her people by marrying the prince of the sea. North of Rosario Head is a beach much favored by scuba divers. The trail to Pass Lake begins north of the campground.

The Maiden of Deception Pass, on Rosario Head. This side of the story pole shows her hair transformed into kelp by her life in the sea.

There's more state park across the bridge, as described above in the entry for Cornet Bay.

Sharpe Cove ★★★★★

Charts: 18421, **18427**, 18429

This tiny bight is northwest of Bowman Bay, inside the knob of Rosario Head and the low isthmus that joins the head to the rest of Fidalgo Island. Sharpe Cove is separated from Bowman Bay by a reef that terminates at Gull Rock, connected on shore by a steep half-mile trail. Though Sharpe Cove is shallower and more exposed than Bowman Bay, it has the advantage of a dock and float.

Approaches. From Northwest Pass, enter northwest of Coffin Rock. Watch for kelp off Rosario Head. If approaching from Bowman Bay, stay south of Gull Rock. Pass between Gull and Coffin Rocks carefully, or better yet, go around Coffin altogether.

Anchorage, Moorings. The park float is on the northwest side of the cove, just east of the story pole. The float is about 60 feet long, for shallow-draft vessels only, and is pulled out of service for winter. Sharpe Cove shallows rapidly, and its west side is foul with rocks and reefs. Anchorage is not good; depending on your

Sharpe Cove southeast of Rosario Head. The state park floats have been removed for the winter.

draft, you may find yourself outside the cove before you've got enough depth and swinging room. Nearby Bowman Bay is a better choice.

The cove north of Rosario Head is exposed and small, a favorite for divers but a poor anchorage.

Getting Ashore. All shoreline is public.

For the Crew. An outdoor shower is outside the restrooms of the nearby campground. Hot showers are in the restrooms at the head of Bowman Bay, a half-mile east.

Things to Do. The activities described in the Bowman Bay entry above apply as well to Sharpe Cove. Park activities and facilities south of Deception Pass are described in the Cornet Bay entry.

Burrows Bay

Charts: 18421, **18427**, 18429

This long, wide bay on the west side of Fidalgo Island is sheltered at its north end by Burrows Island and Allan Island, but otherwise exposed to the southwest and the Strait of Juan de Fuca. The main attraction for boaters is the large marina in Flounder Bay.

Approaches. Approaches are clean with hazards well marked. Stay 200 yards away from the National Wildlife Refuge of Williamson Rocks, south of Allan Island. Currents can be strong around these rocks, as well as in Allan Pass and Burrows Pass.

Telegraph Bight

Charts: 18421, **18427**, 18429

This tiny bight lies just outside the south entrance to Burrows Bay, below Biz Point. There's good depth but no protection here. The rocky, steep shore and the reefs on both sides of the entrance magnify the surge off the strait. All tidelands are private.

Langley Bay ★ No Facilities

Charts: 18421, **18427**, 18429

The east side of Burrows Bay is irregular, exposed, and foul with shoal and rock. The shoreline is steep, with broad shallow areas of beach that dry at low and minus tides. The only anchorage worth noting is at the south end—Langley Bay—inside the hook formed by Biz Point. However, this small bay is not recommended. A private dock and private mooring buoys fill the only suitable anchorage in the west corner. The area east of the nearby reef is exposed.

Approaching Langley Bay, stay well north of the reef and kelp off Biz Point. Take care not to drift too far east toward the unmarked reef about 200 yards off the south shore; another reef is about 300 yards north. All tidelands are private.

Allan Island

Charts: 18421, **18427**

This rocky, steep-sided island in Burrows Bay is surrounded by reef. The only good anchorage—on the east side—is off-limits to casual visitors. A sign on the floating breakwater across the entrance warns outsiders not to anchor within 300 feet. Another sign on the dock inside the bight warns visitors that they are under surveillance. All of Allan Island is private.

Burrows Island ★ No Facilities

Charts: 18421, **18427**, 18429

The sheer rock face of Burrows Island is as dangerous as it is beautiful. Reefs surround the entire island, and currents are strong, especially in Allan Pass. A 40-acre undeveloped state park is at the lighthouse, but there is no safe access for boats. All other tidelands are private.

Peartree Bay, on the southeast side of Burrows Island, has room for one boat only; a private mooring buoy is set in the best anchoring spot. A house dominates the beach, which is posted with private property signs.

Alice Bight, on the east side of Burrows, has room inside the 10-fathom line, but you'll need to get quite close to shore for protection from the southwest. The bottom is rocky, and the view of the heavily-developed housing on the hillside across Burrows Bay is unattractive. All tidelands are private.

Flounder Bay ★★ All Facilities

Charts: 18441, **18427**, 18429

The dredged harbor of Flounder Bay is filled with private homes, condominiums, docks, and large, private Skyline Marina. For most boaters this is a jumping-off spot rather than a destination; many from lower Puget Sound lease slips for the summer in order to be close to the fine cruising of the San Juan and Gulf islands.

Approaches. From any direction, the barreled roof of the former dirigible hangar west of the marina and the masts of boats inside the concrete-and-rock breakwater are clear landmarks. The entrance is at the east end of the breakwater, between the pilings marked with green and red lights. A confusing tide gauge on a piling, with a "Leave No Wake" sign, marks the turn to port into the bay; no one seems to know what this gauge is for, or what the numbers mean. Pay attention to your own depthsounder rather than the gauge as you make your turn. Depths are deeper inside than in the entrance channel. Those with deep-draft vessels should take care at minus tides.

Moorings. Pull up to the fuel dock, and check in there or at the marina office for a slip assignment. Skyline Marina has no designated guest moorage, but instead gives tenants credit for transients moored in their slips. Reservations are a good idea in summer—(360) 293-5134—especially if you'll be arriving after working hours. Do not pull into an empty slip without prior arrangements.

There is no anchoring room inside Flounder Bay.

For the Boat. Skyline Marina offers a full range of haulout and repair services. The store inside the marina office is fairly well supplied. Covered repair and storage is inside the old dirigible hangar.

For the Crew. Showers and laundromat are on the east side of the marina office. A few snack items are sold in the marina store; for more variety walk about a block north to the deli grocery at the service station. The nearest supermarket is in Anacortes, almost four miles away. A restaurant is south of the marina office.

Things to Do. A good walking destination is Washington Park on Fidalgo Head, about a half-mile west. This popular Anacortes city park has playground equipment and a two-and-a-half-mile loop trail with extraordinary views of Rosario Strait. The launching ramp on the north shore of the park is flanked by two short floats; this area is a cable crossing, and not good for anchoring.

Swinomish Channel

Charts: 18427

For boaters, long and narrow Swinomish Channel is a popular route between Skagit Bay and Anacortes, especially when conditions are rough "outside" on the straits. Even those in a hurry find La Conner difficult to pass by.

Approaches. Mudflats extend several miles south and north of Swinomish Channel. The channel is well marked through these mudflats; to avoid grounding it's important to stay inside the marks, no matter how high the tide. Whether you enter from the southwest or from the north, keep red marks to starboard and green to port. The colors reverse at the concrete highway bridge that spans the north (Anacortes) end of the channel; northbound ves-

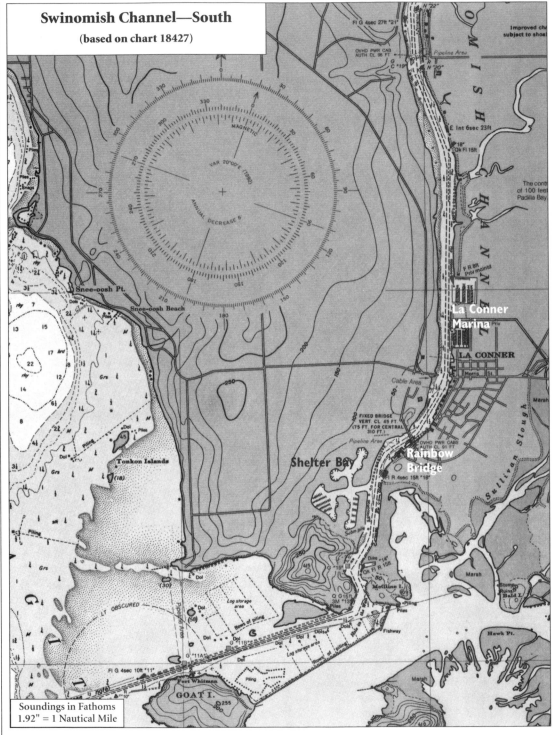

Swinomish Channel—South
(based on chart 18427)

Soundings in Fathoms
1.92" = 1 Nautical Mile

sels keep red to port and green to starboard *north* of the highway bridge, while southbound vessels keep red to port and green to starboard *south* of the highway bridge.

Controlling depth for the entire channel is charted at 10 feet 9 inches; those with deep-draft

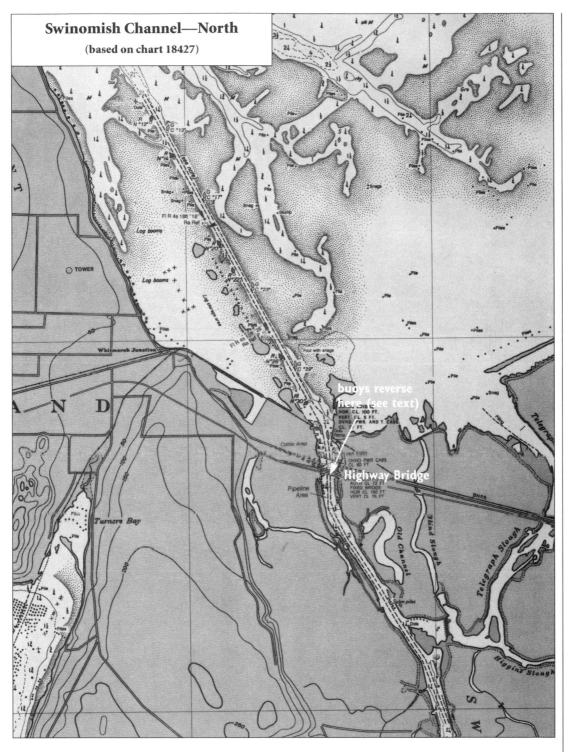

Swinomish Channel—North

(based on chart 18427)

buoys reverse here (see text)

Highway Bridge

vessels should take care during low tide. The bottom is corrugated by current, and shallow areas have been reported at the south end, notably around the entrance to Shelter Bay.

The strong current in Swinomish Channel deserves respect. No one seems able to explain or predict it. Some say it floods north and ebbs south, about an hour before (or after) Anacortes. Generally. Others say it floods and ebbs from both ends. Usually. Where it meets is anybody's guess. Most locals refuse to be pinned down to specifics: "It goes this way, it goes that way, it does stuff in between." Everybody has the same good advice: "Watch it." Before approaching a dock or pulling away, always take time to observe the water, the buoys, and the way your own boat handles. Watch, and maneuver accordingly.

Approaching from the southwest, the dredged channel begins between Whidbey Island's Dugualla Bay and Goat Island. At green "1" and red "2," make a sharp turn to the northeast. Use the range behind you in Dugualla Bay to line yourself up. West of Goat Island, the channel is marked with red daymarks on pilings and green light "11A;" east of Goat are three green daymarks on pilings and a log boom on the south side. At green "13," turn north into the canyon-like passage known as Hole in the Wall. From here the channel is more obvious, and the graceful arch of the Rainbow Bridge will soon come into view, the town of La Conner beyond. The fixed

Rainbow Bridge has a clearance of 75 feet at the center of the span. Watch for boat traffic from the launching ramp on the east shore under the Rainbow Bridge, and observe the no-wake speed limit.

Approaching from the north, pick up the channel in Padilla Bay at red "2," about a half-mile north of March Point. From here you'll pass the towers, derricks, and tanks of the oil refinery on the west shore, and one of the richest saltwater estuaries in the country east of you in Padilla Bay. South of red "30," the channel continues past the timbers of the railroad swing bridge. This bridge is kept in open position for boaters unless a train is on the track.

The state highway bridge south of it has a fixed clearance of 75 feet. Watch for boat traffic from the launching ramp on the east shore behind the breakwater, under the highway bridge. Note that the navigation marks reverse south of this bridge, and keep the red marks to port for the remainder of the channel. From here to La Conner the land is low and grassy, almost like a prairie. Homes on the east shore face the land of the Swinomish Indian Reservation on the west. Watch for the no-wake speed limit signs and observe them.

La Conner ★★★★★ All Facilities

Charts: 18427

The town of La Conner sits straight and proud on its pilings, on the southeast bank of the Swinomish Channel. In the early 1900s, La Conner was a hub of commercial activity. Steamboats navigated to and from the farmlands in the surrounding sloughs, and fishing boats delivered their catch to the canneries. Today the town prospers as a tourist destination, with colorful false-front shops, inns, and restaurants, original wood-framed historic homes, and several museums.

Moorings. The Port of Skagit County operates a large marina on the north side of town consisting of two moorage basins separated by an industrial peninsula. Visitor moorage is on

both sides of the outer float for each basin. These floats are each about 700 feet long, connected to land at their south ends. A fee box is at the top of each ramp; a dock attendant will leave an envelope on your boat for payment, or you can walk to the marina office located between the two basins. The marina does not take reservations.

If your stay is short and you want to be right in town, use one of the three city floats at the street ends along the channel. Pay at the fee box located at each float. Floats vary in length anywhere from 20 to 70 feet, and have no electrical hookups. There is no overnight moorage on these city floats. Overnight moorage is available at the Swinomish Indian Tribal Park

La Conner, from south of the Rainbow Bridge. (U.S. Army Corps of Engineers)

floats at the south end of town. Use the fee box at the head of the ramp. Moorage is limited to 12 hours.

Several restaurants have floats along the channel, including one on the west (Swinomish Reservation) side. Private floats are clearly posted.

Shelter Bay, the large, three-lobed marina south of the Rainbow Bridge, is entirely private and has no visitor moorage.

There is no room—or quiet water—for anchoring in Swinomish Channel.

For the Boat. The fuel dock is between the north and south basins. Just north of the fuel dock is a well-stocked marine supply store with its own float for visitors; a privately maintained arrow points in the direction of the current there. Full-service boatyards are on both sides of the north basin. There's also a boatyard about a mile south of town, just north of Hole in the Wall.

For the Crew. Showers and laundry for the north basin are on the ground floor of the marina office; for the south basin these facilities are across the parking lot, near the public phone. The closest grocery is about a block south of the south basin, at the first intersection. This store has a float on the channel for boat-side deliveries. Another grocery is a few blocks east. The only problem with restaurants in La Conner is choosing one.

Things to Do. La Conner is about one-and-a-half square miles in size, a walking town with shops and restaurants interspersed with picnic tables and views of the channel. Pick up a visitors' guide at the Chamber of Commerce to help you locate La Conner's many historic homes and structures. The Chamber of Commerce is located in the "mall" just south of the blinking light at First Street and Morris. A Fireman's Museum is in the middle of the main commercial block, near the public restrooms and stairway to Second Street. Walk all the way south on First Street, then east up the hill to the old City Hall and the turreted, 22-room Gaches Mansion, now open for visitors.

Farther uphill to the northwest is the Skagit County Museum, worth a visit for its panoramic views alone. From here you can see how La Conner was once an island, and can trace the dikes that hold back the river and its tideflats to form the rich agricultural lands of the Skagit Valley. In spring, the fields are brightly patched with yellow squares of daffodils, and the deep pinks and golds of tulips.

The North Cascades and Mt. Baker frame the eastern horizon.

Special events are held year round, including a Swinomish Channel fireworks display on the Fourth of July, a Boat and RV Christmas Parade in early December, and a two-week Tulip Festival in early spring that attracts enormous crowds to the entire valley. A sign near the Fireman's Museum lists the specific dates of these events; for Tulip Time it suggests you "ask God."

Anacortes ★★★★ All Facilities

Charts: 18421, **18427**

The city of Anacortes is centered on the northeast tip of Fidalgo Island, bordered by Fidalgo Bay and Guemes Channel. Once the site of many canneries—this was the largest cod fishery on the West Coast in the early 1900s—the area is now a commercial center for the nearby San Juan Islands. Its most visible industry is the oil refinery on March Point. Tankers dock at the piers in Fidalgo Bay, and at night the refinery towers glitter like a futuristic Oz.

For most visitors, Anacortes is the gateway to the San Juan Islands, via the state ferry terminal in Ship Harbor and the Guemes ferry on the north edge of town. Boaters are drawn by the facilities for commercial and pleasure craft that line the shore along Fidalgo Bay and Guemes Channel. Of the many marinas here, Cap Sante Boat Haven, operated by the Port of Anacortes, is the only one with floats for visitors.

Approaches. Cap Sante Boat Haven is tucked behind the prominent cliff of Cap Sante, the northwest point of Fidalgo Bay. Approaching from Swinomish Channel, clear red "2" at the north end of the channel before turning west toward Cap Sante. Give the refinery piers and the tugs and ships operating there a wide berth. Past the piers, stay north of red nun buoy "2" and north of red-and-green buoy "A." Buoy "A" lines you up for the marked entrance channel into Cap Sante Boat Haven, as well as for the private marinas to the south.

Approaching from the north, you'll first see the private marinas on the west shore of Fidalgo Bay. Head for red-and-green buoy "A." The Boat Haven will gradually emerge from behind the cliff, north of the charted stack.

Enter Cap Sante Boat Haven between the rock jetty and the timber breakwater. A detached breakwater is just inside, with a sign directing visitors to "C" dock. Make a sharp turn to port past the south end of this detached breakwater (there are rocks to starboard), and then another turn to starboard past "B" dock. The floats at the end of "C" dock are for visitor check-in; moor on either side.

Moorings. After tying up at the end of "C" dock, report to the harbor office at the head of the ramp for a slip assignment. Reservations are taken a half-hour before arrival on VHF Channel 66 (U.S.). After hours, night-time security personnel will check you in on "C" dock.

Overnight moorage is not available at Anacortes Marina, nor at Fidalgo Marina, farther south behind the concrete breakwater.

For the Boat. The fuel dock is under the hoist between "C" and "B" docks. A marine supply store and full-service boat repair yard is right across the street. The most notable marine store in Anacortes—and one of the oldest on the West Coast—is north on Commercial Avenue and 2nd Street.

Gas, diesel, and repairs are also available

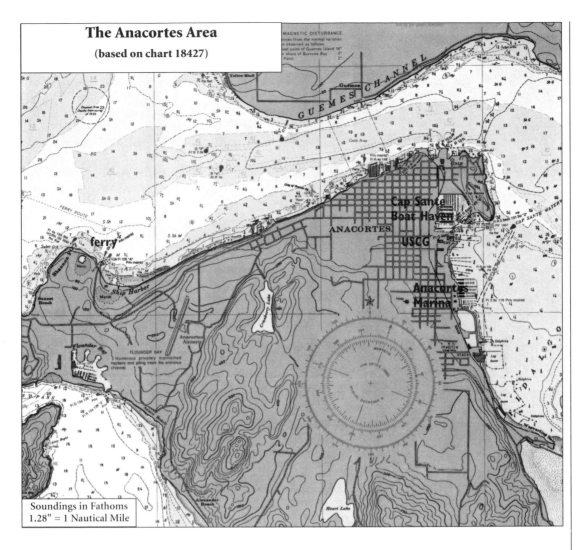

The Anacortes Area
(based on chart 18427)

Soundings in Fathoms
1.28" = 1 Nautical Mile

south of Cap Sante at Anacortes Marina. Enter via the dredged channel that branches southwest from red-and-green buoy "A," outside Cap Sante Boat Haven. This channel is marked but made somewhat confusing by one-way traffic signs on pilings and on the timber breakwater. The entrance to Anacortes Marina is at the south end of this breakwater; the fuel dock and boat hoist are inside, directly ahead. The exit is to the north. Both entrance and exit are narrow, with no room for two-way traffic.

In Guemes Channel, gas and diesel are available at Wyman's Marina, just east of the tall white stack painted with signal flags. Enter east of the three dolphin pilings, and fender well; the floats are exposed to wind and the wakes of passing boats. Depths are OK for shallow-draft vessels. Wyman's also has a small store and repair facility, but no overnight moorage. The float for the nearby restaurant is in disrepair.

For the Crew. Cap Sante Boat Haven has showers and laundries in two locations: at the north end of the harbor office on the west shore, and between the ramps for "J" through "Q" docks on the north shore. There are restaurants, delis, and shops in the retail complex around the harbor office, and many more in town, a short walk west and north. A supermarket is close by, on Commercial Avenue and 12th Street.

The steam train approaches the depot in Anacortes, past the sternwheeler W. T. Preston. *For 52 years the* Preston *removed snags and other navigational hazards from the waters between Olympia and Blaine. The masts in the background are of boats moored in Cap Sante marina.*

Things to Do. The northwest corner of the boat harbor has several attractions. Take a self-guided tour of the dry-docked *W. T. Preston*, the Northwest's last operating steam-driven sternwheeler. The old railroad depot just north of the *Preston* is now a cultural arts center, with a farmers' market that operates every Saturday from April through October. A narrow-gauge steam train takes visitors from here into town, less than a mile away, on weekends and holidays from mid-June through Labor Day. The locomotive and its twinkling, turn-of-the-century passenger cars were built by the engineer.

Many of the buildings in Anacortes are painted with murals depicting the people and events of the town's early days.

If you're up for exercise, walk east and south to the harbor jetty, where you can pick up the steep park trail to the top of Cap Sante. From here the view is unbroken south and east, and Mt. Baker seems to lean northward, as though pushed by the peaks on its southern shoulder.

Anacortes hosts a Waterfront Festival at Cap Sante Boat Haven in late May, and an Arts and Crafts Festival in early August.

Ship Harbor ★

Charts: 18421, **18427**, 18429

Ship Harbor is at the west end of Guemes Channel, east of Shannon Point. On the west

shore is the state ferry terminal for the San Juan Islands. A marina development is planned for

Ship Harbor, but currently there are no facilities other than a snack bar at the ferry terminal, and a couple of restaurants at the top of the hill.

Approaches, Anchorage. About half of Ship Harbor dries at low tide, with a steep shelf edging the deep water. Abandoned pilings extend well out from the middle of the beach; others are west, nearer the ferry dock. In addition to watching for these hazards, it's important to stay out of the way of ferry traffic and to give the ferry dock a wide berth.

The anchorage here—slightly east of the mid-harbor pilings and slightly south of the ferry dolphins—is not good. Expect no protection here from wind, current, or wake. The *Coast Pilot* warns against dragging anchor here, as the holding ground is poor.

The beach below the waiting lanes for the ferry is public.

REGION 9

GUEMES ISLAND

TO POINT ROBERTS

Mt. Baker, with the south shore of Guemes Island
in the foreground.
(Delores Foss photo)

INCLUDING BELLINGHAM BAY

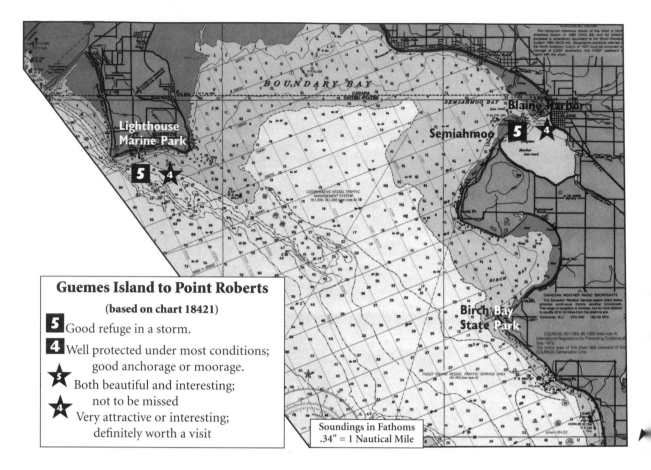

Guemes Island to Point Roberts

(based on chart 18421)

5 Good refuge in a storm.

4 Well protected under most conditions; good anchorage or moorage.

★**5** Both beautiful and interesting; not to be missed

★**4** Very attractive or interesting; definitely worth a visit

Soundings in Fathoms
.34" = 1 Nautical Mile

East of Rosario Strait, from Guemes Island and Cypress Island north to the Canadian border at Point Roberts and Blaine, is a region often bypassed by Pacific Northwest cruisers. The lure of the nearby San Juan Islands draws most boaters west, so unless you or your boat reside here it's generally an area to slip through rather than to savor. Like any place that's off the track, there are wonderful surprises for those who take the time to explore these waters.

To best appreciate this eastern portion, it helps to recognize a few of its defining characteristics. The most apparent is Mt. Baker. In clear weather, or in conditions of high overcast, this 10,788-foot peak seems to occupy half of the eastern horizon. From other parts of Puget Sound, Mt. Baker has a peek-a-boo, distant beauty. Here the mountain is constant and dominating, the tallest peak by far on a horizon of jagged white peaks that form the North Cascades, a living volcano whose last activity, steam plumes, occurred in 1975. Known as Kulshan by the Indian tribes that have lived in its presence for more than 2,000 years, as heavily shrouded in spirit and legend as it is in snow and ice, the mountain is a powerful reminder of the wilderness. You can almost sense the cougar, the mountain goat, the elk and the black bear that live in its shadow. You can almost feel the chill that descends from its flanks.

Even when Mt. Baker isn't "out," its presence is visible in the form of clouds stacking up against the Cascades, heavy with moisture. Where the San Juan Islands average about 25 inches of precipitation annually, the Bellingham area receives more than 33. Be prepared for a bit more rain.

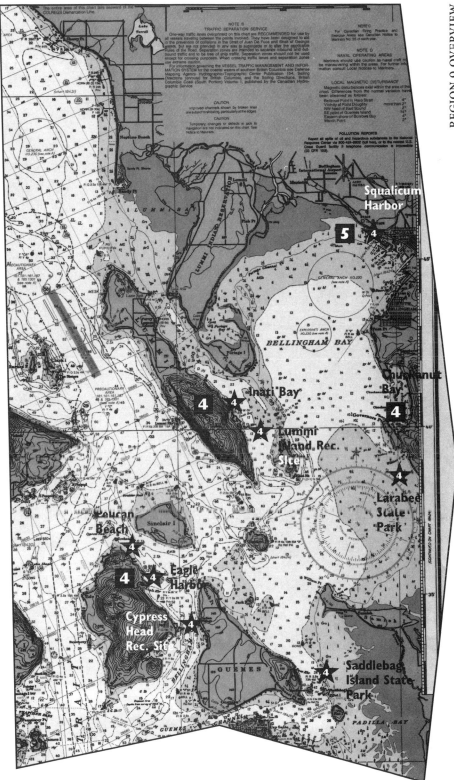

Soundings in Fathoms
.34" = 1 Nautical Mile

Open water is also a factor. The Strait of Georgia extends more than 100 miles northwest, the direction of prevailing summer winds—good news for sailors at this time of year. But fair weather here doesn't always mean fair sailing. The mountains on Vancouver Island and on the U.S./Canadian mainland increase the velocity of the wind and consequently the height of the seas at the southern end of the strait. This condition is further exaggerated on a flood tide, when wind and current are opposed—potentially dangerous even in summer, and certainly uncomfortable for boaters who prefer their inland water relatively flat. Add to this the scarcity of protected anchorages along the eastern shore, and the open water of the Strait of Georgia quickly becomes as much an object of respect and awe as Mt. Baker.

This region consists roughly of two areas. The islands at the south, geologically part of the San Juan archipelago, are rocky; many, but not all, are steep-sided. The area along the mainland is bordered by extensive, largely unnavigable tideflats fed by the many rivers and creeks that flow from the Cascade foothills.

Guemes Island

Charts: 18421, **18424**, 18427

On the chart, Guemes Island looks like a rounded right triangle. With trees and homes dotting low golden hills, the island has a rural look even from a distance. It seems untouched by the industry and development of nearby Anacortes, despite the county ferry that scuttles regularly between the town and the south end of the island.

Most of Guemes is private. Its smooth shores do not invite anchoring, nor do the tideflats that extend south, west, and northeast, many of them marked with shoals and rocks. The flat terrain of the island does steepen toward the southeast tip, where the only two suitable anchorages are located.

Boat Harbor ★★★ [2] No Facilities

Charts: 18421, **18427**

Boat Harbor (also called Square Harbor) is a tiny squarish cove on the southeast side of Guemes Island. Madrona and fir snags cling to steep rock walls that descend almost perpendicularly into the water. The small gravel beach is piled with driftwood. Once tucked into this cove, the southeast point of Guemes Island shields you from an industrial view of the Anacortes refinery, though graceful Rainbow Bridge in La Conner is visible. The entire effect is that you seem much farther away from civilization than you really are.

Approaches. The 100-foot cliff immediately north of Boat Harbor makes it easy to find. From the southeast, aim straight for the center of the small crescent beach.

Anchorage. Unless your boat draws very little, drop anchor abeam of the north cliff. This should put you in 20 to 30 feet of water. Boat Harbor is about 100 feet wide, with room for one or perhaps two boats. Check that your swing won't put you on shore or against the rock wall to the south.

While protection from north wind is satisfactory here, wave action will turn in to this pocket-size harbor.

Getting Ashore. The state Department of Wildlife has designated the shoreline of Boat Harbor an endangered wildlife species area. Landing is prohibited and NO TRESPASSING signs ring the beach. The closest public beach access is not on Guemes at all, but at the state park on Saddlebag Island, about a mile to the southeast.

Cove Southwest of Huckleberry Island ★★ ⬚2 No Facilities

Charts: 18421, **18427**

Though less picturesque than Boat Harbor, this cove offers more depth and swinging room and may be a good alternative if anchorage at Boat Harbor or at Saddlebag Island is full. Private homes perch on the bluffs above you here, and the gravel beach is private.

Approaches. From the south, stay clear of the marked shoals and kelp off Southeast Point. The cove itself is clean.

Anchorage. Anchor anywhere within the bowl of this 2-fathom cove. You may be more exposed than you expect to southwesterlies wrapping around Southeast Point and to swells from either north or south.

Getting Ashore. The tidelands of this cove are private. The nearest public beach access is at the state park on Saddlebag Island, about a mile east.

Saddlebag Island State Park ★★★★ ⬚2 No Facilities

Charts: 18421, **18427**

This tiny, beautifully undeveloped island located about a mile off the southeast tip of Guemes Island was established as a state park in 1974. Saddlebag is shaped like its name, with coves north and south of a low neck of land, humps on both ends. The shoreline looks like a child's construction, squarish blocks of stone piled on each other and then pushed over. Accessible only by water, the island is popular with small craft, kayaks, and canoes; off-season and midweek it can be isolated and lovely.

Approaches. Saddlebag is on the very edge of a steep underwater shelf, and needs to be approached with caution. The bottom rises abruptly from between 10 and 14 fathoms to less than 1 fathom. From the north or south, head for the navigational mark on the west side. Stay west, in deep water, until either cove is clearly visible. When approaching the south cove, take special note of charted rocks and reefs, and be ready for sudden changes in depth.

Anchorage. The south cove is extremely shallow, exposed to southwest winds and swell and to the view of the Anacortes refinery. It is not a good spot to anchor. The north cove is much preferred, though you may need to anchor outside the bight of the cove itself in order to have enough depth and swinging room. The bottom rises abruptly just within the cove. You're totally exposed to the north here, the lee shore is close and rocky, and Padilla Bay to the east is extremely shallow.

Getting Ashore. The entire island is public.

Things to Do. A mile of trail wanders over the humps of Saddlebag Island, through cool woods and out to grassy points that are ideal for picnics or naps in the sun. Firepits, campsites, and pit toilets are located on the island.

Saddlebag is a popular crabbing and fishing spot; its location on the shelf means there's a lot of activity below the surface. The expansive flats of Padilla Bay form one of 17 National Estuarine Sanctuaries in the country, with 241 species of birds and 14 species of mammals. Black brant, among others, stop here on their migrations between Mexico and Alaska. Respect adjacent Dot Island, a National Wildlife Refuge, by keeping at least 200 yards away.

Cypress Island

Charts: 18421, 18433, **18424**, **18430**

More than any other, Cypress Island embodies much of what the San Juan Islands used to be: heavily wooded, quiet, remote. Steep terrain, scarce water, and the lack of ferry service has discouraged individual development. Recent citizen action has led to setting aside most of the core of the island and some of its prime beaches as the Cypress Island Natural Resources Conservation Area. A management plan is currently being developed.

The "cypress" the island was named for is actually juniper, misidentified by the 1792 Vancouver Expedition.

Things to Do. Cypress is a beautiful place for fairly serious hiking. Literally miles of trails—mostly former logging roads—are accessible from Foss Cove, Pelican Beach, and Eagle Harbor. This network wanders the full length of the island, through older second-growth forest that occasionally reveals the huge stumps left behind when Cypress was logged. Only a few of the trails on the island are marked, and you may need a compass to keep your bearings. The trail to Phoebe Lake, for example, is a vigorous three miles or so, with an elevation gain of 1,400 feet; it's easy to take a wrong turn and never find it. Other destinations are Duck Lake (shown as a marsh on the chart) and Eagle Cliff, though the latter trail is closed from February through July to ensure that endangered wildlife is undisturbed.

Nearby Cone Islands, east of Cypress, form an undeveloped state park. Currents around these islands are treacherous and access is difficult.

There are only a few anchorages on Cypress, a fact that is likely to keep the island pristine and uncrowded.

Strawberry Bay ★ ⬚1 No Facilities

Charts: 18421, **18424**, **18430**

Strawberry Bay is a long, sloping beach circled with private homes that faces southwest into Rosario Strait. The bay was named for the wild strawberries found here by the Vancouver Expedition in 1792. Despite the presence of Strawberry Island to the west, this bay is entirely open to weather and wave from the Strait of Juan de Fuca, to the shipping lanes, and to the wakes of ferry traffic between Anacortes and the San Juan Islands.

Approaches. A kelp bed extends off the south shore. Otherwise the bay is clean.

Anchorage. There is no sure shelter in Strawberry Bay. The *Coast Pilot* describes the anchorage most accurately as "indifferent" and seldom used. The mooring buoys in the bay are private.

Getting Ashore. The beach is private, with prominent signs warning against trespassing.

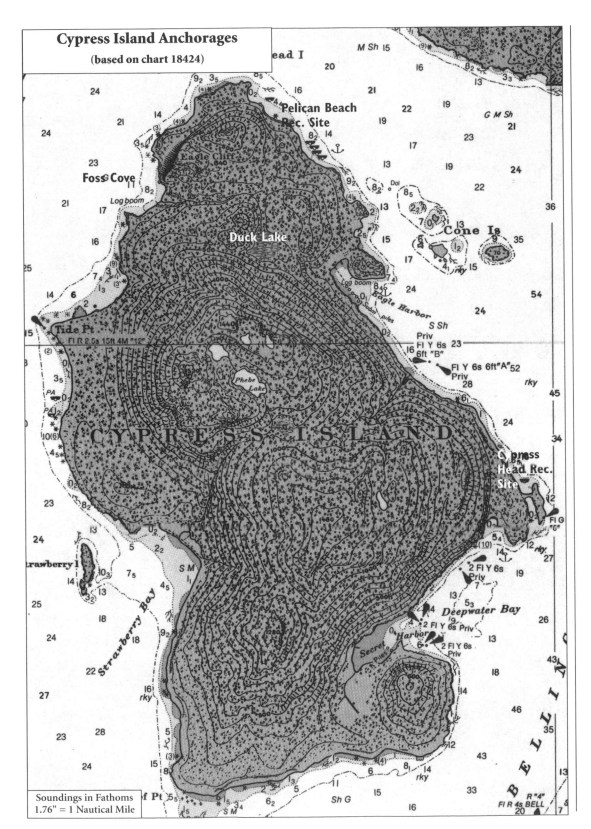

Cypress Island Anchorages
(based on chart 18424)

Pelican Beach Rec. Site

Foss Cove

Eagle Cliff

Duck Lake

Cone Is

Eagle Harbor

Tide Pt
Fl R 2.5s 15ft 4M "12"

Phebe Lake

Priv
Fl Y 6s 6ft "B"

Fl Y 6s 6ft "A"
Priv

CYPRESS ISLAND

Cypress Head Rec. Site

Fl G "0"

Strawberry I

Strawberry Bay

2 Fl Y 6s Priv

Deepwater Bay

2 Fl Y 6s Priv

Secret Harbor

2 Fl Y 6s Priv

BELLING

R "4"
Fl R 4s BELL

Soundings in Fathoms
1.76" = 1 Nautical Mile

Sheer and rocky Strawberry Island is public, a popular destination for kayakers. Watch for submerged rocks and strong tidal currents, especially at the south end.

Coves North of Tide Point ★★★ No Facilities

Charts: 18421, **18424, 18430**

The two coves north of Tide Point are unsuitable for anchoring, for many of the same reasons that affect Strawberry Bay. The southern cove especially is fouled with reefs, submerged rocks, and kelp. The north cove, locally referred to as Foss Cove, is cleaner, but currents are strong and you will need to be quite close to shore to anchor in less than 50 feet. Its setting is dramatic and rugged, with Eagle Cliff above and the woods below opening to a gravel beach, all of which is public. This cove is best explored by anchoring or mooring at Pelican Beach on the other side of Cypress Island and hiking across. Note that Foss Cove is closed from February to mid-July, as is the trail from Foss Cove to Duck Lake that leads on to Pelican Beach.

Pelican Beach ★★★★

Charts: 18421, **18424, 18430**

The Department of Natural Resources maintains a modest, beautiful recreation site on a stretch of gravel beach about a half-mile southeast of Cypress Island's northern tip. A small number of campsites, picnic tables, firepits, and pit toilets are located on or near the beach. An extensive network of trails connects this site with Eagle Harbor, Phoebe Lake, Duck Lake,

Eagle Cliff, on north Cypress Island.

and with Foss Cove below Eagle Cliff on the west side of the island. The trail from Duck Lake to Foss Cove is closed from February to mid-July.

The beach offers an unobstructed view of Mt. Baker to the east.

Approaches. From the north, watch for the charted shoal about 400 yards north of the mooring buoys. From the south, stay clear of the kelp bed off the beach's southern point. Pelican Beach can be located from the east by sighting below and just south of the 750-foot prominence of Eagle Cliff.

Anchorage, Moorings. Four mooring buoys are located off the beach. The southernmost buoy provides the deepest swinging room

toward shore, and possibly the best protection from south winds. Deep-draft vessels might feel more comfortable anchored out and slightly south of the buoys.

Pelican Beach offers absolutely no protection from the north, the prevailing wind in good summer weather. Even when the wind is not particularly stiff, swells that build over the length of the Strait of Georgia steepen when they wash onto Pelican Beach and can make an overnight anchorage extremely uncomfortable. Be prepared to move if settled conditions change.

Getting Ashore. The sloping gravel beach is an ideal place to land your skiff.

Coves Between Pelican Beach and Eagle Harbor ★★★ No Facilities

Charts: 18421, **18424**, 18430

Three tiny coves are tucked in behind a mushroom-shaped island distinguished by a ragged hole on its east face. Two of the coves offer protection from the north and south for about one boat apiece.

Approaches, Anchorage. A kelp bed is charted just north of the little island. The southern cove is mostly shoal. Both the middle and

north cove have gradually rising bottoms that abruptly shelve to less than 1 fathom. Check these coves out at low tide to be sure there is enough depth and swinging room for your boat.

Getting Ashore. Take your skiff around to either Pelican Beach or Eagle Harbor, as there is no shore access from any of these coves.

Eagle Harbor ★★★★ 4 No Facilities

Charts: 18421, 18424, **18430**

Eagle Harbor looks like a perfect anchorage; a steep head of land wraps protectively to the northeast, and all the bulk of Cypress Island stands between you and southwesterly winds. However, it is not entirely as it seems. The west and southwest shorelines shoal out extensively in the former log booming area; some submerged pilings remain. There is also a surprising shoal in the center of the harbor.

Approaches, Anchorage. Enter slowly and

with care, favoring the north shore. Watch for the hazards described above. If at all possible, enter at low tide. Verify enough depth for swing, especially if you are close to the northeast cliff.

Getting Ashore. The shoreline of Eagle Harbor is public.

Things to Do. Trails from Eagle Harbor connect to Pelican Beach Recreation Site, Phoebe

Lake, Duck Lake, and to Foss Cove below Eagle Cliff. The trail from Duck Lake to Foss cove is closed from February to mid-July. Fires are not permitted on Eagle Harbor beaches.

Cypress Head Recreation Site ★★★★

Charts: 18421, **18424**, **18430**

The peninsula of Cypress Head juts like a hammerhead into Bellingham Channel from the easternmost point of the island. The head itself has a few firepits, picnic tables, pit toilets, and campsites. A slice of the main island is also public, though it does not connect with the core of public lands and beaches to the west and north. This recreation site is best suited for small boats, especially kayaks and canoes.

Approaches, Anchorage, Moorings. On the north side of Cypress Head the beach is steep and the currents strong enough to create tidal overfalls. There are five mooring buoys placed close together in this small bay. The bay on the south side, shallow and obstructed by kelp, is not recommended.

Getting Ashore. The shoreline of Cypress Head is public.

Deepwater Bay ★★

Charts: 18421, **18424**, **18430**

Deepwater Bay is not a welcoming place for recreational boats. A private boys' home occupies the shoreline of Secret Harbor, which is full of eelgrass, and dry at low tide. Three large privately owned salmon pens occupy the most protected area at this end of the bay; cables and buoys radiate from them. Workers and their skiffs busily tend the farming operation, and the salmon swim at a dizzying pace back and forth within their net cages. The strong currents of Deepwater Bay—ideal for salmon farming—further discourage anchoring.

The north cove offers the only anchorage in the bay.

Approaches, Anchorage. Head for the private dock in the north cove. Anchor well south of the dock, in about 20 to 30 feet of water. The current, flowing like a river, should set your hook well. You will be protected only from the north here; a south fetch can build when the wind rounds the southern end of the bay.

Getting Ashore. The shoreline of Deepwater Bay is private.

Sinclair Island ★★★ No Facilities

Charts: 18421, **18424**, **18430**

Northwest of Cypress Island is flat, triangular Sinclair Island. Reefs, rocks, and extensive shoals lie off the northwest and northeast shores of Sinclair. A county dock at the tiny community of Urban on the west side provides the only suitable boat access to the few roads and public land.

Approaches, Anchorages, Moorings. Approach the concrete floating dock from the north; there is a piling breakwater and a charted rock just to the south. Currents are strong. The dock is small—only about 45 feet long—and stays are limited to one hour in the summer, two hours in the winter. Depths of 12 feet are reported. Anchoring is possible southeast of the dock, in 10 to 20 feet, mud bottom. All mooring buoys are private.

Getting Ashore. Most of the shoreline of Sinclair Island is private. The county dock at Urban is public.

Things to Do. If the square building at the head of the dock is open, the delightful memorabilia displayed there will give you an intimate feel for the island's life and history. Page through the photo albums, examine the old desks and books, and admire the outline of the 40-pound fish caught in 1946.

A few dirt roads serve what are mostly summer homes on Sinclair Island. Original cottages and ancient orchards give a sense of walking back in time. A good destination is the public land and beach—a state wildlife area—on the other side of the island, about two miles east of the county dock, past an airstrip. The public beach extends south of the road and around the southeast tip of the island.

Sinclair Island has no electricity, no stores, and no public amenities of any kind.

Vendovi Island ★★ 1 No Facilities

Charts: 18421, **18424**

Vendovi Island, located a mile-and-a-half south of Lummi Island, is round and steep-sided. Its unapproachable shores are public, while its only cove, a tiny bight behind a jetty on the southwest tip, is private. Prominent signs warn against trespassing.

One of the few islands not named after a European, American, or Native American, Vendovi takes its name from a Fijian chief who was captured by the Wilkes Expedition in the South Seas and then brought with the exploring party to the Pacific Northwest in 1838. Although he was thought to be responsible for the earlier murder of American sailors, during the voyage Vendovi's dignity and friendliness soon made him well liked by the crew.

Eliza Island ★ 1 No Facilities

Charts: 18421, **18424**

Pinwheel-shaped Eliza Island is located less than a mile east of the tip of Lummi Island. Eliza is the terminus of an underwater ridge that runs northwest to Portage Island and the Lummi peninsula. Low and partly wooded, it is more densely populated than neighboring Vendovi Island or Sinclair Island, with an airstrip at its center and vacation homes lining its shores.

Eliza Island is ringed with numerous KEEP OFF—PRIVATE BEACH signs; the dock and mooring buoys are private.

The entire east side is foul, as is most of the low shore facing northwest. The bay on the southern side of the island is clean, but is exposed to the southwest. The *Coast Pilot* describes the holding ground between Lummi and Eliza Island as poor; presumably this would apply here as well.

Eliza Rock, off the southern tip of the island, is a National Wildlife Refuge; boaters should stay at least 200 yards away.

Lummi Island

Charts: 18421, **18424**, 18430

This long, narrow island three-and-a-half miles north of Guemes has two distinct halves. The southern half, which ends in a sharp point, is steep and mountainous. The dramatic 1,500-foot cliffs are scarred with rock slides on the west side, the slopes on the southeast are deep green with fir. By contrast, the northern half of Lummi is low, rolling, and pastoral. Most of the 600 residents live on the north end, though homes are creeping south into the heights.

Lummi Island is connected to the mainland by a Whatcom County ferry that crosses Hale Passage every hour from Gooseberry Point. The island takes its name from the Native American tribe that resides on reservation land northwest of Bellingham. A favorite seal-hunting site off the island was the area beneath Devil's Slide, near Lummi Rocks.

The island has few suitable anchorages, all but one located on the east side.

Legoe Bay ★★ No Facilities

Charts: 18421, **18424**, 18430

The only bay on Lummi Island's steep west side, Legoe Bay opens widely to the shipping lanes of Rosario Strait. On shore, one of the island's few roads follows the contour of the long, gradually sloping beach. Homes cluster along the road. Traditional flat-bottomed reef-net boats are beached everywhere, their lookout towers giving them a top-heavy appearance even on land.

Approaches. A prominent rocky point forms the south hook of the bay. A radar tower stands inland from Village Point, to the north. When approaching from the south, you can begin to turn in gently once you are abeam of the south hook. Don't go too far in; depths that are comfortable for reef-netters may not be for your vessel. If approaching from the north, stay about an eighth of a mile off Village Point; it shallows farther out than you think.

Anchorage. Since Legoe Bay offers no protection regardless of how far in you go, anchor in the quietest water you can find at an adequate depth for your boat. All mooring buoys are private.

Getting Ashore. All tidelands are private.

Cove North of the Ferry Dock ★

Charts: 18421, **18424**, 18430

The cove just north of the ferry dock on the east side of Lummi Island is a poor anchorage even in fair weather. You will have strong current and often wind to deal with, and the depths are not comfortable. However, a shallow-draft vessel may want to anchor temporarily, to allow its crew either to pick up a few groceries at the small store south of the ferry dock, or to eat at the café (open in summer only). There is a library and post office here as well. Gasoline is no longer sold anywhere on the island.

Reef-net boats hauled ashore in Legoe Bay. Reef-net fishing was devised by the early Indians. Nets are spread between boats in shallow water and drawn in when salmon are spotted from the lookout towers.

Approaches, Anchorage. Stay clear of the ferry dock. If a ferry is in, wait until it leaves in order to avoid its wash. Head in with caution, as the shoreline is steep. Watch for the shoal at the north end of this cove.

Getting Ashore. The stairs that descend to the rocky beach, flanked by boundary signs, are public.

Coves North of Inati Bay ★ No Facilities

Charts: 18421, **18424**

There are a handful of coves on the east side of Lummi Island north of Inati Bay. However, for a number of reasons these are not particularly good choices. Many of them are extremely shallow. Through the narrow section of Hale Passage, the wind and current are often strong (you get a hint of this by watching the county ferry crabbing its way across from Gooseberry Point). In addition, most of the tidelands are private, giving boaters little access to shore. The most promising anchorage, just north of Inati Bay, is unfortunately the site of an industrial rock quarry.

Inati Bay ★★★★ ☐4☐ No Facilities

Charts: 18421, **18424**

This lovely, square bay, the best anchorage on Lummi Island, is a fine anchorage by any standard. Though it faces north, headlands protect it from strong winds coming down Hale Passage. Locals say it is secure in everything except winter northeasterlies, though the wind sometimes skitters around the points. A perfect day-sail from Bellingham, Inati Bay is a favorite year-round destination from that busy harbor. The Bellingham Yacht Club maintains the firepits and pit toilets for public use, as well as the short trail that connects the beach to the main road system.

It's possible to walk four miles north to the Lummi Island ferry dock, where there is a small store and a café (the café is open in the summer only). Few bother, as the chief activity in Inati Bay is to relax and gaze eastward at Mt. Baker. Anyone who's been waiting for the right place to learn to skip rocks will find an endless supply of flat shale stones on the beach.

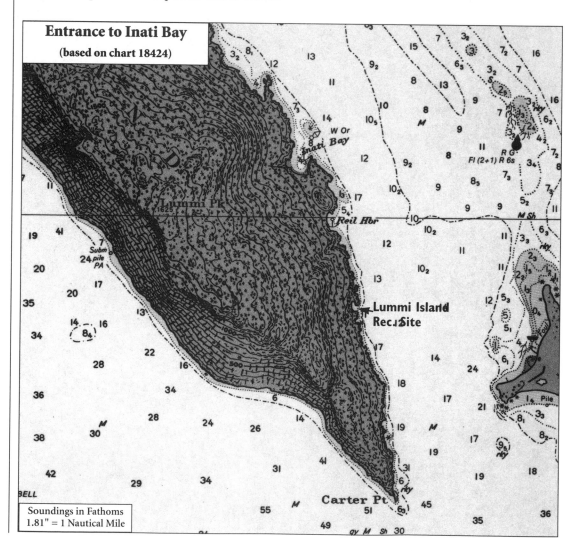

Entrance to Inati Bay
(based on chart 18424)

Soundings in Fathoms
1.81" = 1 Nautical Mile

Inati Bay.

Approaches. Inati Bay is located beneath Lummi Island's highest peak, so it is fairly easy to head for, especially if you're approaching from the east. A white buoy marks the south end of a reef that sits dead-center about 100 yards northeast of the entrance. A pile marks the north end of the reef, but it is submerged at high tide. There are also unmarked rocks that extend from the north point of the bay. To be safe, always enter south of the white buoy.

Anchorage. There's room for a fair number of boats on the gradually rising mud-and-shale bottom of Inati Bay. Depending on what you're comfortable with, you can anchor in 2 to 30 feet of water. During summer months only, the Bellingham Yacht Club places three mooring buoys in the bay for general use.

Getting Ashore. The tidelands of Inati Bay are public.

Reil Harbor ★ 　1　 No Facilities

Charts: 18421, **18424**

Reil Harbor is open and unprotected, with no facilities and no public beach access. Like the coves north of Inati Bay, it is not recommended.

Lummi Island Recreation Site ★★★★

Charts: 18421, **18424**

A tiny bight south of Reil Harbor (about halfway between Inati Bay and Carter Point) is maintained by the Department of Natural Resources as the Lummi Island Recreation Site. Loop trails connect through fir and madrona to other pocket-size beaches, all of them nestled among rocky bluffs. There are pit toilets, picnic tables, and campsites. Standing on one of the rocky knolls that overlook Hale Passage, you'll feel as if you could leap across to Mt. Baker.

Approaches, Moorings. The entrance is clean, but the bight itself is tiny, with room for only one boat at the single mooring buoy. It is possible to anchor farther out, but a better alternative is to anchor in Inati Bay, about a mile to the north, and motor or row your skiff around. In any case, be prepared to move if the weather worsens, especially from the south. Lummi Island Recreation Site is ideal for small, beachable craft.

Samish Island ★★ No Facilities

Charts: 18421, 18423, **18424**

Samish Island is a narrow peninsula extending between Samish Bay and Padilla Bay. An isthmus, protected by dike and bulkhead, connects it to the mainland. The waters north and south are shallow—less than 1 fathom—and often bare at low tide. Most boaters avoid this area, though fishing vessels with local knowledge thread their way through the flats to the mouth of the Samish River.

The only anchorage is in the small cove southeast of William Point, on the north side of Samish Island.

Approaches, Anchorage. From the south, stay well west of Samish Island; avoid making a straight shot from Saddlebag Island, as this course could put you over the shoals. North of William Point you can begin to round the north tip, but try to stay in about 5 fathoms as there are reefs and rocks extending from shore. Continue east until you see the stairs descending from the high bank. At high tide the gravel beach is submerged. The underwater shelf is steep.

Getting Ashore. The 1,500 feet of beach east of the stairs is public land. At the road are picnic tables and pit toilets. There are no other public facilities on the island; signs politely and firmly describe the surrounding properties as private property.

Wildcat Cove (Larrabee State Park) ★★★★ No Facilities

Charts: 18421, **18424**

Wildcat Cove, about a mile south of Chuckanut Bay, is beach access for beautiful, heavily wooded Larrabee State Park. The park uplands can accommodate large numbers of people; there are picnic sites, campsites, restrooms, and a performance amphitheater. Trails along the rocky shore offer spectacular views of Samish Bay and the San Juan Islands. More hiking trails extend upland. In spring, abundant rhododendrons explode red, pink, and purple against the deep-green forest.

Across the highway from the park is the Interurban Trail, a five-mile foot and bicycle path that links Larrabee with Bellingham to the north.

Approaches, Anchorage. A large, square house juts obtrusively from the rocks just north of the cove. Watch for submerged rocks around this area and around the point to the south. You won't be able to enter too far into Wildcat Cove before it shoals. Set your hook slightly south so you'll be out of the way of the launching ramp. If your boat is large and your skiff has an engine, you'll probably feel more comfortable anchoring in Chuckanut Bay and motoring around.

Getting Ashore. The shoreline is public.

Chuckanut Bay/Pleasant Bay ★★★ ◻4 No Facilities

Charts: 18421, **18424**

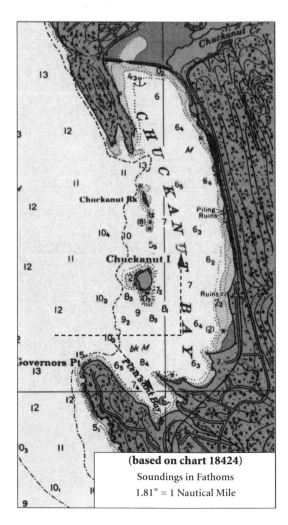

(based on chart 18424)
Soundings in Fathoms
1.81" = 1 Nautical Mile

Chuckanut Bay opens its large jaws to the west. Its pleasing Native American name means "small cliffy bay next to big bay." A short distance from Bellingham, Chuckanut is ringed by private homes, many on steep rock cliffs. The railroad and highway rim the length of the shore. The entrance to the bay, though wide, is obscured by Chuckanut Rock, by a reef extend-

Firs grow from the sandstone cliffs of Chuckanut Bay.

ing southward, and by Chuckanut Island, a public nature preserve managed by Western Washington State University.

Approaches. Enter south of Chuckanut Island or north of Chuckanut Rock. There is deep water between the island and Chuckanut Rock, but the reef that extends from the rock is unmarked. Once inside the bay, you have several choices for good anchorages.

Anchorage. Pleasant Bay and the bay created by its eastern finger offer the best protection in Chuckanut against southwesterly winds. Depth and holding ground are good. Pleasant Bay is tranquil but not very private; you'll feel like you're in the front yards of the fine homes on the steep shore, and they in yours.

Watch for the rocks off the tip of the eastern finger of Pleasant Bay. The western shore is steep.

Getting Ashore. All shoreline is private.

Chuckanut Bay—North Coves ★★★ 3 No Facilities

Charts: 18421, **18424**

The north end of Chuckanut Bay, especially the area north of the trestle, has some of the most beautiful sandstone rock formations found anywhere. In many places, the rock appears to have been poured like batter and frozen in mid-flow. Madrona and fir cling to the steep cliffs. In good weather this area is a favorite among locals for sunbathing and clamming. A development of large private homes that spreads over the lagoon is the only obtrusive element in the scene.

Approaches, Anchorage. This end of the bay is fairly clean, but stay about 100 feet offshore to avoid the shoals. Depth is a steady 6 fathoms until you approach the trestle. Holding ground is good and you can anchor anywhere, but a north wind can williwaw over the ridge; you'll be more protected from it—and any southwesterlies—if you anchor closer to the west cliff.

An alternate anchorage for a single boat is in the tiny, V-shaped cove northwest of Chuckanut Rock. Depth is good to about halfway in. You'll feel more secluded here, but are considerably less protected. The steep cliffs rising above you are private land.

Getting Ashore. Tidelands north of the trestle are public, part of an undeveloped park. The lagoon dries; if possible go in on a rising tide or you may end up dragging your skiff back through the silty muck. The northeast end of the lagoon connects with a short, quiet residential street off the main highway.

A trail from the northwest end of the trestle takes you up a steep bank, over the railroad tunnel via wooden stairs, into a new residential development. You can pick up the trail on the other side of the road and follow it west and north about two miles along the railroad tracks into the Fairhaven Historical District. This trail eventually leads into downtown Bellingham. As always around active railroad tracks, use care and common sense.

Bellingham ★★★★ 2 (anchorage) 5 (marina) All Facilities

Charts: 18421, **18424**

The city of Bellingham spreads over the northeast "corner" of Bellingham Bay. The port has long been active with timber, coal, and fishing. At one time, canneries and logging dominated

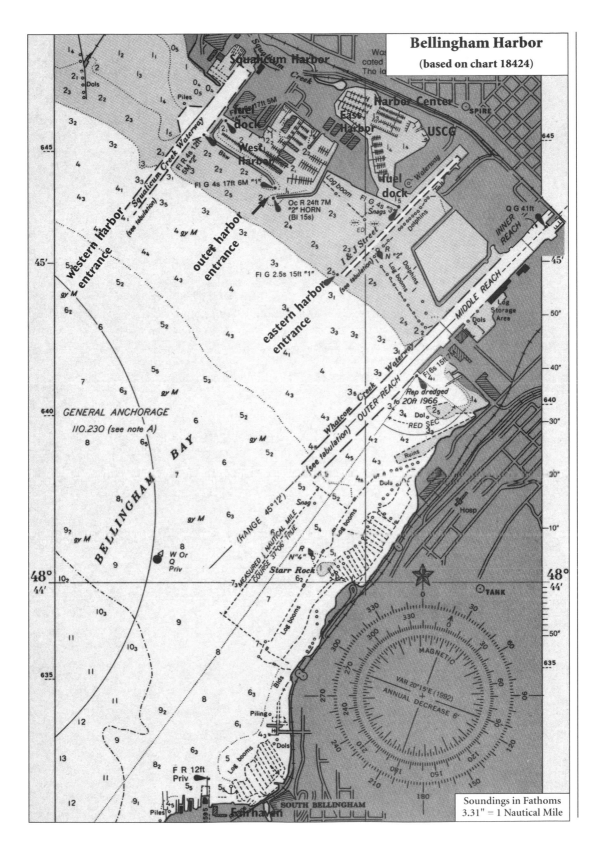

Bellingham Harbor

(based on chart 18424)

Squalicum Harbor

Harbor Center

East Harbor

SPIRE

Float 17ft 5M

dock

West Harbor

USCG

Fl R 4s 2½
5M "3"

Fl G 4s 17ft 6M "1"

Oc R 24ft 7M
"2" HORN
(Bl 15s)

Snags

fuel dock

Waterway

QG 41ft

western harbor entrance

outer harbor entrance

eastern harbor entrance

Fl G 2.5s 15ft "1"

Squalicum Creek Waterway

(see tabulation)

Fl G 4s

Dolphins

ED

I & J Street

2 J Street

R N "2"

Log booms

Dolphins

(see tabulation)

INNER REACH

MIDDLE REACH

Log Storage Area

Dols

Whatcom Creek Waterway

OUTER REACH

(see tabulation)

Fl 6s 15ft

Rep dredged
to 20ft 1966

Dol

RED SEC

Ruins

GENERAL ANCHORAGE
110.230 (see note A)

BELLINGHAM BAY

gy M

(RANGE 45°12')

Snag

Log booms

Dols

Hosp

W Or
Q
Priv

(MEASURED NAUTICAL MILE
COURSE 370°6' TRUE)

Starr Rock

R
N "4"

Log booms

TANK

330

330

300

30

270

MAGNETIC

30

VAR 20°15'E (1992)
ANNUAL DECREASE 6'

240

60

210

150

180

120

90

F R 12ft
Priv

Log booms

Dols

Piling

Bids

Piles

SOUTH BELLINGHAM

Fairhaven

Soundings in Fathoms
3.31" = 1 Nautical Mile

the southeast shore. Fairhaven (South Bellingham) was a separate city, its brick commercial buildings and fine homes built in the 1880s on the speculation that the Great Northern Railroad would choose to site its terminus there (it chose Seattle). On the hill above the Georgia Pacific lumber mill is Western Washington State University.

Though parks now occupy the area once jammed with log booms, the waterfront is still largely industrial. Bellingham boasts the largest drydock ship-repair facility between Seattle and Vancouver, B.C., and is the southern terminus of the Alaska Marine Highway, with ferries departing weekly up the Inside Passage. The main shipping terminal has two deep waterways for ships, tugs, and barges. Commercial fishing vessels fill half the slips of Squalicum Harbor. The industrial park surrounding the harbor offers fish processing, the largest cold storage on the West Coast, and marine supplies, service, and repair. An inter-national airport is north of town, and Interstate Highway 5 is to the east. During the summer, a private passenger ferry offers scheduled departures from Squalicum Harbor to the San Juan Islands.

What makes this harbor attractive to commercial vessels also makes it attractive to pleasure craft: first-rate marine repair services, with convenient automobile access north and south.

Approaches. As you approach from the southwest, you will immediately be able to pick out several distinct landmarks: the airport two-and-a-half miles northwest of Bellingham, the white stack and building slightly south of the airport, and the green copper church spire just uphill of Squalicum Harbor in the middle of town. Head for the spire. Once you're north of Post Point you'll be able to make out the large drydock and round brick Cruise Terminal building on the southeast shore.

The commercial fishing docks in West Squalicum Harbor, Bellingham.

Continue bearing toward the church spire. If you keep the white-and-orange buoy to starboard, you'll stay out of the way of commercial vessels heading into or out of Whatcom Creek Waterway. The float at the head of this waterway is closed to pleasure craft.

Moorings. Squalicum Harbor is the only harbor with moorage for pleasure boats. Squalicum is actually two harbors separated by a jetty, with three entrances. The East Harbor is entered via the dredged I & J Street Waterway channel, with a turn to port at the rock breakwater. The West Harbor is entered either via Squalicum Creek Waterway—the western harbor entrance—or slightly south through what is called (despite its middle location) the outer harbor entrance. All entrances are well marked.

Both harbors have moorage for visitors. In the East Harbor, a long visitors' float can be seen after you turn into the basin. This float is convenient, with lots of turning room, but a southwest gale may pound you into the dock here. There is additional visitors' moorage under the restaurant near the launching ramps, west of the Coast Guard facility. In the West Harbor, where the commercial fleet is moored, guest moorage is not so immediately visible. If you use the middle (outer) entrance, proceed straight north past the fishing vessels; visitors' moorage is near the elevated wooden walkway and square cupola, beneath the restaurant. From the western entrance follow the length of the breakwater and then turn to port toward the restaurant buildings and cupola.

It is possible to call the harbor office on Channel 16 just before you enter either harbor. If someone is monitoring the radio at the time, they will try to direct you to an empty slip. Expect the harbor to be full in summer.

Once docked, register at the drop box located at either the Harbor Center Building or in the Squalicum Mall. One day per month is free. Water and power are included.

Anchorage. There is no protected anchorage in Bellingham Harbor, but two alternatives are available on the southeast shore in settled weather. A few boats anchor in the cove below Fairhaven, north of the Cruise Terminal building. A public launching ramp provides shore access; during summer a float is attached to the concrete pilings. Use of the float is limited to 15 minutes. This cove is a former log-booming ground, so be alert for submerged piles. The surrounding land is private industrial property, and the mooring buoys are private. It's a short walk from here to Fairhaven's restaurants and supermarket, and to Marine Park south of the Cruise Terminal building.

The tiny bight behind Starr Rock is another fair-weather anchorage. A small dock extends here from Boulevard Park during the summer months.

For the Boat. The 250 acres of revitalized industrial park around Squalicum Harbor provide every marine service and supply you will probably ever need. Most of the marine businesses plan their inventories for commercial as well as pleasure boats, so the selection is fairly wide. If you have work done on your boat by a Bellingham Port tenant, up to three days of moorage is free.

The fuel dock (gas and diesel) is located at the west end of the West Harbor. Aluminum and cardboard recycling bins are located in both harbors, and a waste-oil drum is at the West Harbor ramp.

A fuel dock that sells gas only is located in the I & J Street Waterway, east of the entrance to the East Harbor.

For the Crew. Showers, restrooms, and a laundry are located near the drop boxes in both harbors. Restaurants at Squalicum range from deli to formal dining. The nearest supermarket is almost two miles away, at Meridian Street and Illinois. This is a large store, worth the walk and taxi fare for serious provisioning. A small but well-stocked food co-op is located downtown at Holly and State Streets, about a mile from Squalicum. Some groceries are available at the gas station deli a few blocks away on Broadway and Eldridge, but this is mostly a beer-and-cigarettes kind of place.

A map of the city on the south side of the Squalicum Mall at the West Harbor can help you get your bearings.

Things to Do. Even if you don't have much time in Bellingham, visit the Marine Life Tank under the breezeway in Harbor Center, in the East Harbor. A kid-height concrete tank is alive with tidepool creatures—starfish, urchin, anemone, and seaslug. Surrounding tanks display other forms of "Life Between the Tides," including shy, translucent, tube-shaped fish camouflaged in eelgrass.

If you take the half-hour walk into town (or wait for the bus), you'll be rewarded with a broad range of activities, many of them perfect for rainy days. From the harbor, walk southeast on Eldridge and continue after it turns into Holly. Turn left at "C" street, which soon dead-ends at the Salmon Life Cycle Facility of the Bellingham Maritime Heritage Center. Here, a series of rearing and holding ponds guides you along an interpretive walk up Whatcom Creek.

To continue on into town, cross the creek and take the footpath up toward the concrete bridge. You'll be on Dupont and Prospect there, almost in the center of town. As you head east you'll pass the post office, City Hall, and library. South on Prospect is the Children's Museum, with hands-on exhibits, a crafts room, and gift shop. On the same block is the brick Whatcom County Museum (originally City Hall). In the surrounding blocks you'll find cafés, shops, and a bookstore—more than enough to entertain a cabin-weary crew. The more adventurous might want to bus or taxi south to Fairhaven, a restored brick commercial district built in the 1880s that's managed to hold on to a certain woolly funkiness despite its popularity with tourists.

Special events in Bellingham include Opening Day in early May, a Boat Show and Maritime Festival in late May, and the "Blast Over Bellingham Bay" fireworks on July 4.

Portage Bay

Charts: 18421, **18424**

Portage Bay lies on the west side of Bellingham Bay, between the Lummi peninsula and Portage Island. The bay is shallow, and the entrance through Portage Channel foul with rocks and shoals.

Like Lummi Bay on the north side of the peninsula, Portage Bay and Portage Channel are inside Lummi Indian Reservation boundaries. Anchoring, as well as harvesting clams, oysters, or crab, is for tribal members only.

Fisherman Cove ★★  (gas only)

Charts: 18421, **18424**

Fisherman Cove lies south of Gooseberry Point at the north end of Hale Passage, between Bellingham Bay and Lummi Bay. All of the peninsula and surrounding bays are Lummi Indian Reservation land. A community and commercial area is clustered around the ferry dock here. The newest business is the casino run by the Tribal Council. The casino draws customers from Vancouver, B.C., Bellingham, and beyond; the atmosphere inside is mirrored, hushed, and intense.

During fishing season, Fisherman Cove is a busy place, with commercial boats pulling up to the Icicle Seafood processing dock. Year-round, the Whatcom County ferry makes hourly runs to Lummi Island.

The site of an early Indian village, Fisherman Cove is host to the Stommish Festival each June. During this event, which is open to the public, members of some dozen Northwest Indian tribes race their graceful 50-foot cedar dugout canoes to Portage Point.

Approaches, Anchorage. A plain, square building with the words BEER ICE FOOD is north of the ferry dock. Watch the depths, as the bay quickly shallows, and be prepared for some swift current. The anchorage is for use by tribal members only. You're welcome to stop for fuel or groceries at the float attached to the pier just west of the ferry dock; depths of 4 feet are reported.

For the Boat. Gas is available at the head of the pier west of the ferry dock. This pier also has a light-duty marine lift. There are gas pumps at the grocery store across the parking lot.

For the Crew. There's a fair variety of groceries and sundries at the store next to the gas pumps. The café inside the casino is open 24 hours a day.

Sandy Point ★ ⬜5 No Facilities

Charts: 18421, **18424**

Sandy Point is a treeless residential community extending south into the flats of Lummi Bay. The privately dredged channels are lined with boats belonging to the community residents.

The entrance is well marked, with a dredged depth of 6 feet reported. At one time a service dock operated here, but there is no longer any visitor moorage or facilities.

Birch Bay ★★★ ⬜1 🎁 🛒 🚿

Charts: 18421

This large, smooth, and open bay faces west to the Strait of Georgia. The north and east shores are lined with homes and resort cottages. South is the densely wooded marsh area of Birch Bay State Park, its southern boundary marked by a square building; the park is open year-round. Mt. Baker centers herself regally here; at dusk and dawn the lighted towers of the Cherry Point oil refineries to the south and the radio towers to the north sparkle at her feet.

Approaches. Respect the depths around Birch Point and Point Whitehorn when approaching from the north or south, especially at low tide. Keep to the center of the bay, slightly south. It shallows rapidly to 2 fathoms or less; you're barely inside the bay when you run out of water. Silt accumulates and shifts during winter, so use the chart as an aid to your own instruments and senses. Locals describe tides so low the herons stand half-way out in the bay.

Anchorage. Unless your boat draws less than a foot or two, you'll need to anchor a half-mile or more off shore. Near the state park, the depths are charted at a ¼-fathom, with a sobering wreck to remind you not to push your luck. Expect to feel completely exposed to the Strait of Georgia, which you are. If you choose to anchor overnight, be prepared to move to shelter in Drayton Harbor, some eight miles north. Winter storms have been known to wash out the perimeter road of Birch Bay; summer gales should be taken seriously.

There is a private marina at the north end of the bay, with an entrance marked by pilings. Dredged and maintained by Birch Bay Village, it is for property owners and their guests only, accessible to them at high tide.

Getting Ashore. Work around the tides or you'll end up dragging your skiff through the sandflats. The shoreline of Birch Bay State Park, and two small county parks on the east shore, provide beach access. Tidelands are public.

For the Boat. There are no marine facilities in

Birch Bay. The closest fuel and other services are in Blaine.

For the Crew. Restrooms and showers are available at Birch Bay State Park, within each trailer-camp loop. There is a small grocery store inland past the park's east entrance on Helvig Road, about a mile away.

Things to Do. Birch Bay is a resort community that abounds in recreational activities during the summer: bicycle rentals, golf and mini-golf, shopping, and dining. Miles of unobstructed sandflats invite kite-flying, sailboarding, water-skiing, and swimming in what the local Chamber of Commerce describes as the "warmest, safest saltwater beach on the Northwest Pacific Coast." There's clamming,

crabbing, and fishing in season. Local events include a CLAMpetition in mid-July, and sandcastle contests in late July and mid-August.

Wooded Birch Bay State Park has 167 campsites. Demand for these is high; reservations for their use from Memorial Day weekend through Labor Day must be made in writing. The day-use area along the shore has tables, barbecue grills, and fire rings, and three open picnic shelters with electricity. The Terrell Marsh Trail, a half-mile, self-guided interpretive trail, winds through one of the few remaining saltwater/freshwater estuaries remaining in Puget Sound. Great blue herons and red-winged blackbirds are a common sight, especially when the trail isn't crowded.

Drayton Harbor

Charts: 18421

Drayton Harbor is located just inside the U.S. border, through a narrow channel that opens to the northwest. Its navigable portion is actually quite small; tideflats that bare at low tide fill most of the harbor. The town of Blaine occupies the north shore, its marine facilities clustered on a landfill jetty. The sprawling Canadian city of White Rock is visible beyond. A luxury resort on Semiahmoo Spit guards the south entrance at Tongue Point; the remainder of the spit is a county park. On a clear day Mt. Baker dominates everything.

Approaches. The entrance to Drayton Harbor is well marked, but is nevertheless somewhat tricky. Shoals extend well off the north and south shores. If you're approaching directly from the west, you may not be able to see the entrance clearly until you are within a mile or so.

The gabled roofs of the resort are a help, but gas station signs on the freeway, the International Peace Arch, and other border marks are more prominent than the navigational aids. A 27-foot fixed daymark (a black-and-white diamond on pilings) indicates the edge of the south shoal, but this may be difficult to see against the gray-and-white buildings behind it, and is easily confused with the 37-foot tower to the north that marks the international border. Confirm your position amid all this: Look south toward Birch Point, find the red nun buoy, then find the green can north of the entrance. As you enter, favor the north side of the channel to avoid the shoals extending off Semiahmoo Spit.

It is possible to anchor in Drayton Harbor, but most boaters prefer the comfort and convenience of the marinas at Blaine or at Semiahmoo.

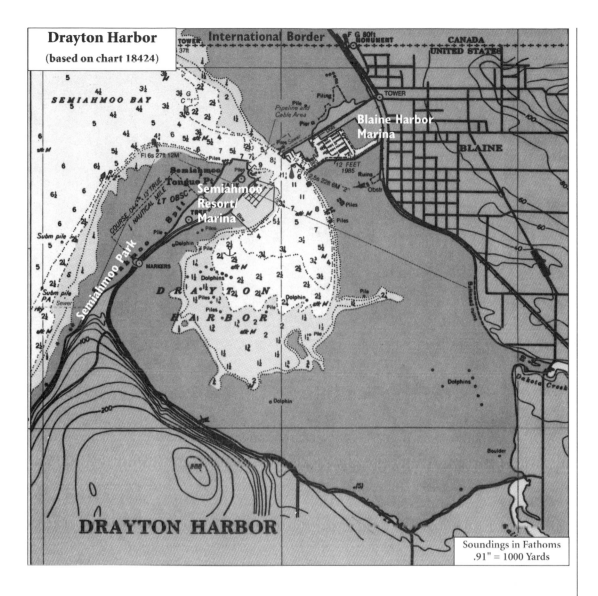

Blaine Harbor Marina ★★★★ ⬚5 All Facilities

Charts: **18421**

Separated from the San Juans by the Strait of Georgia, tucked well inside Drayton Harbor, the town of Blaine isn't on the way to anywhere for most boaters. Facilities are geared to commercial use, for the fishing and crabbing vessels that harvest the Strait of Georgia and—

increasingly—the waters of Alaska. Many of the pleasure boats moored here are owned by Canadians who drive down to cruise and shop. This combination of active commercial fishing fleet and pleasure boat departure point makes Blaine a fine place to provision, restock,

Ghostly Mt. Baker hovers above Semiahmoo, south of the entrance to Drayton Harbor.

and repair. Perhaps this combination has saved it from the resort atmosphere that now overlays the once working ports of Friday Harbor on San Juan Island or Poulsbo on the Kitsap Peninsula.

Blaine was originally a lumber town. Ruins of the mill can still be seen along the edge of Drayton Harbor. The town enjoyed a brief boom during the Fraser Gold Rush in 1858. At the turn of the century, one of the largest private salmon-fishing fleets on the West Coast was centered here. Fish processing, once concentrated in the cannery across the channel on Semiahmoo Spit, is now located (on a much reduced scale) at the end of the north jetty.

Approaches. Immediately upon entering Drayton Harbor, turn to port. The Blaine Marina is protected by a timber-and-stone breakwater that angles off to starboard. Follow this breakwater some 500 yards past the commercial docks, shipyard, and fishing-boat

moorages; you'll see a sign on the breakwater and another on a boathouse that indicates a sharp port turn to the visitors' dock in front of the harbormaster's office.

Moorings. The visitors' dock is a concrete float about 150 feet long that lies parallel to shore and perpendicular to its approach. There is water, but no power for visiting boats. The first 24 hours' mooring each month is free. A small disadvantage to this location is that you'll be moored under bright lights at the foot of the main ramp, and will hear everyone walking past or using the dumpster.

Blaine Harbor plans to dredge someday for an additional 100 to 200 slips. The harbor is operated by the Port of Bellingham.

For the Boat. The fuel dock is located near the harbor entrance. This is a commercial facility; you'll tie to creosoted pilings, climb a ladder, and be handed down the gas or diesel hose. A marine store near the fuel dock and another just east of the marina provide most of what your boat needs. Two marine repair service facilities are available for large and small vessels, respectively. In town you'll also find a complete hardware store.

A tidal grid for bottom work was recently rebuilt, but environmental concerns limit its use. Check with the harbor office before using it.

For the Crew. Restrooms and showers are located in the harbor office. Town is a 10-minute walk away; there you'll find a laundromat, groceries, a bank, and a variety of restaurants and stores. It's a longer walk to the big malls, built to attract Canadian shoppers, east of the main highway.

Things to Do. Walk across to the Semiahmoo Bay side of the jetty at low tide and try your hand at clamming. You'll need a good shovel and a strong back to dig out the horse clams that spit at your every step. There are crabs off the pier at the harbor entrance, and fish in Boundary Bay. If you'd rather buy your seafood, a retail outlet on the harbor jetty specializes in locally caught fish and shellfish in season.

The closest park within walking distance is Peace Arch State Park on the U.S.-Canadian border. On weekends you can watch the long lines of Canadian vehicles waiting to enter the U.S., and the equally long lines of U.S. vehicles waiting on the opposite side. The arch itself is the first structure of its kind in the world, built in 1920 with volunteer labor from both countries; the surrounding grounds were funded by individual donations of no more than 10 cents from Washington and British Columbia schoolchildren.

A Marine Park and Marine Education Center is sited on the Semiahmoo Bay side of the jetty, with shelters, gravel walkways, and an interpretive center.

Within a few minutes of docking, someone will probably recommend the Harbor Café. With reason: the portions are large, the service brisk, the atmosphere friendly, noisy, and busy. If you ask questions about the history of the town you'll be directed to the Café International on Blaine's main street, where old photos and logging gear line the walls.

Of course, all the activities at Semiahmoo Spit are also available on the other side of the harbor entrance.

Semiahmoo ★★★★ All Facilities

Charts: **18421**

The most prominent structure on Semiahmoo Spit is the resort complex, located on the site of a former salmon cannery; a few of the original buildings have been handsomely restored. This is a place to visit if you want to pamper yourself with luxury surroundings set against the sandy beaches of the county park.

Approaches. After clearing the entrance to Drayton Harbor, turn to starboard at the signed entry piling. The visitors' float is immediately to starboard, both east and west of the fuel dock.

Moorings. Check at the fuel dock for a moorage assignment. Generally you'll be sent on to a slip with a power hookup. You can telephone

ahead—(360) 371-5700—24 hours in advance to reserve a slip. Expect to pay twice the price you would pay in Blaine. With the exception of the concrete breakwater float itself, which is used by gulls and other sea birds for clam-crushing and feasting, the marina is of dazzling yacht quality, with trim floats and landscaped grounds.

For the Boat. The marina operates a full-service haulout and repair facility, with supplies available at the chandlery adjacent to the marina office. Fuel is only slightly more expensive here than in Blaine, on a breakwater float that is more accessible for pleasure boats.

For the Crew. Impeccable restrooms, showers, and a laundromat are located at the head of the dock. A small grocery and gift shop is combined with marine supplies near the marina office.

Things to Do. The marina operates separately from the resort; the swimming pool, as well as tennis, racquetball, and squash courts, are for resort patrons and members only. Talk to the marina office about bicycle rentals. The nearby golf course, Arnold Palmer–designed, is open to the public. To get there, walk the paved path through the county park and up the hill.

Both resort restaurants have expansive views west toward the Strait of Georgia and the Canadian Gulf Islands. The hallways that connect the restaurants with conference rooms and lobbies are hung with charts of the area and with photos of the old salmon cannery.

Semiahmoo Park begins at the resort entrance and continues to the base of the spit. Picnic tables and firepits face both beaches. A small museum and gift shop are located in former cannery bunkhouses relocated from the resort area. Clamming on the Strait of Georgia side is excellent. On quiet days, a birdwatcher might spot loon, grebe, heron, and harlequin duck on the Drayton Harbor side. A boardwalk that extends south to Birch Point is planned.

Drayton Harbor Anchorage ★★★★ ☐3 All Facilities

Charts: 18421

The extensive mudflats of Drayton Harbor limit the area available for anchoring. Most boaters prefer the convenience and comfort of the marinas at Blaine or Semiahmoo.

Approaches, Anchorage. Once inside the harbor, motor southeast around the low floating breakwater of Semiahmoo Marina. Drop your hook east of the dolphin pilings, in 2 to 4 fathoms of mud. Anchoring anywhere else exposes you to wave action off the Strait of Georgia that comes through the entrance and is exaggerated by the extreme shallows of the harbor itself. Semiahmoo

Spit offers little protection from the wind.

Getting Ashore. Commercial fishing traffic can be heavy in Blaine Harbor, and officially no rowing is allowed inside the breakwater. This makes getting ashore at Blaine a challenge if your skiff doesn't have a motor. Semiahmoo is a private marina; for security's sake a key is required to re-enter even the fuel dock from shore. If you use your skiff to go to lunch at one of the resort restaurants, the marina office will let you back in.

The Semiahmoo Park beaches are public.

Point Roberts ★★★★ ☐5 All Facilities

Charts: 18421

Point Roberts juts south into the Strait of Georgia from the Canadian mainland, a five-square-mile rectangle of land overlooked by the United States and Britain during the "54-40 or fight" border negotiations of 1846. For U.S. boaters, Point Roberts is completely out of the way to or from anywhere. Arriving by land is even more inconvenient, as you must clear cus-

toms into Canada and then back into the U.S.; Point Roberts' children do this twice a day to attend school in Blaine. Not surprisingly, most of the homes and boats here are owned by Canadians. The chief attraction is beautiful Lighthouse Marine Park.

Approaches. From a distance, Point Roberts appears as a flat island fattened by central bluffs. A forest of sailboat masts marks the location of the marina. When approaching from the south or east it is important to find red buoy "4" off the southeast tip of the point; the buoy is almost two miles offshore, and marks the edge of dangerous shoals. Unless you have good local knowledge, don't pass between the buoy and the shore; the repair yards in Point Roberts and Blaine are kept busy with boats that try to do so.

The *Coast Pilot* reports extensive night drift-fishing in the area, which makes navigation difficult.

Entrance to the marina is on the west side of a rock breakwater. Keep the pilings to port, and stay mid-channel. Flagged sticks at the turn in the privately maintained channel mark a spot missed in the recent dredging operations.

Moorings. Visitors' moorage is on "H" dock, to starboard as you enter, just beyond the fuel dock. Currents set strongly within the marina, and turning room can be tight. Check in with the harbormaster at the fuel dock once you have tied up. Commercial boats have priority for dock space during fishing season; from July through September it may be a good idea to telephone ahead—(360) 945-2255—to arrange for a slip.

For the Boat. The repair yard has a 30-ton travel lift and a tower for mast work. The marine supply store is well equipped.

For the Crew. The showers and laundry require a key; get one from the harbormaster when you check in. A large supermarket is only a five-minute walk away, north on Tyee Drive. There is a café in the marina building and the peninsula has several night spots; the liveliest is north of Lighthouse Marine Park.

Things to Do. Lighthouse Marine Park, about a 20-minute walk west from the marina, is sited among sand dunes and beach grass. It has a marvelous open feel, with extensive views of Georgia Strait, the mountains of Vancouver Island, and the San Juan Islands. There are firepits, picnic tables, a playground area, and a boardwalk. A SunSweep sculpture, one of three spanning the 2,778 miles of U.S.–Canadian border, is set among the dunes. A small informative display describes the three pods of orca whales that frequent the area in summer; climb the 30-foot wooden viewing tower to scan for them. Clamming is good at minus tides on the south beach.

A couple of miles north on Marine Drive is Monument Park, undeveloped and overgrown, with an obelisk that marks the border between the U.S. and Canada—the first such marker to be placed on the 49th parallel.

The flat terrain of Point Roberts makes it a perfect spot for bicycling.

REGION 10

THE SAN JUAN ISLANDS

Mount Baker emerges beyond Obstruction Pass. From left to right the islands are: Orcas, Obstruction, Cypress, Blakely, and Lopez.
(Janis Dyment photo)

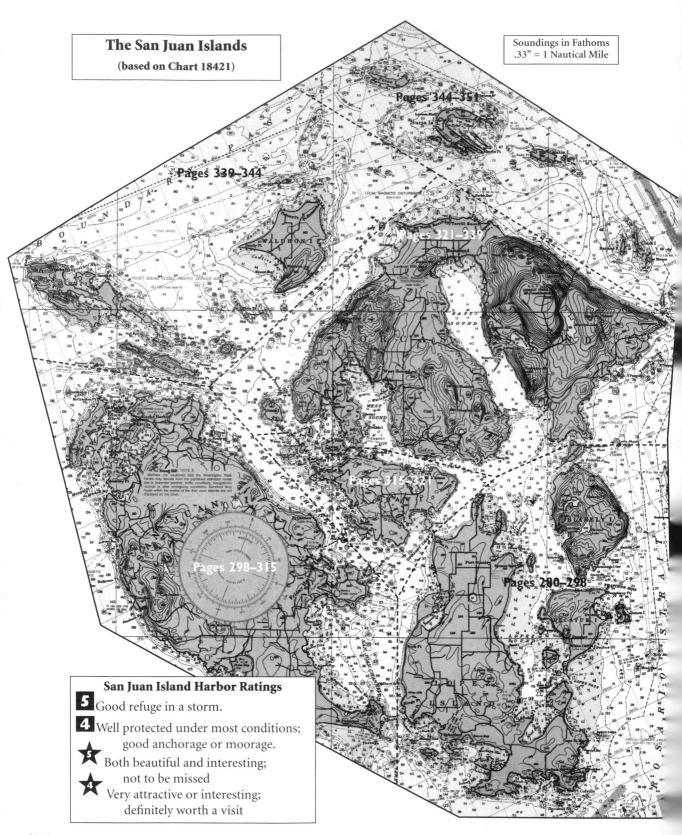

The San Juan Islands
(based on Chart 18421)

Pages 344–351

Pages 339–344

Pages 321–339

Pages 315–321

Pages 298–315

Pages 280–298

San Juan Island Harbor Ratings

5 Good refuge in a storm.

4 Well protected under most conditions;
   good anchorage or moorage.

★**5** Both beautiful and interesting;
   not to be missed

★**4** Very attractive or interesting;
   definitely worth a visit

The San Juans are the premier cruising grounds of Puget Sound. Shaped and fit like intricate pieces of a jigsaw puzzle, the shoreline of one inevitably leads to encountering another, and another after that. There are 172 islands in all—some little more than over-sized rocks, some large enough to support farms, tracts of homes, and towns. Around them are more than three hundred miles of shoreline.

The islands are a partially submerged mountain range, once covered like the rest of Puget Sound by a river of ice more than a mile thick. When the last glaciers retreated, the mountains rose; fossil shells dating back millions of years have been found well above sea level throughout the islands. Names like Fossil Bay and Iceberg Point are reminders of this geologic history.

From a boat, it's easy to believe that the San Juan archipelago consists of gigantic, submerged mountains. For the most part, the islands are forested, rugged, and steep-sided. Where they face open water, their shorelines often seem on the verge of collapse, as though calving off in chunks like a glacier. Scrub oak, twisted evergreens, and dead snags cling to the thin soil. In summer the grasses are golden dry. In fall the oak goes reddish, briefly matching the peeling tissue-paper skins of the madronas.

People often speak of how the San Juans have been ruined by development, but these islands haven't been "the same" since the mid-19th century, when homesteaders moved in. Some staked out farms and planted crops. Many logged their claims, then platted and sold. Canneries near the fishing grounds in the Strait of Juan de Fuca employed hundreds of people; on some of the islands the population and level of industry was higher in the early 1900s than it is today.

Tourism is the major "industry" now. This takes the form not only of inland bed-and-breakfast inns but also of marina resorts, tour boats, guided kayak and canoe trips, and whale-watching and fishing charters. Marine facilities are most crowded from mid-July through September. Fortunately, in the last half of the 20th century, public land has been set aside for parks and recreation sites, many of them geared for boaters. Serious efforts have also been devoted to preservation. More than 80 islands, rocks, and reefs are now protected as National Wildlife Refuges, and parcels on some of the larger islands are set aside for protection of wildlife and biological research.

The San Juans are not only beautiful, they are also dry. Benefiting from the rainshadow of the mountains on Vancouver Island and the Olympic Peninsula, this area receives less rainfall than most of Puget Sound—an average of only 25 inches per year, most of it falling from October through March. It's no wonder boaters choose to spend their vacations here. However, this rain shadow does make for water shortages. Fill your water tanks before you leave for the islands, and be prepared for restrictions. In many harbors, using water for such tasks as washing down boats is strictly prohibited. Beach fires are generally not allowed in summer.

Weather in the San Juans tends to come from either the Strait of Juan de Fuca or the Strait of Georgia. As in most of Puget Sound, southeasterly and southwesterly winds usually bring wetter weather, but "northeasters" are considered the worst conditions in winter. North winds off the Strait of Georgia occasionally reach gale force in summer, and should be respected.

For sailors, winds in the San Juans can be frustrating at any time of year. A westerly is easily turned into a southerly or a baffling easterly by a high cliff. As the land masses warm up and cool down, winds shift as well, swirling and moving in inexplicable ways.

Currents behave likewise. The archipelago is bounded by the Strait of Juan de Fuca, Haro Strait, the Strait of Georgia, and Rosario Strait. As these waters move through the islands, strong currents and eddies result. The *Coast Pilot* is filled with caution on this subject: "Tidal currents have great velocity in places, causing heavy tide rips that are dangerous." Compass courses are of little value, it concludes, and a reliable engine for sailboats "is an absolute necessity"—advice that applies to power boats as well.

Navigating in this boating playground is rarely straightforward. It's easy to lose your way among the islands and rocks, or to become disoriented by the many bays, coves, channels and sounds that branch off in every direction. In this watery maze, it's important to stay alert while under way. Learn to recognize a few of the higher peaks, and the buoys and landmarks of the major channels. Don't simply follow the ferries around and assume you'll "get there." Above all, don't rely on other boats to lead you safely through a tricky passage; they may be less experienced than you are. Use your charts, your instruments, your good sense.

In this chapter, entries are arranged one island at a time, beginning with Lopez and ending with the northern islands that cap the archipelago. The map on page 276 can help you navigate through this chapter.

Approaches to the San Juans

All the routes into the San Juan Islands involve crossing a major strait and then navigating a relatively narrow passage. Currents in most of the straits and passages are strong; always check the current tables.

Beginning from the east, the major passages are:

Rosario Strait

Though only four miles across at its widest point, Rosario is a serious body of water and should be treated as such. Hazards are well marked, but currents of up to 3 knots are common; the *Coast Pilot* warns of heavy tide rips and swirls off Black Rock, Obstruction Pass, Peapod Rocks, and Lawrence Point. Anywhere in Rosario, rough conditions result when wind opposes the current. Rosario is a major shipping lane; more than 500 oil tankers pass through Rosario each year, bound to and from the refineries at Anacortes and Cherry Point. Use special caution in fog. The Vessel Traffic System (VTS) operates the full length of the strait, and monitors VHF Channel 5A. For more information on VTS, see page 8.

Obstruction Pass and Peavine Pass

These narrow passages lie between Orcas and Blakely, on either side of Obstruction Island. In both passages, flood currents are stronger than the ebb. The *Coast Pilot* estimates velocities of more than 6 knots "at times," with "heavy" tide rips east of Obstruction Island. Of the two, the straighter Peavine Pass is considered safer. Approaching Peavine from Rosario Strait, stay east and north of Spindle Rock. Note the reported submerged rock off the Blakely shore, about halfway through Peavine. When conditions are rough in the strait, these passes are often used to avoid crossing beam-on to the seas.

Thatcher Pass

Almost a half-mile wide and well marked, Thatcher is the cleanest approach into the San Juan Islands from Rosario Strait. Ferries use Thatcher as the main route to and from Anacortes, and the *Coast Pilot* describes it as "free of danger," with the noted exception of Lawson Rock, marked with a daybeacon. This rock is about the middle of the pass on the east side of the entrance, north of Fauntleroy Point.

Lopez Pass

This pass between Decatur Island and Lopez Island is narrow—less than 500 yards across. Depths are good, and most hazards are marked. Currents are about the same as in Obstruction Pass and Peavine Pass. Three small islands line up across the west side of Lopez Pass: Ram, Cayou (Rum), and Rim. Steep-sided Rim and Cayou (Rum) are National Wildlife Refuges; Ram Island is privately owned. Stay in mid-channel through the pass. There's good depth between Rim and Decatur, but most boaters enter Lopez Sound via the south side of Ram. The submerged rock southwest of Ram is marked, but the reef that extends from Ram's east side is not.

The Strait of Juan de Fuca

In fair weather, the Strait of Juan de Fuca is the most direct route to the San Juan Islands from Admiralty Inlet. The major hazards (and waypoints) in this 15-mile stretch of open water are Hein Bank and the shoals around Smith Island and neighboring Minor Island. All are marked. When crossing, correct for the current, which sets vessels east toward Whidbey Island on the flood and west on the ebb. A more complete description of the Strait of Juan de Fuca is given in the introduction to Region 11, on page 354.

San Juan Channel (Cattle Pass)

This half-mile wide channel between the south end of Lopez Island and San Juan Island is often referred to as Cattle Pass. It is notorious for its strong current; at times all the water in the Strait of Juan de Fuca seems to be flushing through here. The channel is deep, but there are many rocks and shoals on both sides and south of the entrance. These create heavy tide rips and eddies that can be dangerous, especially in bad weather or whenever wind and current are opposed. A slack tide is always recommended. To determine slack, use the current tables titled "San Juan Channel (south entrance)."

Approaching from the south, look for the lighted mark on Iceberg Point on the east (Lopez) side, and for the lighted mark three miles northwest at Cattle Point, on the San Juan Island side. Cattle Pt. is low, sloping, and almost treeless. Between these two marks are Hall Island, Long Island, and Whale Rocks—all unmarked. The deepest and cleanest approach is west of Whale Rocks.

Haro Strait and Boundary Pass

These two channels form the boundary between Canada and the United States, and are exceptionally deep—over 100 fathoms. Hazards in both channels are well marked.

Currents are strongest west of Kellett Bluff at the south end of Henry Island, and off Turn Point at the west end of Stuart Island. The *Coast Pilot* warns of "heavy dangerous tide rips" between East Point (Saturna Island) and Patos Island. Haro Strait and Boundary Pass are used regularly by freighters moving between the Strait of Juan de Fuca and the Strait of Georgia; use special caution in fog. A vessel traffic system is monitored by the Canadian Coast Guard on VHF Channel 11.

Mosquito Pass

The *Coast Pilot* has good reason to recommend this short cut between Haro Strait and Roche Harbor "only to small craft with local knowledge." The pass is narrow, depths are irregular, and currents are fairly unpredictable. However, most hazards are marked, and navigating Mosquito Pass can be straightforward if you pay attention to where you are. Those with deep-draft vessels will probably feel more comfortable if the tide is rising.

From the south or west, begin by positioning yourself in the middle of the pass. Note the numerous charted, unmarked rocks scattered a quarter-mile off the southeast tip of Henry Island, and give them a wide berth. As you enter Mosquito Pass, slightly favor San Juan Island.

The rocks and shoals between Hanbury Point and Delacombe Point are marked; stay west of these. Off White Point, red nun buoy "6" marks a 1-fathom hump.

Slightly favor Henry Island as you pass west of "6," then go mid-channel as you curve northeast around the next unnamed peninsula off San Juan Island. Note the reef that extends southwest of this small peninsula.

Expect strong current as you proceed north toward the islet in the middle of Mosquito Pass. The islet is surrounded by an extensive reef. Stay east of this islet, favoring San Juan Island. You're free of the channel past Bazalgette Point.

The Strait of Georgia

This large body of open water deserves as much respect as the Strait of Juan de Fuca. Give the area around Alden Bank a wide berth, especially when current and wind are opposed. For additional information on the Strait of Georgia, see the introduction to Region 9, on page 248.

Lopez Island

Charts: 18421, **18429, 18430, 18434**

Lopez Island, low and rolling, has long been a farming community. Its population is relatively small—half that of Orcas—and virtually all its shops and services are centered on Fisherman Bay. Most of the large farms are slowly being parceled into vacation homes, but the rural spirit persists, and people still wave to each other on the country roads.

From the fishtail of its south end to the horns at its north, Lopez has almost as many anchorages as San Juan Island. The most popular are Fisherman Bay and Spencer Spit State Park.

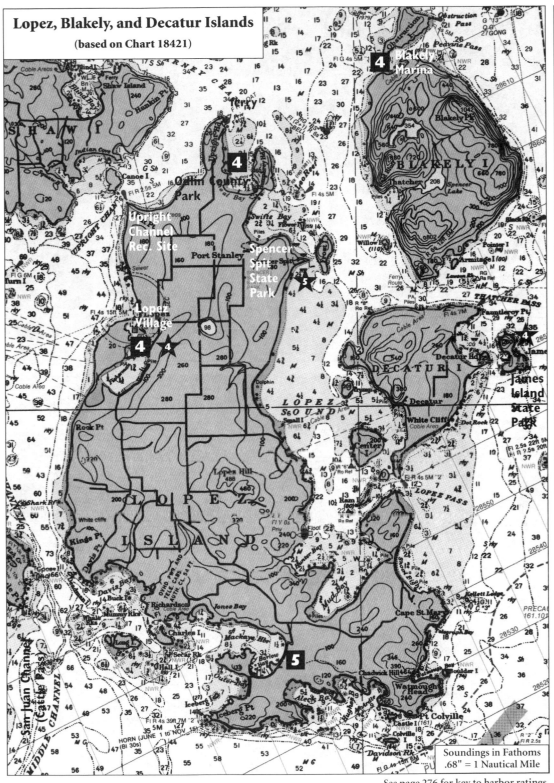

Lopez, Blakely, and Decatur Islands
(based on Chart 18421)

Soundings in Fathoms
.68" = 1 Nautical Mile

See page 276 for key to harbor ratings.

Spencer Spit State Park ★★★★★

Charts: 18421; **18429, 18430**

Spencer Spit is one of the most popular state parks in the San Juans. The quarter-mile spit is slightly triangular and encloses a tidal lagoon. Driftwood is piled on the silvery beach grass, and in summer the sandy shoals are warm enough for wading. The wooded uplands of the park, with their trails and campsites, cover more than 120 acres. At the end of the spit is a tiny cabin, originally built by the park's namesake, who homesteaded here with his family in the 1880s. The cabin has been rebuilt to look as it did then. The spit continues beyond; a walk to its very tip will put you almost within arm's length of boats parading by.

Approaches. From the south, the spit is so low it may not be visible at all. Look for the hump of Frost Island. Flower Island, low and bare, is on the other side of the spit. The boats you see are likely to be tethered to the buoys that parallel both sides of the spit.

From the north, the spit and the small cabin on the tip are more discernible. The cleanest approach is between Flower Island and Frost Island, east of Leo Reef.

The narrow channel between Spencer Spit and Frost Island is passable and surprisingly deep. Favor Frost Island, which plunges straight down into the sea. Expect to feel the tug of current.

Anchorage, Moorings. All of the mooring buoys at Spencer Spit are in deep water. There are nine on the south side of the spit; depth at the far west buoy is 10 feet greater than at the

Looking north past the log cabin at Spencer Spit State Park.

far east buoy. The seven buoys on the north side of the spit are comparable, with the deepest water west toward the Lopez shore.

If you anchor, stay outside of these buoys. The bottom rises gradually from 2 fathoms to less than 1 fathom on the south side of the spit, more abruptly on the north side.

Pay attention to the weather. This anchorage is exposed to the north and the south, and though the spit gives protection from waves, it does not protect from wind. If a gale kicks up, the closest protection from a southerly is in Swifts Bay; from a northerly the closest protection is in Brigantine Bay off Decatur Island.

Getting Ashore. The long beach of Spencer Spit has a sandy bottom that's easy on skiffs. Frost Island is private. Flower Island is a National Wildlife Refuge, aflutter with noisy, nesting gulls—stay at least 200 yards away.

For the Crew. Spencer Spit State Park has picnic areas, firepits, restrooms, and campsites, but no showers. The campground is closed from November through February.

There are no facilities within walking distance.

Coves South of Small Island

Charts: 18421, **18429**

About halfway down the east shore of Lopez, south of Small Island in Lopez Sound, are a series of pocket-sized coves. The first of these is a double cove separated by a tiny peninsula. Both sides of the peninsula are shallow and exposed, and the surrounding land is private. The peninsula itself is private, part of the San Juan Preservation Trust. It is dedicated to naturalist and photographer Gretchen Comstock Goodner; a small sign requests that visitors "please nurture it as she would have."

South is a deeper cove that opens toward Center Island. Private floats extend from the homes on shore, and there are a few private mooring buoys. The north half of this cove is deeper, but has less swinging room. There is no public shore access.

Jasper Bay is box-shaped, with steep sides and a view of Mount Baker through Lopez Pass. There are a couple of homes and a gazebo set on the rocks here, at the end of a winding road. This "bay" is shallow and tight, with room for one small boat at most. There is no public access to shore.

Hunter Bay ★★★ ⬚3 No Facilities

Charts: 18421, **18429**

Hunter Bay is the best anchorage at this southeast end of Lopez Island. It has good depth, public shore access, and is reasonably protected. The shores are steep; from here you can see east beyond Decatur Island all the way across Rosario Strait, and north up Lopez Sound to Spencer Spit.

Approaches. Approaches are clean from Lopez Sound, and from Lopez Pass once clear of red "4" southwest of Ram Island. Watch for the aquaculture pens against the west shore. From Mud Bay, go around the outside of Crab Island, a National Wildlife Refuge surrounded by rocks and reefs.

The approach through Lopez Pass is described on page 279.

Anchorage. Anchoring is good most anywhere in Hunter Bay, in about 2 fathoms. Stay out of the west bight, which shallows abruptly inside. A 3- to 4-fathom trench lies parallel to the southeast shore, west of the county float. Much of this area is occupied by private mooring buoys—it may take some time to find a spot here.

Except in a northeasterly, protection is good in Hunter Bay. The county float on the southeast shore is for loading and unloading only—no overnight stays are permitted.

All mooring buoys in Hunter Bay are private.

Getting Ashore. Use the county float. Depths are good to the float, about 4 feet shallower at the ramp. All other floats in Hunter Bay are private.

For the Boat, Crew. There are no facilities within walking distance. The Islandale store is more than two miles away, toward Mackaye Harbor.

Mud Bay ★★ [2] No Facilities

Charts: 18421, **18429**

Mud Bay is wide, reasonably deep, and perfectly named, so muddy you can't see bottom 2 feet down. On a minus tide the mudflats stretch halfway out, exposing public tidelands that are popular for clamming. The northwest side of Mud Bay has an extraordinary view of Mount Baker all the way down to its foothills.

Approaches. Stay between Crab Island and the daymark set on the edge of a shoal off the east shore. Inside Mud Bay, a wreck is charted on the west shore, and both sides are peppered with rocks.

The approach through Lopez Pass is described on page 279.

Anchorage. Deepest anchorage is in the north half of the bay. Protection is not especially good. Mud Bay is open to the north, and a strong southerly can blow from Mackaye Harbor across the low south isthmus. In these conditions, better protection is in Hunter Bay.

All floats and mooring buoys in Mud Bay are private.

Getting Ashore. A street end on the southeast shore, between a blue-gray house and a wooden fence, is used by local residents to reach the public tidelands. The road, however, is private. There are no facilities within walking distance.

Cove East of Fortress Island (Camp Nor'Wester)

Charts: 18421, **18429**

North of Hunter Bay and Mud Bay, east of Fortress Island, is a small bight with an islet in the center. The Indian longhouse, the carvings, and the artfully groomed grounds are part of Camp Nor'Wester, a private summer camp. Anchoring is permitted but not encouraged, as the entire cove is used for camp activities.

Approaching, keep a respectful distance off the islet (known locally as Skull Island), and don't go in too far; there's kelp and a submerged rock northeast of Skull. The mooring buoys are private; leave adequate swinging room around them.

The "bay" to the south is less than a fathom, and most of it dries at low tide.

All tidelands are private. Visitors to Camp Nor'Wester must have an appointment. Both Skull Island and Fortress Island are National Wildlife Refuges.

Telegraph Bay

Charts: 18421, **18429**

Telegraph Bay is a small bight on Lopez Island's rugged southeast shore, south of Cape Saint Mary. The headlands are steep, and beyond the crescent of beach at the head of the bay is a grassy field. Shallow, exposed to the southeast and to the freighter wakes in Rosario Strait, this bay is not recommended as an anchorage.

Approaching from the north, watch for the extensive kelp bed west of Kellett Ledge. Note the rock charted just inside Telegraph Bay, on the south point.

This bay has no public upland access.

North of Telegraph is Shoal Bight, which is exposed and foul with submerged pilings.

Watmough Bay ★★★ 1 No Facilities

Charts: 18421, **18429**

Wedged between the steep cliffs of Chadwick Hill and Watmough Head, this northeast-facing bay on the southeast side of Lopez is one of the most dramatic in the San Juans. Boulder Island leans toward the Strait, as though it had been pushed off the tip of Lopez. At the head of the bay is a low marsh. In 1792, part of the Spanish Eliza Expedition anchored here to observe the emergence of one of Jupiter's moons.

The *Coast Pilot* describes protection from the west and south as "good," and commercial fishers use Watmough as a haven from Rosario Strait. However, it is not recommended. Even on a calm day the water is restless here, and the wakes of freighters wash onto the beach, spraying the steep sides and covering the rocks around Boulder Island with foam. Watmough is a dangerous place in a northerly blow.

Approaching, do not attempt to pass between Boulder Island and Watmough Bay. The bottom is rocky, and rises abruptly at the entrance.

Hughes Bay and McArdle Bay ★★★ 2 No Facilities

Charts: 18421, **18429**

These twin bays on the south shore of Lopez are rimmed with trees and steep rock. Some of the homes here have a playful, elfin look. The bays themselves are small and exposed.

Approaches. The entrance to these two bays is about a mile west of the Davidson Rock mark. The cleanest approach is midway between Colville Island and Swirl Island. Give the unmarked, charted rocks east of Swirl a wide berth. From the northeast, the passage is deep between Colville Island and Castle Island.

On any approach, watch out for kelp, and be prepared for whirlpools. All these small islands and rocks are National Wildlife Refuges—stay 200 yards away.

Anchorage. In both bays the bottom rises gradually but steadily. Of the two, Hughes Bay is the better anchorage, with a 3- to 5-fathom basin and more protection from southerlies; note the submerged rock charted off the east shore. Both Hughes and McArdle are exposed to the swell off the strait and should be used in settled conditions only.

All mooring buoys and floats are private.

Getting Ashore. At the southeast corner of McArdle Bay is the pocket-size public beach of "Blackie" Bradie County Park. Wooden stairs angle up the high bank to a grassy clearing. There are no facilities within walking distance.

Aleck Bay ★★★ No Facilities

Charts: 18421, **18429**

Rectangular-shaped Aleck Bay is steep-sided at its entrance, gradually lowering to a marsh at its head. The view eastward is a fairyland; when clouds are low one can easily imagine castles and sea serpents among the islands that guard this entire south shore, and the Strait of Juan de Fuca seems to disappear over the edge of the earth.

The *Coast Pilot* describes protection as good here in all but "heavy" southeast wind. However, it is a good idea to avoid this bay when southeasterlies of any strength are predicted.

Approaches. Nothing is marked along this south shore of Lopez except Davidson Rock and Iceberg Point, more than three miles to the west. The many islands and headlands make this area confusing to navigate. From the south, the cleanest approach is between Colville Island (one mile west of Davidson Rock) and Swirl Island.

Aim for the peninsula between Hughes Bay and McArdle Bay until past Swirl Rocks. Note the unmarked, charted rocks east of Swirl Island, and give them a wide berth. It's possible to pass between Swirl Island and Aleck Rocks, and even west of Aleck Rocks, but these routes are more hazardous. When approaching from the east, Castle Island's vertical sides and pinnacle top are a prominent landmark; there's good depth between it and Colville Island.

Pinnacles below the surface create whirlpools everywhere. All of the small islands in this area are National Wildlife Refuges—stay a minimum of 200 yards away, a good idea anyway, considering the rocks, kelp, and shoals around them.

Anchorage. The inside of Aleck Bay is cleansided. Best protection is toward the south shore. Stay east of the rocks charted at the head of the bay, where it is shallow and dries at low tide.

Getting Ashore. All the land around Aleck Bay is private. The closest public access is east in McArdle Bay.

Coves West of Aleck Bay

Charts: 18421, **18429**

From Aleck Bay west to Iceberg Point are a series of rocky coves mercilessly exposed to the Strait of Juan de Fuca and filled with kelp, logs, and deadheads. Currents are strong. If you want to explore this area, do so in calm conditions only, in a small sturdy boat, and use caution. Flint Beach, the only likely place to go ashore, is private.

Outer Bay ★★★ ⬜1 No Facilities

Charts: 18421, **18429**, 18434

This squarish bay lies between Iceberg Point and Johns Point, and is open to the west. Above the beach are many small, closely packed homes. Agate Beach County Park is toward the center of the bay; stairs lead to a picnic area, and a short trail loops through the trees and wild roses.

Outer Bay is too exposed to the Strait of Juan de Fuca for comfortable overnight anchorage. Waves break steadily on the beach, polishing the stones. All the surrounding land is barren, and the evergreens lean eastward.

Approaches. From the south, stay well off Iceberg Point, which is surrounded by reef, rock, and kelp. Pass either side of Iceberg Island. From the north, keep to the south side of the bay; the north half is foul with rocks, shoals, and kelp.

Anchorage. Anchor in the south half of the bay, in 2 to 5 fathoms. The bottom, scoured by wave action, is hard.

Getting Ashore. Use the county park beach. There are no facilities within walking distance. The nearest store is almost two miles away, at Islandale.

Mackaye Harbor and Barlow Bay ★★★

Charts: 18421, **18429, 18434**

Mackaye Harbor curls east and south into Barlow Bay, forming an ideal refuge from the Strait of Juan de Fuca and the current of San Juan Channel (Cattle Pass). Even the *Coast Pilot* describes Barlow as an "excellent shelter." The area was originally a Lummi settlement, and a thriving fishery in the 1900s. Fishing boats still moor here, but the last of the fish-buying stations has been sold, and the commercial flavor of this harbor is fading.

Approaches. From the south, the fuel tanks at Richardson are visible past Iceberg Point. Head slightly east of Richardson to avoid the rocks off Charles Island. As you turn east into Mackaye, keep several hundred yards off the south shore, away from the reefs and a string of unmarked rocks.

From the northwest, you can thread your way past Mummy Rocks and between Long Island and Charles Island, but the cleaner approach, especially when currents are strong, is as described from the south. The narrow passage between Lopez and Charles Islands is marked, but note the many rocks that are unmarked, and take care. Overhead are power lines, with a charted clearance of 54 feet.

Anchorage. Protection is good in the 2- to 5-fathom basin of Barlow Bay. Four docks extend into deep water from the south shore; the area between them dries at low tide. There are plans to expand one of these into a larger marina, with guest moorage and a dinghy dock, but for now all the floats and beaches in this corner of the bay are private.

Getting Ashore. All tidelands in Barlow Bay are private. Public access is on the east shore of Mackaye Harbor, at the county launching ramp. A white diamond marks the end of a rock jetty here. The beach is strewn with boulders at the high-tide line; pick your landing spot carefully, and keep the launching ramp clear.

For the Boat, Crew. A half-mile uphill from the launching ramp is the Islandale Store, which carries a fair selection of groceries and has a café and a deli. Hard ice cream from a local dairy is a specialty. The store also sells fishing gear and a little hardware. A gas station is attached. The nearest diesel fuel is at the Richardson pier.

Richardson and Jones Bay ★★

Charts: 18421, **18429**, 18434

In the early 1900s, Richardson was the most active port on Lopez Island, with a hotel, a store, and a cannery that employed 400 workers. Until recently the most notable remnant of that boom time was the Richardson Store. Perched on the pilings overlooking the strait, the store was famous throughout the San Juan Islands for its worn wooden floors, its shelves crammed with dry goods and groceries, and for its hard ice cream.

In 1990, one of the aging refrigerator compressors sparked and blazed; volunteer firefighters managed to save the fuel dock and its tanks, but the store burned to the water. The entire island mourned.

Today, Richardson is a scattering of homes around a dead-end road. Other than the fuel dock, there is nothing to tempt the boater to stop.

Approaches. From the south, the fuel tanks at Richardson are visible past Iceberg Point. Head slightly east of Richardson to avoid the rocks off Charles Island. From the northwest, you can thread your way past Mummy Rocks and between Long Island and Charles Island, but the cleaner approach, especially when currents are strong, is as described from the south. The narrow passage between Lopez and Charles Islands is marked, but note the many rocks that are unmarked, and take care. The overhead power lines have a charted clearance of 54 feet.

Anchorage. Jones Bay, east of Richardson, has room and depth for a couple of boats to anchor, but there's no protection. Driftwood is piled high along the beach, attesting to the vigor of southerlies here. You can try to tuck in behind the west headland, but take care: tideflats fill most of the northwest portion of the bay, and private mooring buoys are set in the best spots. Entering Jones Bay, strongly favor the east shore to avoid the two submerged rocks charted to the west, one of them in the center of the entrance. Glass-fronted homes gaze unblinking from the east shore, and all tidelands are private.

Between Richardson and Charles Island are two bights separated by an islet. The east bight is unprotected from the restless water of the strait, and is not recommended. The west bight is crowded with private mooring buoys and a seaplane float, part of the Davis Bay Head Resort community. There is no public access to shore in either bight.

For the Boat. The Richardson fuel dock is open weekday afternoons from 1 P.M. to 4 P.M., a little later in the summer. There's plenty of depth at the pier, but no float. You'll have to tie to the pilings and climb the ladder—an awkward maneuver if a swell is running off the strait.

Davis Bay ★★ No Facilities

Charts: 18421, **18434**

Davis Bay opens widely to the Strait of Juan de Fuca and the turbulence of San Juan Channel (locally known as Cattle Pass). Rocks are scattered off the entrance and inside, the bottom is hard, and there is kelp everywhere. With Mackaye Harbor so close by, there is little reason to anchor here. All tidelands in Davis Bay are private.

From the south, the cleanest approach is between Long Island and Whale Rocks, then on either side of Mummy Rocks. From the east, pass between Secar Rock and Hall Island, and continue along the north side of Long Island and Mummy Rocks. The narrow passage between Lopez and Charles Island is marked, but note the many rocks that are unmarked, and take care. The overhead power lines have a charted clearance of 54 feet.

From the northwest, stay 500 yards off Davis Point—a popular scuba diving area, with numerous rocks and shoals. From any direction, expect strong tide rips.

Entering, stay in the middle of Davis Bay, and don't expect to find protection or quiet water.

Fisherman Bay ★★★★ All Facilities

Charts: 18421, **18430**, 18434

Lagoon-like Fisherman Bay, halfway up the west side of Lopez, is the only anchorage on the entire island with a full range of boating facilities. There are two marinas with guest moorage, room for anchoring, and restaurants within walking distance. A mile north is the commercial center of Lopez Village.

Approaches. The entrance to Fisherman Bay is narrow, shallow, and—as the *Coast Pilot* so accurately describes it—tortuous. Boaters should study the detailed chart before entering, and choose a rising tide with some margin for maneuvering. Anyone who runs aground here—a fairly common occurrence—does so in view of the town. Those with deep-draft vessels should note that the inside of the bay is charted at less than 2 fathoms; you may need to

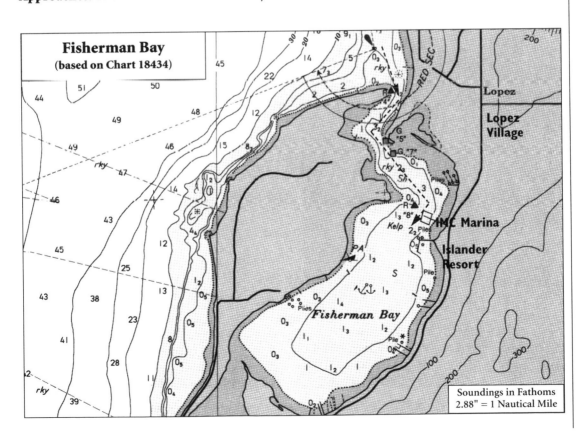

Fisherman Bay (based on Chart 18434)

Soundings in Fathoms
2.88" = 1 Nautical Mile

The entrance to Fisherman Bay. In this photo, Lopez Village is at the far left (north), and the two marinas are at the center.

bypass Fisherman Bay altogether during periods of minus tides.

From the middle of San Juan Channel the entrance to Fisherman Bay is not immediately apparent. Head for the square white church tower, which is topped with four turrets, until the red-and-white entrance mark is clear. If approaching from the north, stay at least 200 yards off the Lopez shore in order to avoid the string of rocks (some submerged) that lie between Flat Point and the entrance.

The red-and-white entrance mark is on a piling set in shallow water about 300 yards north of the spit. Enter north and east of this mark, about midway between it and the shore. This mark is lighted.

Within 100 feet of the next mark ("4"), slightly favor the spit. Take care to avoid the submerged rock on the east shore without drifting on to the shoal that extends east off the spit. This is the shallowest portion of the channel.

Past "4," favor the east shore. Make your course around green "5" and "7" slightly curved rather than straight. At "7," look south toward the marina to locate red "8" on a piling, which marks another spit. Stay east of "8" as you head into the bay.

Moorings. Island Marine Center (IMC) is the first (most northerly) marina on the east side. The hoist and boatyard across the street are visible from the water, and its black pilings are topped with pointed white caps. A yellow arrow points south to the guest floats (T1 through T10), which are labelled on the south side of the marina. The long outside float (T0) is also guest moorage. Pull all the way into an empty guest slip and check in at the office across the street. In summer, reservations are strongly recommended; call (360) 468-3377. IMC also monitors VHF Channel 69. Expect to raft up as the marina fills. The outside (west) slips are about 5 feet deeper than inside (east). All slips have power and access to water.

South of IMC is the marina and fuel dock of the Islander Restaurant and Resort. In summer, call ahead on VHF Channel 78; in the off-season, arrange for moorage at the resort office across the street from the restaurant. The Islander takes reservations for guest moorage (360) 468-2233. All slips have power and water. Depth at the fuel dock and at the inside floats is about 4 feet shallower than at the outside float.

The Galley Restaurant and Tavern, halfway down the bay on the east side, has overnight moorage for patrons. The floats are in shallow water, suitable for small craft only; check the tides. These floats have no power or water.

Protection in Fisherman Bay is not as good as it seems at first glance. Strong winds funnel over the low isthmus at the south end of the bay, and waves build up in the shallow water. Boats at either marina may have a rough ride.

Anchorage. Anchoring is good anywhere in the center of the bay, but it is shallow—less than 2 fathoms—and may not be deep enough for your boat during a minus tide. The south quarter of the bay is a fathom or less, and the lagoon beyond dries at low tide.

Protection is good except in strong southerlies.

Getting Ashore. The Islander Resort has an area for dinghies at the south end of the fuel dock, almost under the pier. IMC has limited space for dinghies from July through September; it's OK to land at their beach.

The Galley Restaurant and Tavern has a small float for patrons, in shallow water. The Galley is located halfway down the bay on the east side. The pier and float to the south is private, as are all others in Fisherman Bay. All tidelands inside the bay are also private.

The street end just outside the entrance to Fisherman Bay is public, but the bank is steep and there is no way to get up to Lopez Village without trespassing on private land.

For the Boat. The Islander fuel dock is on the north side of the main pier, in water about 4 feet shallower than at the marina's outside float. In the off-season, use the phone at the dock store to call for service.

Full-service marine repair services are available at IMC, with free transportation provided to the ferry. IMC's well-stocked marine store is open seven days a week from Memorial Day to Labor Day, on weekdays during the rest of the year.

For the Crew. IMC has showers for paying moorage customers only. Boaters moored at the Islander may use the resort showers, jacuzzi, pool, and laundry. There are also showers at the public restroom in Lopez Village, west of the grocery store.

The closest restaurants are the Islander and the Galley; both have moorage for patrons (see Getting Ashore above).

The dock store on the Islander pier sells a few snack items and ice; IMC also has ice. A fully stocked grocery store is a mile north in Lopez Village, where there are also gift shops, a bookstore, more restaurants, and a bakery. North of the village is the post office, a hardware store, and a pharmacy with a soda fountain. The island's historical museum, located near the village, is open afternoons in summer, Friday through Sunday. A bicycle rental is near the Islander.

Lopez celebrates the Fourth of July with a parade through town. A Saturday farmers' market is held in summer.

Upright Channel Recreation Site ★★★

Charts: 18421, **18430**, 18434

This day-use park on the east side of Flat Point makes the most of its narrow parcel of land. Three mooring buoys are set in deep water off the sand-and-cobble beach. A plaque identifies the public tidelands that continue to the east, and encourages a walk to Odlin County

Park, two miles away. Uphill is a groomed trail that leads past a series of terraced picnic sites and eventually to the road.

Approaching, look for the park some 500 yards east of the Flat Point mark. Private mooring buoys are set off the homes that crowd together on the point. The three yellow park buoys are to the east, about 75 feet apart.

The bottom rises steeply off the park; to the east is a 5- to 10-fathom shelf broad enough for anchoring. Protection is good here, but boat traffic in Upright Channel is fairly steady; be prepared to roll.

There are no facilities within walking distance.

Odlin County Park ★★★

Charts: 18421, **18430, 18434**

One of the most popular public beaches on Lopez Island is Odlin Park. It has a sunny western exposure, broad sandy tideflats, and a road right down to the driftwood that makes it easy for families to spread out their picnic gear. The nearby playing field has a volleyball net, a baseball diamond, and a cooking shelter for large groups. On the wooded ridge to the west are campsites and trails. North of the beach is a launching ramp and pier with a 40-foot float for temporary tie-ups. Offshore are four mooring buoys.

Approaches. Odlin Park is located on the southwest side of Upright Head, in the "corner" of the cove. The head is well-named, rising from the water like the forehead of a whale. From the north, approaches are clean and deep. The main surprise to watch for is the ferry, which often passes close to Upright Head on its way to and from the ferry dock. From the southwest, stay 300 yards or so off Lopez to avoid the broad shoal.

The park, with its ballfield, its bleachers, its flagpole and pier, is easy to identify.

Anchorage, Moorings. Four mooring buoys

are set in a diamond pattern toward the west half of the beach. Depths are good. The buoys are for boats 40 feet long or less, with a limit of two boats per buoy. There is a charge for using these buoys; pay at the fee box located at the head of the launching ramp, or at the park office up the road.

If you anchor, set your hook north or in line with the buoys; south of them the bottom rises abruptly to less than 1 fathom. Protection is good from southerlies and fair from the north, but boat traffic is steady here, especially in summer.

A 40-foot float is on the south side of the pier. Tie-ups are limited to two hours. Depths are good, about 6 feet shallower at the ramp.

Getting Ashore. Use the float or the beach. If you land at the beach, leave the swimming and wading areas clear.

For the Crew. The park has outhouses, but no showers. A mile north up the road is the ferry dock, where a takeout restaurant operates in summer. There are no other facilities within walking distance.

Shoal Bay ★★★ 4 No Facilities

Charts: 18421, **18430, 18434**

This bay between Humphrey Head and Upright Head is wide, and despite its name is fairly deep. Homes are set close together along its western and southern shores. Beneath the cliff of Humphrey Head is a small marina protected by a rock breakwater. Eagles and herons argue incessantly about nesting rights in the trees above.

Approaches, Anchorage. The approach is clean and deep around Upright Head. The waters around Humphrey Head are likewise clean and deep, but watch for the aquaculture pens north of the breakwater. From any direction, check to see if a ferry is approaching, and stay out of its way; ferry landings at Upright Head can be tricky, often sideways to wind and current.

Holding ground is good anywhere in Shoal Bay, in 2 to 3 fathoms. The best protection from the north—and from the ferry wakes—is slightly behind the marina breakwater.

The marina has no guest moorage. All other floats and all mooring buoys in Shoal Bay are private.

Getting Ashore. Shoal Bay has no public shore access. The marina and all the tidelands are private.

Swifts Bay (Port Stanley) ★★ 3 No Facilities

Charts: 18421, **18429, 18430**

Swifts Bay opens widely to the northeast, between Humphrey Head and Spencer Spit. It has an irregular bottom, and many large rocks along its shores. At the head of the bay is Port Stanley, which once had a post office, a store, and a kelp plant. The kelp plant operated briefly during World War I, extracting potash for use in explosives. Today, all that's left of the settlement is a line of modest homes.

With Spencer Spit State Park so close, Swifts Bay is usually ignored as an anchorage. However, it can be a good alternative when a southerly kicks up.

Approaches, Anchorage. From the north, note the submerged rock charted 3 feet below the surface, west of Leo Reef. From the east, stay clear of the rocks scattered north of Flower Island. If approaching from Spencer Spit, stay 100 yards or so off the Lopez shore to avoid the shoals and rocks off the headland.

The best protection from southerlies is toward Port Stanley. Southerlies tend to turn east into this bay, making the northeast shore uncomfortable. Swifts Bay is completely exposed to the north.

Getting Ashore. All tidelands in Swifts Bay are private. The nearest shore access is at Spencer Spit State Park. Flower Island is a National Wildlife Refuge—stay 200 yards away or more.

Obstruction Island

Charts: 18421, **18430**

Obstruction Island is shaped like a triangle, with steep shores and almost no beach. Homes are built around the entire island. All floats, mooring buoys, tidelands, and uplands are private.

A description of Obstruction Pass and Peavine Pass is given on page 278.

Blakely Island

Charts: 18421, 18429, **18430**

Blakely Island is mountainous and steep. It has no public ferry service or even county roads. Originally homesteaded by the Spencer family (of Spencer Spit) the island has since been divided into parcels, and remains a private enclave. This reclusive spirit is reinforced by the shoreline: only three coves dent its perimeter, only one has guest moorage.

Approaches, via Rosario Strait, Thatcher Pass, and Peavine Pass, are described on pages 278 and 279.

Blakely Marina ★★

Charts: 18421, **18430**

The only place on Blakely Island where the general public is welcome is at the private marina off Peavine Pass. This marina is tucked behind a low peninsula and attached headland that bends west to almost touch the square, south point. Inside the narrow entrance is guest moorage for about 70 boats, with fine protection from almost any weather. The grounds are green and meticulously trimmed, the concrete floats appear to have been scrubbed, and signs are everywhere. A chain link fence confines visitors to the marina grounds.

Approaches. The entrance to the marina opens to the west between two rock breakwater jetties. Approaching from the east, you can see the boats on the other side of the low peninsula. The marina entrance itself is quite narrow, and the current can be strong. If a northerly is blowing you may feel the wind here. The entrance has a controlling depth of 8 feet at zero tide. Depth inside is about the same as at the entrance, roughly half as deep as at the fuel dock.

Approaches to Peavine Pass are described on page 278.

Moorings. Blakely Marina has both covered and uncovered slips, set east-west off two main floats that branch from a single ramp. Man-euvering room is tight. Depth is steady throughout, a couple of feet shallower south of the southernmost float. Unless you have a reservation, tie up at the fuel dock and register at the store; be prepared for strong current at the dock. For after-hours arrivals, a fee box and a list of available slips are posted on the door. All slips have power and water. For reservations, call (360) 375-6121.

On the whole, protection is good here. The fuel dock, however, is exposed.

Getting Ashore. Shore access is limited to the marina grounds. A sign on the chain-link fence at the far end of the parking lot reminds you that Blakely is a private community.

For the Boat. The fuel dock is south of the marina entrance, in deep water. Approaching, be prepared for strong current. From January through mid-February, call a few days ahead for service—(360) 375-6121. The store sells a few boat supplies.

For the Crew. Everything in the Blakely Marina is clearly labelled: the ice machine at the head of the ramp, the restrooms and showers on the north side of the main building, the garbage and pet areas. The marina store specializes in gourmet items and gifts. South of the store is a barbecue and picnic shelter. The launching ramp may be used for a fee.

Cove Behind Armitage Island ★★ ☐2 No Facilities

Charts: 18421, **18429**, **18430**

On the southeast tip of Blakely is an unnamed cove behind Armitage Island. Private floats and mooring buoys are set in front of the fine homes; surrounding lawns are groomed like those of a country club.

There's enough depth and room for several boats to anchor in this cove, but little protection from the wakes off busy Thatcher Pass. Except for a small area north of Armitage, this cove is exposed to the south and southeast.

Approaches are clean on both sides of Armitage Island. There is no public shore access.

Thatcher ★★ ☐2 No Facilities

Charts: 18421, **18429**, **18430**

When the wind blows from the north, the quiet water in this bay on the west side of Blakely Island might tempt boaters to duck in for protection. However, only those with shallow-draft vessels should do so. Less than 50 feet inside the entrance, the bottom rises alarmingly from 8 fathoms to just over 1 fathom. The bay itself is shallower than charted. The northeast corner is foul with pilings and the ruins of an old log skid. This area was once an active logging operation; the island timber was cut so completely that run-off from the denuded slopes filled the bay with silt.

Approaching, Willow Island is a distinctive landmark. From the north, Bald Bluff is a mostly bare rock face, deeply lined from glacial grinding. Stay at least 100 yards off this north bluff as it rounds into the cove, in order to avoid the shoal and charted rock.

There is no public shore access. Willow Island is a National Wildlife Refuge—stay at least 200 yards away.

Decatur Island

Charts: 18421, **18429**

Decatur Island lies between Lopez Sound and Rosario Strait. The island has a high, bulbous north end that tapers to a low curving tip. Decatur has a small schoolhouse, but no public ferry service, no town, and no store. The private nature of this island does not encourage visiting boaters. In any case, there are few anchorages along its shores.

Cove at the Southwest Tip ★★★ ☐2 No Facilities

Charts: 18421, **18429**

At the south tip of Decatur is a tiny cove inside a wooded headland. An islet in the center of the cove has an intriguing concrete structure on its west side—the remains of an old kelp

295

plant that was once use to extract potash for explosives. It's possible for a single small boat to anchor just northeast of the islet in about 2 fathoms, but shoals surround this cove on three sides, and swinging room is limited. Strong southeasterlies from Rosario Strait blow across the low isthmus that connects the headland to Decatur. The area south of the islet dries at low tide.

Approaching from the south, note the 1-fathom shoal located in mid-channel between Center Island and the wooded headland off Decatur. There's good depth between Decatur and Rim Island, but currents can be strong.

From the north, take care through Reads Bay, where there is an unmarked rock charted 5 feet below the surface, and a shoal that extends east from Center Island. Note the shoal off Decatur, about 100 yards north of the islet.

All tidelands are private. The isthmus and the attached headland are a private preserve belonging to the San Juan Preservation Trust, accessible only with permission.

Reads Bay ★★

Charts: 18421, **18429**

This bay northwest of Center Island is the most active area on Decatur. Read Brothers Shipyard has operated here since 1895; its travel lift and shop buildings are clustered in the southeast corner. The entire east shore is shallow, gradually turning to marsh; a private airstrip is on the other side of the beach grass. There are several piers extending into deep water, and many private mooring buoys.

Approaches. Approaching from the south, note the 1-fathom shoal southeast of Center Island. There's good depth between Decatur and Rim Island, but currents can be strong. From the north, take care through Reads Bay, where there is an unmarked rock charted 5 feet below the surface, and a shoal extending east from Center Island.

Anchorage. The best anchorage is north of the cable area, slightly to the north of Center Island, in 2 to 4 fathoms. Protection is fair here from the north and south, but strong winds can blow across the low isthmus at the south end of Decatur. All floats in Reads Bay are private; a sign on one states unambiguously that temporary moorage requires "dated written permission of property owners."

Getting Ashore. There is no public access to Decatur Island in this bay. Center Island is encircled by public tidelands, but all floats and all uplands are private.

For the Boat. Read Brothers Shipyard operates as a full-service yard from September 1 through May 31. Limited work can be done during the summer. Access is via a float south of the travel lift, at high tide only. Call ahead if you can, either by phone—(360) 375-6007—or on CB Channel 14.

Brigantine Bay ★★★ No Facilities

Charts: 18421, **18429**

Brigantine Bay is protected from the south by Trump Island and from the north by Decatur. Though wind may come over the saddle of land from Sylvan Cove, this is a good place to duck into when northerlies kick up at Spencer Spit. Depths are good—5 to 10 fathoms—and the bottom is mud. The private beach is for members of the Decatur Northwest community only. A few homes are along the shore, and private mooring buoys are set along the 5-fathom shelf.

Approaching from the north along the Decatur shore, note the rock charted 7 feet below the surface, close to shore. Rocks are charted north and south of Trump Island as well.

Anchor west of the buoys. The bottom rises steeply—give yourself enough swinging room from shore.

All tidelands in Brigantine Bay are private. Trump Island is encircled by public tidelands, but all uplands are private.

Sylvan Cove ★★★ 3 No Facilities

Charts: 18421, **18429**

Sylvan Cove indents the northwest shore of Decatur Island. Its east and west shores are rocky and steep, with a number of artfully placed homes. The south shore slopes gently from a small pier and float; white clapboard buildings dot the smooth grass. This private community of Decatur Northwest looks like a tiny town.

Approaches, Anchorage. Sylvan Cove is filled with private mooring buoys, but there is room and depth for anchoring. Approaches are clean. Note the shoal on the west side of the cove, and watch for kelp there.

Sylvan Cove gives pretty good protection from southerlies, but winds from that direction do funnel over the saddle of land, touching down about the middle of the bay. There is no protection here from the north.

Getting Ashore. All tidelands in Sylvan Cove are private. A small sign on the pier warns that its use is for members of Decatur Northwest only.

Cove Between Fauntleroy Point and Decatur Head ★★ 2 No Facilities

Charts: 18421, **18429**

There's little to attract boaters to this wide bay on the east side of Decatur Island. The shores are fairly crowded with homes, the west side is shallow and foul, and protection is minimal. However, there's more room and holding ground than at James Island State Park, making this an alternate anchorage when the float and mooring buoys there are occupied.

Approaches, Anchorage. The best anchorage in this bay is at the southeast end, toward Decatur Head. Approaching, head for the street end on the southwest shore until you can see across the isthmus. As you round the northwest side of Decatur Head, stay at least 100 yards offshore to miss the shoals. Avoid the west shore, where a submerged rock is charted.

This bay has an irregular bottom, and shallows rather quickly to less than 2 fathoms. The rock awash, charted off the west shore, extends into the bay farther than you'd expect. Pilings are charted toward the isthmus—don't go in too far.

The isthmus protects you from southerly waves but not southerly winds. There is no protection in this bay from northerlies or from ferry wakes.

The buoy charted in the middle of the bay is used by the Coast Guard.

Getting Ashore. A county launching ramp is at the street end on the south shore. Adjacent tidelands are private. There are no facilities within walking distance.

James Island State Park ★★★★   🛶

Charts: 18421, **18429**

This hourglass-shaped island east of Decatur is a marine state park, rustic and delightfully unimproved. Along the trails that wander throughout its 113 acres of second-growth timber are picnic tables, firepits, and campsites. Pit toilets and a shelter are located in the center of the island. A sign warns of marauding raccoons.

Approaches. Currents are strong around both coves. Depths are good, though there are many rocks close to shore.

Anchorage, Moorings. The park float is in the west cove, about 50 feet long and in deep water. There is only one buoy, close to shore in deep water. Anchoring is possible but not recommended, as the bottom is steep and rocky and the currents are strong. Watch for an unmarked rock off the south shore of this cove.

The east cove has four buoys, the northern two in water 8 to 10 feet deeper than the others. Anchoring is possible east of the buoys. Both coves are exposed to the currents and weather off Rosario Strait.

Getting Ashore. In the west cove, use the park float. In the east cove you can land on either of the two gravel beaches. The trail across the island to the other cove begins on the north beach.

Fees are charged for the park float and

The state park float in the west cove of James Island. The east cove has mooring buoys only.

buoys, from May 1 through September 30. The fee box is at the head of the ramp in the west cove.

San Juan Island

Charts: 18421, **18433, 18434**

San Juan Island tapers from a broad head to a narrow, curling tail. Its southwest shores are steep, wind-swept, and completely exposed to the Strait of Juan de Fuca. North and east, the land is lower, with more protective harbors.

This second largest island in the archipel-

ago was the first encountered by European explorers, and the first to be settled and farmed. Today almost half the population of the county lives here. The island is blessed with dry weather, but wells have now lowered to alarming levels, and strict water-conservation rules are in effect.

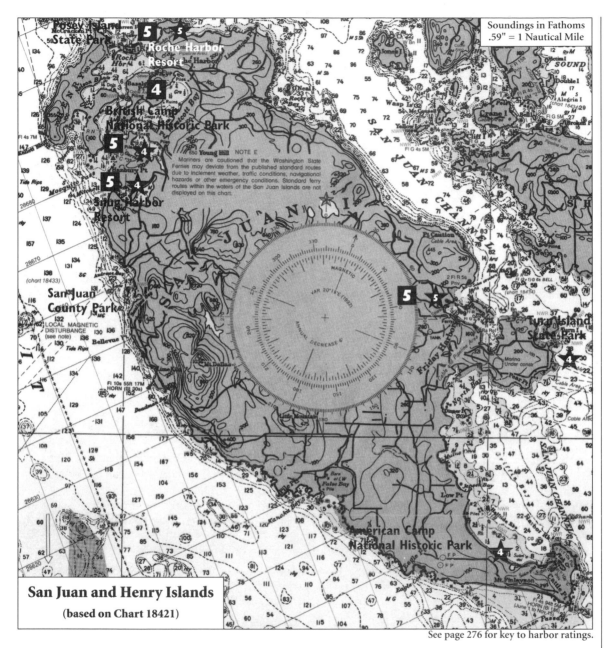

Soundings in Fathoms
.59" = 1 Nautical Mile

San Juan and Henry Islands
(based on Chart 18421)

See page 276 for key to harbor ratings.

For most boaters, San Juan Island is noted for the lively town of Friday Harbor, and the resorts at Roche Harbor and Mitchell Bay.

Friday Harbor ★★★★★ ☐4 (anchorage) ☐5 (marina) All Facilities

Charts: 18421, **18434**

In all the San Juan Islands, Friday Harbor is the liveliest, most crowded port, with the largest variety of services and shops. In summer, everything seems to happen here at once.

299

Fishing and pleasure boats come and go around the fuel dock and marinas. Excursion boats full of tourists share the breakwater with vessels clearing customs. Seaplanes taxi through the north channel as ferries arrive and depart. Boats anchor where they can.

Those who cruise the San Juans to "get away from it all" often swear they'll avoid Friday Harbor, but sooner or later they happily submit to its pull. It may be the desire to wander aimlessly among bookstores, shops, and galleries, or the need to clear customs, or the crew's demand for some choices in restaurants. A large part of its allure is its appearance: two- and three-story wooden buildings that step uphill from the harbor in pleasing disarray.

Approaches. In San Juan Channel, look for the green-and-red buoy that marks Reid Rock when approaching from the north, and for green "3" on Turn Rock, east of Turn Island, when approaching from the south. Friday Harbor itself can be approached either southeast or northwest of Brown Island (locally known as Friday Island).

The narrow passage southeast of Brown Island should be entered in mid-channel. A reef connected to the south tip of Brown Island is marked with a red triangle ("2") on pilings; a series of reefs surrounds the opposite point on San Juan Island, with numerous rocks charted east to the green square daymark. If you use this approach and your destination is the Port of Friday Harbor, be prepared to thread your way between mooring buoys and anchored boats. Watch for traffic crossing to Brown Island.

The passage northwest of Brown Island is wider, and is used regularly by ferries, tour boats, and seaplanes. There are fewer hazards, but note the charted 5-foot shoal and the submerged rock on the west side of Brown Island. Strobe lights flash on Brown and on the opposite point (just east of the Oceanographic Laboratories) when seaplanes are taking off or landing.

In both these passages, current is often strong, and tends to run clockwise around Brown. Watch your drift.

Moorings. Friday Harbor has a number of marinas. The only one with moorage for visitors is the large marina operated by the Port of Friday Harbor. In terms of transient "boat nights," it is reportedly the busiest on the West Coast. The marina is located northwest of the ferry dock, directly in front of you if you enter northwest of Brown Island. It is protected by two floating breakwaters that overlap to create an entrance toward the north end of the marina. This entrance can be found by looking for the windsock on the small hut at the end of the north breakwater; the entrance is just south of this hut.

Guest moorage is in several locations: on both sides of the north breakwater, on the inside of the longer south breakwater, on both sides of "G" dock, and on the south side of "H" dock. For shallow-draft vessels less than 24 feet long, there is additional guest moorage toward shore on "C" dock.

The outside of the south breakwater is reserved for U.S. Customs, for tour boats, and for seaplanes.

To help reduce congestion during summer, boaters are encouraged to call the Port on VHF Channel 66A (U.S.)—not 66—when they are within sight of the marina. Moorage assignments are also made from the hut at the end of the north breakwater.

Pay stations are located at the head of "G" dock, on the main pier, and in front of the harbor office. The harbor office is the blue-roofed building at the head of the main pier.

The Port of Friday Harbor takes reservations for overnight moorage, provided you call at least 48 hours in advance and your boat is less than 40 feet long. It costs almost twice as much per foot if you reserve a slip. From July 15 to Labor Day, it's advisable to make reservations. The phone number is (360) 378-2688.

All slips have power and water. Water use is severely limited—no washing down of boats. Plaques near the spigots warn of a stiff fine.

If your stay is short (four hours or less) you will not be charged for moorage, but you are expected to check in with the harbor office.

Southeast of the ferry dock are a number of private marinas. None has overnight guest

The Port of Friday Harbor. This photo was taken soon after the marina was expanded, and it is uncharacteristically empty. Note the entrance between the floating breakwaters at the far right (north). The harbor office is at the head of the wide pier. (U.S. Army Corps of Engineers)

moorage. All mooring buoys in the harbor are also private.

Anchorage. Anchorage is good in Friday Harbor, but it takes some care to find a spot among the many boats at anchor, and the many private buoys. The cove to the west of the University of Washington Oceanographic Laboratories shallows, as charted, to 10 feet and less; if your boat is deep-draft, anchor just outside this cove. The area inside (west) of the marina is even shallower. Southeast of the ferry dock is a 5- to 10-fathom basin; here, it's important to stay out of the cable and pipeline area and to keep the ferry channel clear. Mooring cables spider out from the port breakwater—do not anchor within 300 feet.

Regardless of where you anchor, take time to set your hook well. Currents are strong and shifting, and many an anchor has corkscrewed out of the mud.

Getting Ashore. A dinghy float is in front of the port office, on the northwest side of the main pier. A tideflat makes beaching impractical near the gazebo at Waterfront Park. All other floats and tidelands in Friday Harbor, including those at the University of Washington Oceanographic Laboratory, are private.

For the Boat. There are two fuel docks between the harbor office and the ferry dock. Approach south of the breakwater. The fuel dock closest to the ferry dock is currently out of service.

A complete marine supply store is one block up Spring Street. There is a well-stocked hardware store up the hill on the same street. A sail loft and a marine electronics shop are northwest of the harbor office building.

Full-service repairs are available at Jensen's Boatyard, in the south "cove" of the harbor.

The U.S. Customs hut on the breakwater is staffed during the summer. The main office is on shore, northwest of the harbor office, in the two-story building at the end of the parking lot.

301

For the Crew. Restrooms with showers are on the ground floor of the port office building. The closest laundromat is a half-block up Spring Street, in a retail alley next to the San Juan Inn; within a block are two others. Two grocery stores almost face each other across Spring Street.

Friday Harbor also has a dive shop, a micro-brewery, and numerous restaurants, cafés, and delicatessens. A fresh seafood market operates in summer at the foot of the ramp, off the main pier.

Things to Do. Friday Harbor is a compact, walkable town, with gift shops, galleries, and a movie theater—plenty of diversions for rainy days. It is also a "real" town, with a lumber store, drug store, and post office, and is the seat of county government.

If you want to stretch your legs and at the same time learn about the town's history, pick up a walking-tour map at the visitors' center on Spring Street. One of the historical buildings, a two-story clapboard overlooking the harbor office, houses the Whale Museum. This museum is scaled for people and geared for children. The entry stairwell is painted all around with underwater scenes; above, the ceiling is painted like the sky. Display rooms are small, with a refreshing lack of wordy captions. You'll learn a little about whales in general, and a great deal about the three pods of orcas that reside in Puget Sound. You'll come away relaxed, feeling more connected to these giant creatures than overwhelmed. The Whale Museum is open seven days a week.

For exploring beyond the town, Friday Harbor has bicycle and moped rentals, and a shuttle taxi to Roche Harbor. Scheduled air service is available at the nearby airport. Seaplane services also are available. During the summer, passenger boats make scheduled runs to Orcas Island, Bellingham, and Seattle; catch these at the south breakwater. Washington State ferries make a daily run between here and Victoria, British Columbia, and several runs to and from other islands and Anacortes.

In order to prevent interruption of research and classes, the University of Washington Oceanographic Laboratories (generally known as the Friday Harbor Labs) ask visitors to stay away.

Special events in Friday Harbor include Whale Week in early May, a parade and fireworks on the Fourth of July, and—most popular of all—the Jazz Festival on the last weekend in July. The San Juan County Fair is held in mid-August; the fairgrounds are within walking distance of the harbor.

Turn Island State Park ★★★★

Charts: 18421, **18434**

This small state park less than a mile southeast of Friday Harbor attracts many boaters. It has picnic tables, firepits, and a few campsites. The west side of the island is low, with two beautiful beaches; the steep east side overlooks San Juan Channel. A perimeter trail wanders beneath evergreens and sinuous madronas, punctuated here and there by enormous boulders left behind by glacial retreat.

Turn Island is jointly managed as a park and a wildlife refuge by the U.S. Fish and Wildlife Service and the Washington State Department of Parks and Recreation. Please stay on the trails (no rock climbing), and do not pick flowers or other vegetation. Keep your pets on your boat.

Approaches. The cleanest approach to the island is from the north. From Friday Harbor, respect the San Juan shore, where a string of rocks—some submerged—are charted. Do likewise when approaching from the south. Depth is good between Turn Rock and Turn Island. The passage south of Turn Island, constricted by rock and reef, is narrow and not advised for most vessels. Note that the south-

A hooded merganser surveys the anchorage from the beach at Turn Island State Park. The islet joins the beach at low tide.

west tip of Turn Island is surrounded by tide-flats, and the islet south of the mooring buoys is connected to Turn at low tide.

Anchorage, Moorings. Three mooring buoys are set off the west beach. The north buoy is in deepest water, the middle buoy about 5 feet shallower. Don't use the south buoy if your boat is deep-draft. This buoy is in shallow water (15 feet shallower than the north buoy) and uncomfortably close to the rocks that spill off the islet.

There's good anchoring depth west of these buoys, in 5 to 10 fathoms. However, the cur-rent is swift, and the rocks that line all the shores suggest a rocky bottom. If you anchor, set your hook well.

Though there's depth and room to anchor in the cove south of Turn Island, kelp and rock make it difficult to set a hook. All mooring buoys in this area are private.

Getting Ashore. The low gravel beach on the west side of Turn Island rises at a perfect angle for landing a skiff. The nearby tidelands on San Juan Island are private, with the exception of a street end, southwest of Turn. There are no facilities within walking distance.

North Bay ★ ☐2 No Facilities

Charts: 18421, **18434**

By San Juan Island standards, this is not an attractive anchorage. North Bay is predomi-nantly industrial, the back side of Friday Harbor. East of Little Island is a working gravel pit, with piles of sand spilling toward the long spit of Jackson Beach park. Tugs and barges loading from the gravel pit often anchor nearby. The pier on Little Island—connected to San Juan—is built like a fortress on a concrete bulkhead, with a row of fuel tanks and a few floats inside. This is still an operating cannery.

Approaches. From the south, the main hazards to watch for are two rocks charted at 5 feet below the surface, one about 500 yards southeast of Dinner Island, another 1,000 yards east of Dinner. Passage on the west side of Dinner Island is complicated by several unmarked reefs and rocks, some of them submerged; according to the *Coast Pilot* this passage should not be attempted. The cleanest approach is from the north, provided you stay several hundred feet off Pear Point.

Anchorage. The 3- to 5-fathom anchoring basin is between Little Island and Dinner

Island. Protection is fair from the northeast, but you're exposed to south wind funneling up San Juan Channel. Dinner Island gives some protection from the southeast.

Getting Ashore. Beach your skiff at Jackson Beach, a stretch of sand on the isthmus connecting Little Island with San Juan. The park has sand volleyball courts, and a few picnic tables and firepits. The airport and county fairgrounds are a mile away, up Argyle Avenue; the town of Friday Harbor is a half-mile farther.

The launching ramp on the other side of the isthmus is public. Most of the area inside the lagoon is a biological preserve for the University of Washington. No plants or animals (including clams) should be removed.

All other tidelands are private, including Dinner Island. The reefs surrounding Dinner are a National Wildlife Refuge—stay at least 200 yards away.

Merrifield Cove, Mulno Cove, and Jensen Bay ★★ No Facilities

Charts: 18421, **18434**

These three coves on the west side of Griffin Bay have little to recommend them as anchorages. All are surrounded by homes, all are shallow, and none offers much protection.

The best anchorage is in Merrifield Cove, south of the charted rocks. Dinner Island gives some protection from the north, but not from the northeast. To avoid the reefs and rocks

around Dinner Island, approach Merrifield Cove from the southeast.

As much as half of Mulno Cove and Jensen Bay are dry at low tide. Jensen Bay is especially foul with submerged rocks.

All tidelands in these three coves are private.

Griffin Bay Recreation Site ★★★

Charts: 18421, **18434**

On the west shore of Griffin Bay, about a half-mile south of Low Point, is a 15-acre Department of Natural Resources (DNR) park. This park has a few campsites and picnic tables. The beach here is fairly small, and quite rocky.

Approaches. On the chart, find Halftide Rocks and North Pacific Rock; the park is about halfway between, at a reef and dense cluster of rocks near shore. A midway course toward shore, between Halftide and North Pacific rocks, should avoid four charted pilings and several unmarked, submerged rocks. As you approach, watch for the DNR sign with white lettering on the bank, and for the two park mooring buoys.

Anchorage, Moorings. Two park mooring buoys are set in shallow water (less than 2 fath-oms), and are encrusted with barnacles and kelp. East of these is good depth for anchoring, but virtually no protection.

Getting Ashore. Thread your way carefully among the rocks. Mudflats extend about 100 yards from shore. There is no public access to the main road. Adjacent tidelands are private.

American Camp National Historic Park ★★★★ ☐3☐ No Facilities

Charts: 18421, **18434**

American Camp is San Juan Island's largest park, over 1,200 acres of woods and open grassland. On Griffin Bay the park stretches roughly from North Pacific Rock to Fish Creek, and includes three lagoons. It extends across the island to the Strait of Juan de Fuca.

This has long been an inhabited area. Native American artifacts found here date back three thousand years. In 1860 some 500 American soldiers encamped here to oppose the growing British force in Garrison Bay. The border dispute in question came to be known as the "Pig War" and lasted 12 years, without casualties or battles. (For more on the "Pig War," see page 309.) Old Town—a rowdy settlement also referred to as San Juan Town—developed around the garrison activity; it burned in 1890.

Today nothing remains of the town, and little of the structures that housed the soldiers. The deserted fields, set apart by split-rail fences, have been left relatively unaltered. The only residents are birds, rabbits, and deer.

American Camp National Historic Park is most commonly visited by land. Although there are no facilities here for boats, there is good anchorage in Griffin Bay.

Approaches, Anchorage. From Dinner Island to North Pacific Rock, Griffin Bay is foul with rocks and pilings. The cleanest approach to American Camp is between North Pacific Rock and Harbor Rock. The beach in this area is bordered by a stand of thick evergreens. Beyond, the land rises gently some 300 feet, to the knoll of Mount Finlayson.

Approaching from San Juan Channel (Cattle Pass), stay north of Harbor Rock, and be prepared for swirling currents. For a description of Cattle Pass, see page 279.

The best anchorage in the bay is roughly between the middle and east lagoons, which are shown on the Park Service map as Jackle's Lagoon and Third Lagoon. The charted mooring buoy is used by the Coast Guard. Don't get too close to shore, as submerged piles are charted in this area. San Juan Island will protect you from southerlies as well as from current. However, many of the trees twist northward, as though trying to escape from the winds off the strait. Storms have piled driftwood in a thick tangle around the lagoons. Don't underestimate a northerly.

Getting Ashore. Go ashore anywhere on the park beach. The steepest area, and the easiest for landing a skiff, is at the smooth cobble beach off Third (east) Lagoon. A park boundary marker is about two-thirds of the way east. Off Jackle's (middle) Lagoon the beach is flatter; depending on the tide, you may need to land as far out as 200 yards.

Northwest of the west lagoon (known as Old Town or First Lagoon), is a sandy, sloping beach and a grassy field. Picnic tables are set in a meadow surrounded by wild rose bushes. A split-rail fence separates this area from a dirt road that joins the main road. There are many

305

rocks southeast along the beach, and the mudflats are extensive. Be prepared to wade if you go ashore here.

Fish Creek is thick with private docks and mooring buoys, and surrounded by homes. Depth at the entrance is about 4 feet shallower than inside. There are no public facilities here or within walking distance. To avoid the submerged cables, do not anchor within 150 feet of the entrance.

Things to Do. From any of the three lagoons you can pick up trails that connect the lagoons and curve south around Mount Finlayson. The Exhibit Center and the Interpretive Trail are to the west, near the flagpoles, on the other side of the main road; guided walks and historic re-enactments are held here in summer. A closer destination by foot is across the island to South Beach. This sandy stretch has the expansive feel of an ocean beach, with piles of driftwood, a steady west wind, and a limitless horizon across the Strait of Juan de Fuca. This is a good place to check on weather conditions in the strait. Wherever you walk, watch for rabbit holes.

There are no campgrounds in the park, and no facilities within walking distance. Beach fires are allowed at the beach north of Old Town (west) Lagoon.

Eagle Cove

Charts: 18421, **18434**

The public beach at Eagle Cove, with its open views across the Strait of Juan de Fuca, is a beautiful place to visit by land, but should be avoided by boaters. Rocks and kelp extend several hundred yards offshore, and the swells off the strait break steadily on the sand. Reefs and rocks clutter the small eastern bight known as Grandma's Cove.

Eagle Cove is bordered on its steep east side by the National Historic Park of American Camp, and on its west by a tract of homes. A trail leads up the ravine to a small parking area. The entrance to American Camp is less than a half-mile north.

False Bay and Kanaka Bay

Charts: 18421, **18433**, **18434**

About a third of the way up its rugged southwest shore, San Juan Island indents deeply at False Bay. Perfectly named, this entire bay is dry at low tide. Reefs and rocks lie across its entrance. False Bay is a biological preserve of the University of Washington. No plants or animals (including clams) should be removed.

A third of a mile west of False Bay is the small bight of Kanaka Bay, named for the Hawaiian Islanders brought here by the Hudson's Bay Company. Like most of the "coves" on this side of the island, Kanaka Bay is shallow, exposed, and foul with unmarked rocks, reefs, and shoals. All tidelands are private.

Deadman Bay (Limekiln State Park)

Charts: 18421, **18433**

This V-shaped "bay" south of the lighthouse at Lime Kiln Point has extensive reefs along its steep north shore, and is too exposed for anchoring. The state park on the point is a popular whale-watching site. Here, everyone faces west, waiting. The only sounds are the rush of the waves on the rocks and the fog signal. Cheers erupt when whales appear in Haro Strait.

Kayakers visiting Deadman Bay can reach this park by way of a short, steep trail.

Smallpox Bay (San Juan County Park) ★★★ No Facilities

Charts: 18421, **18433**

Smallpox Bay, U-shaped and shallow, is a tiny bight a mile-and-a-half north of Lime Kiln Point. Surrounding it is San Juan County Park, one of the few public campgrounds on the island. A prominent feature of this park is the steep rock headland north of the bay, topped with twisted cedar and madrona. The view west across to Vancouver Island is spectacular at sunset.

The bay's name recalls a smallpox epidemic among the Native Americans who once lived here. Burning with fever from a disease they had no immunity to, the Indians are said to have plunged into the cold waters of Haro Strait. Two European sailors who had been sent ashore, and who had been cared for by the tribe, were among the few survivors of the epidemic.

Approaches. From the south, watch for a break in the steep shore north of Lime Kiln Point. Approaches from this direction are clean. From the north, the park begins a little over a half-mile south of the Andrews Bay mark, a short white obelisk erected as a boundary reference in the early 1900s. Road maps show this as Sunset Point. A shoal is charted south of Low Island, which is surrounded by a reef. Watch for divers, as this is a popular scuba area.

At the head of Smallpox Bay is the park office—a log house with a red metal roof—and a launching ramp. Depths are good outside the entrance, shallowing quickly to the height of eel grass. The bottom is rock and mud.

Anchorage. Exposure, depth, and steep shores make both Smallpox Bay and nearby Andrews Bay unsuitable for overnight anchoring. Boaters will probably feel more comfortable visiting by skiff from Mitchell Bay or Garrison Bay.

Getting Ashore. Beach your skiff at the head of Smallpox Bay, keeping the area clear for 8 to 10 feet around the launching ramp. The bight on the north side of the headland, with its steeper bottom and gravel beach, is easier for landing. In this bight, stay south to avoid trespassing on adjacent private property.

The tidelands in Andrews Bay to the north are private.

For the Crew. The park has picnic tables and barbecues, but no showers. There are no facilities within walking distance.

Mitchell Bay (Snug Harbor Resort) ★★★★   (gas only)

Charts: 18421, **18433**

Mitchell Bay, shallow and tight, twists into San Juan Island from Haro Strait. Private homes stare across the water, and private docks extend beyond the mudflats that line the entire bay. Just inside the entrance, on the south shore, is the aptly-named Snug Harbor Resort.

Approaches. From the south, approaches to the outer (Mosquito) bay are clean. North from Mosquito Pass, stay west of the marked rocks between Delacombe Point and Hanbury Point. Approaching from the west, stay at least a quarter-mile off the southeast tip of Henry Island, where there are many unmarked rocks. At low tide these rocks appear to have been scattered by a careless giant.

Mosquito Pass is described on page 280.

Enter the outer (Mosquito) bay in mid-channel. In the middle of the entrance to Mitchell Bay is a faded rectangular sign with an arrow that points left (north) toward the channel. This sign stands on a reef that extends from the south shore. The reef is covered at high tide, and extends north of the sign. To avoid this reef, strongly favor the north shore as you proceed into Mitchell Bay, and slow down.

Depth at the entrance is charted at 1 fathom. If your destination is the resort, keep to the middle of the bay until abeam of the marina. Boaters with deep-draft vessels should check the tides.

Anchorage, Moorings. The resort marina is on the south shore. Its wooden floats are attached to a central pier that leads directly to the store and guest cabins. Pull into the fuel dock on the end of the west float, and inquire at the store about a slip. All slips have electricity. The marina reports depths of 8 feet on a zero tide. The resort takes reservations for guest moorage—(360) 378-4762.

Anchorage is good anywhere you can find enough depth. Check the tides if your vessel is deep-draft. It's about 5 feet deeper toward the inner cove, which shallows rapidly inside. Beyond the mudflats at the head of this cove Young Hill rises, rounded and green.

Getting Ashore. The marina floats are for resort guests and store patrons. All other tidelands are private.

For the Boat. The fuel dock (gas only) is on the end of the resort's west float. On shore is an engine repair shop that specializes in outboards and small diesels. There's water at the fuel dock, but it comes from the resort's own well, and guests are asked to conserve—no washing down of boats.

For the Crew. The store has snack foods, but no real groceries. The specialty here is fishing gear, probably everything you'll need to entice and land fish in Haro Strait. The walls around the cash register are covered with photographs of beaming guests displaying their catches: golden cabezon, lingcod and salmon, giant purple starfish, a flat leathery skate. A small picnic and barbecue area is at the head of the pier, next to a hut containing video games. RV campsites overlook the beach; there are more uphill, behind the cabins. The resort rents fishing gear and skiffs, and can refill scuba tanks.

There are no other facilities within walking distance.

Horseshoe Bay ★★ [4] No Facilities

Charts: 18421, **18433**

This bight west of Garrison Bay and Westscott Bay has anchoring room for a couple of boats at most. The shores are wooded, and surround a fairy-tale cottage. Approaches are clean from Mosquito Pass. All mooring buoys and tidelands are private.

Mosquito Pass is described on page 280.

Garrison Bay (British Camp) ★★★★ [5] No Facilities

Charts: 18421, **18433**

Though close to Roche Harbor, this protected bay is generally under-used by boaters. Its shallow anchoring basin is one reason; lack of facilities is probably another. However, a visit to

Mosquito Pass, Roche Harbor, and Vicinity
(based on Chart 18433)

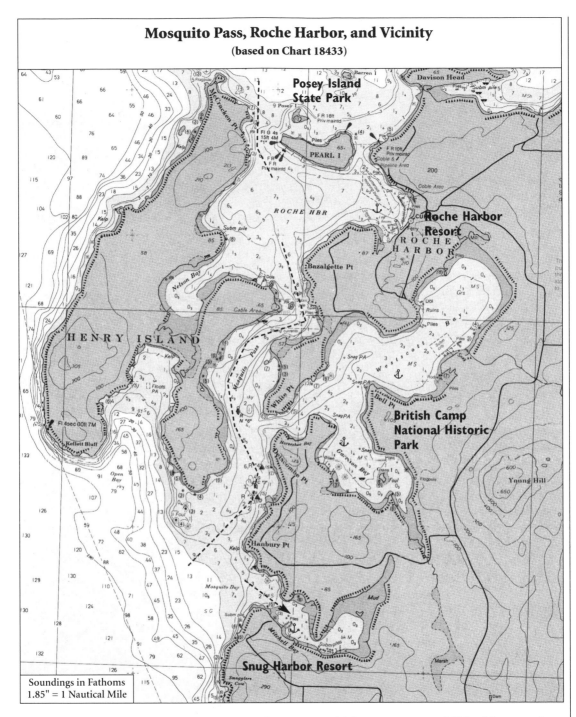

Soundings in Fathoms
1.85" = 1 Nautical Mile

Garrison Bay is worthwhile. Here at the National Park of British Camp (and at American Camp on the opposite end of the island) is an opportunity to get close to something rare in history: a war that was averted by international negotiation, with no human casualties.

British Camp was established in 1860 for a "token force" of British soldiers to oppose the U.S. troops in American Camp, south on Griffin Bay. The dispute, known as the "Pig War," began when an American settler killed a pig rooting in his garden. The animal belonged to the Hudson's Bay Company, and its demise brought the unresolved territorial issue to the surface: Did the islands belong to Britain or the United States?

The earlier Oregon Treaty established "the channel" boundary, but failed to specify Rosario Strait (the British interpretation) or Haro Strait (the U.S. interpretation). Troops and warships mobilized on both sides. The dispute was referred to the German monarch Kaiser Wilhelm I, and settled 12 years later, in 1872. The National Park brochure includes photos of the dour men who postured and negotiated through it all. The pig is not pictured.

Approaches. Several snags and deadheads are charted on both sides of the entrance to Garrison Bay, so it's best to stay in mid-channel. If your vessel is deep-draft, favor the west shore, where there are a number of homes with docks. An uncharted orange diamond marks a rock awash off the southwest shore; more rocks are beyond. On the east shore are the distinctive garrison structures of British Camp.

Mosquito Pass is described on page 280.

Anchorage. The anchoring basin in Garrison Bay is roughly between the entrance, the marked rock, and Guss Island, in 1 to 2 fathoms. The mooring buoy shown on the chart does not exist. The float at the park is for dinghies only. All mooring buoys in Garrison Bay are private.

Once larger, this basin silted up after the surrounding hills were denuded to fuel the Roche Harbor lime kilns. An alternate anchorage for deep-draft vessels is north in Westcott Bay.

Getting Ashore. You can land on the park beach, but it's more convenient to use the float on the northeast shore. This float was donated by an International Yachting Fellowship on Vancouver Island, as a gesture of "Hands Across the Border." Depth at the float is only a couple feet at zero tide.

Guss Island is a national preserve, with NO TRESPASSING signs posted above the tideline. Note that the south tip of Guss is connected to San Juan Island by an isthmus that bares at low tide. The inlet southeast of Guss Island is a University of Washington biological preserve; no plants or animals (including clams) should be removed. Crabbing in this inlet is strongly discouraged, as it disrupts the scientific research.

Things to Do. Photos of Garrison Bay during British occupation show it busy with ships, officers, and enlisted men. Today, silent evergreens surround the remains of the British garrison: a blockhouse on the bank above the beach, a picket fence enclosing a tiny formal garden, and an enormous maple that stands guard over everything. The interpretive center offers a slide show and guided walks in summer. The park has a few picnic tables and restrooms, but little else; camping and fires are not allowed. Before clamming, note the signs or inquire at the ranger's office. The park brochure warns of yellow jackets.

British Camp can be best experienced by hiking its trails. These lead through the forest, northwest to Bell Point and east past the cemetery to the top of Young Hill. From here you can survey Haro Strait and beyond to Vancouver Island, as the British soldiers must have done, waging peace.

Westcott Bay ★★★ ▢4 No Facilities

Charts: 18421, **18433**

Westcott Bay angles northeast from Mosquito Pass, and is larger and deeper than neighboring Garrison Bay. A portion of its south shore is part of the National Historic Park of British Camp. The rafts of a large oyster farm east of the park extend almost halfway across the bay. Homes are widely spaced around the remaining shores. The surrounding orchards and low hills beyond give the entire area a rural feel.

Westcott Bay is a good alternative for those with deep-draft boats who want to visit British Camp. Chart 18433 uses the spelling "Westscott."

Approaches, Anchorage. Enter in mid-channel to avoid the submerged rock and snags charted on both sides. Stay north and west of the oyster operation, marked on the chart as piles and "Subm crib." The cribs are supported by buoys that look like hundreds of black balloons on the surface, and may be difficult to see at dusk.

Mosquito Pass is described on page 280.

Depth is good for anchoring, especially toward Bell Point. Protection is also good, though the low head of the bay can funnel a north wind.

All mooring buoys in Westcott Bay are private.

Getting Ashore. Land on the park beach, anywhere between Bell Point and the sign in the trees that marks the park boundary. The park dinghy float is about a half-mile south in Garrison Bay. All other tidelands are private.

Roche Harbor ★★★★★

Charts: 18421, **18433**

Roche Harbor is one of the major destination resorts in the San Juan Islands. Its original buildings—the hotel, restaurant, and chapel—are over a hundred years old, sparkling white against the deep green trees that surround them. The addition of several new condominiums, and the busyness of its airstrip and marina, don't seem to detract from the quaint comfort here. It's almost impossible to suppress a smile while walking the firebrick path around the hotel's lush flower garden, or listening to the decidedly secular carillon tunes played from the chapel at sunset.

The historic buildings were originally part of the Roche Harbor Lime Works, which supplied "nearly pure" limestone to British Columbia, Portland, San Francisco, and Hawaii. From the 1880s to the Great Depression, this was a flourishing industry, employing hundreds of workers and consuming the surrounding forests to fuel the kilns. A few of the kiln tunnels are visible south of the hotel and pier. The small square houses north of the chapel were built as cottages for the company workers; what is now the restaurant was the grand main residence.

Approaches. From the south, heed the cau-

tions about Mosquito Pass on page 280.

For those approaching from the northeast or northwest, the first prominent landmark is Battleship Island, off the tip of Henry Island. Especially from the east, this bare island with its few trees resembles a battleship heading south in Haro Strait. A strong tide rip occurs when the east-bound flood of Spieden Channel meets the northwest-bound flood of San Juan Channel. Boaters crossing Spieden Channel from Stuart Island should be prepared for tide rips between Danger Shoal and Center Reef.

Both sides of Pearl Island are passable, but the west channel is deeper and has fewer obstructions. When using the east channel, favor the Pearl Island side, but take care also to stay clear of the unmarked, submerged rock charted off Pearl's northeast shore. Those with deep-draft boats will breathe easier entering west of Pearl.

Once inside the harbor, your eye will be drawn to the resort, its white clapboard cabins, the spire of the chapel, the green roofs of the restaurant and hotel, and the delicate white railings on the piers—all accented with brilliant flowers. The singularly unattractive metal building is used by U.S. Customs.

The chapel and restaurant of Roche Harbor Resort. The visitors' slips begin left (north) of the ramp.

Moorings. Guest moorage is on both sides of the long float set north-south beneath the resort restaurant and hotel. There are lots of slips—enough for 80 or more boats—and depths are good; the inside is a few feet shallower, and has a limited turning basin. Pull into slip "8" at the hut in the middle of the guest float, and check in with the harbormaster there or at the hotel lobby.

All slips have power and water, with power included in the fee. Also included is the use of the resort's recreational facilities (pool and tennis courts). From late May through September it's a good idea to reserve a slip. Call ahead: (800) 451-8910. During summer the marina monitors VHF Channel 78A (U.S.)—not 78. Off-season, rates are half-price, but call ahead to find out what resort facilities are open.

Overnight moorage is not allowed on the fuel dock. You will be charged if you stay overnight at the Customs dock.

The "Numerous mooring buoys" noted on the chart are maintained by the resort. The five strings total more than 50 buoys. The outside (westernmost) buoys are in deeper water than those inside (to the east). Fees are charged for using these buoys, and include use of the resort pool and tennis courts.

All other floats and mooring buoys are private.

Anchorage. The anchorage in Roche Harbor is excellent, but somewhat congested by the resort buoys and by traffic in and out of the marina. Set your hook well and check your swing.

The bight south of the hotel has slips for permanent moorage and a launching ramp. It is also an active log rafting area; do not obstruct the channel into this bight.

Getting Ashore. Tie your dinghy to the float underneath the "wheelhouse" above the fuel dock, which is prominently marked with a crossarm and flags.

All other surrounding property is private, including Henry Island and Pearl Island.

For the Boat. The fuel dock is located below the crossarm and flags at the end of the main pier, southwest of the hotel. It's about 7 feet deeper at the west end of the fuel dock than at the eastern end, at the hut. In summer, excursion boats moor temporarily at the fuel dock.

The store at the head of the pier has some marine supplies. Repairs, though not available on site, can be arranged.

The U.S. Customs float is south of the fuel dock and distinguished by its red tie-rails.

For the Crew. The store at the head of the main pier has a well-stocked grocery with fresh produce. A laundromat and restrooms with showers are on this same pier, tucked among the gift shops, fast-food stalls, and post office. There are more gift shops on the ground floor of the hotel. Both the hotel and the restaurant are on the National Historic Register.

Unless you are paying to use a slip or mooring buoy, you will be charged for garbage disposal.

Things to Do. Tennis courts are north of the chapel, with play equipment nearby. The pool is a little way up the hill.

In summer, a shuttle service runs hourly to the town of Friday Harbor. An intriguing destination for a walk is the mausoleum, northwest along the beach trail and beyond the tennis courts. This mausoleum was built by the lime company's most memorable owner, Robert McMillan, a businessman with an apparently romantic—if not eccentric—bent. Infatuated by the sunset afterglow, he designed the family's final resting place to resemble their dining arrangement: a table with six chairs facing westward, the ashes of the departed in the seats.

Posey Island State Park ★★★ ☐1 No Facilities

Charts: 18421, **18433**

This one acre of state park is north of Pearl Island, between the north tips of Henry and San Juan. Access to this fragile area is restricted to human-powered beachable watercraft.

Posey Island is surrounded by reefs on all but its south side, where there is a sloping gravel beach. Ashore are a couple of campsites with firepits and weathered picnic tables, and a privy. An old wood hut, bleached silver-grey, overlooks the west beach. In early spring, tiny wildflowers are everywhere.

Pearl Island, and Barren Island to the north, are private.

Cove Behind Davison Head ★★ ☐3 No Facilities

Charts: 18421, **18433**

Davison Head is connected to the north end of San Juan Island by a narrow isthmus, and from a distance appears to be a separate island. Shoals spread east from the isthmus, leaving only about half the cove deep enough for anchoring. This cove is surrounded by homes and private docks, and studded with mooring buoys—all private.

Approaching, note the reef and rock off the northeast tip of Davison Head, and give this area a wide berth. East of the mooring buoys, depths are somewhat greater than charted, but it may be difficult to find swinging room far enough into the cove for northerly protection.

All tidelands are private.

Limestone Cove (Lonesome Cove)

Charts: 18421, **18433**

Two bights lie between Davison Head and Limestone Point, on either side of an unnamed point and reef. The bight to the east is identified on the chart as Limestone Cove, but maps and local residents call it Lonesome Cove. Lonesome Cove Resort, with its inviting gazebo and small orchard, has a few floats here in summer. However, these are reserved for guests staying at the resort. Anchoring on either side of the reef is possible but tricky, and protection from strong eddies is dubious. All tidelands are private.

Ruben Tarte County Park ★★★ No Facilities

Charts: 18421, **18433**

This county park on the northeast side of San Juan Island, halfway between Limestone Point and O'Neal Island, is little more than a low rocky headland. Driftwood piles up impressively on both sides; a steep road downhill provides access to shore. The 5- to 10-fathom shelf is broad enough for anchoring, but the area is too exposed to recommend. Note the two submerged rocks charted south of the point.

Ruben Tarte County Park is named for the man who originally turned Roche Harbor into a resort. The park has no facilities.

Rocky Bay ★★★ No Facilities

Charts: 18421, **18433**, **18434**

Rocky Bay is well-named, lined with rocks and reefs, exposed to current and wind funneling through San Juan Channel. On shore are a fair number of homes and private docks. Some protection from the north (but not the northeast) is available in the "corner" of the bay; approach from the southeast, and note the charted reef and submerged rock. Better protection from the south is toward the bight at the southeast end of the bay, but private buoys occupy the best anchoring areas.

There is no upland access anywhere in Rocky Bay. O'Neal Island, in the middle of the bay, is private.

Henry Island

Charts: 18421, **18433**

Henry Island lies northwest of San Juan, curving softly north and east to protect Roche Harbor. The island is vaguely H-shaped, so deeply indented north and south that it is almost divided in two. This is a private island, with no public ferries or other facilities. Public tidelands on the west and north shores are steep and almost non-existent.

Open Bay ★★★  No Facilities

Charts: 18421, **18433**

This well-named, steep-sided bay has a rugged, remote feel. Trees cling to the thin soil, their branches growing northward, and the beach is piled with driftwood. The *Coast Pilot* describes Open Bay as having good holding ground and protection from north and east weather. However, it is completely exposed to prevailing southerlies, and even a north wind can funnel over the isthmus.

Approaches, Anchorage. From the south, head directly into the bay, slightly favoring the clean shore around Kellett Bluff. Coming north from Mosquito Pass, stay at least 500 yards off the unnamed southeast tip of Henry Island, where the rocks are numerous and unmarked. Some are wickedly submerged.

Open Bay has a gradually rising bottom. Watch out for logs and deadheads, which seem to collect here.

Nelson Bay ★★ ③ No Facilities

Charts: 18421, **18433**

Though only a short distance overland from Open Bay, Nelson Bay is entirely different. Its banks are low and gentle, and there are many homes and docks here, as well as boats at anchor. It is also shallow—most of it less than 1 fathom—and surrounded by broad mudflats. Private mooring buoys are set in the relatively deep core of the bay.

Protection is fairly good in Nelson Bay, but choppy seas can build up from the north, across Roche Harbor, and southerlies funnel over the low isthmus. A larger anchoring basin of similar depth is in the bight just north of Nelson Bay.

There is no public access to Henry Island. The small marina southeast of the entrance is a Seattle Yacht Club outstation.

Approaching Nelson Bay, stay in the center. Deepest water is just inside the entrance. Expect the bay to shallow to less than 1 fathom about halfway in.

The approach from Mosquito Pass is described on page 280.

Shaw Island

Charts: 18421, **18434**

Although set in the middle of the San Juan Islands, Shaw is not a hub of activity. There are only a few businesses on the island: a small store and gas pump at the ferry dock near Blind Bay, a sheep farm and dairy run by Catholic nuns, a small plant that manufactures salmon tags. Shaw has no other store, no restaurants, no resorts.

With a population of fewer than two hundred, the island is empty and quiet, and wants to stay that way. Most of its shoreline is off-limits, either privately owned or set aside by the University of Washington for biological research. But even a desire for seclusion cannot

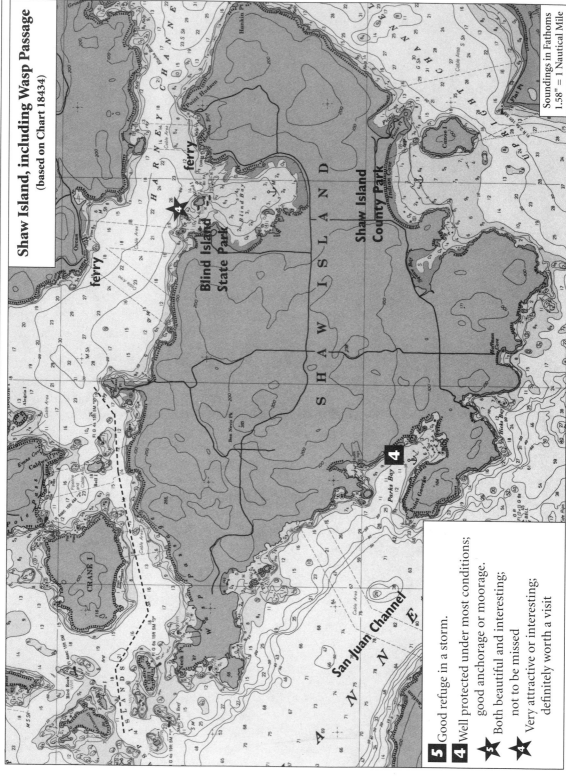

Shaw Island, including Wasp Passage
(based on Chart 18434)

Soundings in Fathoms
1.58" = 1 Nautical Mile

Blind Island State Park

Shaw Island County Park

S H A W   I S L A N D

ferry

ferry

San Juan Channel

5 Good refuge in a storm.

4 Well protected under most conditions;
good anchorage or moorage.

⭐**S** Both beautiful and interesting;
not to be missed

⭐**4** Very attractive or interesting;
definitely worth a visit

change the fact that Shaw is in the center of the San Juans. Boaters are inevitably drawn to its protected anchorages in Blind Bay and Parks Bay, and to the county park at Indian Cove.

Blind Bay (Blind Island State Park) ★★★★

Charts: 18421, **18434**

This large bay on the north side of Shaw is one of the best on the island. Blind Island State Park has mooring buoys, the anchorage is good, and there is a small store at the Shaw Island ferry dock. The town of Orcas, which has a larger store and more facilities, is just across Harney Channel.

Approaches. Blind Bay has an unfortunate entrance, foul with submerged rocks and shoals. Navigation takes care, but no special skill.

The passage east of Blind Island is the preferred entrance. The most notable hazard here is a long, low rock about halfway between the ferry dock and Blind Island that covers at high tide. This rock, which still snags an occasional pleasure boat, is marked with a privately maintained white diamond on a tripod pole. Rocks also lie off Blind Island. At low tide these rocks are visible, ghastly but more easily avoidable. Enter between the mark and Blind Island. If the tide is high, slightly favor the white diamond mark, but only slightly. Go in slowly, and expect a temporary but significant shallowing—as much as 20 feet. Don't forget to watch for ferries, and stay out of their way.

The passage west of Blind Island is used by a few boaters. Do not attempt this route without first checking out the rocks in this passage (all of them unmarked) at low tide.

Anchorage, Moorings. Four mooring buoys wrap around the south side of Blind Island. The two eastern buoys are in water 5 to 6 feet deeper than the western buoys. All are set fairly close to the island. There's enough swinging room, but you may feel uneasy when wind picks up from the south.

Anchorage is good throughout the central core of the bay, in 2 fathoms to 6 fathoms. The bottom is charted as mud, but the seaweed may be difficult for some anchors to penetrate. Best protection from a southerly wind is at the southeast end. Stay east of the islet, and note that tideflats extend several hundred feet from shore on all sides.

Hudson Bay, northeast of Blind Bay, is all reef and shallow water; enough room for a private dock but no "bay" at all for anchoring.

Getting Ashore. The only public landing is at Blind Island State Park. You can take a skiff to the tiny marina just east of the ferry dock, but be mindful that this marina is private, and don't stay without permission—ask at the store.

A small section of tideland toward the middle of the west shore in Blind Bay is public. All other tidelands are private, including the beach at the south end.

For the Crew. Blind Island State Park has a few picnic tables and an outhouse. This two-acre island is a good place to stretch out and watch the steady parade of boat traffic in Harney Channel.

The country store at the ferry dock, run by Franciscan nuns, is tidy and simple. The wooden floors are polished, the glass in the oak refrigerator cases twinkles, and fresh fruit beckons from the baskets. Some of the dairy items sold here are produced on the island. Just outside the store is a post office, and nearby are gas pumps.

Picnic Cove ★★★ No Facilities

Charts: 18421, **18430, 18434**

Picnic Cove is small and narrow, with reefs on both sides, a tideflat at its head, and a few homes along the shore. Its most distinctive feature is the tiny islet off Picnic Point. There is room here for only one or two boats to anchor; halfway in, the cove shallows to 1 fathom.

Approaching, head straight in to avoid the reefs, and stay a couple hundred yards off the end of Picnic Point. The main exposure here is to the wakes of ferries and other boats in Upright Channel.

All tidelands in Picnic Cove are private.

Indian Cove
(Shaw Island County Park) ★★★ No Facilities

Charts: 18421, **18434**

The county park at Indian Cove is one of the few public shores on Shaw Island. The park, which includes a separate portion on the west peninsula, has campsites, picnic tables, a cookhouse, and some rustic play equipment. The beach is glorious sand and driftwood.

Approaches. Approaches are clean from the southwest. If approaching from the east, note the rock awash charted 300 yards off the southwest tip of Canoe Island. Those with shallow-draft boats can pass between Crane Island and Picnic Cove, but should note the charted reef and 5-foot shoal, and stay safely between them.

To find the park, look for a set of wooden stairs down to the beach. The blue shed is a cookhouse. A public launching ramp is at the east edge of the park, next to a yellow house.

Anchorage. Anchoring is good in the gradually sloping bottom toward the west half of the

cove. Toward the east half, the shelf is steep; check your swing if you anchor toward Canoe Island. All mooring buoys are private. Indian Cove is exposed to the full length of San Juan Channel, and is uncomfortable in a stiff southerly.

Squaw Bay, which branches west from Indian Cove, is dry at low tide. The entrance is crowded with pilings, private docks, and private mooring buoys. All tidelands are private.

Getting Ashore. The sand-and-gravel park beach is kind to skiffs. The land east of the launching ramp and west toward the bluff is private property. The county park includes portions of the west peninsula; you'll need to walk west and south on the road in order to reach it without trespassing on private land.

The steep tidelands of Canoe Island are public, but there is no public upland access.

Hoffman Cove ★★★ No Facilities

Charts: 18421, **18434**

Hoffman Cove is little more than a square-shaped notch. It is shallow—just over 1 fathom—and open to the south, with reefs along its eastern and western shores. The bot-

tom rises abruptly at the entrance. The mooring buoys here—all private—are almost aground on a minus tide. Not much room is left over for anchoring.

At the head of the cove is a broad beach, with a dark-brown boatshed on the west shore, a trail up the bank to the street end on the east shore, and tall poplars beyond. The east half of the street end may be used for public access to the Cedar Rock Preserve, an old farmland now managed as a biological preserve by the University of Washington. At the gate is a small guest book in a box and a list of simple rules: no dogs, no smoking, no flower picking. This is a meditative place, the only sounds the birds, the rustle of the unmown grass, and your footsteps on the path.

All other tidelands and uplands are private.

Hicks Bay ★★ ▢2 No Facilities

Charts: 18421, **18434**

This V-shaped bay gives protection from the north, but like others on this side of Shaw Island, it is exposed to the full length of San Juan Channel, and to the wakes of ferries and other boat traffic. Hicks Bay has depth and room for several boats to anchor in 5 to 10 fathoms. Around the bay are a few homes and many signs identifying the land as a biological preserve of the University of Washington, for use in scientific research. Fishing is restricted here; only salmon and herring may be taken (no bottom fish). All tidelands are private.

Approaching, slightly favor the west shore to avoid the submerged rocks charted 200 yards off the east shore.

Parks Bay ★★★ ▢4 No Facilities

Charts: 18421, **18434**

Only two miles east of busy and crowded Friday Harbor, Parks Bay is a favorite alternate anchorage. Protection and holding is good, and the shoreline is completely wooded. This is a fine place to swing on the hook, but that's all you can do here, as the surrounding tidelands are a University of Washington biological preserve. Fishing is restricted to salmon and herring (no bottom fish), and no plants or animals (including clams) should be removed. Crabbing is strongly discouraged, as it upsets the biological research being done in this area. Signs that ring the bay remind boaters (and their dogs) not to trespass on the tidelands.

Approaches. From the north, Point George is prominent. Note that southwest of Tift Rocks the bottom is shallow and filled with kelp; stay 500 yards away to avoid this area. The islet on the north side of the entrance to Parks Bay (locally known as Little Shaw) is connected to Shaw at low tide.

From the south, approaches are clean past Reid Rock. Note the rock awash charted off the tip of Point George.

Anchorage. Set your hook about two-thirds of the way into the bay, in 5 to 10 fathoms. The bottom shallows beyond the rock-and-grass outcropping on the east shore; the area beyond is cluttered with pilings. The piers and floats are privately owned. The inlet that branches north just inside the entrance to Parks Bay is shallow and foul with submerged pilings.

All tidelands in Parks Bay are private.

Coves North of Parks Bay

Charts: 18421, **18434**

Between Parks Bay and Wasp Passage are a couple of bights that provide limited northerly protection, used primarily in summer.

The shallow bight just outside the entrance to Parks Bay, north of the islet, is locally known as Post Office Cove. A pair of submerged rocks are charted on the south shore of this bight. The mooring buoys are private.

Farther north, behind Tift Rocks, is a bight less than 1 fathom deep. When approaching, stay 500 yards southwest of Tift Rocks, where there are shoals and kelp, and note the submerged rock charted east of Tift Rocks. Tift Rocks are a National Wildlife Refuge—stay at least 200 yards away.

Around Neck Point are several more bights, all of them foul or shallow (or both). A few have private docks. None are recommended anchorages. Many of the nearby islets are National Wildlife Refuges.

All tidelands and uplands in these coves are private.

Broken Point ★★★ No Facilities

Charts: 18421, **18434**

Broken Point is a distinctive knob of land on the end of a narrow isthmus that lies west of Blind Bay. The point is perfectly named—the east side of the rock face appears to have been sheared off with a giant chisel.

Anchoring is possible on both sides of the point. On the east side is a small 5- to 10-fathom basin toward the "corner" of the cove. Anchoring is trickier west of the point, in a deep pocket between the unnamed island and the rocks charted off the tiny peninsula to the west. In both these coves the bottom rises fairly steeply toward shore, and while there is protection from the south, the north wind funnels down from West Sound. Ferries make frequent runs through the passage, adding their wakes to those of other boats speeding through.

Approaches to Broken Point are clear from Harney Channel and West Sound. From the west, respect the east shore of Crane Island, and don't cut between Bell Island and green "5." If passing between Bell Island and Caldwell Point on Orcas, favor Bell Island.

There is no public shore access in either cove, and all mooring buoys and floats are private.

The Wasp Islands ★★★ No Facilities

Charts: 18421, **18434**

Between Shaw and Orcas lies a cluster of smaller islands that take their collective name from narrow, twisting Wasp Passage. All of these islands are steep-sided and surrounded by reefs. All are either National Wildlife Refuges or private. The channels between them are peppered with rocks, most of them unmarked, many submerged. It's no surprise that the *Coast Pilot* emphasizes the hazards here. Few boaters linger in this area, but from late March to early June, some stop to pay homage to the extraordinary wildflowers on Yellow Island.

Yellow Island belongs to the Nature Conservancy, a private, nonprofit organization dedicated to land preservation. The island is open to the public for serious wildlife observation and appreciation. Yellow was never grazed, nor does it have a resident deer population. These factors, combined with its isolation, account for the unusual abundance of wildflowers here, a thick patchwork of indigo, yellow, white, and pink.

Approaches, Anchorage. Shore access to Yellow Island is best on the south beach, where there is a 2-fathom "cove" and enough room for a handful of boats to anchor. The cleanest approach is from the south. From the east, thread your way carefully between Crane Island and Shaw, then continue south of Crane Island and north of Cliff. Stay in deep water (10 fathoms or more) as you pass midway between Coon Island and Nob Island. Abeam of the mark on Shirt Tail Reef, head slightly south until abeam of Low Island; then turn into the "cove" of Yellow Island. This should help you avoid the submerged rock and the 1-foot shoal that lie several hundred yards east of Yellow Island. The stone-and-driftwood house that overlooks the beach here was built by the original homesteaders, Lew and Elizabeth Dodd, and is now used by resident caretakers.

You can also anchor and go ashore at the spit on the east side of Yellow Island. Approach with care. A piling and a rock are charted off the northeast beach.

Both anchorages are exposed to weather and current, and should be used only temporarily. The mooring buoys (one north and one south of the island) are for use by Nature Conservancy vessels only.

The west side of Yellow Island, foul with reef, is not recommended.

Getting Ashore. The gravel beaches mentioned above are good for landing a skiff. Be mindful that Yellow Island is a wildlife preserve, not a park. There is no picnicking allowed, no camping or overnight anchoring, no smoking, no fires, and no pets. Even an activity that seems as harmless as turning over beach rocks or skipping stones into the water can disturb the animals and disrupt the environment. To reduce human impact even further, groups are limited to five. If your party is larger, you will have to take turns walking the trails.

An alternative public shore is at McConnell Rock, on the northwest tip of McConnell Island. This rock is an undeveloped state park. No camping is allowed.

Orcas Island

Charts: 18421, **18430**, 18432, 18434

On the chart, Orcas appears to have been folded over on itself, and is often described as a saddlebag or a horseshoe. From the water, this largest land mass in the San Juans looks like many separate islands. Orcas is distinctly mountainous, with the tallest peak in the archipelago—2,400-foot Mount Constitution—and several waterfalls. Its complex topography creates many miles of shoreline and a number of good anchorages.

Though said to have been named for a Spanish noble, most locals have adopted the orca whale as the island's namesake.

Orcas (Orcas Landing) ★★★

Charts: 18421, **18434**

The small town of Orcas (locally known as Orcas Landing or Orcas Village) is built up from the ferry landing on Harney Channel, near the entrance to West Sound. The ferry is

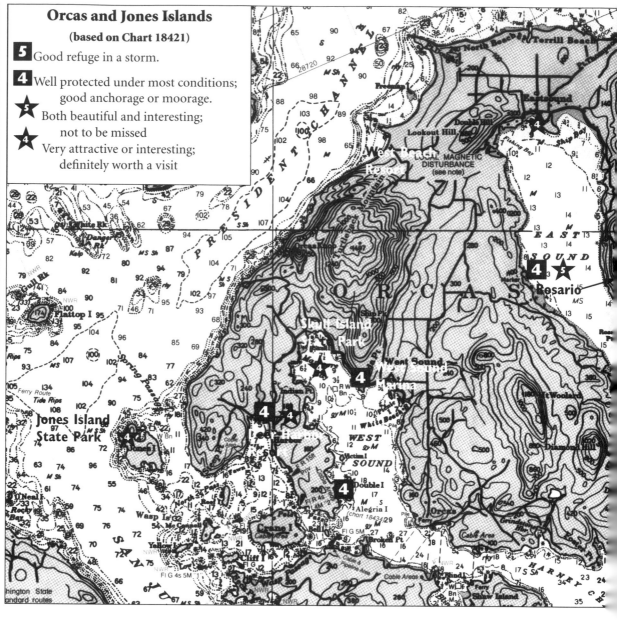

Orcas and Jones Islands
(based on Chart 18421)

5 Good refuge in a storm.

4 Well protected under most conditions; good anchorage or moorage.

★**5** Both beautiful and interesting; not to be missed

★**4** Very attractive or interesting; definitely worth a visit

the main event here; Orcas Island has the second-largest population in the San Juans, and the businesses clustered around the ferry landing cater to tourists and weekenders. The fuel dock has a visitors' float that also makes this a convenient stop for boaters.

Approaches. From the east, the prominent landmarks are the white Orcas Hotel with its red roof, and the fuel tanks on shore. From the west, the wing walls of the ferry dock come into

view before the hotel. On either approach, note the reefs off the steep shores. Look around for ferries, and stay out of their way.

Anchorage. There's good holding ground toward the east side of the bay, in 5 to 10 fathoms. The bottom rises abruptly toward shore; don't go in too close.

Protection from prevailing winds is pretty good here, but boat traffic in busy Harney Channel, combined with the ferry wakes, can

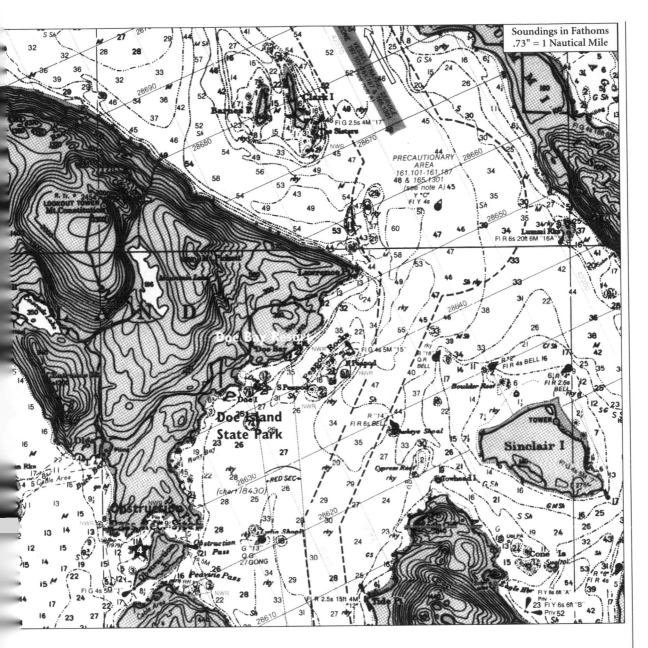

Soundings in Fathoms
.73" = 1 Nautical Mile

make it rougher in summer than in winter. You'll have a quieter night if you anchor across the channel in Blind Bay.

The float at the fuel dock has no overnight guest moorage. The marina behind the break-water is for tenants only. All mooring buoys are private.

Getting Ashore. The private float west of the fuel dock may be used for short-term stays. This float is about 150 feet long, and set paral-

lel to shore. On the outside, the west end of the float lies in water almost 10 feet deeper than at the ramp; depths are slightly less on the inside. Check the tides if your vessel is deep-draft.

All tidelands in this cove are private.

For the Boat. Look for the fuel dock west of the ferry landing, at the east end of the long float. The fuel dock float is set perpendicular to the long float; tie up on either side. Depths are good, but check the tides if your boat is deep-draft.

In summer, fuel is available every day during working hours. From October through May, the fuel dock is open part-time; call to make arrangements—(360) 378-4430.

For the Crew. The grocery store near the fuel dock is well stocked, with a meat counter and fresh produce. Gift shops, a bakery, and a few restaurants are nearby. Picnic tables are across the street and up the stairs, near the ferry terminal restrooms. Bicycles may be rented east of the ferry dock.

West Sound

Charts: 18421, **18434**

As a boating destination, West Sound is superior to East Sound. The sound is broken into many protected coves, with half-a-dozen islands off its steep shores. The wind funnels north and south, but not too strongly. Throughout the day, shadows move across Turtleback Mountain, transforming its wooded and grassy slopes into tortoise shell designs.

Approaches. From the east, the approach to West Sound is fairly clean. From the west, pass south of Bell Island, and the marked rock east of it, before turning into the sound. There's enough depth north of Bell Island, but two 1-fathom shoals off Caldwell Point make it a somewhat trickier approach.

Cove East of Oak Island ★★ No Facilities

Charts: 18421, **18434**

This small cove east of Oak Island has good depth and fair protection from southerlies. There are a few homes and private floats here, and an inner cove that dries at low tide. Approach west and north of Oak Island.

All tidelands in this cove are private.

White Beach Bay ★★★ (anchorage) (marina)

Charts: 18421, **18434**

White Beach Bay opens widely into West Sound, about halfway up on the east side. It takes its name from an abundance of clamshells noted by the early explorers—the remains of Indian feasts. Picnic Island (locally known as Sheep Island) lies in the center of the bay. East of Picnic are the skids and booms of a commercial logging operation. North of it is a marina with guest moorage, a fair-sized anchoring basin, and a county dock at a small public beach.

Approaches. From the south, the tan clubhouse of the Orcas Island Yacht Club is more prominent than the marina, which is hidden behind Picnic Island. Approaches are clean west of Picnic. From the north, look for the Harbor Rock mark in the middle of Massacre Bay. This rock is charted 4 feet below the surface.

Moorings. West Sound Marina has guest moorage on both sides of its south float, with power and limited water. Toward Picnic Island, the rocks are fairly close; large boats may have difficulty maneuvering here. It's 10 feet shallower at the ramp than at the west end of this float. Expect a lot of activity; the area near the ramp is used as a fuel dock, and the float at the ramp itself is reserved for seaplanes.

Follow the signs up the ramp to the marina office, where you can check in or use the fee box.

West Sound Marina takes reservations by phone up to 24 hours in advance—(360) 376-2314. For boats 50 feet or more in length, reservations can be made further in advance with a deposit.

Anchorage. West of the marina is a fair-sized anchoring basin with good depth. Picnic Island provides some protection from southerlies. All mooring buoys are private.

The area south of Picnic Island is foul with submerged pilings, and is not recommended as an anchorage.

Getting Ashore. Use the county float on the north shore, west of the Orcas Island Yacht Club. This dock, which is known as Buddington's Dock, has an 80-foot concrete float for day-use only. The adjacent beach to the west is also public.

West Sound Marina has a float at its south end for short-term visitors who are using the marina facilities.

For the Boat. The fuel dock is at the head of the south float in West Sound Marina. This is also the marina's guest float, and may be somewhat congested. The service yard here does full-service haulouts and specializes in engine repairs. The marine store is well stocked.

For the Crew. A store is about 100 yards west of the county dock. This is more of a delicatessen and café than a grocery store, with sandwiches, beverages, and a few snack items. Outside the store is a mailbox and pay phone. Ice is available here and at West Sound Marina.

West Sound Marina has restrooms with showers, located near the parking lot. These are for paying guests only; get a key from the marina office.

The park across the street from the county dock is part of the yacht club, and not for public use.

There are no other facilities within walking distance.

Massacre Bay (Skull Island State Park) ★★★★ ⬚3 No Facilities

Charts: 18421, **18434**

This far end of West Sound is not a particularly good anchorage, but Skull Island is worth a visit. The undeveloped state park here is a treasure, with rocky steps leading up to grassy knolls from a crescent of shell beach. The low junipers lean west, away from the prevailing wind. The bare rocks on top of the island are strewn with clamshells. In early spring, the camas flowers are bursts of blue—almost purple—against new green stalks, and the bees hum loudly.

In the mid-1800s marauding Indians from the north, reportedly on a slave-gathering expedition, destroyed the Lummi villages here. The grim names in this area are reminders of the slaughter.

Approaches. Look for the Harbor Rock mark in the middle of Massacre Bay. This rock is charted 4 feet below the surface. Pass either side.

Anchorage. Massacre Bay has a number of pocket-size coves along the west shore. North of Skull Island is a tight, shallow cove almost completely surrounded by rocks. West of Skull, there is better anchorage; stay south of the charted pile, and away from the west shore, which is foul with rock and reef.

Better protection from the north and the south is in the next, longer cove. The islet toward the center is topped with a square hut and surrounded by a reef. Check your swing

The beach at Skull Island State Park.

when anchoring, as the bottom rises quickly toward shore.

Getting Ashore. The best way to get ashore on Skull Island is at the beach on the southeast tip.

The entire island is surrounded by an irregular reef; look out for rocks as you approach this beach. All other tidelands in Massacre Bay are private.

Cove South of Indian Point ★★★ [3] No Facilities

Charts: 18421, **18434**

South of Indian Point is a long, deep cove—almost 10 fathoms deep—with a steep underwater shelf. Reefs line the shore. The best protection from northerly winds is toward the north end, where a weathered totem stands on shore. Best protection from southerly winds is to the south, with good depth toward the flagpole. Take care in this area, and make sure your swing doesn't put you on one of the surrounding rock clusters.

All tidelands in this cove are private.

Cove North of Victim Island

Charts: 18421, **18434**

For almost 70 years the cove north of Victim Island has been a watery playground for two summer camps: Westward Ho (boys) and Four Winds (girls). Their floats, canoes, and rafts make anchoring here difficult; in summer the cove is busy with camp activity. There is no public landing place at the lodge, and no facilities for visiting boaters.

Cove Between Victim Island and Double Island ★★★ ☐ [4] No Facilities

Charts: 18421, **18434**

Tucked in between two islands, this cove provides the best all-round protection in West Sound. The anchoring basin is large enough for a number of boats, and has good depth, between 3 and 10 fathoms. The impressive home on the west shore is the former mansion of the Kaiser (aluminum and shipbuilding) family.

The cove south of Double Island is a cable area and not suitable for anchoring.

Approaches. Approach from the east, giving the north tip of Double Island a wide berth. A stone marker, painted white, is topped with a signpost. The reef off this point is underwater at low tide.

Southwest of Victim Island a reef extends several hundred yards off the Orcas shore.

The narrow channel west of Victim Island is passable with care at high tide. The channel west of Double Island, constricted by a reef and shoal, is not recommended.

Getting Ashore. Victim Island is an undeveloped state park, thickly wooded. You can go ashore on its rocky beach, but the bank is steep and difficult to climb.

All of the Orcas shore is private. The tidelands on Double Island and Alegria Island are public, but so steep they are basically non-existent; there is no public upland access to either of these islands.

Deer Harbor ★★★★ ☐ [4] 🛢 🚰 🍞 🔧 ⚓ 🛒 ⛵ 🍴

Charts: 18421, **18434**

One of the finest anchorages on Orcas Island is V-shaped Deer Harbor. It is well protected from the north and the south. A resort marina on the east shore provides facilities for boaters, and a repair shop is nearby. A plaque at the foot of the resort's cross-arm flagpole sums up the pace here: ON THIS SITE IN 1897 NOTHING HAPPENED.

Approaches. There are three main approaches to Deer Harbor: from the south, west, and east. The simplest approach from the south is between Crane Island and Bird Rock. If approaching from the west, favor Steep Point on Orcas to avoid the rocks west of Reef Island. Use caution through the Wasp

Islands; for this approach, see page 321.

The cleanest approach from the east is south of Bell Island. North of Bell are two 1-fathom shoals with kelp; take care if you go that way.

Pole Pass, the channel between Orcas and Crane Island, seems impassable at first glance. However, it is well marked and commonly used. The rocks on the north side of the pass are marked with a red "2." On the southwest side is a jetty. The pass is only about 150 feet wide, but deep in mid-channel. Expect current to be strong here. Once through the narrowest portion, favor the Orcas side. Pole Pass is named for the duck-hunting method used here by the Indians,

327

who strung snare nets on high poles across the pass.

Inside Deer Harbor, stay at least 300 yards off the east shore in order to avoid the shoals.

Anchorage, Moorings. Deer Harbor Resort is easy to spot—a spread of low white buildings and white guest cabins on the east shore. The slips at the resort are attached to two main floats that branch off a central pier. Slips on the south float are for guest moorage; those on the north are for permanent patrons. Report to the fuel dock on the end of the central pier for a moorage assignment. Depths are good on the south float, and all slips have power and water. The marina takes reservations by phone—(360) 376-4420—and monitors VHF Channel 16. If you arrive after hours, check in with the harbormaster in the morning. Dogs should note the sign on the ramp, reminding them to keep their owners leashed.

All other floats in Deer Harbor, including those in the marina north of the resort, are private and have no guest moorage.

Anchorage is good anywhere in the harbor, in 3 to 10 fathoms, mud bottom. The islands to the south give reasonable protection from southerly winds.

The inner lagoon at the far north end is obstructed by a bridge, and bares at low tide.

Getting Ashore. Inquire at the fuel dock about going ashore at the resort; there is generally no problem if you keep your dinghy out of the way.

All tidelands in Deer Harbor, including those on Fawn Island, are private. The launching ramp on the northwest shore is not for public use.

For the Boat. The fuel dock is on the end of the resort's central pier, open only from June through September. The repair yard at Deer Harbor Boatworks, north of the resort, is accessible for most vessels at high tide. The yard has a marine store, and can haul out boats up to 50 feet in length. Boaters are welcome to do their own work, and use the showers and laundry while in the yard.

For the Crew. Deer Harbor Resort has showers at the head of the main pier, but no laundromat. Groceries, ice, and some fresh produce are across the street, in a country store that specializes in deli items. A restaurant overlooks the harbor; another is up the road. Behind the post office is the resort's gift shop and main office.

Use of the resort facilities is included in the moorage fee. These include the group barbecue area, the spa, and the pool. Small boats can be rented from the resort.

Lovers' Cove

Charts: 18421, **18432**

Like most of the indentations on the west side of Orcas Island, this is not a real cove. Its steep sides and many reefs make it a popular spot for scuba divers, but as an anchorage it should be avoided.

West Beach ★★★   (gas only)

Charts: 18421, **18432**

On the northwest side of Orcas Island is a low, wide crescent of sand known as West Beach. The small resort here has cabins and campsites, a small-craft marina, and several mooring buoys.

Approaches. Approaches are clean from the

south. From the north, stay 300 yards or so off the point just north of West Beach to avoid the shoals charted there. Toward West Beach the bottom shallows gradually.

Anchorage, Moorings. The marina is in shallow water—less than 1 fathom at low tide—and is for small craft only. It is minimally protected by a floating log breakwater. Tie to the fuel dock on the north ("A") float, and inquire at the office about moorage. West Beach Resort recommends reservations by phone—(360) 376-2240.

The resort has more than a dozen mooring buoys, set south and east of a cluster of pilings. A fee is charged for their use. If your vessel is deep-draft, use the westernmost buoys. Make sure you're on a buoy that is anchored firmly enough to hold your boat. If you anchor, set your hook some distance out, in 2 fathoms or more.

Protection at West Beach is fairly good from all directions except the southwest.

Getting Ashore. You can use the resort float if you are on a buoy or shopping at the resort store. All tidelands are private.

For the Boat. The fuel dock is on the north ("A") float, in shallow water. Only gas is available; the nearest diesel fuel is in Deer Harbor.

For the Crew. The resort store sells a few groceries, and a variety of fishing tackle and bait. A laundromat is behind the store. Showers and an outdoor hot tub are near the campground.

Fishing and diving are the main activities here, with air compressors for scuba tanks and an outdoor shower available for divers. A chalkboard on the pier lists the fish caught each day, and where.

Coves South of Point Doughty ★★★ 2 No Facilities

Charts: 18421, 18432

On the northwest tip of Orcas Island is the sharp finger of Point Doughty. South of it are two crescent beaches separated by Freeman Island. Camp Orkila spreads around the shore in the north cove; the south cove is filled with private mooring buoys.

Both coves have gradually sloping bottoms and enough depth for anchoring. There's protection from the north here, but none from the southwest.

Steep-sided Freeman Island is an undeveloped state park, approachable only by beachable craft. The finger of Point Doughty is an undeveloped recreation site.

Inlet West of Terrill Beach

Charts: 18421, 18430

At the top of Orcas Island is a narrow inlet, with a private, small-craft marina inside that has no overnight or even short-term moorage. Around this inlet are beachfront residences and a few bed-and-breakfast inns. A street end east of the inlet is the only public landing; check the tides, as the rocky beach extends out several hundred yards at low water. From here, it's about a mile across the island to the town of Eastsound.

When approaching, keep a respectful distance from Parker Reef, and watch your drift. A 2-fathom shoal is charted west of the reef. Two stone jetties protrude north from the entrance to the inlet; the inlet itself has a reported depth of 8 feet.

Point Lawrence Recreation Site

Charts: 18421, **18430**

Point Lawrence is an undeveloped recreation site, wild and overgrown, with a few deer trails and an energizing view across Rosario Strait to Mount Baker. Landing a skiff is possible only at low tide, and there is no protected anchorage.

Pt. Lawrence was named for James Law-rence, the U.S. Navy Commander who is best known for the phrase: "Don't give up the ship."

The cabins at Sea Acres, a former resort south of Pt. Lawrence, are now privately owned, and offer no beach access.

Doe Bay ★★★

Charts: 18421, **18430**

Like the animal it is named for, this bay halfway down the southeast side of Orcas Island has a soft, quiet look. A green lawn rolls up from the beach at the south end. To the north is Doe Bay Resort, its weathered gray buildings scattered among the trees and in the open field. Flower-boxes are placed here and there. Signs are hand-lettered and whimsical. On the north side of the resort is a shallow inlet fed by a waterfall. A giant, wood-carved lion on the bank greets visitors who arrive by water.

Doe Bay Resort caters to kayakers rather than to general boaters (there are no slips or mooring buoys), but what amenities it has it shares gladly.

Approaches. From any direction, look for Doe Bay north of Doe Island. Stay clear of Peapod Rocks; only the northern Peapod rock is marked, and there are reefs and shoals around the entire group. Outside Doe Bay, to the east, is a charted 11-foot shoal.

Anchorage. Depths are good for anchoring, and the bottom is charted as mud. Best protection from the south is toward the south end of the bay. The north inlet is shallow—less than 1 fathom—and is not recommended. Doe Bay is not a good anchorage in a southeasterly, and in any weather you may feel the wakes of freighter traffic in Rosario Strait.

Getting Ashore. Beach your skiff on the gravel beach beneath the old boathouse, south of the carved lion. The stairs lead up to the resort buildings.

The southern half of Doe Bay is private property.

For the Crew. The storefront building—a former post office—has a welcoming lobby with worn, overstuffed furniture, a café, and a small store that sells a few groceries and gift items. You can arrange for a sauna bath or hot tub, explore the grounds, or simply sit on the porch awhile. The resort offers guided kayak tours.

Doe Island State Park ★★★

Charts: 18421, **18430**

Doe Island sits off the east shore of Orcas. The island is small and completely surrounded by reefs. Storms have thinned its trees. Here and there are picnic tables and firepits. The Orcas shore is relatively crowded with homes, but from the east tip of Doe Island all you will see is Rosario Strait, the islands beyond, and Mount Baker.

Approaches. The best approach is from the east. Only those with shallow-draft vessels should attempt the channel on the west side of Doe Island.

Anchorage, Moorings. On the north side of the island is a state park pier with a float that extends into deep water from a short ramp. This float is removed from October through April.

There's room and depth for anchoring north of Doe Island, with reasonable protection from the south and north (not the north-east). You may feel the wakes of freighter traffic in Rosario Strait. All mooring buoys are private. One, on the east side of the island, is guarded by a sculptured dragon.

The cove south of Doe Island shallows abruptly from a steep shelf, and is not recommended. Boats here are exposed to the south.

Getting Ashore. Use the state park float. When it is removed in winter, access across the reefs and up the steep bank is difficult.

The nearby tidelands on Orcas Island are private.

Buoy Bay

Charts: 18421, **18430**

This slight curve into the east shore of Orcas Island has little to recommend it as an anchorage. The bay is peppered with rocks off its south and north shores. You're reasonably out of the current here, but exposed to weather from the north and south, and to freighter traffic in the strait. Private mooring buoys are set along the 2-fathom shelf. There is no public access to shore.

Cove North of Obstruction Island ★★★

Charts: 18421, **18430**

Obstruction Pass curves north around Obstruction Island, shaping a cove into the Orcas shore. A small resort rents cabins here, and maintains a small marina for permanent moorage. A public launching ramp and county dock are east of the resort. This is a low-key community, at the end of the road. A sign on the resort office attempts to pin down "working hours," with no success.

Approaches. Obstruction Pass is deep and the approaches are straightforward. Stay south of Brown Rock, which is more of an islet than indicated on the chart, its grassy top visible at almost any tide.

Anchorage. Anchorage is good in 5 to 10 fathoms, mud bottom. There is current here, but you may be able to escape it toward the Orcas shore. Obstruction Island does not protect this cove from either southeast or southwest winds.

All mooring buoys are private.

Getting Ashore. A county pier and float lie northeast of the Lieber Haven Resort, in shallow water suitable for dinghies only. The float is for loading and unloading—no overnight stays are permitted. To the west is an unpaved public launching ramp off a parking lot. Adjacent tidelands, and those on Obstruction Island, are private.

For the Crew. The Lieber Haven Resort has a small grocery. Boat rentals and fishing charters are available. A public phone is near the county pier. In summer, a passenger ferry makes scheduled runs from the resort float to Friday Harbor and Bellingham.

Obstruction Pass Recreation Site ★★★★

Charts: 18421, **18430**

Between two prongs of rock at the west end of Obstruction Pass is a splendid park. This 10-acre, walk-in campground is maintained by the Department of Natural Resources (DNR). The campsites overlook the pass, and a narrow, worn trail that seems to go on and on skirts the steep west shore. Sunset glows through the thick foliage. Three mooring buoys set off the south shore invite boaters to enjoy the rustic beauty here.

Approaches. From the east, once clear of Obstruction Pass look for a low, gray, beach cabin and a pier on the west point. This private property borders the park. Slightly east is a brown DNR park sign on the bank, and stairs that descend to the beach.

Approaching from the west, stay in deep water (10 fathoms or more) until the DNR sign is visible. This will help you avoid the reported submerged rock charted southwest of the point. If you're approaching from East Sound, note the rocks charted off the west shore, and keep a safe distance away—about 500 yards. The islet indicated on the chart is a rock awash at low tide. Expect tide rips in this area.

The approach through Obstruction Pass is described on page 278.

Anchorage, Moorings. Three mooring buoys are set in deep water off the south beach, with enough anchoring room for several more boats. The current of Obstruction Pass flows visibly beyond the anchorage, like a river, but leaves this little cove surprisingly undisturbed. Protection from north winds funneling down East Sound is excellent. There is no protection from prevailing southerly winds.

Getting Ashore. The steep gravel-and-sand beach is ideal for landing a skiff. Note that the east side of the cove, as well as the tip of the west peninsula with its beach cabin and pier, is private land.

For the Crew. Obstruction Pass Recreation Site has campsites, pit toilets, and fire rings above the beach. There are no other facilities. Groceries can be found a half-mile east by boat, at Lieber Haven Resort.

East Sound

Charts: 18421, **18430**

East Sound is long and narrow, with high mountainous sides. It is famous—some would say notorious—for its wind. Southerlies funnel north, and the long fetch builds up waves in the shallows of Fishing Bay and Ship Bay. Northerlies sweep over the low head from the Strait of Georgia, picking up speed as they move south. It can be relatively calm everywhere else in the islands, yet brisk here.

Along both shores of this long reach are many pocket-size coves with rocky headlands and private beaches. The most popular destination in East Sound is the resort at Rosario.

Approaches. From the southwest, stay about 500 yards offshore until past Shag Rock. From the southeast, keep a similar distance to avoid the unmarked rocks around the southeast tip.

Olga ★★★

Charts: 18421, **18430**

In the 1800s, Olga was a thriving little town at the south end of East Sound, with a hotel above the shore and a strawberry-packing plant inland. Today it is a cluster of residences around a post office and seasonal store. This is a sleepy place from October through May, a bit livelier in summer, when tourists wander to this end of the island. A public float off a tiny park and gazebo invites boaters to do likewise.

Approaches. From the south, the homes around Olga and Buck Bay can be seen south of Entrance Mountain's twin humps. From the north, start looking for Olga about two miles south of Rosario, across the sound from Twin Rocks.

Anchorage, Moorings. The Olga dock is tucked in east of a steep headland, near a private pier and float. The dock has a 100-foot wooden float secured between a pier and a stout dolphin piling. Thread your way carefully among the many private mooring buoys to either side of the float; gusty north winds may make maneuvering tricky. East of the Olga dock, the bay shallows rapidly as charted.

At the ramp is a sign welcoming boaters to tie up, and explaining that the dock is main-tained with community labor and moorage fees. Stays are limited to three days. On the east side, depth at the ramp is about 10 feet shallower than at the end; on the west side it's about 6 feet shallower. The float has no power. Water is available at a spring-loaded spigot located at the foot of the ramp.

Southeast of the public float is a good-sized, 5- to 8-fathom anchoring basin. A shallow shelf extends out from shore about as far as the float. As charted, this shelf is abrupt, and much of this area, including all of Buck Bay, dries at low tide.

The obvious exposure here is to the south. Don't expect much protection from the north, either—gusts swing around from the west.

All mooring buoys are private.

Getting Ashore. Use the public float. All other tidelands are private.

For the Crew. The small store at Olga sells deli sandwiches, ice, and ice-cream cones, but has few grocery items. The store opens for a short summer season only. Up the road is a country café, and a gift shop that specializes in local arts and crafts. Other than a post office, there are no facilities nearby.

Rosario (Cascade Bay) ★★★★★

Charts: 18421, **18430**

This resort halfway up East Sound is one of the most famous in the San Juan Islands. Rosario is built around a historic mansion and has a formal appearance, with trimmed lawns, a pool, and tennis courts. Guests who arrive by boat may moor at the marina or secure to one of the resort's mooring buoys.

Approaches. The white, three-story mansion with its globe lights is a distinguishing landmark on Rosario Point. From the south, head slightly east of the mansion. From the north, give a wide berth to Rosario Point in order to avoid the reef that wraps around it.

The Moran mansion at Rosario. The entrance to Cascade Bay is to the right (east) of this headland.

Moorings. The marina is protected on its south side by a rock breakwater extending from the west shore. In addition, two floats are set east of the jetty, making for a narrow entrance into the marina.

At the head of the bay is a triangular pier with a fuel dock and harbormaster's office. Check in here for moorage. You will be directed to a marina slip or a mooring buoy. From fall through spring, pull into an empty slip and register at the main desk in the mansion.

The marina has room for about 30 boats. If you use a slip on the south side of the main float, stay north of the white poles inside the breakwater; these mark a ledge of rock that limits turning room. There's more turning room on the north side of the main float. Depth in the marina is about 1 fathom shallower than it is at the end of the fuel dock.

More than a dozen mooring buoys are set in deep water along the east shore of Cascade Bay. A free launch service to shore is provided by the resort. These buoys are exposed to southerlies.

All slips have power and water. Fees charged for slips or buoys include use of the resort facilities (pool, showers, spa, and tennis courts).

Rosario Resort takes reservations for moorage—(800) 562-8820.

Anchorage. Cascade Bay has plenty of room for anchoring, though you may need to drop your hook in more than 10 fathoms during busy summer months. Keep the channel to the marina and fuel dock clear. Seaplanes use the float east of the fuel dock. Protection is fairly good from the north, but there is none from the south.

Getting Ashore. A landing fee is charged for boaters at anchor who wish to use the marina floats. Payment includes up to five passes per boat for use of the resort facilities. Additional passes may be purchased.

For the Boat. Fuel is available at the triangular pier east of the marina, with pumps on both sides. Depths are good. The nearest repair facilities are in West Sound.

For the Crew. A small café and store is at the head of the marina ramp, open in summer only. The store mainly sells snack items. Behind the store is a laundromat. Showers are north of the ramp, in the small gray building next to the outdoor swimming pool.

In the mansion is a restaurant, lounge, and music room.

Things to Do. The resort has an outdoor pool, play equipment, and tennis courts. An elaborately tiled indoor pool is located in the mansion, along with exercise rooms and a pampering spa. Organ concerts are held most evenings in the music room on the second floor. Van service to Eastsound is available for a fee.

The mansion alone is worth exploring. All the grounds, indeed much of this part of the island, was once the estate of the prosperous Seattle shipbuilder Robert Moran. Warned in his late 40s that he was dying from overwork,

Moran retired to Rosario, where he went on to live another 40 years, channeling his energy into building the estate. He designed the mansion to be fireproof, electrified with power generated at nearby Cascade Lake, and built to last. The walls are 12-inch thick concrete, the roof is covered with copper, the links of the mansion fence fashioned from the anchor chain of the USS *Nebraska*. In the early 1920s, Moran donated the considerable spread of land around Mount Constitution for a state park.

From the resort, Moran State Park is an energetic walk away. A half-mile trail heads up past the condominiums and tennis courts to Rosario Lagoon, and continues around Cascade Lake. In summer, the lake has a swimming area, a food concession, and paddleboat rentals. You'll feel far inland here, in deep woods. Don't be surprised if you find yourself drawn across the road toward the 2,400-foot peak of Mount Constitution; the 360-degree view from the stone tower there is worth the day-long trek.

Coves South and North of Giffin Rocks (Coon Hollow)

Charts: 18421, **18430**

South and north of Giffin Rocks are two small coves with a few private mooring buoys. The south cove has a private float, but neither has enough room or depth for anchoring. A private salmon hatchery operates at a stream outfall in the south cove, with a siphon running off

the beach. The blue sign on shore hopefully proclaims LONG LIVE THE KINGS.

North of Giffin Rocks, Coon Hollow is a shallow bed of eelgrass. According to Lummi legend, the first deer was created in this area of East Sound.

Ship Bay ★★ ☐2 No Facilities

Charts: 18421, **18430**

This bay at the head of East Sound, east of Madrona Point, is encircled by a low beach and skirted by a road. There is good depth for anchoring toward Madrona Point, but the bay quickly shallows—don't try to go in very far. All tidelands here are private except for Madrona Point, which is too steep for landing a skiff. Your best bet is to use the public float on

the west side of the point, which is within easy walking distance of the town of Eastsound.

Ship Bay offers no protection from southerlies. You'll get wind overland from the north, but no wave action.

For a description of the town of Eastsound, see the following entry.

Fishing Bay (Eastsound) ★★★★ 🖼️ 2 🎁 🛒 🍽️

Charts: 18421, **18430**

This bay on the west side of Madrona Point provides the best access from the water to the town of Eastsound. An islet, locally known as Indian Island, is in the middle of the bay, connected to the beach at low tide. A road runs along the head of the bay.

By San Juan Islands standards, Eastsound is a "big" town, with sidewalks and a few crosswalks. Though smaller, its growth has paralleled that of Friday Harbor, and to this day Eastsound has its own newspaper. The town is focused inland, but the white church spire and the two-story Outlook Inn—both historic structures—are visible from the water. A small county float on the west side of Madrona Point invites boaters to stop for a while and explore.

Approaches, Anchorage. Approaches are clean into Fishing Bay. Stay south of Indian Island; a rock is charted 3 feet below the surface, off the south tip, and the "coves" on both sides quickly shallow. Anchor south of this islet, in 5 to 10 fathoms. There is no protection here from southerly winds, which pick up speed as they move up the sound; in these conditions, the best protection is to the west, in Judd Bay.

The county float on the west side of Madrona Point is for day-use only—no overnight stays are allowed.

Getting Ashore. The most convenient shore access is at the county float on the west side of Madrona Point. This short concrete float is in

Fishing Bay at Eastsound, looking south. To the left (east) of Indian Island is the county dock and the Madrona Point Preserve.

shallow water. A short road leads from the pier to a small parking area, then north to the center of town.

The beach around and west of Indian Island is part of a small San Juan County Park. You can land here, but the tideflats are extensive at low tide.

For the Boat. Other than a gas station at the road and a hardware store in town that sells some fishing gear, there is little for boats in Eastsound.

For the Crew. The supermarket is about a block north of the main road, on Prune Alley. Along the way and beyond are bookstores, a bakery, a hardware store, and many restaurants, galleries, and shops. The laundromat is at Airport Center, more than a mile north of the bay—not especially convenient for boaters.

The town of Eastsound has several parks. In the commercial center is an open field known as Village Square, used on summer Saturdays as a farmers' market. The log cabin here is a historical museum, open each afternoon from Monday through Saturday. The county park at the head of Fishing Bay includes Indian Island, which is accessible at low tide. Madrona Point, once a Lummi Indian burial site, is still considered a sacred place. Trails wander through the tall grass of this preserve, and the view south makes the sound look like it goes on forever.

Special events in Eastsound include a parade on the Saturday before the Fourth of July, and a Library Fair on the second Saturday in August. Plays and concerts are held year round at the community center on Mount Baker Road.

Judd Bay ★★ ☐3☐ No Facilities

Charts: 18421, **18430**

This bight southwest of Fishing Bay is not especially attractive, but it is the only anchorage in this end of East Sound with southerly protection. The head of Judd Bay is jammed with log booms, and quickly shallows. Approaching, watch for the rock and piling charted off the south point. Anchor south and east of the log-boom pilings. From here you can see the town of Eastsound, and are exposed to wind from that direction. The distance is not enough, however, to build up much wave action.

All tidelands in Judd Bay are private. The nearest place to get ashore is in Fishing Bay.

The series of driftwood cabins around the point south of Judd Bay are part of a private camp.

Coves Between Judd Bay and White Beach

Charts: 18421, **18430**

Along the west shore of East Sound, between Judd Bay and White Beach, is a series of bights. Some, such as Dolphin Bay, are deep and big—enough for a boat or two. Many have private mooring buoys, occasionally a dock. In a few areas the tidelands are public, but nowhere is there any public access to the shore. Numerous signs remind boaters not to trespass.

The mountains across East Sound turn both north and south winds toward these small coves, making protection here doubtful.

Coves Near Twin Rocks and White Beach ★★ No Facilities

Charts: 18421, **18430**

Near the entrance to East Sound, around Twin Rocks and White Beach, are two small coves. Of these, the cove north of Twin Rocks is the most appealing, with good depth and views of undeveloped Twin Rocks State Park, of Rosario, and of the steep folds of Entrance Mountain and Mount Constitution. There's no protection here from northerlies, and minimal protection from the south, though the rocks do break up the wave action somewhat. Twin

Rocks is public, but so steep-sided that it is difficult to go ashore. All other surrounding tidelands are private.

The "cove" south of Twin Rocks is too shallow for anchoring; you'll hit bottom if you go in very far. White Beach, wider and deeper, has a private pier and a mooring buoy. There is no protection here, and no upland access.

Guthrie Bay ★★ No Facilities

Charts: 18421, **18430**

This small bay near the entrance to East Sound is deeper and easier to enter than Grindstone Harbor, its neighbor to the west. Homes are perched on the rocky shores; at the head of the bay is a beach with an islet in the middle. All tidelands and mooring buoys are private.

Protection is good here from the north, but southerlies may funnel in.

When approaching, give the rocks and reefs off Foster Point a wide berth. Shag Rock to the east is marked. When entering, slightly favor the cleaner east shore.

Grindstone Harbor ★★ ☐ No Facilities

Charts: 18421, **18430**

Descriptions of Grindstone Harbor always mention the knife-sharpener who once lived here, but even without this reference the name fits. The harbor is full of stones, with reefs off both shores, a rock and reef off its entrance, and another rock and reef in the center, about halfway in. None of them is marked.

In keeping with the underwater topography, the shores are steep. The narrow entrance widens at the head of the harbor; depth is charted here at just under 2 fathoms, enough for anchoring a small boat, provided you can find room among the private mooring buoys.

The best time to enter Grindstone Harbor is at low tide, when the rocks and reefs are exposed. Take it slowly. The tricky part is about a quarter of the way in, between the rock in the middle and the reefs on either shore.

Grindstone Harbor is well protected from the north. Southerlies may funnel in from Harney Channel, but the waves are broken up by the rocks.

All tidelands in Grindstone Harbor are private.

Jones Island State Park ★★★★ 2 (south cove) 3 (north cove)

Charts: 18421, **18434**

Jones Island lies off the southwest shore of Orcas, at the north end of San Juan Channel. The entire island is a state park, with picnic areas, campsites, and pit toilets. Trails connect the north and south coves.

This popular marine park was devastated in 1990 by a severe winter storm. The low center of the island is now thinly wooded; trails have been re-routed around the enormous, circular root systems of the toppled fir and cedar.

Approaches. From the south, an open, grassy area (the group campsite) marks the cove on this side. A rocky knob extends from the island, about the middle of the cove. Note the unmarked, submerged rock charted south of this knob.

The most distinctive feature in the north cove is the park float. The approach from the north is clean. Stay clear of the white mark on the piling east of the entrance, where there is a submerged rock. Boaters approaching from Spring Passage should do likewise.

Anchorage, Moorings. The south cove is small, and open to San Juan Channel. Three buoys are set in deep water, two west of the unmarked rock, one east. The underwater shelf is steep; if you try to anchor in less than 10 fathoms you may be uncomfortably close to the rocks. This cove is completely exposed to southerlies.

The north cove is larger, with a 100-foot float that's deep enough for most vessels, and four mooring buoys. Deepest water (by over 10 feet) is at the buoy closest to the float. These buoys are set fairly close together; boats over 40 feet may swing into one another with the current. There's anchoring room and depth south of the buoys, and in the area slightly northwest of the float. The obvious exposure in this cove is to the north.

Fees are charged for the park float and buoys, from May 1 through September 30. The fee box is on shore, at the head of the ramp in the north cove.

Getting Ashore. In the north cove, the park float is the best place to land a skiff. The south cove has a narrow strip of beach among the rocks at high tide.

Stuart Island

Charts: 18421, **18432**

Stuart Island is aimed like an arrowhead at the Canadian Gulf Islands. It rises from the confluence of Boundary Pass and Haro Strait to the rounded peak of its most distinctive feature, 640-foot Tiptop Hill. Much of Stuart Island is private, with steep and unapproachable shores. The island has no town, no ferry service, no restaurant, no store or repair shop. This lack of facilities doesn't deter boaters, however, as Stuart is blessed with two outstanding harbors that flank the isthmus of a popular state park.

Stuart Island State Park has mooring buoys and floats in both harbors, as well as firepits, restrooms, and over a dozen campsites. There are trails throughout the park's 150 acres of cedar, fir, and madrona. Clamming is good at

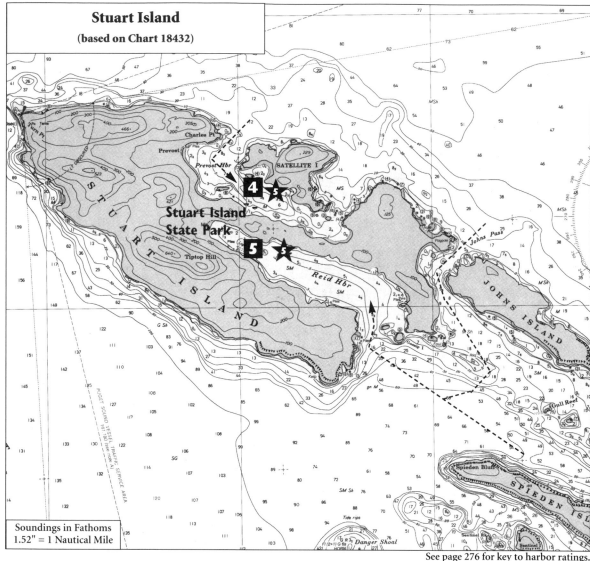

See page 276 for key to harbor ratings.

the head of Reid Harbor. In the quiet of dawn and dusk, deer browse on the cliffs.

Ambitious hikers who want to explore beyond the park can do so without trespassing on private land by starting from the county street end, at the west corner of Reid Harbor. To the north, about a mile along the road, is the school and cemetery; two more miles north and west is the Turn Point lighthouse. Adjoining roads and all surrounding lands are private. There is no public access to the summit of Tiptop Hill.

Note that some of the park trails continue on to private land.

Approaches. Currents around Stuart are strong and should be respected. Tide rips are especially impressive off Turn Point; within a mile of this point is the deepest water in all of Puget Sound.

Specific approaches to Reid Harbor and Prevost Harbor, including Johns Pass, are described in the following entries.

Reid Harbor ★★★★★

Charts: 18421, **18432**

Of the two anchorages on Stuart Island, Reid Harbor is the most popular. A boat in here is almost land-locked, protected in any weather. The harbor itself has good depth, a mud bottom, and no navigational hazards. Even the cautious *Coast Pilot* describes it as "free of danger."

Approaches. From the east, the most conservative approach is between Spieden Island and the Cactus Islands. Strongly favor the Spieden side of the channel to avoid the reefs along the Cactus side. Current boils through here—expect tide rips. Tiptop Hill and the entrance to Reid Harbor are dead ahead, with Gossip Island appearing mid-channel. Gossip is actually east of the entrance; wait until the second, smaller island emerges from behind it before turning in. The passage east of these islands, as well as between them, is foul. Stay in mid-channel until you're past the pilings on the west shore.

An alternate, though narrower, approach from the east is along the south shore of Spieden Island.

Johns Pass is a tempting shortcut for those approaching from the north, but it is not a good idea if your boat is slow (under 10 knots), as the currents are strong. Stay in mid-channel, out of the kelp. Once through the pass, head for Gull Reef until almost abeam of Spieden Bluff, then turn south and west toward Reid Harbor. This should help you avoid the rocks charted 700 yards off the east tip of Stuart; the outermost is indicated as "Rks" on the chart.

Boaters approaching from the south should give a wide berth to the many marked and unmarked reefs that lie between Roche Harbor and Spieden. Once abeam of Spieden Bluff, the approach to Reid Harbor is clear. Take note of the entrance hazards described above.

Anchorage, Moorings. You can anchor almost anywhere in Reid Harbor, but most boaters head for the west half, where there are several park floats. The float connected to land is toward the head of the bay on the northwest shore, in fairly shallow water. Check the tides if your boat is deep-draft. Toward the center of the bay are two detached floats, one straight, the other X-shaped; the X-shaped float is in slightly deeper water. During summer, boats raft all around, and the floats themselves may be obscured.

Two rows of mooring buoys, seven buoys per row, are set east of the park floats. The outermost buoys are in water about 10 feet deeper than those closest to the head of the bay.

Fees are charged for all park floats and buoys, from May 1 through September 30. The fee box is on shore at the head of the ramp.

Reid Harbor has plenty of room for boats to anchor.

The detached float southeast of the main dock is for sanitary pump-out only.

Getting Ashore. The state park encompasses the marsh at the head of the bay and about half the isthmus. Gossip Island, at the entrance to Reid Harbor, and the smaller island (known locally as Cemetery Island), are also public. All other tidelands are private.

Things to Do. All the amenities of Stuart Island State Park described earlier in this section are accessible from Reid Harbor. In addition, Gossip and Cemetery Islands are within reach. The clear and rocky waters around these islands attract scuba divers, and the grassy knoll of Gossip, fragrant with wildflowers in spring and summer, offers lovely views south and east. No camping or fires are permitted on either island.

Prevost Harbor ★★★★★

Charts: 18421, **18432**

Prevost Harbor is slightly deeper than Reid Harbor, and almost as protected. It has a complex shape and variable bottom, with hazards inside that make for a somewhat tricky approach to a relatively small anchoring basin. For these reasons, Prevost Harbor is usually less crowded.

Approaches. Enter west of Satellite Island, in mid-channel. Head for the house with the red roof on the far south shore. Stay on this heading until you're abeam of the pier at the small community of Prevost on the west shore. When you can clearly see the far east end of the harbor (the low spot there is an airstrip), turn southeast toward the state park float, slightly favoring Satellite Island. This should help you stay between two submerged, charted but unmarked reefs—one off Satellite, the other off Stuart. Go slowly and watch your depth sounder. You may want to try this the first time on a rising tide.

Do not enter Prevost Harbor via the channel east of Satellite Island, which is constricted with rocks, reefs, kelp, and strong current.

A description of Johns Pass is given on page 341.

Anchorage, Moorings. The state park float is on the south shore, about 100 feet long and with enough depth for most vessels. The seven park buoys are all in deep water. Fees are charged for the park float and buoys, from May 1 through September 30. The fee box is on shore at the head of the ramp.

Anchorage is good north and east of the

A calm morning at the state park float in Prevost Harbor.

buoys, but don't go much beyond the east bight on Satellite Island, as the harbor shallows. The best anchorage is in the 5- to 6-fathom basin slightly northeast of the park float.

Strong northerly winds can wrap around Satellite Island, but protection is generally good.

Getting Ashore. The state park extends east to about the center of the isthmus. All other shoreline is private. There is a county dock at Prevost, but all other land is private. Satellite Island, which shields the anchorage from Boundary Pass, is a YMCA Camp.

Things to Do. All of the amenities of Stuart Island State Park described earlier in this section are accessible from Prevost Harbor.

Johns Island

Charts: 18421, **18432**

Johns Island, separated from Stuart by narrow Johns Pass, is entirely private. A sign on one of the homes accurately describes it as a SELF-SER-VICE ISLAND. There are no facilities for boaters, or harbors to recommend. The two bights on the north side are exposed, quickly become shallow, and are filled with private mooring buoys.

For a description of Johns Pass, see page 341.

Islands North of Spieden Channel

Charts: 18421, **18433**

Between San Juan and Stuart is a cluster of steep-sided islands with no coves to attract passing boaters. Currents throughout these islands are strong, and tidal overfalls are common. All land is private.

Spieden Island is the largest of these islands. In the early 1970s, exotic animals wandered on its high grassy slopes; a Seattle taxidermy firm flew in big-game "hunters." The business lasted only a few years, but some of the animals remain. Today the island is a private marine-science camp.

Nearby Sentinel, Flattop, and the Cactus Islands are similarly grassy, dry enough to grow cactus. Sentinel is best known as the old homestead of June Burns, a writer whose loving chronicles of the San Juans helped preserve some of them for public use.

Waldron Island

Charts: 18421, **18432**

With no ferry or telephone service, no town, no parks and no boating facilities, Waldron seems to have removed itself from the rest of the San Juan Islands. Residents value their remoteness and privacy, and the geography of the island helps them: The southeast shore is steep, the north shore is foul, and the only two anchorages are exposed.

Cowlitz Bay ★★ [2] No Facilities

Charts: 18421, **18432**

The wide crescent of Cowlitz Bay opens to the southwest. From the dramatic cliffs of Point Disney—a cormorant nesting area—the shore gradually lowers to sandy bluffs. Past the county dock and the cluster of buildings charted as "Waldron," it is low and wooded. On shore is a post office, but no store, no gas station, and no telephone.

Sandstone quarried at Pt. Disney was used to construct the jetties on the Columbia River.

Approaches, Anchorage. From the south, Pt. Disney is a steep and prominent cliff. Watch for the submerged reef of Danger Rock, located halfway between Flattop Island and Pt. Disney, and for unmarked Mouatt Reef, about a half-mile northwest of the same point. Boaters approaching from the north should be able to spot the uncharted tower on Sandy Point. Give the shoals and rocks south of this point a wide berth.

Anchor northwest of the county dock at Waldron. The float at this dock is for loading and unloading only. All mooring buoys are private.

Getting Ashore. There is no public access to Waldron Island except at the county float. The main roads are public, but all land is private, including the parcels owned by the Nature Conservancy. Serious wildlife watchers may walk the private Nature Conservancy beach, located roughly between the two marshes charted north of the county dock. This is not a park; there is no picnicking allowed, no camping, no smoking, no fires, no pets, and no groups may visit without prior arrangement. This beach cannot be reached by land without trespassing on private property—approach by water only.

Mail Bay ★★ [2] No Facilities

Charts: 18421, **18432**

This small, double bay on the east side of Waldron Island was formerly used by the mail boat from Orcas. It has a pretty, wooded shore, a few private homes, but too many rocks and submerged pilings to invite anchoring. Where depth is suitable for anchoring, Mail Bay offers little protection from any direction except the west. Some protection from the north may be found nearer the north shore. All buoys and tidelands are private.

Patos Island State Park ★★★★

Charts: 18421, **18431**, **18432**

For freighters bound through Haro Strait, Patos is an important light marking the north end of Boundary Pass. The island is small and narrow, the northernmost of the San Juans, and the most remote. Under the steady siege of water and wind, the trees on Patos are stunted and twisted. Reefs surround its rocky shores.

Along with Little Patos, the entire island is a state park. However, it has only one anchor-

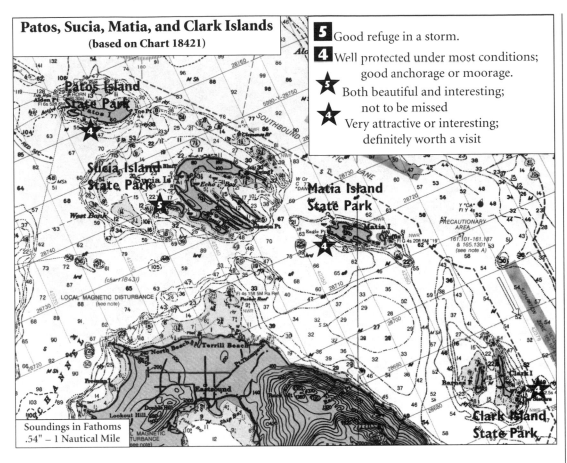

Patos, Sucia, Matia, and Clark Islands
(based on Chart 18421)

5	Good refuge in a storm.
4	Well protected under most conditions; good anchorage or moorage.
★5	Both beautiful and interesting; not to be missed
★4	Very attractive or interesting; definitely worth a visit

Soundings in Fathoms
.54" – 1 Nautical Mile

age—tiny Active Cove—and draws far fewer boaters than nearby Sucia.

Approaches. The approach to Active Cove should be made from the west only. Be prepared for tide rips; the Spanish explorers described the currents on this side of the island as "rapid and violent," with "such whirlpools that without exaggeration there seems to be a small vortex." These swift currents, as well as rocks, make the south passage between Patos and Little Patos dangerous.

As you enter Active Cove, stay in mid-channel; reefs extend from both islands.

Anchorage, Moorings. Two park buoys are placed in deep water near Little Patos Island. There is swinging room for one or two additional boats in the anchorage.

Though actually named for a survey ship in the mid-1800s, the word "Active" suitably describes this cove. You're out of the current

here, but the wakes of ships in Boundary Pass may roll into the anchorage, and there's less protection from southwesterlies than you might expect.

Getting Ashore. The entire island is public. The best landing spot is at the head of Active Cove. A one-and-a-half mile loop trail begins here, and there are a few campsites. If you want to walk out to the lighthouse, beach your dinghy east of the old lighthouse pier; it will be pounded by wakes if you tie it to the pier itself.

Things to Do. With few campsites and limited anchorage, Patos is likely to be an empty place. Take advantage of the solitude. Hike the trail east to Toe Point. Walk the overgrown sidewalk path to the abandoned lighthouse buildings, and gaze across the strait to the undulating landforms of the Canadian Gulf Islands. Listen to the foghorn, and the silence.

Sucia Island/Sucia Island State Park

Charts: 18421, **18431**

Sucia Island is the crown of the San Juans and of the entire marine state park system. It is shaped like a welcoming hand—thumb to the north, fingers to the south—and has a surprising number of bays, each with its own personality. You can happily spend a week here, anchored in a different cove every night, hiking a different trail every day, eating every meal on a different beach.

Among Sucia's many attractions are its magical landforms. The north shore is steep-sided, with cliffs that drop perpendicularly into the Strait. The rest of the island appears to have been gently sculpted by the sea. Small cobbles, dropped from the sandstone, have left behind a

surface that resembles lace. Wind and wave have carved out pillars and caves. The hard rock that remains drips like frosting over the undercut, softer stone.

For thousands of years these islands were Indian seal-hunting grounds. The present name was given in 1791 by the Eliza Expedition (*sucia* means "dirty" in Spanish), warning mariners of the island's many rocks and shoals.

In the early 1900s, a sandstone quarry here employed a thousand workers; when the stone, used for paving Seattle's streets, was found to be too soft, the operation was abandoned. Sucia Island remained in private hands until the 1960s and 70s, when it was purchased with

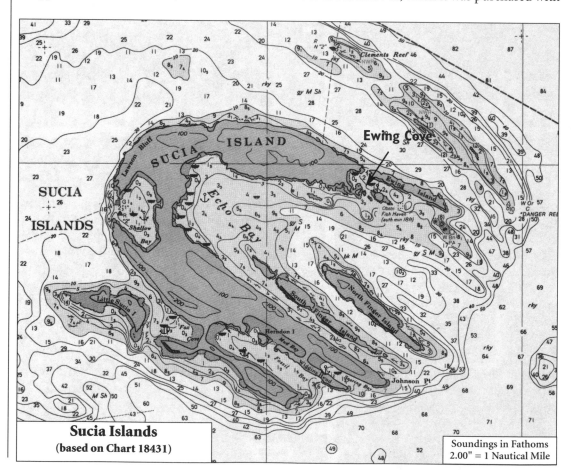

Sucia Islands
(based on Chart 18431)

Soundings in Fathoms
2.00" = 1 Nautical Mile

funds raised by Puget Sound yacht clubs and donated to the state for a marine park. Today, only North Finger and South Finger are private.

Approaches. Approaches to Sucia from the east and west are fairly clean. The island has an especially distinctive appearance from the southeast, looking like a giant foot on the water with its toes reaching toward you. From the north, watch for the red nun buoy ("2") marking a 1-mile string of rocks called Clements Reef, and another buoy almost a mile to the southeast that marks the end of Danger Reef. These reefs are part of the San Juan National Wildlife Refuge—stay at least 200 yards away. When approaching from Orcas Island, watch for Parker Reef. It is well marked and also a National Wildlife Refuge.

Things to Do. Sucia Island covers more than 500 acres, and has a shoreline almost 9 miles long. Hiking trails and dirt roads meander through forest, wetlands, and numerous sand and gravel beaches. The park has firepits, picnic tables and shelters, restrooms, and more than 50 campsites. Water use is limited. A map of the entire park is displayed between Fox Cove and Fossil Bay, and another between Shallow Bay and Echo Cove. A fish haven for scuba divers is south of Ewing Island.

Moorage fees are charged for all park floats and buoys, from May 1 through September 30. Fee boxes are located on shore, near the floats in Fossil Bay. From October to May, the water system is turned off, and the west float is removed.

Fox Cove ★★★★★

Charts: 18421, **18431**

This cove on the southwest side of Sucia is protected by Little Sucia Island, though it is somewhat exposed to southwesterlies. Sunset views are lovely here, and the sculptured sandstone on the north beach is some of the finest on the island. At high tide you can see across the low isthmus to Fossil Bay.

Approaches. The cleanest entrance is from the west, north of Little Sucia. Favor the Sucia Island shore. Give the west tip of Little Sucia a wide berth; the reef that extends about a quarter-mile is marked only by the seals that often haul out there at low tide. The south entrance has sufficient depth for most boats, but it is constricted by kelp. The currents here are strong.

Anchorage, Moorings. Four mooring buoys are set in a square pattern at the head of the cove. The southwest buoy is in deepest water, the northeast buoy shallowest. There's room to anchor west of these buoys; to the east the bay shallows rapidly.

Getting Ashore. All shoreline around Fox Cove is state park land. Little Sucia is closed to the public from January 1 to August 15 to protect nesting areas.

Shallow Bay ★★★★★

Charts: 18421, **18431**

Shallow Bay offers the best sunset views of any anchorage on Sucia, and the warmest water for swimming. Regular visitors consider it one of the quietest as well, removed from the crowds and parties that fill Echo Bay and Fossil Bay in summer. Despite its name, Shallow Bay is no

A pedestal of sandstone at Fox Cove.

shallower than Fossil or Snoring.

Approaches. The red and green entrance marks are visible for some distance. These marks are on pilings; expect an abrupt change in depth as you cross over the shelf.

Anchorage, Moorings. Shallow Bay has eight mooring buoys. Those nearest the entrance are in slightly deeper water than the others. There's anchoring room as well, but the basin is smaller than it appears on the chart. Be careful to leave enough swinging room from the shore, and keep in mind that almost a third of the bay is less than 1 fathom deep. Deep-draft vessels may bottom out on a minus tide. A strong southeasterly wind can come over the lowland of the marsh, but swells from traffic in Boundary Pass are usually not a problem.

Getting Ashore. All shoreline around Shallow Bay is state park land.

Ewing Cove ★★★★★

Charts: 18421, **18431**

Ewing Cove lies off the northeast "thumb" of Sucia, bounded by Ewing Island and a group of rocks and islets known as the Cluster Islands. This may be Sucia's most spectacular anchorage, with a fantasy of small-scale sandstone sculptures exposed at low tide. It is also the most exposed, and has the trickiest entrance.

Approaches. There are two entrances, both with hazards. If you enter from the southeast, slightly favor Ewing Island. Rocks that submerge at high tide extend northwest of the white mark on the piling, and there is an unexpected underwater hump between this mark and the southeast tip of Ewing Island.

If you enter from the south (the approach preferred by many boaters), find the uncharted white can that marks the fish haven. Stay in deep water east of this can, and take care not to drift toward the rocks described above.

Regardless of the entrance used, slow speed and a rising tide are recommended.

The narrow, rocky passage between Ewing and Sucia is not advised.

Anchorage, Moorings. The four mooring buoys here are set in a line, the easternmost almost 10 feet deeper than the buoy at the head of the cove. Anchoring room is limited. Expect a rocky bottom.

Getting Ashore. All shoreline around Ewing Cove is state park land.

Echo Bay ★★★★★

Charts: 18421, **18431**

Echo Bay is the largest and deepest on Sucia Island, with enough room for anchoring on even a crowded weekend.

Approaches. The entrance to this wide bay is clean, but watch for reefs off the tips of the "fingers," and for the marked reef southeast of Ewing Island. Inside Echo Bay is a reef near the north shore. Passage is clean between North and South Finger Islands, as well as between South Finger and Sucia.

Anchorage, Moorings. A dozen mooring buoys are set in an irregular crescent at the head of the bay. Those farthest from shore along this crescent are in deepest water.

Anchoring is good in mud bottom anywhere in the bay. The buoy charted in the center of the bay is used by the U.S. Coast Guard.

Getting Ashore. North and South Finger Islands are private. All other shoreline is state park.

Snoring Bay ★★★★★

Charts: 18421, **18431**

Narrow and steep-sided, Snoring Bay is like a canyon. The south face is shingled; the north rounded, with volcanic rock forming a crust over the undercut sandstone. The bay's high sides and low ends create a funnel that increases wind here, and exaggerates wave action. If there's a stiff wind coming up Rosario Strait you may have a bouncy night.

Snoring Bay is said to have been named by park officials who found a ranger napping here.

Approaches. Head directly into this bay from the southwest. There are reefs off the points on both sides of the entrance. The flagpole visible at the head of the bay is across the marsh, near the ranger station in Mud Bay.

Anchorage, Moorings. This narrow bay has two mooring buoys, with anchoring room for only a few more boats. The bay is shallow—a little over 1 fathom—and should be avoided by deep-draft vessels during minus tides.

Getting Ashore. All surrounding lands are state park.

Fossil Bay ★★★★★

Charts: 18421, **18431**

With two floats and plenty of buoys, Fossil Bay is easily the most popular anchorage on Sucia. The bay takes its name from the fossils found in the surrounding bluffs. Little Hernden Island once served as a "guest book" for Sucia, with visitors scrawling the names of their boats on its rock face. The practice is now prohibited, but some of the writing is still visible.

During summer, boats raft thickly, and the floats are cluttered with lawn chairs and barbecues. The west float is removed from October through April.

Approaches. Head directly in from the southwest, keeping to the middle of the bay. Watch for the reef off the tip of E. V. Henry Point. You'll be able to see Fox Cove and Little Sucia Island beyond the low isthmus at the head of Fossil Bay.

Anchorage, Moorings. Fossil Bay has two floats, each about 100 feet long, one at the head and one across the entrance to Mud Bay. Depths are about the same on both sides of these floats, slightly shallower toward shore. Fifteen mooring buoys are set in two parallel lines, all in similar depths. There's good anchorage southeast of these buoys.

All of Fossil Bay is less than 2 fathoms; deep-draft vessels may be aground during minus tides.

Mud Bay, behind Hernden Island, dries at low tide.

Getting Ashore. All surrounding lands are state park.

Matia Island ★★★★ (float)  (anchorage)

Charts: 18421, **18430**, **18431**

Matia Island is less than two miles east of popular Sucia. Though equally beautiful, it attracts fewer people—deliberately. The island is jointly administered by the U.S. Fish and Wildlife Service and the Washington State Department of Parks and Recreation, and is designated primarily as a refuge for seabirds, eagles, and seals.

Along with Turn Island (located southeast of Friday Harbor), this is the only National Wildlife Refuge in the San Juans open to the public. On Matia, human activity is restricted to five acres of state park land, where there are a few campsites, picnic tables, firepits, and a composting toilet. Hiking is limited to the loop trail (no rock climbing), and no pets are allowed on the island. Anchoring is also restricted (see below). The remaining 140 acres of Matia are the exclusive preserve of puffins and oyster catchers, seals and otters.

Despite its restrictions (or perhaps because of them), Matia is well worth a visit. The one-mile loop trail takes you inland through old-growth forest. The untrampled vegetation is thick, and offers satisfying glimpses of wildlife, especially if you walk quietly. Past a settler's ruins (the famous—and misnamed—"Hermit of Matia" rowed weekly to socialize on Orcas) is a tiny, keyhole-shaped cove that invites you to linger, and to daydream.

Approaches, Anchorage, Moorings. Boats may anchor only in Rolfe Cove, in the smaller cove southwest of Rolfe, and in the larger cove on the southeast side of Matia.

Rolfe Cove opens directly toward Sucia; boats at the dock or on the buoys can be seen from Echo Bay. You can enter Rolfe Cove on either side of the smaller island that shelters it from the west, but the south passage is the wider, preferred approach. Currents are strong. Watch for reefs off all shores. A 60-foot park float extends into deep water from the beach at the head of the cove. Watch for rocks close to shore when maneuvering around the float.

Two mooring buoys, also in deep water, are set close to the south shore; pay attention to tides and check your swing. Fees are charged for the park float and buoys, from May 1 through September 30. The fee box is on shore at the head of the ramp. *Matia* means "no protection" in Spanish, but Rolfe Cove is reasonably protected from southerlies. Protection from the north is not good. There is less protection on your own hook, west of the float or buoys.

Anchoring is also permitted in the cove southwest of Rolfe Cove. Favor the south shore to avoid the reef on the opposite side.

The larger cove on the southeast side of Matia has sufficient room for four or five boats. Approach with care; unmarked reefs extend 200 yards off the south entrance point, and 500 yards off the north. About halfway in, the cove shallows to less than 1 fathom. Don't expect any protection from southerlies.

Getting Ashore. In Rolfe Cove, go ashore only at the park float. In the southeast cove, shore access is permitted only at the head of the cove, where the island's loop trail touches the beach. No landing is permitted in the small cove southwest of Rolfe, in either cove on the south side of the island, or anywhere else on Matia. Signs all around the island remind you to stay at least 200 yards away.

Barnes Island

Charts: 18421, **18430**

This small island is about a mile northeast of Orcas, west of Clark Island. It has no protected anchorage, and is surrounded by rocks, reefs, and shoals. The north and west shores are especially foul. All uplands are private.

Clark Island State Park ★★★★

Charts: 18421, **18430**

Narrow Clark Island, located about a mile northeast of Orcas, bends slightly east at its south tip. From a distance it seems to have been thrust up from the Strait of Georgia. Much of its shoreline is fissured, the rocks shaped and fit together like pieces of a three-dimensional puzzle.

All of Clark Island is a state park, with campsites on the east shore, picnic tables, and firepits. The trails are overgrown with salal, maple, and madrona, and in some places they tunnel through thickets of wild roses. From the west beach you can see Mount Constitution on Orcas, with its tower and rock fortress.

Park buoys are located on either side of Clark's pinched waist.

Approaches. From the south, Clark Island presents a somewhat confusing aspect, with the cluster of islets known as the Sisters seemingly connected to its south tip. The green mark is on the north Sister; note the rock charted about 200 yards north of it.

Depending on the anchorage you've chosen, head east or west of the Sisters. Do not pass between them and Clark. There is depth enough, but currents are strong, and the islets are a National Wildlife Refuge. Pass around them, at least 200 yards away.

If your destination is the east anchorage, don't turn in until you're almost abeam of Clark Island's highest point. This approach should keep you well clear of the unmarked rocks that extend northward from the southeast tip of Clark.

Approaches from the north are more straightforward. Note the charted reefs and rocks on both sides.

Anchorage, Moorings. In the east anchorage are six mooring buoys, set close together. The depth at the far south buoy is about 5 feet shallower than at the far north buoy. There's anchoring room north of these buoys. The beach is a gradually sloping gravel crescent.

On the west side of Clark are three buoys, all set in deep water at the edge of the shelf. Be prepared for strong current here. The beach on this side is steep and sandy.

Clark Island is too low to offer much protection in either of these anchorages. On the east side you're exposed to the wakes of freighter traffic even in calm weather.

REGION 11

THE EAST PORTION OF
THE STRAIT OF JUAN DE FUCA

The New Dungeness Lighthouse, looking north from Dungeness Bay.

FROM DISCOVERY BAY TO PORT ANGELES

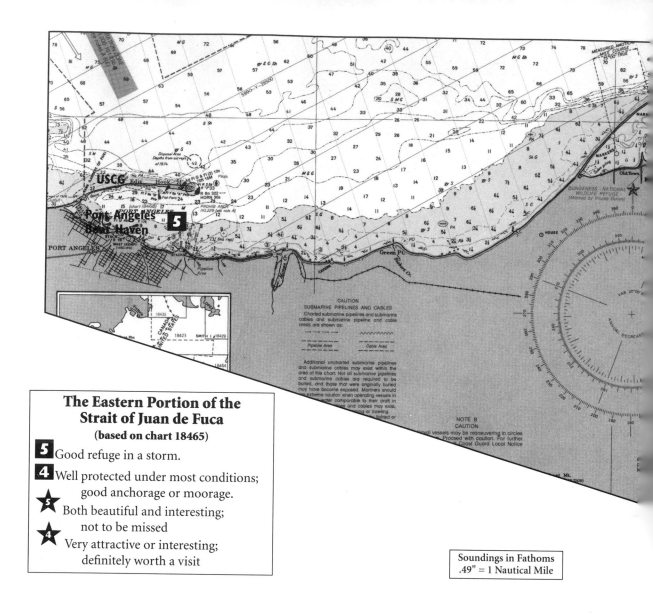

The Eastern Portion of the Strait of Juan de Fuca
(based on chart 18465)

5 Good refuge in a storm.

4 Well protected under most conditions;
good anchorage or moorage.

⭐**5** Both beautiful and interesting;
not to be missed

⭐**4** Very attractive or interesting;
definitely worth a visit

Soundings in Fathoms
.49" = 1 Nautical Mile

The Point Wilson light north of Port Townsend marks the end of Admiralty Inlet and all the protected waters to the south. Ahead lies the Strait of Juan de Fuca, some 15 miles across and 80 miles long—the ocean entrance to Puget Sound, the highway for commercial traffic off the North Pacific.

Influenced by ocean and mountain, the Strait of Juan de Fuca has many moods. It can be glassy and flat, but most often it's not. Wind and wave build from the west; on an ebb tide the seas steepen. In late summer, fog is common. The *Coast Pilot*, not generally given to extremes, speaks sternly on this subject: "In few parts of the world is vigilance of the mariner more called upon than when entering the Strait of Juan de Fuca from the Pacific in fog." This "thick weather" moves into the strait along the south shore, creating hazardous conditions for pleasure boats groping across crowded shipping lanes.

Even under fair conditions, most cruisers hurry across the strait early in the morning

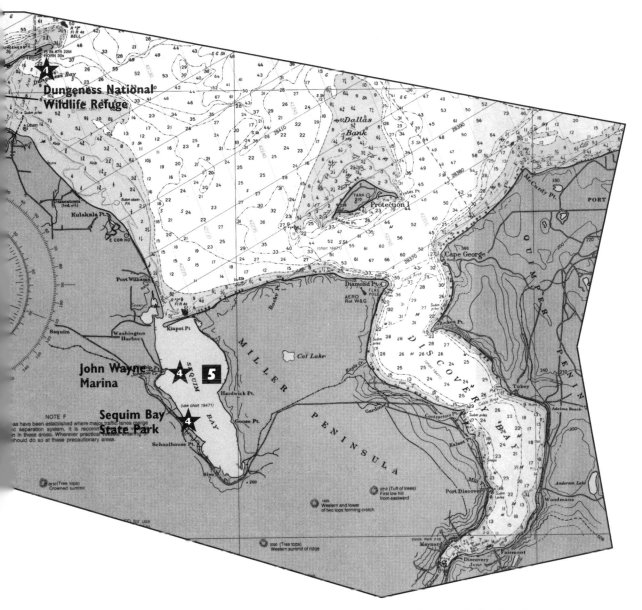

when it's generally calmer; everyone breathes easier once they reach the San Juans or Admiralty Inlet. Many avoid the strait altogether, taking the longer but considerably more protected route on the east side of Whidbey Island. Commercial skippers agree with this strategy: "Why be out there if you don't have to?"

There are good reasons to be "out there." For sailors, the open water of the strait is inviting and challenging. You can sail all day on long, often exhilarating reaches; possibly the only real sailing you'll have during your summer vacation, and a good shakedown for ocean hopefuls. If you linger here you'll be rewarded with peaceful anchorages, especially around holiday weekends that draw most cruisers north. Fishing, crabbing, and clamming are excellent. The big water and chance of big weather will sharpen your boating skills, your wariness, and your enjoyment.

Discovery Bay

Charts: 18441, 18465, **18471**

Discovery Bay is eight miles long, shaped like a bent leg with its knee pointing west. Inside the wide entrance, depths are consistently 20 fathoms or more. The bay has few protective coves, only one public beach access, and virtually no boating facilities. These factors, combined with close proximity to Port Townsend and Sequim Bay, probably account for its surprising emptiness. You will encounter few other pleasure boats here, and with only a little imagination can look upon the rolling hills that surround you as Captain Vancouver saw them when he dropped anchor in 1792—his first anchorage in Northwest waters—and named this bay after his ship.

Approaches. From the west, look for the green can southwest of Protection Island. This buoy will appear more distant from the island than you expect. Keep the can to port. The low buildings and flagpole on Diamond Point, a former military reservation and quarantine station, are visible as you approach.

From the northeast, take care locating red nun "4" north of McCurdy Point off the Quimper Peninsula; charted dolphin pilings are easily confused with this buoy. Stay a half-mile or so from Cape George to avoid the rocks and shoals there. Once inside Discovery Bay, you'll feel like you're cruising down a wide channel, and will find only a few suitable anchorages.

Cape George Marina

Charts: 18441, 18465, **18471**

Tucked away on the south shore of Cape George, a small marina and launching ramp operates for Cape George Colony residents only. No public access is permitted.

Cove South of Beckett Point ★★ No Facilities

Charts: 18441, 18465, **18471**

Beckett Point, densely crowded with summer homes and flagpoles, sits low on the horizon beneath a 500-foot bluff. The "cove" south of this sandspit will protect you somewhat from the swells off the Strait of Juan de Fuca in settled weather. There are numerous shrimp pots off the point in season, but otherwise the approach is clear. Underwater the shelf is steep, with a gravel bottom. Take care that your anchor is firmly hooked in 10 fathoms or so and that your swing won't put you on the beach at low tide. You'll experience some swell on even the calmest nights, and will waltz with the current. All tidelands in the cove are private, except for a public beach on the north side of Beckett Point, with water access only, almost a mile northeast of the charted pond.

WORKING THE WATER: THE VIEW FROM A CONTAINER SHIP

At first the small, square speck on the horizon seems too distant to worry about. Moving at a steady 22 knots, the container ship is abeam before you're ready, its rolling wake rocking your boat, its towering hull robbing your wind. Across its stern is the name of a distant port: Singapore, Sydney, Seoul.

One hundred feet up on the bridge is a pilot who hails from a less exotic spot—usually Tacoma or Seattle. Puget Sound pilots are hired by shipping agents to guide all foreign (and most domestic) vessels in and out of Puget Sound. With the pilot is the ship's quartermaster at the wheel, and often the first mate and captain. The atmosphere on the bridge is all business. Even the excitement of pulling away from the dock doesn't generate much chit-chat. No one speaks loudly or moves quickly. Eyes gaze outward through enormous windows, scanning the horizon, confirming with binoculars or brief study of the radar.

It's a perspective so different from a pleasure boat that everything seems new. After a tug-assisted departure from the dock, the 55,000-ton mass of the ship moves imperceptibly at 5 knots—top speed for some cruising sailboats. There is only a mild sensation of speed at 22 knots, and absolutely no sound of an engine. The landforms are more chart-like; you look down on points, across the tops of hills. You're so high above the water you're part of the sky; low-flying aircraft appear on the radar screens. The inland water appears flat or gently corrugated. In fog, the ship itself—more than 800 feet long and 100 feet wide—becomes your whole world, the only color anywhere the orange and rust of the containers that stretch hundreds of feet forward to the bow, where a mast protrudes like a gunsight.

From this height, most pleasure boats blend into the water like pelagic birds. A gray raft would be invisible, a white yacht on the horizon hardly distinguishable from a whitecap or haze. A runabout appears as a tiny dot on the ship's radar, disappearing altogether when there's surface chop.

The large ships that enter and leave Puget Sound work hard to avoid even the appearance of crowding each other. They communicate frequently with the Coast Guard's Vessel Traffic System to confirm their course in the shipping lanes, with the state ferries to agree how to cross paths, and with each other when passing or overtaking. No one wants a close call.

You can do a lot to help ships avoid you by avoiding them.

"Think of the shipping lanes as a major highway," advises one pilot. "Get across as directly and quickly as you can." If there's any doubt about clearance, pass astern of the ship rather than in front. The speed of a large mass is deceptive and difficult to gauge—a container ship can cover almost a mile every couple of minutes. At that speed, it takes a long time to turn or stop. If you choose to cross a ship's bow, remember that its blind spot may extend hundreds of feet ahead; if you're in it, you won't be seen by anyone on the bridge.

Try not to fish or sail within the lanes. Stay closer to shore, leaving the lanes to ships that need the deep water. Especially at night or in fog, stay away from the mid-channel turning buoys; big ships aim for them.

Like many jobs done well, the Puget Sound pilot's does not attract outside attention. The only glimpse of the job you're likely to catch is off Ediz Hook at the entrance to Port Angeles harbor. Here, sturdy pilot boats, topsides painted bright red and boldly lettered, rendezvous with incoming and outgoing ships. While the pilot is transferred, the crew on the bridge above and on the pilot boat below focus on the complex maneuvers that bring the vessels together for as brief a time as can be safely managed. The Strait of Juan de Fuca is a dizzying rush of water between them. The pilot, who embarks or disembarks by way of a rope ladder, is suddenly a small human against the enormous wall of the hull, moving deliberately along the scored wooden rungs. For a moment, all sense of scale and speed is suspended. The entire process takes only minutes, and is as gracefully executed as a dance.

Everything about these freighters deserves healthy respect, but not fear. Gliding in and out of Puget Sound as though on a conveyer belt, they follow a predictable course. Monitor VHF Channel 14 (Channel 5A north of Marrowstone Island) and you'll know where many of them are—a good idea in fog. They maintain a steady speed and direction. And you can count on their pilots knowing more about local conditions than you do; as part of their licensing they must draw—from memory—every buoy, rock, and fathom line onto a blank chart.

The next time you spot a large ship, imagine the view from that bridge: the wide expanse of Puget Sound, your boat something small and unpredictable below on the water, and all those eyes, scanning and watching.

Adelma Beach ★★ ☐2 No Facilities

Charts: 18441, 18465, **18471**

The gradually sloping bottom of Adelma Beach (the "heel" of Discovery Bay) is somewhat open to northwesterlies, but the view to the west toward the Olympic Mountains is lovely in fair weather. The approach is clean. All mooring buoys are private. There are many homes along the shore, and no public access.

South End of Discovery Bay ★★ ☐3 No Facilities

Charts: 18441, 18465, **18471**

The southern toe of Discovery Bay terminates in the mud flats of Salmon and Snow Creeks. The shallows are spanned by power lines and littered with ruins and pilings, many submerged at high tide. Highway 101 is visible beyond. This valley was once an active logging area, with a sawmill and railroad that fed the now quiet communities of Maynard, Uncus, and Discovery Junction.

Approaches, Anchorage. Between 5 and 10 fathoms there is a broad, sloping sand-and-gravel bottom suitable for anchoring. The approach is clean as long as you stay in these depths. Below 5 fathoms, the bottom rises abruptly; a charted wreck on the south shore marks the shelf there. This anchorage offers good protection from the northwest, but southwesterlies can funnel up from the valley. There is no public shore access.

Cove South of Mill Point ★★★ ☐3 🛥 🍽

Charts: 18441, 18465, **18471**

Along with the empty beauty of Discovery Bay, the reward for exploring this area is the restaurant at Mill Point. The Original Oyster House (formerly the Discovery Bay Inn) is cut into the hill above a newly rebuilt dock that offers free moorage for diners, fresh local seafood, and a small-town friendliness unexpected in an establishment with white linen and china.

Approaches, Anchorage, Moorings. From the north, you'll first spot the condominiums that flank the north side of the restaurant. You can tie up on either side of the wooden float, but watch for charted submerged pilings when approaching the shore side of the dock; watch, too, for a dangerous submerged wreck about 300 feet south. A private launching ramp descends from the restaurant parking lot. Condominium owners have priority at the dock. If you need to anchor after dinner it is possible to do so in 5 to 10 fathoms to the south; your safest bet is to anchor further south toward the toe of the bay.

The dock at the Original Oyster House in Discovery Bay.

Cove Between Contractors Point and Kalset Point ★ 2 No Facilities

Charts: 18441, 18465, **18471**

The slight indentation between Contractors Point and Kalset Point may provide protection from the fetch coming off the strait, but is not recommended for anchoring. A substantial private dock extends south of Contractors Point. The shelf is fairly steep, littered with charted rocks, pilings, old ballast, and a wreck—a good spot for diving. There is no public access to shore.

Gardiner ★★★ No Facilities

Charts: 18441, 18465, **18471**

The launching ramp at Gardiner, some two-and-a-half nautical miles south of Diamond Point, provides the only public shore access within Discovery Bay. The steep bottom makes for a good ramp site but a poor anchorage. However, a brief stop in settled weather is worth the effort: There is magic inland. Walk north and west along the road and you'll soon spot the carved mushrooms and gnomes. Tall fence posts that line the road as it rises up the hill are carved with mermaids, witches, and wizards. The fairy-tale grounds and embellished homes are strictly private, but you can see more than you'll ever be able to describe from a respectful distance. An enormous cyclops stands watch over a garden. Trolls stalk the paths and fields, and support the roof of a large barn. The castle at the top of the hill is guarded by dragons, and the bus stop across the street has been changed into a swing.

This troll haven is a tiny spot on the way to nowhere. When you return to your boat, turning your attention to the open water and green bluffs of Discovery Bay, don't be surprised if you feel somewhat disoriented, as though you have drifted from one dream only to find yourself in another.

Protection Island

Charts: 18441, 18465, **18471**

Protection Island, a mile-and-a-half long and 200 feet at its highest west bluff, rises like a fortress across the entrance to Discovery Bay. Once privately owned and platted for substantial development, it is now an important refuge for birds and seals; an astonishing 75 percent of all the seabirds in Puget Sound nest here. The island provides nesting burrows for the rhinoceros auklet and tufted puffin, open nesting for over 9,000 pair of glaucous-winged gulls (the largest gull colony in Washington state), and for other seabirds such as oyster catchers, scoters, and harlequin duck. The spits on both ends of the island are nurseries for harbor seal.

The northwestern three-quarters of Protection Island is managed as a National Wildlife Refuge by the U.S. Fish and Wildlife Service. Boaters should stay at least 200 yards offshore. No landing is permitted; the few people occasionally seen on the beach are caretakers, researchers, or others with special permission. The inlet on the southeast side—dredged from a former wetland by land speculators before the island became a refuge—is also off-limits. The west end of the island is the 48-acre Zella M. Schultz Seabird Sanctuary managed by the Washington State Department of Wildlife.

You can best appreciate Protection Island at a distance by observing the varied seabirds in the surrounding waters. The rhinoceros auklet can be seen everywhere, diving with an almost comical fuss, raising thin arm-like wings in alarm, then curving downward with a splash. The north end of Discovery Bay is also an especially fine area to watch tufted puffins; on an overcast day their bright orange-and-yellow parrot beaks and spiked hairdos are startling against the muted gray-green sea.

Sequim Bay

Charts: 18471

Sequim Bay, almost four miles long, lies in the rain shadow of the Olympic Mountains. With only 17 to 19 inches of rainfall a year, this is the driest area in Puget Sound, so dry that its annual celebration is an Irrigation Festival. The entrance to Sequim Bay is narrow, constricted by two sandspits. Once inside, the west shore rises briefly into a high bluff that has recently yielded the bones of mastodons that roamed here 11,000 years ago.

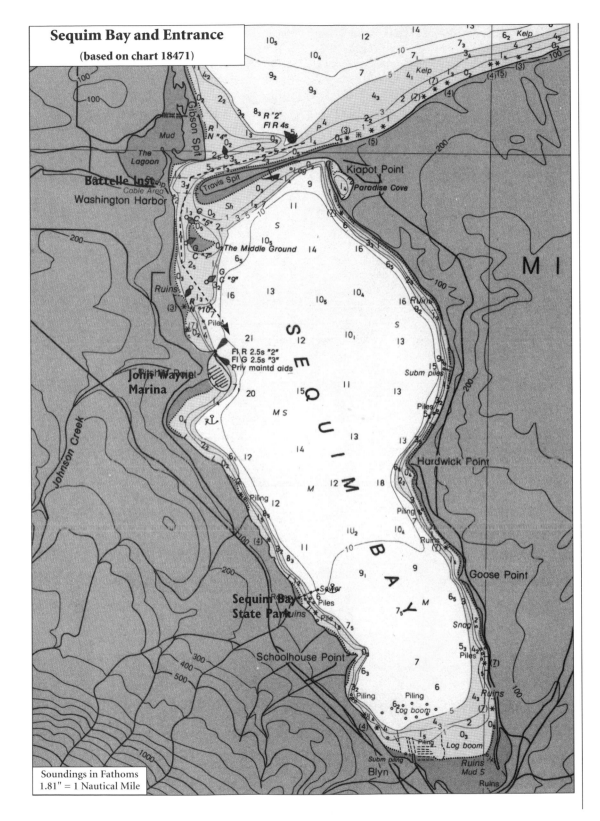

Sequim Bay and Entrance

(based on chart 18471)

Soundings in Fathoms
1.81" = 1 Nautical Mile

Most of the shoreline is private and gently sloped, with manicured lawns and an occasional dock. The foothills of the Olympics to the south are a patchwork of clear-cut logging. This area is not yet infested with tract homes, and the overall effect is of peaceful solitude.

Approaches. Because Travis and Gibson Spits overlap, you won't be able to see the entrance when approaching from the northwest. From this direction it's a good idea to aim slightly east, toward the middle of the Miller Peninsula's north shore, as tideflats extend from Dungeness Bay to Sequim Bay. Approaching Sequim Bay from the northeast, the main hazards are the shoals north and west of Protection Island. The entrance itself is narrow and winding, marked by buoys that must be closely followed. Begin by finding the two red buoys that parallel Travis Spit. The outermost (east) buoy is lighted; to find it in daylight, try looking against the slight rise of land on Travis Spit, near the headland of Kiapot Point. Leave both these buoys to starboard, staying as close to the center of the channel as

possible. Stay in mid-channel as you round Travis Spit, past the marine research center of the Battelle Institute. You'll then pick up three green can buoys and one red nun. As you wind past these, favor the west shore to avoid an area called "The Middle Ground" that bares at low tide. Watch your depth sounder, and expect shallowest water between southernmost green can "9" and red nun "10." Considerably deeper water lies just beyond.

It's a good idea to enter Sequim Bay on a rising tide. The *Coast Pilot* twice recommends you obtain local knowledge when entering, and warns that entrance buoys are occasionally towed under by strong currents. Certainly the shoals off Gibson and Travis Spits are continually shifting and reshaping.

In the language of the native S'Klallam Indians, Sequim means "quiet water," and the bay is aptly named. There is good anchorage almost anywhere, in about 5 to 10 fathoms with a mud bottom. Recommended sites are the John Wayne Marina at Pitship Point, the state park dock and mooring buoys north of Schoolhouse Point, and the areas nearby.

Cove Behind Travis Spit ★★★ [1] No Facilities

Charts: 18471

The sunset view from the northeast corner of Sequim Bay south of Travis Spit can be dramatic, and certainly the spit itself is beautiful, but as an anchorage this spot is not recommended. You are unprotected from the wind that invariably blows off the Strait of Juan de Fuca. There is virtually no shore access; the lagoon of Paradise Cove is private, and what

public land exists on Travis Spit lies outside Sequim Bay or is put off-limits by Battelle's marine research lab. The bottom is surprisingly steep, shallowing rapidly from 5 fathoms.

When approaching, beware of "The Middle Ground" shoal that lies between this cove and the entrance to Sequim Bay.

Sequim Bay State Park ★★★★ [2]

Charts: 18471

This 90-acre park north of Schoolhouse Point rises above a narrow beach, its waterfront limits bounded roughly by a launching ramp to

the north and a pier with a float to the south. From the water, the park seems densely wooded and undeveloped. Ashore, cedar-

Sequim Bay State Park's public pier and float. The mooring buoys are north (left) of the dock.

shadowed trails and roads wander through ingeniously sited recreation and camping areas.

Sequim Bay State Park is open year round.

Approaches. The most visible landmark is the launching ramp. The pier and float south is part of the park; the pier beyond is private. Between the state park mooring buoys and the shore, the bottom rises a bit too quickly for deep-draft vessels.

Anchorage, Moorings. Five mooring buoys parallel the shore, the middle two in deepest water. Fees are posted at the nearby dock, where a drop box for payment is located. The surrounding area is good anchorage, in mud between 5 and 10 fathoms. If you can tuck in to the south behind Schoolhouse Point you'll be more protected from the customary afternoon breeze off the Strait of Juan de Fuca, but you'll also be more exposed to the noise and lights of nearby Highway 101.

The park float itself, which is about 60 feet long, is recommended for shallow-draft vessels only.

Getting Ashore. Take your skiff to the park dock. There is a float next to the ramp, but this is for the convenience of those launching their boats and is best left uncluttered by dinghies.

For the Boat. No facilities for boats are available at the park. Fuel and some marine supplies can be purchased at the John Wayne Marina less than two miles north. Propane and gas are sold at the general store on the highway, 800 feet south of the park entrance.

For the Crew. Sequim Bay State Park is an ideal destination for a cruising family. Not only are the chances of dry weather greater here than in most areas of Puget Sound, but the park itself offers surprisingly varied on-shore recreation opportunities. Trails wander everywhere. There are play areas, picnic shelters, more than 80 campsites, restrooms with hot showers, and an amphitheater that features educational and entertainment videos. A walkway tunnel leads under Highway 101 to tennis courts and a ball field.

A general store 800 feet south of the park entrance has ice and a few groceries. A mile-and-a-half farther, at the south end of the bay, is the Jamestown S'Klallam Tribal Center. An art gallery features quality paintings, sculpture, weavings, and jewelry, as well as books and pamphlets describing the S'Klallam ("Strong People") who have lived in this area for thousands of years.

The nearest restaurant is about a half-mile north of the park entrance.

John Wayne Marina ★★★★

Charts: 18471

       [3] (anchorage) [5] (marina)

This beautifully designed marina at Pitship Point may come as a surprise compared to the rustic feel of Port Townsend or the industrial busyness of Port Angeles. The unlikely image of the cowboy hero John Wayne in Sequim Bay comes of the late actor's own passion for cruising Pacific Northwest waters. His boat, the *Wild Goose*, anchored here frequently. After his death, his family donated land to the Port of Port Angeles specifically for this marina. The result: well-groomed docks, landscaped public walkways, and a service building that rises gracefully from the gravel shore. The entire facility is polished without seeming primped, exclusive-looking without being so, and remarkably suited to its serene setting. The marina is completely protected by a stone jetty that encircles it like a scythe.

Approaches. Entrance to the harbor is at the north end of the circular jetty, between the privately maintained red and green day marks. The red mark on the point will be visible immediately upon entering Sequim Bay. Both marks are lighted at night. Pilings inside and outside the jetty indicate shoals; keep these to port as you enter the marina itself.

Anchorage, Moorings. The concrete guest float is immediately in front of you as you enter, with tie-ups on both sides. This outer float is also open to the public for fishing and crabbing. Additional guest moorage is directly beneath the harbormaster's office, which is located in the large blue-roofed service building. Total guest moorage capacity is about 22 boats.

If you prefer anchoring, the wide cove outside and south of the jetty offers protection from wind and swells in 5 to 10 fathoms. Take care to keep off the steep shelf. This anchorage has an unfortunate western view of the road, an RV park, and the marina parking lot, but in other directions the scene is open and lovely. You'll hear the highway noise from here more clearly than from the marina itself.

Getting Ashore. Guest floats in the marina are public. South of the breakwater, you can beach your skiff in the area adjacent to the marina parking lot.

For the Boat. The fuel dock is inside the jetty, just west of the outer guest float. Water is available on all guest floats, power on some. Talk to the harbormaster if you need electricity. Limited marine supplies are available at the marina store. One of the garbage and dock-cart storage areas accepts waste oil and provides recycling bins for aluminum and cardboard. A small-boat repair yard is two miles north, on the main road.

For the Crew. Showers and a laundromat are located in the main service building, and limited groceries in the marina store upstairs. Here also, on ground level, is a café, its decor given over to John Wayne memorabilia. It's a long walk northwest into the town of Sequim, some three miles or more along West Sequim Bay Road to the sprawling strip of malls and motels. More pleasant is the walk along the marina promenade, inhaling the fragrance of honeysuckle in summer. Pitship Point itself, at the head of the outer guest float ramp, is a public park with picnic tables and paths. Picnic tables are also near the south parking lot.

Dungeness Bay ★★★★ No Facilities

Charts: 18465, 18471

Dungeness Bay lies under the curve of slender, five-mile-long Dungeness Spit. One of the longest in the world, the spit takes its name not from the local crab but from the English town of Dungeness that came to mind when Captain Vancouver surveyed the area in 1792. Only the lighthouse still bears the name New Dungeness. The S'Klallam Indians used the spit as a lookout for whales and enemy tribes crossing the strait. Tugs and other commercial boats now use it as a temporary haven from storms on the strait.

In fair weather this is a spectacular spot—desolate, open to the east, with views south to the Olympic Mountains and west to the Strait of Juan de Fuca. The ocean has a real presence here. Even on a calm day the surf pounds on the northwest beach, and the gravel, sucked out with the retreating waves, emits a muffled growl. A confusion of enormous bleached logs is piled thickly on the spit itself. Boats of almost any size will seem small and vulnerable here. And with reason: Beautiful Dungeness Bay—so exposed and shallow—can be a dangerous place.

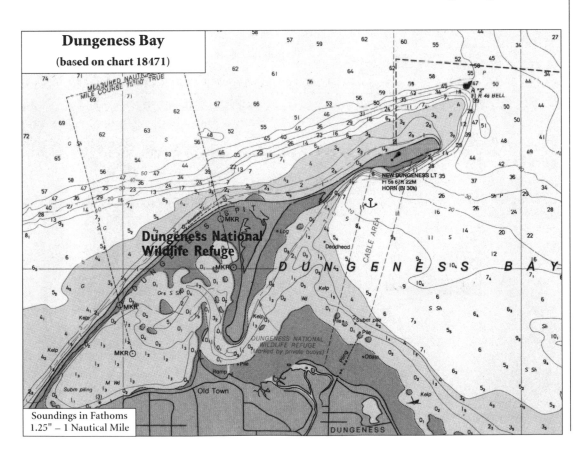

Dungeness Bay
(based on chart 18471)

Dungeness National Wildlife Refuge

NEW DUNGENESS LT 35
Fl 5s 67ft 22M
HORN (Bl 30s)

DUNGENESS BAY

DUNGENESS NATIONAL WILDLIFE REFUGE
(Marked by private buoys)

Old Town

DUNGENESS

Soundings in Fathoms
1.25" – 1 Nautical Mile

Dungeness Bay from the spit. Clouds are piled against the Olympic Mountains.

Approaches. From the west, look for the easternmost end of the trees; this is where the spit starts. You may feel the spit before you see it, as wakes that bounce back from its shallows. As you approach, the spit itself will emerge faintly, like a line of wind on the horizon, with a lighthouse on the far tip. A red buoy about a mile north and east of the lighthouse more accurately marks the true end of the spit. Aim north of this buoy, and guard against an almost mesmerizing drift toward the spit, especially under sail. Boats can and do sail right onto the beach near the lighthouse, a costly mistake on a falling tide in worsening weather.

When approaching from the southeast, head directly north in 10 fathoms or more to avoid the extensive west shoals. From Sequim Bay, a good feature to sight on in clear weather is the high west shore of San Juan Island across the strait. Boaters arriving from the east as well as the southeast will first see the lighthouse and keeper's residence almost as a mirage floating on the strait.

Favor the spit (north) side as you enter the bay; the mainland side shallows rapidly and is foul with kelp and submerged piles. Watch for crab pots.

Anchorage. For such a broad bay, suitable anchorage for all but the most shallow-draft boats is relatively constricted and surprisingly deep—in about 10 fathoms west of the lighthouse and cable area. The bottom shelf is steep, so keep enough distance from shore to stay afloat through shifts of wind and tide. Old crabbing gear that can snag an anchor lies below.

Getting Ashore. The shoreline is public, but bear in mind that this is a National Wildlife Refuge. Take care not to disturb feeding and resting birds, as this is an important stop for migrating waterfowl such as black brant. Access to shore requires a permit, available for a fee at the park entrance uphill from the base of the spit, some five miles away. A more convenient method is to purchase a Duck Stamp ahead of time at any U.S. Post Office.

A small strip of public land on the west side

of Cline Spit, which protrudes from the mainland, is a county park. On the east side of Cline Spit, north of Old Town on the mainland, is a public ramp where you can find a telephone, restrooms, and a retail outlet for oysters and clams.

Things to Do. Dungeness Spit is a wildlife refuge, not a park. Please respect this fragile environment, and be mindful that an activity as innocent as walking may disturb vegetation critical to the existence of the spit itself. Use special care during spring, when birds are nesting. Activities such as jogging, kite flying, board sailing, and jet skiing disturb wildlife and should be done elsewhere. Beach fires are not permitted. Visitors are welcome to fish, catch crab, and dig clams, but all oysters are privately owned and may not be harvested by the public.

The New Dungeness Lighthouse, though automated, is still occupied. Tours are available Thursday through Sunday. It's worth the beach hike to the lighthouse if only to marvel at the tidy residence that seems to defy the wildness with its white picket fence.

The Dungeness National Wildlife Refuge is currently developing a new public-use plan for managing the spit that will maintain its integrity as a refuge in a region where the human population is growing dramatically.

Port Angeles ★★★  (anchorage) (marina) All Facilities

Charts: 18465, **18468**

Port Angeles backs up against the Olympic Mountains from a deep harbor protected by the sand spit of Ediz Hook. Even from a distance it has a determined look. Stout pilot boats charge into the strait and back again, rushing to rendezvous with ocean freighters. The harbor is crowded with cranes, mills, and log booms. The prevailing west wind off the strait blows the white smoke of the mill stacks inland, horizontally. After the emptiness of the strait, all this industrial muscle can be an abrupt surprise.

Port Angeles is a small city, but a real one. It exists more for timber than tourists. You can learn a lot about harvesting trees here without ever leaving the waterfront. Entire forests of logs are piled around you on the harbor breakwater, waiting to be exported, or peeled and flattened into plywood. The smell of sawdust blows from the giant golden mounds surrounding the paper mill. Pleasure boaters can easily feel out of place here.

Approaches. From the north and east, the tall, striped red-and-white stack of the pulp mill is visible for miles. This stack is about a mile east of Port Angeles; heading for it puts you on a

The Port Angeles City Pier and waterfront park.

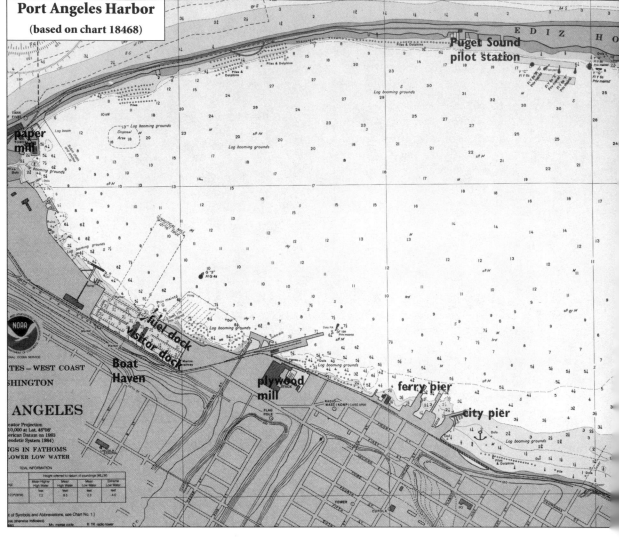

good course to clear the end of Ediz Hook. Once past the red roofs of the Coast Guard hangar and the rotating vessel-traffic tower, head west of the shorter, lone, center stack. Inside Ediz Hook, watch for crab pots and log booms. The *Coast Pilot* urges extra caution due to submerged deadheads.

Anchorage, Moorings. The entrance to the Boat Haven is behind a timber breakwater, just beyond green buoy "3." The masts of boats moored in the marina can be located against the west shore, between the stacks of logs belonging to the plywood mill and the mountain of sawdust belonging to the paper mill.

The visitors' "transit float," to port as you enter the Boat Haven, is marked. Strong gusts off the strait can make turning and docking difficult. Register by filling out an envelope at the head of the dock, or walk over to the jetty to pay the harbormaster directly.

The marina on Ediz Hook is also operated by the Port, but has no visitor moorage. Many of the charter fishing vessels operate from this site.

If you prefer to be closer to downtown Port Angeles at the City Pier, head east of the lone center stack (rather than west as you would for the Boat Haven). The cream-colored, peaked roof of the blue viewing tower marks the end of

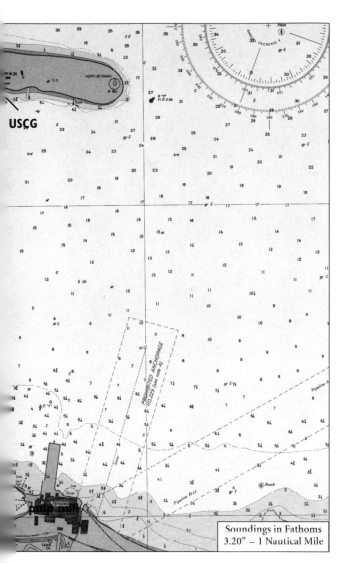

Soundings in Fathoms
3.20" – 1 Nautical Mile

For the Boat. Complete marine facilities are available at the Boat Haven, including a 125-ton marine railway and a tidal grid. There's probably nothing you can't buy or get repaired in Port Angeles, but keep in mind that industries look more toward Highway 101 than to the harbor, so you may have to hunt a bit for what you need.

The fuel dock is just inside the Boat Haven, to port as you enter.

For the Crew. Restrooms and showers are located at the head of the Boat Haven visitors' float. A few steps beyond is the Fisherman's Wharf Café, with its U-shaped counter that promotes cross-conversation (topics are fishing and timber). A convenience store is a short walk east of the harbor. For more restaurants and a wide range of stores, it's about a half-hour walk east into town. The supermarket is a mile away from the Boat Haven, uphill from downtown on Lincoln Street, across from the courthouse. A laundromat is two blocks east of the supermarket.

Things to Do. From the Boat Haven, follow Marine Drive to Front Street and into downtown Port Angeles—about a half-hour walk. The City Pier has a Marine Lab that's especially attractive to children; you can look an octopus or wolf eel in the eye, or stroke a sand dollar. There's a viewing tower to climb, a sandy beach, playground equipment, and picnic tables. A map of the area on the side of the restroom building will help you get your bearings. The Clallam County Museum is about four blocks south of the pier on Lincoln Street; near the museum is the municipal swimming pool.

A passenger/auto ferry makes round trips daily from downtown Port Angeles to Victoria, British Columbia.

For an overlook of the harbor, climb the stairs from Oak or Laurel Street. From this vantage you can easily understand why the city raised itself 14 feet from sea level in the early 1900s. Before this was done, runoff from the surrounding hills combined with high tide to wash the streets with mud and sewage. Some of the old sea-level storefronts

the City Pier. Moorage is on the east (inner) side. Moorage at the concrete floats is free for 24 hours for boats of 40 feet and less. The float design makes it difficult for boats much over 30 feet to tie up comfortably. Protection from westerly winds is best when the Coast Guard cutter is docked outside the pier. Because of weather, floats are removed after Labor Day, replaced before Memorial Day.

The only suitable anchorage for small craft in Port Angeles Harbor is south of the City Pier. A few buoys are placed here. It may be difficult to find water deep enough for anchoring that is out of the surge. In any case, this is a fair-weather anchorage only.

The view from the visitor float inside the Port Angeles Boat Haven.

are still intact beneath the sidewalks.

Port Angeles celebrates Fourth of July with a fireworks display from the City Pier. A Derby Days Festival is held mid-August, and the annual salmon derby around Labor Day.

I n writing this book I benefited greatly from the research and works of others.

The following are books I used and recommend.

History

Buerge, David. *Chief Seattle*. Seattle: Sasquatch Books, 1992.

A compilation of historical photos and selections from Chief Seattle's famous 1854 speech.

Buerge, David. *Mount Rainier*. Seattle: Sasquatch Books, 1992.

Historical photos, Indian legends, and excerpts from the accounts of explorers and mountain climbers.

Burn, June. *Living High*. Friday Harbor, Wash.: Griffin Bay Bookstore, 1992.

A high-spirited, true story of a couple who homesteaded in the San Juan Islands in the 1930s.

Burn, June. *100 Days in the San Juans*. Friday Harbor, Wash.: Longhouse Printcrafters and Publishers, 1983.

A series of articles written in 1946 that chronicle 100 days of rowing and sailing in the San Juans. Gives a decidedly fresh (and at times familiar) view of this popular cruising area. Out of stock indefinitely, but available through some libraries.

Denny, Arthur A. *Pioneer Days on Puget Sound*. Fairfield, Wash.: Ye Galleon Press, 1965.

A description of early Seattle days written by one of the city's founders.

Fisher, Robin. *Vancouver's Voyage*. Seattle: University of Washington Press, 1992.

Illustrated with stunning photos and original engravings, this book describes Vancouver's methods, achievements, and shortcomings, and describes the expedition's interaction with native cultures.

Hilson, Stephen E. *Exploring Puget Sound & British Columbia*. Michigan: Van Winkle Publishing Co., 1975.

Now sadly out of print, this chartbook is richly annotated with historic notes and excerpts from the journals of early explorers.

Kirk, Ruth and Alexander, Carmela. *Exploring Washington's Past: A Road Guide to History*. Seattle: University of Washington Press, 1990.

Historical vignettes of almost every community in Washington State. Though written for those who cruise by land, it is informative and entertaining for boaters as well.

Kruckeberg, Arthur R. *The Natural History of Puget Sound Country*. Seattle: University of Washington Press, 1991

Considered the premier reference book on the natural history of this area. A clearly and beautifully written synthesis of the sound's geology, meteorology, biology, and human history.

Morgan, Murray. *Puget's Sound: A Narrative of Early Tacoma and the Southern Sound*. Seattle: University of Washington Press, 1979.

This lively history of South Sound—from Vancouver's exploration to the present—reads like a novel.

Morgan, Murray. *Skid Road: An Informal Portrait of Seattle*. Seattle: University of Washington Press, 1982.

Considered one of the best-known and best-written (if somewhat irreverent) books on the subject.

Morgan, Lane and Morgan, Murray. *Seattle: A Pictorial History*. Norfolk, Va.: Donning Co., 1982.

Historical photos interspersed with brief narratives.

RECOMMENDED READING

Nelson, Sharlene P. and Ted W. *Umbrella Guide to Washington Lighthouses*. Friday Harbor, Wash.: Umbrella Books, 1990.

Information and anecdotes about all the lighthouses in Washington state, and the men and women who operated them.

Miles, John C. *Koma Kulshan: The Story of Mount Baker*. Seattle: Mountaineers, 1984.

The human history of Mount Baker, including Indian legends, accounts of early explorers, prospectors, and the first ascent.

Satterfield, Archie and Crowley, Walt. *West Coast Workboats: An Illustrated Guide to Work Vessels from Bristol Bay to San Diego*. Seattle: Sasquatch Books, 1992.

Fishing and other working vessels, explained with drawings and text.

Suquamish Museum. *The Eyes of Chief Seattle*. Suquamish, Wash.: Suquamish Museum, 1985.

Historical photos and narratives of tribal life, from European contact to the present. Includes descriptions of traditional methods of food-gathering and preparation, fishing, canoe-carving, basket-making, and weaving.

Warren, James R. *Where the Mountains Meet the Sea: An Illustrated History of Puget Sound*. Northridge, Ca.: Windsor Publications, 1986.

Briskly paced narrative, with abundant historic photos and old maps.

Weather

Renner, Jeff. *Northwest Marine Weather: From the Columbia River to Cape Scott*. Seattle: Mountaineers. 1993.

Clear explanations of how the weather is "made" all over the Pacific Northwest coast, with advice on how to predict it.

Field Guides

There are numerous guides to the animals of Puget Sound. The three I use regularly are:

National Geographic Society. *Field Guide to the Birds of North America* (Second Edition). Washington, D.C., 1987.

Meinkoth, Norman A. *The Audubon Society Field Guide to North American Seashore Creatures*. New York: Alfred A Knopf, 1981.

Osborne, Calambokidis, and Dorsey. *A Guide to Marine Mammals of Greater Puget Sound*. Friday Harbor, Wash.: The Whale Museum, 1988.

Other Guides

Mueller, Marge and Ted. *Afoot & Afloat* series: *South Puget Sound* (1991); *Middle Puget Sound* (1990); *North Puget Sound* (1988); *The San Juan Islands* (1988). Seattle: Mountaineers.

Written primarily for hikers, kayakers, and canoeists, these books describe beaches, towns, trails, and parks. Abundantly illustrated with photos and freehand maps.

Scott, James W. and Reuling, Melly A. *Washington Public Shore Guide: Marine Waters*. Seattle: University of Washington Press, 1986.

A list of all the public tidelands, beaches, and street ends in the state, with overview maps and tables.

Free Booklets and Guides

Marine Yellow Pages—Boaters' Directory.
Published yearly by Kannberg & Associates of Kirkland, Wash. Available free at most boating supply stores, marinas, and port offices.

Puget Sound Public Shellfish Sites.
Published by, and available from, the Washington State Department of Fisheries, Department of Natural Resources, and Parks and Recreation Commission. Includes information about fishing and shellfishing, as well as maps showing the location of public tidelands, launching ramps, fishing piers, fishing reefs, and sewage pumpouts. Available at most state park campgrounds, or through DNR Photo & Map Sales, P.O. Box 47031, Olympia, WA 98504-7031, telephone (360) 902-1234.

Washington State Parks and Recreation Commission. *Washington State Boater's Guide.* Seattle: Outdoor Empire Publishing, 1992.
A compact booklet with information about boating registration, regulations, safety equipment, and rules of the road. Includes a list of sewage pumpout stations. Available at most state parks, wherever boat licenses are sold, and from local marine patrol units. You can also get a copy from: Boating Safety Program, Washington State Parks, 7150 Cleanwater Lane, Olympia, WA 98504-2654, telephone (360) 586-2166.

48° North
A free monthly yachting magazine that publishes an update on saltwater marine state park facilities, and a listing of yacht clubs and boating clubs, in its spring issues. The magazine is available at most marine supply stores. This magazine also publishes a monthly calendar of boating events.

Northwest Yachting
This magazine publishes an updated listing of fuel docks, marinas, and haulout facilities each year in its spring issues. The magazine is free and available at most marine supply stores. Back issues can be purchased by calling (206) 789-9116.

The following tidal current charts cover two areas of Puget Sound: the south part, roughly from Olympia to Blake Island, and the north part, from Blake Island to Point Wilson. These charts are taken from the 1973 (third) editions of *Tidal Current Charts* published by the National Oceanic and Atmospheric Administration. In this book, 10 charts (rather than the original 12) are reproduced for the south part, and 10 for the north.

Current directions are shown with arrows. Current velocity is shown to the nearest tenth of a knot when the maximum current is 3.8 to 4.1 knots at The Narrows (for the southern portion), and when the maximum current is 2.4 to 2.6 knots at Bush Point (for the northern portion). At other times, make corrections using the tables below.

Factors for Correcting Speeds—Puget Sound, Southern Part

When the predicted speed in The Narrows (north end) is—	Multiply speed on chart by—
Knots:	*Factor*
0.2—0.5	0.1
0.6—0.9	0.2
1.0—1.3	0.3
1.4—1.7	0.4
1.8—2.1	0.5
2.2—2.5	0.6
2.6—2.9	0.7
3.0—3.3	0.8
3.4—3.7	0.9
3.8—4.1	1.0
4.2—4.5	1.1
4.6—4.9	1.2
5.0—5.3	1.3
5.4—5.7	1.4
5.8—6.1	1.5

CURRENT CHARTS

Factors for Correcting Speeds—Puget Sound, Northern Part

Flood factors			Ebb factors	
For use with speeds accompanied by solid arrows			For use with speeds accompanied by dashed arrows	
When predicted "Maximum flood" speed (knots) off Bush Point is—	Multiply speed on chart by—		When predicted "Maximum ebb" speed (knots) off Bush Point is—	Multiply speed on chart by—
	Usual factor	Special factor "a"		Factor
(*)_____	0. 0	0. 2	0. 3–0. 4_____	0. 1
0. 3_____	0. 1	0. 3	0. 5–0. 8_____	0. 2
0. 4–0. 6_____	0. 2	0. 4	0. 9–1. 1_____	0. 3
0. 7–0. 8_____	0. 3	0. 5	1. 2–1. 4_____	0. 4
0. 9–1. 1_____	0. 4	0. 6	1. 5–1. 8_____	0. 5
1. 2–1. 3_____	0. 5	0. 6		
			1. 9–2. 1_____	0. 6
1. 4–1. 6_____	0. 6	0. 6	2. 2–2. 4_____	0. 7
1. 7–1. 8_____	0. 7	0. 7	2. 5–2. 8_____	0. 8
1. 9–2. 1_____	0. 8	0. 8	2. 9–3. 1_____	0. 9
2. 2–2. 3_____	0. 9	0. 9	3. 2–3. 4_____	1. 0
2. 4–2. 6_____	1. 0	1. 0		
			3. 5–3. 7_____	1. 1
2. 7–2. 8 _____	1. 1	1. 1	3. 8–4. 1_____	1. 2
2. 9–3. 1_____	1. 2	1. 2	4. 2–4. 4_____	1. 3
3. 2–3. 3_____	1. 3	1. 3	4. 5–4. 7_____	1. 4
3. 4–3. 6_____	1. 4	1. 4		
3. 7–3. 8_____	1. 5	1. 5		

NOTE: if arrows are solid, obtain the predicted speed of the nearest "Maximum flood" from the current tables. If the arrows are dashed, obtain the predicted speed of the nearest "Maximum ebb" from the current tables. Use factor "a" only when the speed on the tidal current chart is followed by the letter "a."

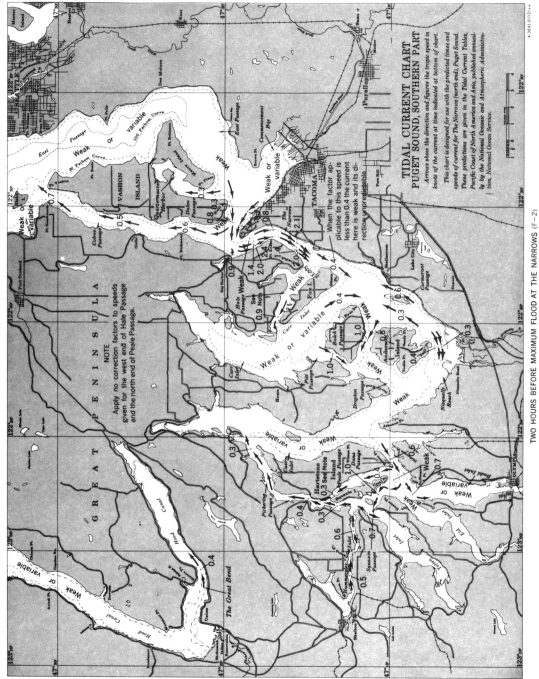

TWO HOURS BEFORE MAXIMUM FLOOD AT THE NARROWS (F-2)

For tables of
adjustment and
information on
how to use this
chart, see page 374.

376

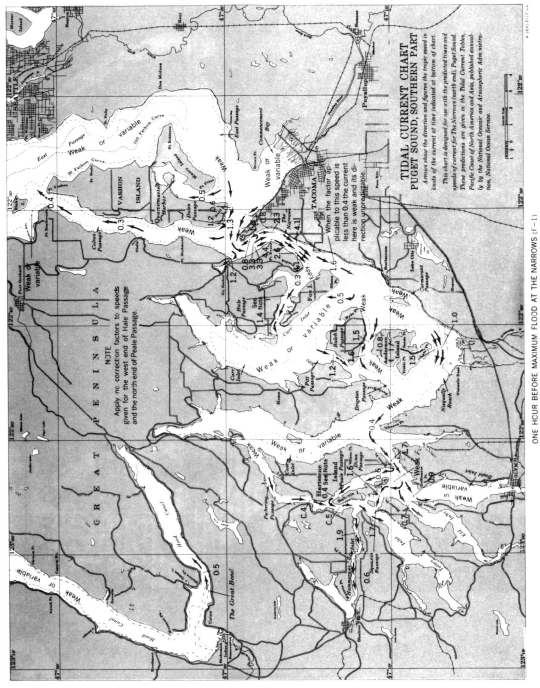

TIDAL CURRENT CHART
PUGET SOUND, SOUTHERN PART

Arrows show the direction and figures the tropic speed in
knots of the current at time indicated at bottom of chart.

This chart is designed for use with the predicted times and
speeds of current for The Narrows (north end), Puget Sound.
These predictions are given in the Tidal Current Tables,
Pacific Coast of North America and Asia, published annually by the National Oceanic and Atmospheric Administration, National Ocean Service.

NOTE

Apply no correction factors to speeds
given for the west end of Hale Passage
and the north end of Peale Passage.

When the factor ap-
plicable to this speed is
less than 0.4 the current
here is weak and its di-
rection unpredictable.

ONE HOUR BEFORE MAXIMUM FLOOD AT THE NARROWS (F−1)

For tables of
adjustment and
information on
how to use this
chart, see page 374.

TIDAL CURRENT CHARTS—SOUTHERN PART

377

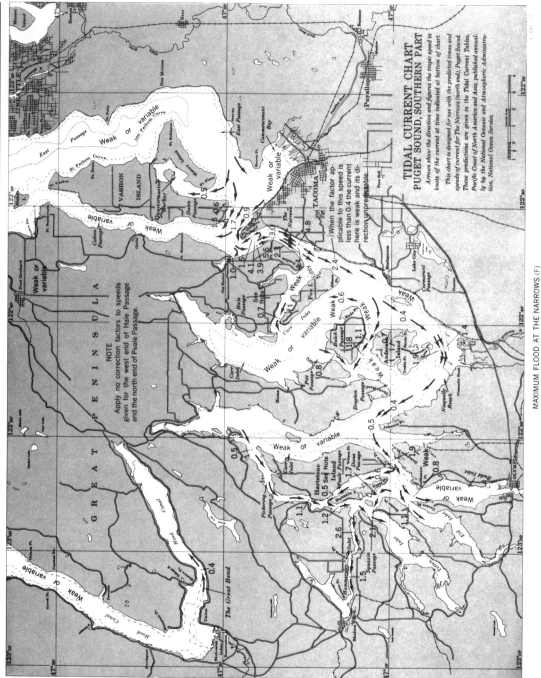

TIDAL CURRENT CHART
PUGET SOUND, SOUTHERN PART

Arrows show the direction and figures the tropic speed in knots of the current at time indicated at bottom of chart. This chart is designed for use with the predicted times and speeds of current for The Narrows (north end), Puget Sound. These predictions are given in the Tidal Current Tables, Pacific Coast of North America and Asia, published annually by the National Oceanic and Atmospheric Administration, National Ocean Service.

NOTE
Apply no correction factors to speeds given for the west end of Hale Passage and the north end of Peale Passage.

When the factor applicable to this speed is less than 0.4 the current here is weak and its direction unpredictable.

MAXIMUM FLOOD AT THE NARROWS (F)

For tables of adjustment and information on how to use this chart, see page 374.

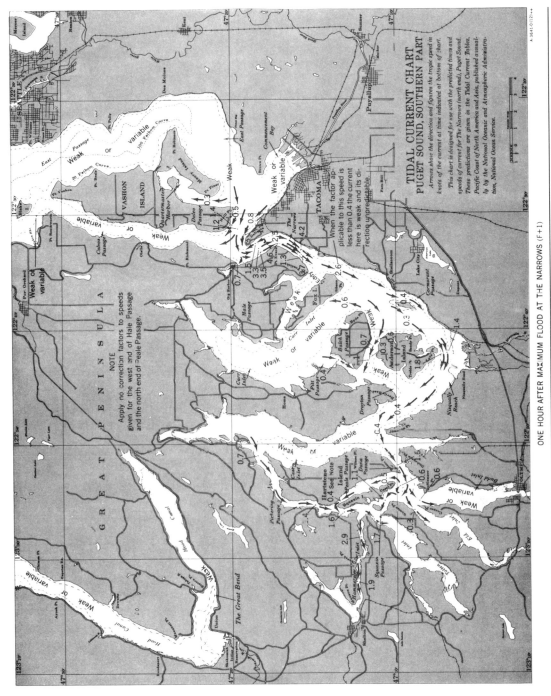

TIDAL CURRENT CHART
PUGET SOUND, SOUTHERN PART

Arrows show the direction and figures the tropic speed in knots of the current at time indicated at bottom of chart.

This chart is designed for use with the predicted times and speeds of current for The Narrows (north end), Puget Sound. These predictions are given in the Tidal Current Tables, Pacific Coast of North America and Asia, published annually by the National Oceanic and Atmospheric Administration, National Ocean Service.

ONE HOUR AFTER MAXIMUM FLOOD AT THE NARROWS (F+1)

For tables of adjustment and information on how to use this chart, see page 374.

TIDAL CURRENT CHARTS—SOUTHERN PART

379

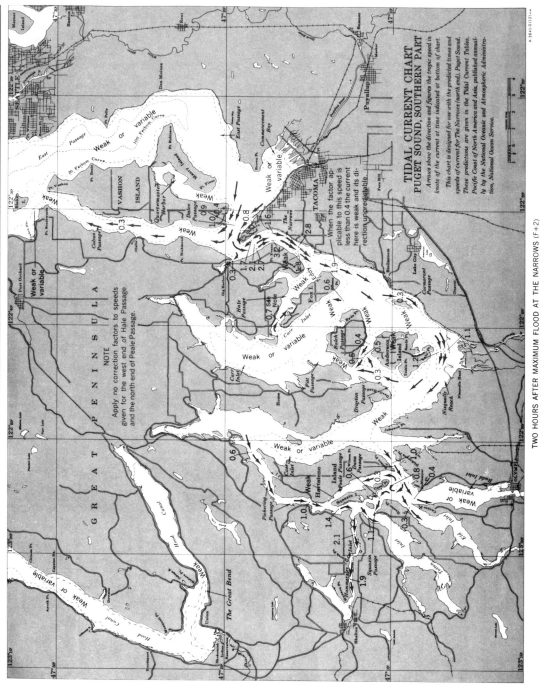

TIDAL CURRENT CHART
PUGET SOUND, SOUTHERN PART

Arrows show the direction and figures the tropic speed in knots of the current at time indicated at bottom of chart.

This chart is designed for use with the predicted times and speeds of current for The Narrows (north end), Puget Sound. These predictions are given in the Tidal Current Tables, Pacific Coast of North America and Asia, published annually by the National Oceanic and Atmospheric Administration, National Ocean Service.

A-3641-0127++

NOTE

Apply no correction factors to speeds given for the west end of Hale Passage and the north end of Peale Passage.

When the factor applicable to this speed is less than 0.4 the current here is weak and its direction unpredictable.

TWO HOURS AFTER MAXIMUM FLOOD AT THE NARROWS (F+2)

For tables of adjustment and information on how to use this chart, see page 374.

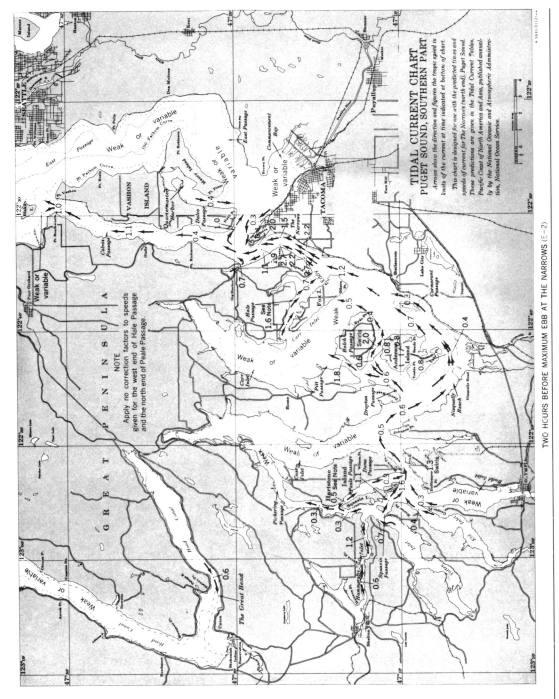

TWO HOURS BEFORE MAXIMUM EBB AT THE NARROWS (E–2)

TIDAL CURRENT CHARTS—SOUTHERN PART

For tables of
adjustment and
information on
how to use this
chart, see page 374.

381

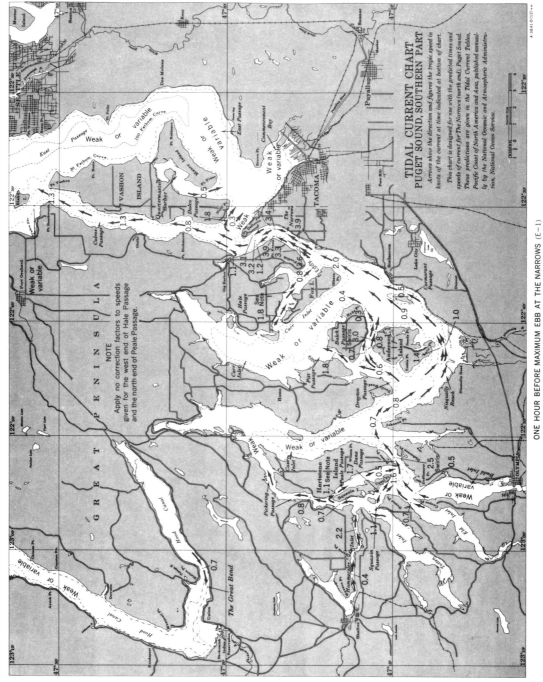

TIDAL CURRENT CHART
PUGET SOUND, SOUTHERN PART

Arrows show the direction and figures the tropic speed in knots of the current at time indicated at bottom of chart.

This chart is designed for use with the predicted times and speeds of current for The Narrows (north end), Puget Sound. These predictions are given in the Tidal Current Tables, Pacific Coast of North America and Asia, published annually by the National Oceanic and Atmospheric Administration, National Ocean Service.

ONE HOUR BEFORE MAXIMUM EBB AT THE NARROWS (E-1)

For tables of adjustment and information on how to use this chart, see page 374.

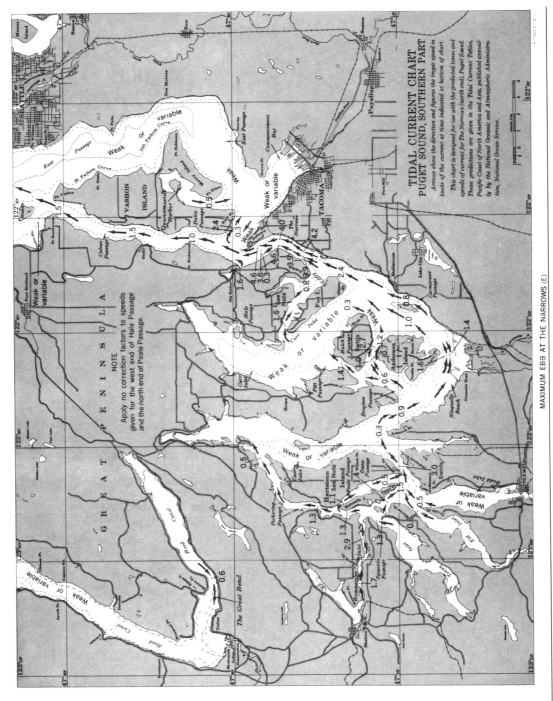

MAXIMUM EBB AT THE NARROWS (E)

For tables of
adjustment and
information on
how to use this
chart, see page 374.

TIDAL CURRENT CHARTS—SOUTHERN PART

383

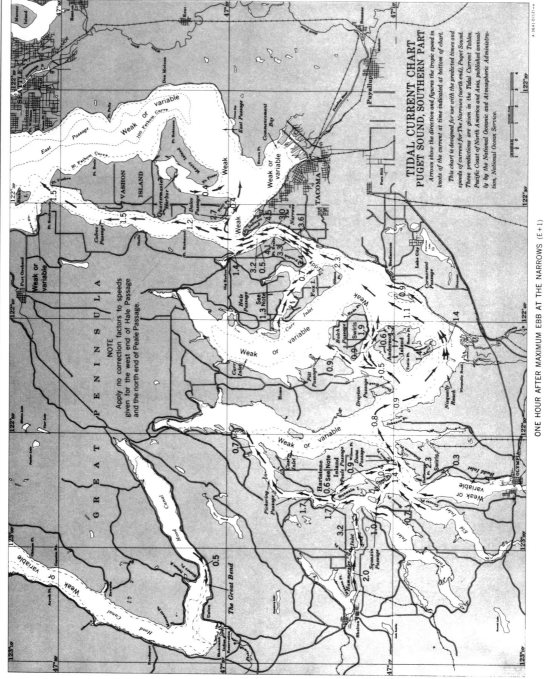

TIDAL CURRENT CHART
PUGET SOUND, SOUTHERN PART

Arrows show the direction and figures the tropic speed in knots of the current at time indicated at bottom of chart.

This chart is designed for use with the predicted times and speeds of current for The Narrows (north end), Puget Sound. These predictions are given in the Tidal Current Tables, Pacific Coast of North America and Asia, published annually by the National Oceanic and Atmospheric Administration, National Ocean Service.

ONE HOUR AFTER MAXIMUM EBB AT THE NARROWS (E+1)

For tables of
adjustment and
information on
how to use this
chart, see page 374.

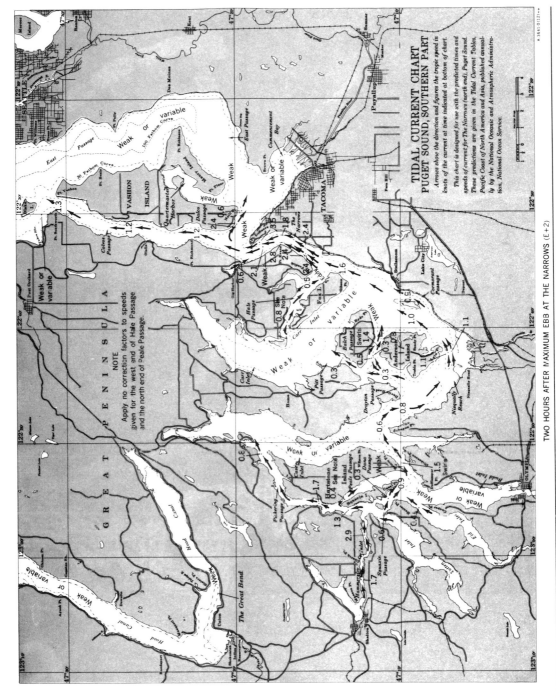

TIDAL CURRENT CHART
PUGET SOUND, SOUTHERN PART

Arrows show the direction and figures the tropic speed in knots of the current at time indicated at bottom of chart.

This chart is designed for use with the predicted times and speeds of current for The Narrows (north end), Puget Sound. These predictions are given in the Tidal Current Tables, Pacific Coast of North America and Asia, published annually by the National Oceanic and Atmospheric Administration, National Ocean Service.

NOTE

Apply no correction factors to speeds given for the west end of Hale Passage and the north end of Peale Passage.

TWO HOURS AFTER MAXIMUM EBB AT THE NARROWS (E+2)

TIDAL CURRENT CHARTS—SOUTHERN PART

For tables of adjustment and information on how to use this chart, see page 374.

385

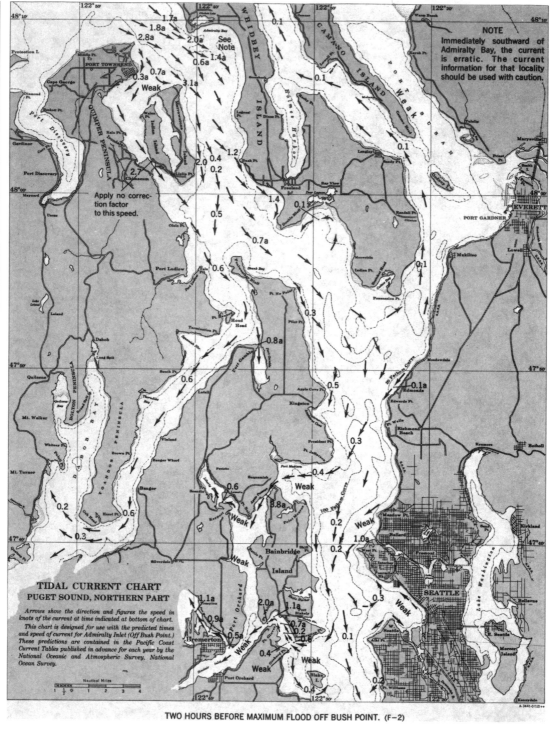

TIDAL CURRENT CHART
PUGET SOUND, NORTHERN PART

Arrows show the direction and figures the speed in knots of the current at time indicated at bottom of chart.

This chart is designed for use with the predicted times and speed of current for Admiralty Inlet (Off Bush Point.) These predictions are contained in the Pacific Coast Current Tables published in advance for each year by the National Oceanic and Atmospheric Survey, National Ocean Survey.

NOTE
Immediately southward of Admiralty Bay, the current is erratic. The current information for that locality should be used with caution.

Apply no correction factor to this speed.

TWO HOURS BEFORE MAXIMUM FLOOD OFF BUSH POINT. (F–2)

For tables of adjustment and information on how to use this chart, see page 375.

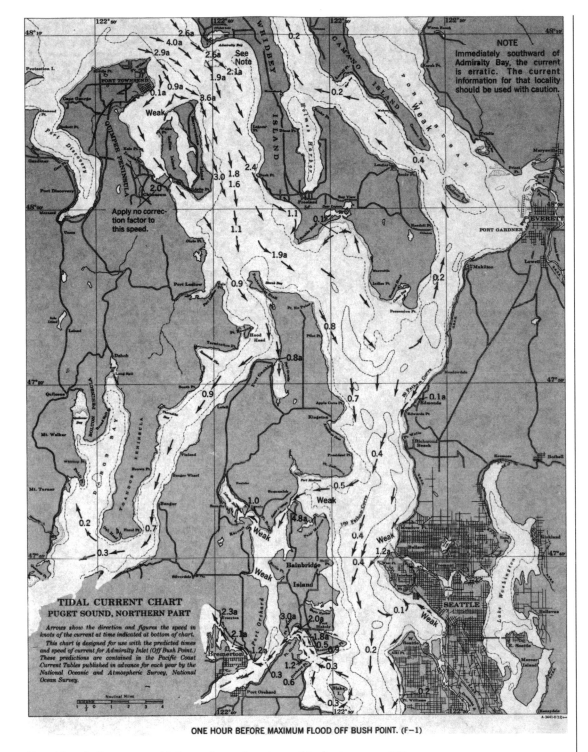

NOTE
Immediately southward of Admiralty Bay, the current is erratic. The current information for that locality should be used with caution.

TIDAL CURRENT CHART
PUGET SOUND, NORTHERN PART

Arrows show the direction and figures the speed in knots of the current at time indicated at bottom of chart.

This chart is designed for use with the predicted times and speed of current for Admiralty Inlet (Off Bush Point.) These predictions are contained in the Pacific Coast Current Tables published in advance for each year by the National Oceanic and Atmospheric Survey, National Ocean Survey.

Apply no correction factor to this speed.

ONE HOUR BEFORE MAXIMUM FLOOD OFF BUSH POINT. (F–1)

For tables of adjustment and information on how to use this chart, see page 375.

387

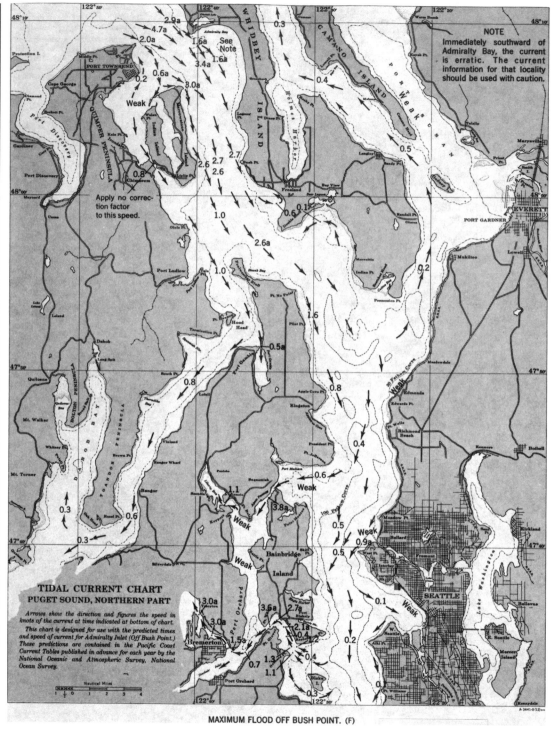

NOTE

Immediately southward of Admiralty Bay, the current is erratic. The current information for that locality should be used with caution.

TIDAL CURRENT CHART
PUGET SOUND, NORTHERN PART

Arrows show the direction and figures the speed in knots of the current at time indicated at bottom of chart. This chart is designed for use with the predicted times and speed of current for Admiralty Inlet (Off Bush Point.) These predictions are contained in the Pacific Coast Current Tables published in advance for each year by the National Oceanic and Atmospheric Survey, National Ocean Survey.

Apply no correction factor to this speed.

Nautical Miles

MAXIMUM FLOOD OFF BUSH POINT. (F)

For tables of adjustment and information on how to use this chart, see page 375.

388

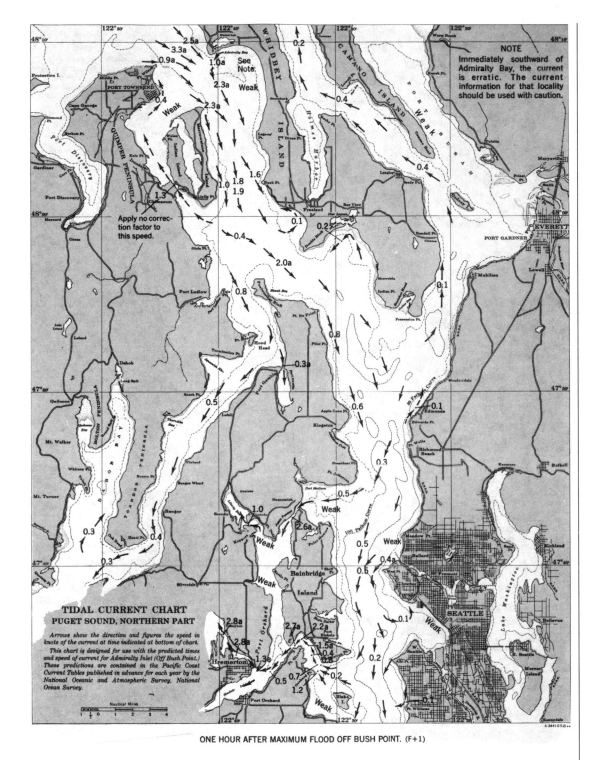

NOTE
Immediately southward of Admiralty Bay, the current is erratic. The current information for that locality should be used with caution.

Apply no correction factor to this speed.

TIDAL CURRENT CHART
PUGET SOUND, NORTHERN PART

Arrows show the direction and figures the speed in knots of the current at time indicated at bottom of chart.

This chart is designed for use with the predicted times and speed of current for Admiralty Inlet (Off Bush Point.) These predictions are contained in the Pacific Coast Current Tables published in advance for each year by the National Oceanic and Atmospheric Survey, National Ocean Survey.

ONE HOUR AFTER MAXIMUM FLOOD OFF BUSH POINT. (F+1)

For tables of adjustment and information on how to use this chart, see page 375.

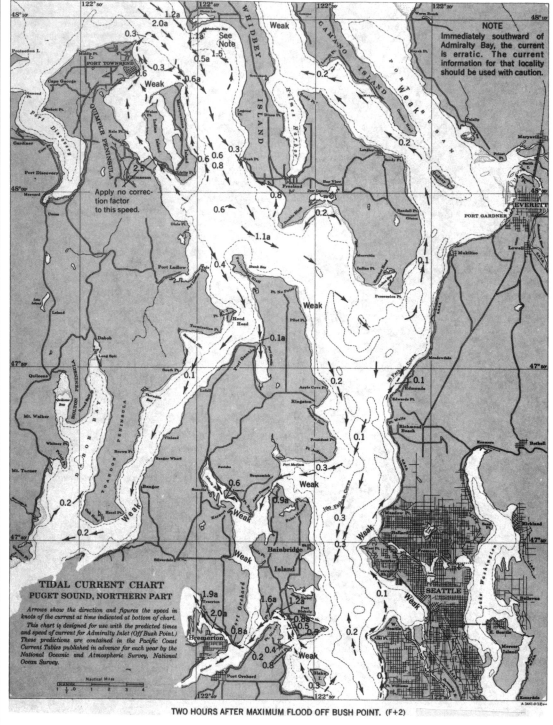

NOTE

Immediately southward of Admiralty Bay, the current is erratic. The current information for that locality should be used with caution.

Apply no correction factor to this speed.

TIDAL CURRENT CHART
PUGET SOUND, NORTHERN PART

Arrows show the direction and figures the speed in knots of the current at time indicated at bottom of chart.

This chart is designed for use with the predicted times and speed of current for Admiralty Inlet (Off Bush Point.) These predictions are contained in the Pacific Coast Current Tables published in advance for each year by the National Oceanic and Atmospheric Survey, National Ocean Survey.

Nautical Miles

TWO HOURS AFTER MAXIMUM FLOOD OFF BUSH POINT. (F+2)

For tables of adjustment and information on how to use this chart, see page 375.

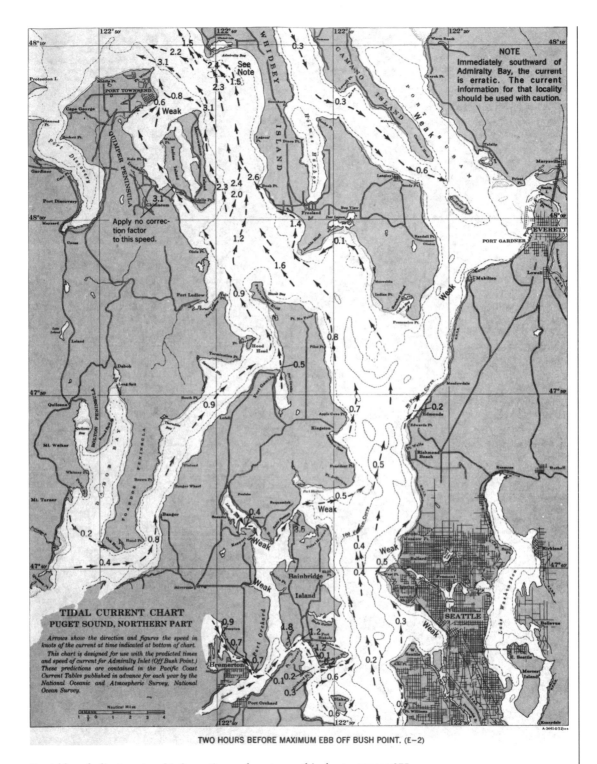

NOTE
Immediately southward of Admiralty Bay, the current is erratic. The current information for that locality should be used with caution.

Apply no correction factor to this speed.

TIDAL CURRENT CHART
PUGET SOUND, NORTHERN PART

Arrows show the direction and figures the speed in knots of the current at time indicated at bottom of chart.

This chart is designed for use with the predicted times and speed of current for Admiralty Inlet (Off Bush Point.) These predictions are contained in the Pacific Coast Current Tables published in advance for each year by the National Oceanic and Atmospheric Survey, National Ocean Survey.

Nautical Miles

TWO HOURS BEFORE MAXIMUM EBB OFF BUSH POINT. (E–2)

For tables of adjustment and information on how to use this chart, see page 375.

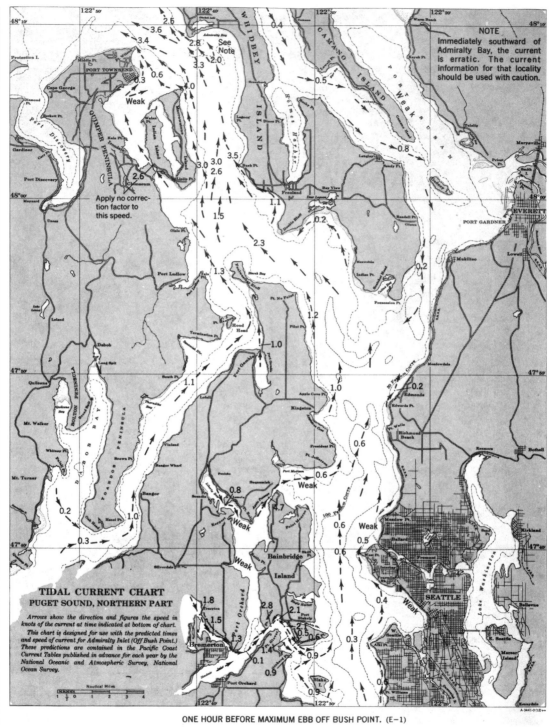

TIDAL CURRENT CHART
PUGET SOUND, NORTHERN PART

Arrows show the direction and figures the speed in knots of the current at time indicated at bottom of chart.

This chart is designed for use with the predicted times and speed of current for Admiralty Inlet (Off Bush Point.) These predictions are contained in the Pacific Coast Current Tables published in advance for each year by the National Oceanic and Atmospheric Survey, National Ocean Survey.

Nautical Miles

NOTE
Immediately southward of Admiralty Bay, the current is erratic. The current information for that locality should be used with caution.

Apply no correction factor to this speed.

ONE HOUR BEFORE MAXIMUM EBB OFF BUSH POINT. (E–1)

For tables of adjustment and information on how to use this chart, see page 375.

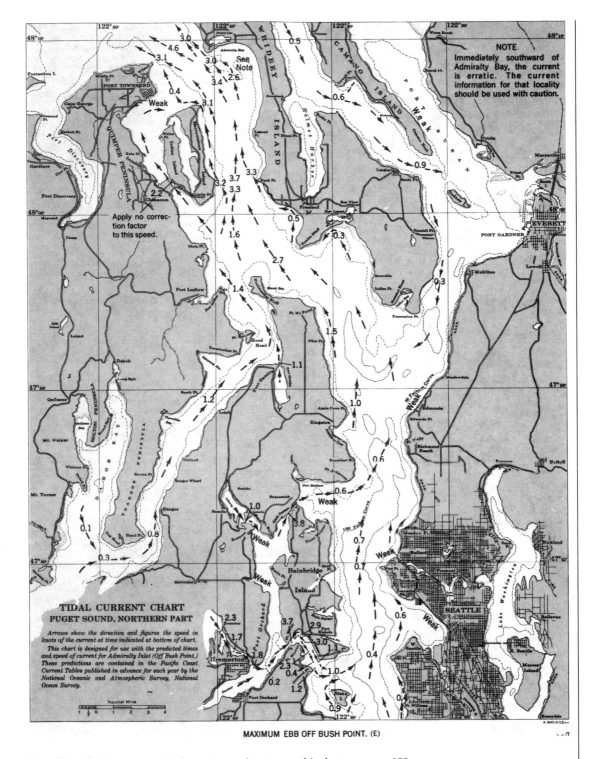

NOTE
Immediately southward of Admiralty Bay, the current is erratic. The current information for that locality should be used with caution.

Apply no correction factor to this speed.

TIDAL CURRENT CHART
PUGET SOUND, NORTHERN PART

Arrows show the direction and figures the speed in knots of the current at time indicated at bottom of chart.

This chart is designed for use with the predicted times and speed of current for Admiralty Inlet (Off Bush Point.) These predictions are contained in the Pacific Coast Current Tables published in advance for each year by the National Oceanic and Atmospheric Survey, National Ocean Survey.

Nautical Miles

MAXIMUM EBB OFF BUSH POINT. (E)

For tables of adjustment and information on how to use this chart, see page 375.

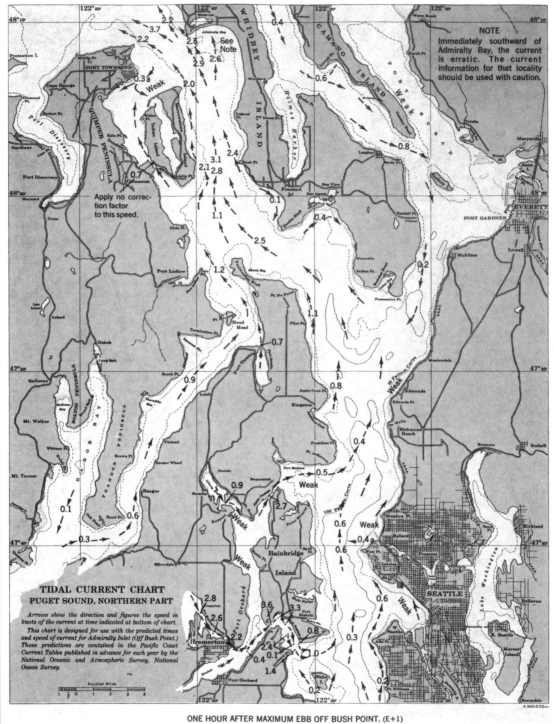

TIDAL CURRENT CHART
PUGET SOUND, NORTHERN PART

*Arrows show the direction and figures the speed in
knots of the current at time indicated at bottom of chart.*

*This chart is designed for use with the predicted times
and speed of current for Admiralty Inlet (Off Bush Point.)
These predictions are contained in the Pacific Coast
Current Tables published in advance for each year by the
National Oceanic and Atmospheric Survey, National
Ocean Survey.*

Nautical Miles

NOTE
Immediately southward of
Admiralty Bay, the current
is erratic. The current
information for that locality
should be used with caution.

ONE HOUR AFTER MAXIMUM EBB OFF BUSH POINT. (E+1)

For tables of adjustment and information on how to use this chart, see page 375.

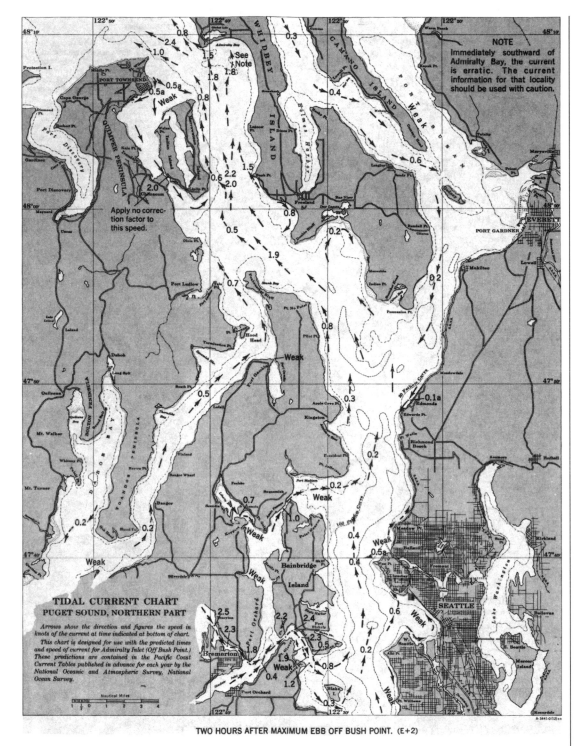

NOTE
Immediately southward of Admiralty Bay, the current is erratic. The current information for that locality should be used with caution.

Apply no correction factor to this speed.

TIDAL CURRENT CHART
PUGET SOUND, NORTHERN PART

Arrows show the direction and figures the speed in knots of the current at time indicated at bottom of chart.

This chart is designed for use with the predicted times and speed of current for Admiralty Inlet (Off Bush Point.) These predictions are contained in the Pacific Coast Current Tables published in advance for each year by the National Oceanic and Atmospheric Survey, National Ocean Survey.

TWO HOURS AFTER MAXIMUM EBB OFF BUSH POINT. (E+2)

For tables of adjustment and information on how to use this chart, see page 375.

INDEX

Note: Boldfaced pages indicate photo or map reference.

400